Mirati Sikandari: Or The Mirror Of Sikandar

Fazlullah Lutfullah Faridi

MIRATI SIKANDARI.

OR

The Mirror of Sikandar,

BY

SIKANDAR, the son of MUHAMMAD, alias

MANJHU, GUJARATI.

———————

TRANSLATED BY

FAZLULLAH LUTFULLAH FARIDI.

———————

PRINTED AT THE EDUCATION SOCIETY'S PRESS,

UNDER THE AUSPICES OF

HIS HIGHNESS MAHARAJA DHIRAJ MOHAN DEVAJI BAHADUR

RAJA SAHIB

OF

DHARAMPUR.

[1899]

TO

HIS HIGHNESS MAHARAJA DHIRAJ MOHAN DEVAJI BAHADUR,

To whose princely patronage and Royal Munificence this work owes its existence, it is most respectfully and gratefully

Dedicated.

PREFACE.

I had the honour in the year 1889 of obtaining several interviews with Colonel J. W. Watson, then Political Agent, Kathiáwáda, in connection with a certain account I had written which was noticed by him with approval. In the course of a conversation on Persian Histories of Gujarát the accomplished Colonel expressed regret at the incompleteness of the English translations of the two works on the history of Gujarát by indigenous writers—the Miráti Ahmedi and the Miráti Sikandari. The valuable translation of the Ahmedi by Dr. Bird was, he said, not complete. In the same way, he observed, Sir Edward Clive Bayley's translation of the Sikandari broke off somewhat abruptly at the end of the reign of Sultán Mehmúd III, omitting unhappily the record of the eventful period that ushered in the Mughal sovereignty. Many of the numerous anecdotes that form the most attractive feature of the "Mirror" of the genial Sikandar, were, he added, omitted. Colonel Watson said he was thinking of writing another translation, but want of time and failing health had come in the way. He advised, nay, asked me to translate the work, offering me all the help in his power. Such a kind hint from the accomplished scholar was tantamount to a command, and I undertook the work with pleasure. To my great regret he, who can be said to have been the father of the undertaking, did not live to see its completion. It is, however, a source at least of some satisfaction to me that some of the earlier chapters of the translation met his approval.

The proofs of this translation have been read by A. M. T. Jackson, Esquire, I. C. S., M. A., to whom, and to Sir James Campbell my very respectful thanks are due for much help and many improvements. My ability for its publication I owe solely to the kind and friendly efforts of Mr. Anopchand Jagjivandás Modi, B.A., LL.B., Sar Nyáyadish, Rajkot, and the munificence of His Highness Mahárája Mohan Devaji Rája Sáhib of Dharampúr.

FAZLULLÁH.

MÍR-ÁTI SIKANDARÍ.

THE first among the ancestors of the Sultáns of Gujarát who became qualified with the honour and distinction of Islám was one Saháran the Táṅk.[1] He was styled Wajíh-ul-mulk, when he became a Muhammadan. "Táṅk" means expelled from caste. The Táṅks were expelled from caste for wine-drinking. Saháran was the son of Harchand who was the son of Harpál who was the son of Kandrapál, son of Harpál son of Dharbhandar son of Kuṅvarpál son of Daríman son of Darsáp son of Kunvar son of Trilok son of Sáláhan son of Múlhan son of Mandan son of Bhogat son of Tágan son of Dúlha son of Máhsu son of Náhsu and thus step by step to Rámchandra whom the Hindus worship as God. Zafar Khán son of Wajíh-ul-mulk was the first of them who sat on the viceregal throne of Gujarát, and the first who sat on the throne of the Sultánate of this country was Sultán Muhammad Sháh son of Zafar Khán called Tátár Khán.

It is related that Sultán Firúz Sháh, the uncle's son of Sultán Muhammad Tughlak Sháh, the king of Delhi, was very fond of hunting. He loved sport perhaps to an extent to which few of his predecessors or successors on the throne of Delhi have done. In fact he is accounted a patron saint of the sport, and people engaging in the pursuit address prayers for success to him. One day before his ascending the throne of Delhi he set out for hunting, and, in the pursuit of a deer, became separated from the body of his followers. At sunset, realizing the difficulty of his position, he began to look out for some place to pass the night in, and saw one of the villages of the Táluka of Thánesar.[2] He turned the head of his horse towards

---

[1] The Bombay Gazetteer History of Gujarát calls the Táṅks a class of Rajpúts claiming to be of the Surya-Vansi race, who, together with the Gújars, appear from very early times to have inhabited the plains of the Panjáb.

[2] In the Sirhind division of the Panjáb.

it ; when he reached it, he saw a number of cultivators sitting outside of the gate. Alighting, he joined them, and asked one of them to pull off his long hunting boots. This man happened to be well versed in the art of physiognomy and palmistry. He happened to glance at the sole of the prince's feet, and he read the lines as indicative of future greatness. He told his companions that the stranger was either a king or a person who would shortly attain to that dignity.

This man was one of two brothers Sádhu and Saháran. They were men of consequence and influence in the town and had much of its management in their hands. They could at a call summon thousands of horse and foot. Both of them kissed the ground before the prince and said, " If the prince is pleased to favour us by accepting our hospitality, it will be a great honour." The prince accepted their offers, and they did their best to give him satisfaction. The wife of Sádhu was a sensible woman. She proposed that although appearances were in favour of the greatness and exalted position of the distinguished stranger, it would be better not to place perfect confidence in him before testing his nobility of soul by the introduction of wine into the entertainment, for wine opens the heart and brings forth the qualities of him who drinks it. Sádhu's sister, who was as accomplished as she was beautiful, filled a cup, and handed it to the prince, who, with great good pleasure, took the cup, and quaffed it. This made the prince unbend and made him social and agreeable to an extent which permitted of the adroit wife of Sádhu plying him with judicious questions from all sides, with the result of by degrees worming out of him all his circumstances. When the prince showed an inclination towards the fair damsel, the wife of Sádhu consented to give her to him in marriage provided he informed her of all relating to himself.

The prince said his name was Firúz Khán, that he was the uncle's son of Sultán Muhammad the son of Tughlak Sháh. That the Sultán had made him his heir-apparent. On the wife of Sádhu giving this information to her husband, he gave his consent readily to the marriage which was forthwith contracted. When the happy husband of this charming young beauty got up in the morning, all his people assembled from all sides and he made ready to depart towards the capital. The brothers Sádhu and Saháran both attached themselve

to the suite of the Sultán and followed in his rotinue. They made themselves so useful to the prince that they seldom left his presence. The
prince also loved his young bride greatly. Eventually the brothers
both of them became converted to Islam, and Sahárán received the
title of Wajíh-ul-mulk from Sultán Firúz, and both brothers shortly
after became the spiritual followers of the great Saint Hazrat Makhdúm
Jehánián. The Sultán also, day by day, conferred greater favours
upon them.

One day it so happened that in the abbey or residence of
the Saint Makhdúm Jehánián, a great crowd of people had collected,
but there was no food to feed them. This information reached
Muzaffar Khán, the son of Wajíh-ul-mulk. He was a spiritual
follower of the saint. He got up at once and sent a large quantity of
food and sweets to the shrine and placed it before the derwishes, who
were so pleased with the savory viands that (by way of grace) they
yelled out such a loud and hearty 'tekbir' "Alláho-Akbar" (God
is Great) that it reached the ears of the saint inside, who thereupon
enquired what it meant. The servants explained. The saint sent for
the donor Muzaffar Khán, who, coming, kissed the ground before him.
The saint said : "Oh ! Muzaffar Khán, the return for this feeding of my
derwishes is the kingdom of the whole of Gujarát which in reward of this
handsome deed, I grant thee., May it be auspicious to thee ! " Saying this
the saint presented him with a bed-cover which was then in his actual
use. Muzaffar brought his forehead to the ground and made obeisance.
Returning home happy and joyous he recounted his adventure to his
wife, a woman of sharp wit and solid sense. She heard his account with
pleasure, but said : " thou art now verging on old age—if thou attainést
" to the rule of Gujarát—how long wilt thou reign ? So hie back to
" the presence of the saint and tell him to pray that the kingdom
" may continue in thy family for generations. To-day the sun of
" the kindness of the saint hath dawned on thee, and I doubt not,
" but that whatever request thou makest shall . be complied with."
Muzaffar Khán went forth with delicate perfumes, sweet smelling
flowers, delicious fruits, and pretty betel-leaves and placed them before
the holy man, who pleased at this elegant tribute, said : " Thou
hast brought us perfumes ! " He gave a handful of dates from
out of the tray presented by Muzaffar to him, saying :—" According to
the number of these dates, shall thy children rule over Gujarát ! " Some
say the number of dates was twelve or thirteen ; others that it was not

more than nine or ten. God knows best. Historians, may God have
mercy on them, relate that in A. H. 747 (A. C. 1345) Sultán
Muhammad Tughlaksháh, while on his way to Thatha in Sindh, and when
he had reached its vicinity, breathed his last. Twelve days after this
event, Sultán Firúz Tughlak mounted the throne and promoted
the brothers, Mazaffar Khán and Shamshír Khán[1]; and they having
obtained his entire confidence, were appointed by him his cup-bearers.
From this circumstance those who call the Sultáns of Gujarát, wine-
makers and sellers, are quite wrong. The fact to which this malicious
report owed its origin was that one year there having accrued
to the Sultán of Delhi an extraordinarily plentiful crop of grapes,
as the whole quantity was going to the bad, the brothers were
ordered to extract wine out of the grapes. Their detractors thus got
reason to connect them with wine-making. But the truth is as described above. They certainly belonged to the tribe or caste of ' Tánk.'
Whatever and whoever they were, they were a goodly race of men,
having pure and virtuous souls, and they performed meritorious actions
and gave numberless endowments, and shewed good-qualities and amiable traits in connection with God's creatures. When Sultán Firúz
Sháh reached the ripe age of four score years and ten, he made over
the affairs of State to his son, whose name was Muhammad Khán, and
occupied himself with the service and worship of the Almighty, and
they began to read the sermon in the names of both (father and son).
In the year 790 A. H. (A. C. 1388) the followers of Sultán Firúz
Shah turned from his son and there was disturbance and Sultán Muhammad Sháh came forth to fight them, but the followers of the old
Sultan brought him out and placed him before the ranks, and when the
army of his son saw him, they were so struck with awe that they fled
leaving the followers of the old Sultan masters of the day. These men
now plundered the palace of Muhammad Sháh and the houses of his
nobles; Muhammad Sháh fled to Sherpúr.[2] In this year Firúz Sháh
died. He reigned eight and thirty years and nine days. After this
the men of Firúz Sháh raised his grandson Ghiásuddín, the son of
Fateh Khán, to the throne at Fíruzabád.[3] They appointed an army to
harrass Sultán Muhammad who, after a little fight, was defeated and fled

---

[1] Shamshir Khan was the Musalman name of Sádhu or Sáhu.
[2] Sir Clive Bayley calls it Sirmor.
[3] The words in the text are " in the Kúshak of Firúz-abád." The word Kúshak in
Turkish means a villa residence and is the original of the English corruption Kiosk.

from Sherpura to Sánka.   On Tughlak Sháh pursuing he fled to Nagar
Kote.   Tughlak Sháh, owing to extreme youth, fell into play and luxury,
and his followers commenced plundering and annoying the people,
till in A. H. 791 (A. C. 1389) Malik Ruknuddín, his minister, killed him
and hung up his head opposite the palace.   He reigned for six months
and eighteen days. After him Abú Bakr, the son of Zafar Khán,
the son of Firuz Sháh, mounted the throne, and between him and
Sultán Muhammad there were many battles, and Sultán Muhammad
was often defeated.   Eventually the army mutinied against Abú
Bakr and went over to Sultán Muhammad, and Abú Bakr fell a
prisoner into the hands of Sultán Muhammad, and died in prison
The Sultanate of Delhi fell again into the hands of Sultan Muhammad.
In this very year A. H. 793 (A. C. 1391) news reached Delhi that
Nizám Mufarrah Khán, whose title was Rásti Khán, had rebelled.   The
Emperor having given him the red insignia sent Mohammed Zafar Khán
to quell this rebellion in Gujarát (of which place Rásti Khán was the
viceroy and farmer), on the 2nd of the month of Rabi-ul-awwal of
the same year.   The Khán moved from Delhi on that day, and pitched
his camp on the bank of the Hawzi-Khás.   On the 4th of the month
Sultán Muhammad came out to bid farewell to the Khán, and adopted
his son Tátár Khan as his own son and kept him with himself.   After
Zafar Khán had gone some stages, he came to hear that a son was born to
his son Tatár Khan, whom he gave the name of Ahmed Khán,[1] and he
went forward thence by forced marches.   When he reached the domain
of Nágore, the people of Cambay, who had come forward to complain
of the tyrannies of Rásti Khán, met him.   He consoled them,
asked them to return and pushed on towards Pattan.   From this
place he sent a letter of advice to Rásti Khán persuading him to return
to his duty, and stating that he himself would be the intermediary to
obtain for him the royal forgiveness.   That ill-fated man replied by
advancing towards Pattan to give battle, which took place at a place
called Kambhoi, a village under the perganah of Pattan.   After a
hard fought battle, victory remained on the side of the Khán, who
returned to Pattan, the Nizám being killed in battle.   This took
place on the 7th of the month of Safar in the year A. H. 794
(4th January A. C. 1392).   After that, Zafar Khán remained in Pattan
for some time, and ordered a town to be founded on the site of the field

---

[1] Ahmed Khán the future founder of Ahmedabad.

of battle and named Jítpúr or town of Victory. This village, so founded, still exists.

Then in A. H. 795 (A. C. 1393) Zafar Khán moved towards Cambay and subdued all the country of Gujarát, then under Musalmán rule. In the year 796 A. H. (A. C. 1394) Sultán Muhammad, son of Firúz Sháh, died. He reigned six years and seven months. In Rabí-ul-awwal of the same year Humáyún Khán, the eldest son of Sultán Muhammad, mounted the throne under the title of Sultán Ala-ud-din. He reigned for six weeks and a day and died. After that, on the 20th of Jamádil Awwal, Mehmúd Khán, the younger brother of the above-mentioned prince, mounted the throne, under the title of Násir-ud-dín Sháh. Shortly after, news reached Zafar Khán that the Rája of Idar had rebelled. He was appointed with an army to subdue the rising. He beseiged the fort and sent armed men on all sides to plunder and harrass the people of the rebel Rája. In the end the Raja made due submission. The Khán returned and thought of sacking and plundering Sómnáth, when news reached him that Malik Násir alias A'dil Khan, the ruler of Asírgarh and Burhánpúr, was transgressing the limits of duty and allegiance and encroaching on Sultánpúr Nazarbár, a dependency of Gujarat. Zafar Khán immediately on hearing this reached the place by forced marches, and when A'dil Khan heard it, he turned back and went to Asír, and the Khán also returned to Anhilwára or Pattan.

In A. H. 797 (A. C. 1394) Zafar Khan marched against Jahrand (Júnágadh) in the country of Rái Bhára, and defeated the infidels of those parts, and then marched against Somnáth, which temple he cast down and introduced Islám in the city of (Somnáth) Pattan.

In the next year (A. C. 1395) information reached him that the infidels of Mándu annoyed the Moslims. He marched against them, and though unable to take the fort of Mándú, he subdued the Rája after a year's siege. Thence he performed a pilgrimage to Ajmer, walking the distance. From Ajmer he went to Sámbhar and Dándwána, and subdued the infidels of these parts. He thence marched against the infidels of Delwara and Jalwáráh,[1] whom punishing, he returned to Pattan.

The author of the history of Mehmúd Sháh has related that after the death of Mohammed, the son of Firúz Sháh, there was great

---

[1] By Jalwárah the historian means the modern principality of Jhálawád in Kathiáwar. Delwara is Mount Abú.

disturbance in the kingdom of Delhi. Every noble entertained hopes of the purple. After a long while, when the rule of Delhi came into the hands of Mallu Ikbál Khán, Tátár Khán, the son of Zafar Khán, was in Pánipat. Ikbál Khán marched towards Pánipat to attack Tátár Khan, who, leaving his baggage in the fort of Panipat, went with an army to besiege Delhi. On the third day Ikbál Khán took the fort of Pánipat and captured the whole of Tátár Khán's baggage. In consequence of this, Tátár Khán, being unable to remain in that country, turned his face towards Gujarát, intending to raise an army in that country and return to oppose Ikbál Khán.

In the meanwhile it came to Tátár Khán's ears that Mirza Moham-med Moghal, [1] having brought an army out to India by the command of Amír Timúr Gúrgán (Tamerlane), was in Multán besieging Sárang Khán, the brother of Ikbál Khán. Thus the intention of marching against Delhi which had nearly taken the form of determination was postponed.

In A. H. 800 (A. C. 1397-98) Zafar Khán marched against Ídar to chastise the infidels. He besieged the fort and plundered the district ; his intention being not to leave the district till he had wholly subdued it, but hearing of Timúr's conquests he concluded peace with the Ídar Rája and returned to Pattan. In A. H. 801 (A. C.1398-99) the Somnáth infidels made incursions into the Musalmán possessions and began to affect independence. Zafar Khán led an army against them and subdued them and established Islám on a firm basis in their country. In this year Mahmúd, the son of Muhammad, the son of Sultán Fíruz Tughlak flying from the power of Timúr, came to Pattan but not obtaining armed aid from Zafar Khán, went to Málwa to Alp Khán. There also he received no aid and went to Kannouj and contented himself with that domain.

SULTÁN MUHAMMAD, OTHERWISE CALLED TÁTÁR KHÁN, SITS ON THE THRONE OF GUJARÁT.

During the unsettled times that followed the Mughal conquest at Delhi, Tátár Khán was always praying of his father Zafar Khán to march against Delhi, but Zafar Khan was always cooling his ardour by objecting, on the ground that such action would be reproved as venially avaricious. At last in A. H. 806 (A. C. 1403) Zafar Khán invested Tátar Khán with

[1] Feristah (II. 855) calls this prince Mirza Pir Muhammad, the grandson of Timúr.

the sovereignty and title of Násirudin Muhammad Sháh, and having handed over to him the treasure, elephants, horses, &c., himself repaired to Asáwal, which city Muhammad Sháh made his capital. In the same week in which he assumed royalty, he left Asáwal on a religious war, and, after humbling the infidels of Nádot, who resided in a mountainous country and did not acknowledge the sovereignty of the Sultáns of Gujarát, he marched against Delhi. Ikbál Khán was alarmed at hearing his intentions, but Muhammed Sháh being suddenly taken ill, died, and his body was brought to Pattan,[1] where he was buried.

But the people of Gujarat say that Tatár Khán, with the desire of mounting the throne, at the instigation of evil counsellors, imprisoned his father Zafar Khán, and caused himself to be proclaimed king by the style and title of Muhammad Sháh. When he set out for Delhi, persons, friendly to Zafar Khán, poisoned him. The title " the Martyred Lord" that he was given after his death also points out to the fact that he did not die a natural death.

It is said that the late Sultán was a spiritual follower of the Makhdum Jahánián. It is related that when Sultán Muhammad sent a large sum of money to the Saint Ganj-Bakhsh (the saint who lies enshrined at Sarkhez) and begged of him to pray for the permanence of his kingdom, the saint rejected the offer, and returned word that the money did not of a right belong to him but to his master, and that he had no right to spend it in any way.

When Muhammad Sháh bade adieu to life, Zafar Khàn again ascended the throne. The nobles gave him obedience, and he, on his part, tried to obtain their love, and returned to his capital. It is related that from that day to the end of his life his eyes were never tearless, and he often wished to give over his kingdom to his younger brother Shams Khán and retire from public life, but, owing to the refusal of the latter, could not obtain his wish. At last he sent Shams Khán to Nágor and ordered him to take over the rule of that place from Jalál Khán Khokhar. He made Ahmed Khán, the son of his son Sultán Muhammad, his heir-apparent and educated him.

On the 17th of the month of Ramazán A. H. 807 (A. C. 1404) it came to hearing that Amír Timúr was dead and that Ikbál Khán

---

[1] Though the author's meaning is vague, it seems that Muhammad Sháh died at some other place and his body was brought to Pattan where it was interred.

had invaded Kanouj with the intention of wresting that province from the hands of Sultán Mahmúd, the grandson of Sultán Fírúz, who had of late contented himself with the piece of territory consisting of Kanouj. Sultán Mahmud entrenched himself within the castle of Kanouj and Ikbál Khán returned to Delhi after some unavailing attempts to reduce the place. In A. H. 808 (A. C. 1405) Zafar Khán prepared an army to go to help Mahmud Sháh. In the meanwhile, however, it came to hearing that in the Jamádil-awwal[1] of the same year there was a battle between Ikbál Khán and Khizr Khán, that Khizr Khan was successful and that Ikbál Khán was killed. Zafar Khán now abandoned his expedition, as Khizr Khán was now established on the throne of his forefathers.

ZAFAR KHÁN MOUNTS THE THRONE WITH THE TITLE OF SULTÁN MUZAFFAR.
A. H. 810 (A. C. 1407).

Three years after the death of Sultan Muhammed Sháh, in consequence of the representations of his nobles, that as the Tughlak dynasty to which he owed fealty was no more, Zafar Khán took to himself the title and insignia of royalty in Bírpúr in the year A. H 810 (A. C. 1407). He proceeded towards Dhár in Málwa to ask Alp Khán, son of Diláwar Khán, to enter into his allegiance, or failing that to leave the country. Alp Khán, however, opposed him, and being defeated in battle betook himself to the castle of Dhár, which was besieged by the Sultán. Finally, however, Dhár was reduced and Alp Khán surrendered himself and was placed in confinement under the charge of Nasrat Khán. About this time news was received that Sultán Ibráhím of Jaunpúr had marched to Kanouj with a view of plundering the Delhi territories. Muzaffar Sháh marched to the assistance of Sultán Mahmúd, son of Sultán Muhammad, Lord of Delhi. On hearing of this Sultán Ibráhím returned to Jaunpúr, and Sultán Muzaffar also on hearing of this returned to his capital. Alp Khán remained a year in prison, when Músa Khán, one of Alp Khán's kinsmen, usurping his authority, Alp Khán begged to be released, and the Sultán consenting, sent his grandson Ahmed Khán with an army to reinstate him. Having done this, Ahmed Khán marched to Mándu, Músa Khán fled, and Ahmed Khán returned to Gujarát.

---

[1] The fifth month of the Arab Calendar.

2 M

In A. H. 812 (A. C. 1409) the Sultán attacked the infidels of
Kunbh Kōt.[1] He asked aid of Sheikh Kásim, a saint. The holy
man having glanced over the list of the army drew lines through the
names of certain persons who, he said, would be killed. As it happened,
the prophesy of the saint proved true.

Sultán Muzaffar Sháh died in the latter part of the
month of Safar[2] in the year A. H. 813 (A. C. 1410). Though
the historians are silent as to it, the cause of Sultán Muzaffar's
death is so related:—The Kolis of the village of Asáwal, having
thrown off their allegiance, took to brigandage and highway robbery.
Muzaffar sent Ahmed Khán to subdue them with an army that was
present at the capital. The prince encamped at Khán Sarovar, and
there calling before him a number of the great Doctors of Law, asked
them whether a person whose father was killed by another without
reason, had over the murderer, the right of retaliation and blood.
All the Doctors unanimously returned a verdict in the affirmative, and
the prince taking care of the paper on which their opinions were
written, suddenly returned to the city the next day and imprisoned
his grandfather and mixing poison in a bowl gave it to him to drink.
The old Sultán said : " My son, why such a hurry ? All that is mine
would have, before long, come to thee without this violence ! "
But the young prince said: " Your time has come" according to the
Koranic verse: " And when their hour cometh, they tarry not
a moment, nor do they hasten." The Sultán then asked him to
hear some advice from him. The first was, to kill the man who
had set him to this act, or if not, at least never to trust him;
next, to abstain from wine; third to kill Sheikh Malik and Shere
Malik who were dangerous men. Sultán Muzaffar was buried
within the city walls of Pattan. It is related that after his grand-
father's death Ahmed Khán was often very remorseful and sorrowful
and ever deplored an act that had been done by him in the rashness
and heat of the prime of youth. Otherwise looking to the general
virtuous tenor of his conduct this act was extremely repugnant to it.

SULTÁN AHMED SHÁH.

On the 14th of the holy month of Ramazán, A. H. 813 (A. C.
1410-11.) Ahmed Sháh, the son of Muhammad Sháh, the son of

---

[1] The Tabakáti Akbari has Kanth Kot, a dependency of Katch. This is probably
correct.

[2] The second month of the Musalmán Calendar.

Muzaffar Sháh, ascended the throne of Gujarát. After some days information came that Moid-dud-din Fíruz Khán, his cousin and ruler of Baroda, having made some nobles to side with him, wanted to dispute with him the sovereignty of Gujarát. His allies were Hi-sám-ul-mulk Bhandári and Malik Ahmed his son, and Malik Sháh, father of Khatri, and the son of the deceased Hasbul-Mulk, and Malik Kásim Khusrao, and Jívandás and Prágdás, who all met him at Nadiád and defeated Bhíkan Khán and Ádam Sultán Afghán Khán who were friends of the king. Jívandás Khatri then induced them to swerve from their allegiance, and assembling the Amírs proposed to attack Pattan, but the others refused; and on Jívandás reproaching them with cowardice a dispute arose, in which Jívandás was killed and the rest sought forgiveness from the king and were forgiven. Moid-dud-din Firuz Khán, however, went to Cambay where he was joined by, Sheikh Malik, called Masti Khán, son of Sultán Muzaffar Khán who was governor of Surat. When the Sultán marched against them they fled from Cambay to Broach, whither the Sultán pursued and beseiged them. On the Sultán's arrival Moid-dud-dín's army went over to him and Masti Khán submitted to him, and after a few days Sultán Ahmed sent for and forgave Moid-dud-dín and returned triumphant. On his return to Asáwal he determined to meet Ásá, the Bhíl, and with the advice of the Saint Khwájah Ganj-Bakhsh began to build Ahmedabad.

In the year A. H. 816 (A. C. 1413) the construction of the city walls began by the hands of four persons of the name of Ahmed. The first was the famous Saint Sheikh Ahmed Khattu; the second, Sultán Ahmed; the third, another Sheikh Ahmed of great sanctity, and the fourth, Mulla Ahmed. The royal palace was the first building to be constructed within the city; the Jámá Mosque near Mának Chouk was begun in the Hijra year 817 (A. C. 1414). The date or the year of the building can be obtained from the numerical value of the word خير (good).[1] The length of its southern court is a hundred *gaz* (a little less than a yard); the breadth of this court is 120 *gaz*. The breadth of the two northern and southern sides

---

[1] The author of the Miráti Sikandari derives the date of the commencement of the construction of the city from the numerical value of the Arabic word *Khair*, (خير) good. Now, according to the Abjad account Kh being equal to 600 ey, = 10, r = 200 makes 810. But the author gives the year in one place as A. H. 813 (A. C. 1410) in another place A. H. 816 (A. C. 1413), whereas Feríhtah gives the year as A. H. 815 (A. C. 1412).

is 120 *gaz.* Deducting the Mulúk-khánah, or the Royal Retiring Chamber, there are 350 pillars, there being two pillars for the doorway of the royal portico. The royal raised portico is supported by 8 pillars. On the northern and southern sides, there are 212 pillars. There are 350 pillars within the mosque. And there are 8 domes without the south side, 77 large ones and 20 small. The minarets have 57 steps.

In A. H. 815 (A. C. 1412), Moid-dud-din Fírúz Khán and Masti Khán joined Rája Ranmal of Ídar and took shelter in the Ídar fortress at the instigation of Badr-i-Ulá. Sūltán Ahmed marched against them to Ídar, and sent Hoshang, called Fateh Khán, a cousin of Sultán Muzaffar, with an army to enter the Ídar country by way of Kherálu.

At this time Moid-ud-dín Khán won over to his side Ibráhím Khán, the son of Nizám, commonly known as Rukn Khán, who was a Thánádár on behalf of the Sultán in the town of Morásá.[1] Badr-i-Ulá and Moid-ud-dín Khán and Masti Khán and Ranmal, the Rájá of Ídar, marched down having joined their forces to the village of Ránakpur (miswritten Rangpúr) under Ídar, about five miles from the town of Morásá, and began strongly to strengthen the fort of Morása, to dig a deep moat round it, and to place at each opening in the castle strong guns and mortars.

The Sultán also came out to the neighbourhood of Morásá and, from natural kindness of heart and fear of God with an eye to mercy sent an emissary, advising the enemy to abstain from the evil ways of disaffection, which would lead surely to ruin, and to make submission and ask for pardon which was sure to be granted. The rebels, however, not giving ear, the Sultán laid siege to the castle, not however without repeating the peaceful advice. The rebels now, pretending to be effected by the Sultán's advice, said that they would submit to the Sultán, provided he sent Nizám-ul-mulk the Vazír, Saadul-mulk, the commander of the right, and Malik Ahmed Azíz-ul-mulk and Nasír Seyf, called Bázdár Khán, to receive their submission and to lead them in safety to the Sultán, as their faults were many and great and they could not bring themselves to believe in such an easy pardon.

The Sultán gave the abovenamed nobles leave to enter the castle, but to take care of the guile of the rebels. When the Amírs abovenamed approached the castle, Badr-i-Ula, having placed some armed and armoured men in ambuscade, advanced to meet them, and began to address them in such sweet and plausible words that he quite

---

[1] Morása, forty miles north-east of the town of Kaira.

removed from their minds the fear of foul play, and asking Nizám--ul-mulk and Saádul-mulk to give him a minute apart, took them aside, when the armed men, rushing from their ambush, secured the two noblemen and took them inside the castle. Before entering it, however, Nizám-ul-mulk called out in a loud voice and told his other companions that whatever he was destined to suffer had passed, but that the Sultán should on no account, owing to his being taken, fall short of anything in the taking of the castle. The Sultán now ordered the castle to be taken by escalade, which was done on the third day of this event; the misguided rebels concealed themselves in the cells of the castle.

At last in A. H. 814 (A. C. 1411-12) Badr-i-Ula and Rukn-Khán were killed, and Fíruz Khan and the Rájá of Ídar fled. Nizam-ul-mulk and Sääd-ul-mulk were released from prison in safety. The Rájá seeing what had happened, and thinking that his safety lay in it, surrendered to the king the elephants and horses and baggage of Moid-ud-dín, Firúz Khán, and Masti Khán, and plundered their camp. Moid-ud-dín and Masti Khán fled to Nágore where they took shelter with Shams Khán Dandani, so called from his teeth being long. Moid-ud-dín was eventually slain in the war beween Rúna Mokal and Shams Khán. On account of the Ídar Rájá acting thus submissively the king forgave his offence, and having levied the tribute agreed on, departed.

After this, in A. H. 816 (A. C. 1414-1415), Usmán Ahmed Sarkhej and Sheikh Malik, son of Sher Malik, who resided in Pattan, and Ahmed Sher Malik, and Sulimán Afgán, called Ázím Khán, and Ísá Sálár rebelling, wrote secret letters to Sultán Hoshang of Málwá that if he would march with the view of the conquest of Gujarát they would join him and seat him on the throne and expel Sultán Ahmed. To strengthen their cause they persuaded the Káthis and Sátarsál, Rájá of Jháláwár, to join them.

Sultán Ahmed sent Prince Latíf Khán his brother and Nizám-ul-mulk, against Sheikh Malik, and himself going to Bándhru in the parganá of Sánvli, ten kos from Chánpáner, encamped there, and sent Imád-ul-mulk against Sultán Hoshang. Sultán Hoshang afraid to risk a battle with Imád-ul-mulk, a slave of Sultán Ahmed's, said that if he was victorious over him he would only have the doubtful honour of beating a slave, but, victory being God-given, if he was defeated by Imád-ul-mulk he would have to bear the opprobium of being routed by a slave. He therefore retired and Imád-ul-mulk after plundering Málwá, returned.

Latíf Khán and Nizám-ul-mulk, having repulsed Sheikh Malik and Sátarsál, drove them into Sorath, which is a Táluká of Mandlik Rájá of Girnár, and leaving the guilty persons to their guilt returned, and the Sultán also returned with joyful heart to Ahmedabád.

Be it known that Sultán Alá-ud-din first spread the light of Islám from Nehrwálá Pattan to the fort of Bharoch (Broach), but the rest of the country remained as it was, in darkness. The Gujarát Sultáns by degrees enlightened the country, and the parts of the country that were thus enlightened through the exertions of Sultán Ahmed were as under.

THE EXPEDITION OF SULTÁN AHMED AGAINST SORATH, HIS ATTACK ON GIRNÁR AND HIS RETURN.

In A. H. 817 (A. C. 1415) Girnár, the famous rock-castle of Sorath, was attacked by Sultán Ahmed. Ráo Mandlik, the Rájá of Girnár, having prepared a strong army gave battle to the Sultán near the foot of the mountain. The van of the Muslim army broke the ranks and scattered the army of the Ráo, who, losing many men in the field, fled and took refuge on the top of the mountain. It is said that though the light of Islám was not brought to the perfection of its refulgence in this expedition, yet the infidels of the place from being militant [1] became tributary, and lost their independence, and the fort of Júnágadh, which is situated at the foot of the mountain, fell into the hand of the Sultán, and the greater part of the Zamindárs of Sorath became obedient and submissive and consented to service. The Sultán returned to Ahmedábád leaving Syad Abul Kheir and Syad Kásim to collect the Zamindars' salámi or tribute.

EXPEDITION AGAINST SIDHPUR. A. H. 818 (A. C. 1416).

In A. H. 818 (A. C. 1416), the Sultán attacked Sidhpúr [2] and broke the idols and the images in the big temple at that place and turned the temple into a mosque. When he satisfied himself with having brought to an end the expedition against Sidhpúr, he in

[1] The words used in the text are the legal Arabic terms Harbi and Zimmi, the first denoting an infidel engaged in active warfare, against a Musalmán power and the second paying tribute or tax to it. This was the Second destruction of the beautiful temple. It was first sacked and destroyed by Alá-ud-din Khilji (A. C. 1295-1315).

[2] On the river Sarasvati, fifty-eight miles north of Ahmedábád.

A. H. 819 (A. D. 1417) invaded Dhár. The reason of his having done so was that while the Sultán was going towards Sultánpur and Nuzarbár to repel an attack of Nasír, the son of Eynul-mulk, the ruler of Asírgar and Burhánpúr, a Gujarát zamindár by name Púnjá, the Rájá of Idar, and Trinbakdass, Rájá of Chámpáner, Satarsál, the Rajá of Jhálâwár, and Siri, Rájá of Nádot,[1] having agreed among themselves wrote to Sultán Hoshang of Mándu, telling him that Sultán Ahmed being absent, and engaged with Nasír Eynul-.mulk, it was an opportunity for the invasion of Gujarát which they would help to render successful by their co-operation. Sultán Hoshang began to prepare an army, and wrote to Shams Khán Dandáni offering him the city of Pattan with its parganás if he agreed to co-operate with him, if not, he stated, that for what had passed Sultán Ahmed was sure to visit upon him his vindictive displeasure. Shams Khán Dandáni, however, wrote to Sultán Ahmed setting forth the intention of Sultán Hoshang, and stating that he was not the man to play fast and loose with the fidelity that he owed to the Sultán who allowed him to rule over a corner of his dominions. The camel-rider of Shāms Khán conveyed this letter to the Sultán from Nágore[2] on the ninth day to Sultánpúr,[3] during which time it also reached the ear of the Sultán that Sultán Hoshang had crossed the boundaries of Gujarát and encamped near Morásá. The Sultán set ferth for Gujarát by forced marches, and in spite of the rainy season reached the neighbourhood of Morásá on the seventh day and encamped opposite to Sultán Hoshang. Sultán Hoshang reproached the confederates for representing to him that the absence of Sultán Ahmed was to be of long duration, and saying that he had lost confidence in them, fled back during the night to Málwa, and the confederate Rájás dispersed regretful and crestfallen. Sultán Ahmed stayed a few days at Morásá, and receiving news that consequent on the incursion of Sultán Hoshang the zamindárs of Sorath refused to pay tribute, and also hearing that Nasír, the son of Ráje, the ruler of Asír, with the connivance of Gheirat Khàn, son of Sultan Hoshang, had laid siege to the fort of Thálner, and by the treachery of Iftikhár-ul-mulk, son of the ruler of the fort, had taken possession of it, and with the aid of the zamindárs of Nádot had

---

[1] This is Nándod, the chief town of Rájpípla in the Reva Kántha Agency.

[2] Nágore in the Rájpútana State of Jodhpur, eighty-four miles north-west of Nasírábád.

[3] Sultánpúr now forming with Nandurbar, the western part of the Khándesh collectorate.

marched towards Sultánpur and Nazarbár and had organised a rebellion, Sultán Ahmed nominated Malik Mehmúd Barki and Mukh-li-
sul-mulk to subdue Nasír, and sent Kháni Aázam Mehmúd Khán with
a strong army to chastise the Sorath rebels. When Malik Mehmúd
Barki reached Nádot he plundered and laid waste its territories, and
when he neared the town of Sultánpur, Gheirat Khán fled to Málwá
and Nasír to Thálner, at which latter place he was besieged by the
Malik and was so hard pressed that in a short time he submitted
to the Sultán, asking forgiveness which the Sultán accorded
with the title of Khán. After some time, to chastise the
transgression that has been above related of Sultán Hoshang, Sultán
Ahmed invaded Málwa. The Rájás, Punjá the son of Ranmal of Ídar,
and Trimbakdass of Chánpáner, and the Rája of Nádot, who were the
confederates of Sultán Hoshang in his late invasion of Gujarát, sent
their agents in the presence of the Sultán to seek forgiveness, and the
Sultán out of policy having pardoned them and having kept Malik
Ziyá-ud-din, Nizám-ul-mulk, the Vazír, as Regent behind him, marched
on towards Málwa, and after many consecutive marches arrived in the
presence of Sultan Hoshang's army, who had by digging a deep moat,
strongly entrenched his position in the neighbourhood of Ujjain. It
is related that on the day of battle Sultán Ahmed Shàh, having
prepared himself mounted his horse, and came to the tent of Faríd,
the son of Imád-ul-mulk, and there pulling in rein, sent word to the
Malík that he had conferred upon him the dress of honour and the
title' of Imád-ul-mulk that was enjoyed by his father. It so happened
that at that particular time Faríd, preparatory to donning his armour,
as was the wont in the warfare of those days, was rubbing oil on his
body and had to send an apology to the Sultán instead of proceeding
personally to join him. The Sultán went on his way and engaged the
enemy. When Faríd reached that place, he found the way across
the stream that ran between the hostile armies so blocked up by
crowds of soldiers, that it was impossible for him to find the
whereabouts of the Sultán. At last he called out if anybody could
point out to him the way to the Sultán. A man came forward
and said there was none except by taking a turn to the rear of the
enemy. Dangerous as this was, Faríd said it was all that he desired
(to retrieve, no doubt, his late slackness in answering the call of the
Sultán) and readily asked the man to lead. When he had made the
dangerous circuit, he found the hostile armies botly engaged, the van
with the van, the right wing with the right wing, the left with the left,

and the centre of the Málwa Sultán was kept as reserve to await the turn of events; but the fate of the day was decided by the bold charge of Faríd who turned the trembling scale in favour of the Gujarát army; meanwhile the van of Sultán Hoshang was dispersed by the van of the Gajarát army, and however much he tried to stem the tide of defeat, he could not restrain his army from flight. The Málwa Sultán was thus utterly routed leaving in the field his elephants and treasure to be captured by the victorious Sultán Ahmed. Sultán Hoshang took refuge in the fort of Mándu, up to the very gates of which he was persued by the army of Sultán Ahmed, who, after staying a short time in the neighbourhood and appointing an army to lay waste the territories of Málwá, returned victorious on the first of Zil-kaad [1] A. H. 821 (A. C. 1418) to his capital. In this year he marched to Chánpáner [2] to chastise the Rájá Trimbakdass, but as the necessity of subduing and taking the territories and the fortress of Mándu was ever present before his mind he did not attempt the capture of the Chánpáner fortress, but after the waste and plunder of the territories and the levy of the fixed tribute, in the beginning of the month of Safar [3] of the same year he went to Bahádurpúr Sank-hedá. [4] He plundered this country and carried away a large amount of booty, and having built mosques and introduced Islám and appointed Kázis, he built a wall round the town of Mángani under Sankhedá, and having left a garrison to take care of the place he drew his army towards the fortress of Mándu. When he reached Dhár, Sultán Hoshang sent Máulaná Músa and Ali Jámdár as ambassadors to crave pardon for his past conduct, and Sultán Ahmed accepted their excuses and marched to the fort of Chánpáner, and after plundering that country returned to Ahmedábád in A. H. 823 (A. C. 1421).

The latter part of this year Ahmed Sháh devoted to bringing his own dominions into thorough subjection, and wherever any one was headstrong he cast down his stronghold, and he overthrew temples and built mosques in their stead, and he also constructed fortified *thánás*, of which he first populated the fort of Chitor [5] in the pargana of Bárásinor and Dohad which is among the hills, and he repaired the

---

[1] The eleventh month of the Musalman calendar.

[2] In the British district of the Panch Mahals and from A. C. 1483 to A. C. 1560 the chief city of Gujarat, now in ruins.

[3] The second Musalman month.

[4] A town on the northern bank of the Or river in H. H. the Gaikwar's territories.

[5] It cannot be determined whether this is Chitor or Jepúr.

fort of Kárehth which had been built by Alaf Khán Sanjar in the year A. H. 704 (A. C. 1304) during the reign of Sultán Alá-ud-din, and named it Sultánábád. Sultán Ahmed besieged the fort of Mesar, At this time Sultán Hoshang had gone to Jájnagar to hunt elephants. The garrison, therefore, hopeless of succour, surrendered the fort. Sultán Ahmed leaving a strong garrison at the place then besieged Mándu, but after a seige of eighteen days on the approach of the rainy season he raised the seige and went to Ujjain which city is the navel (centre) of Málwá. He again besieged Mándu, but Sultán Hoshang now returned from Jájnagar, entered the fort by the Tárápúr Gate and began to strengthen its position. Sultán Ahmed despairing of taking Mándu this time, marched for Sárangpur which he besieged. Sultán Hoshang now sent ambassadors to him and peace was concluded.

On the night of the twelfth of Muharram, (the first Mussalman month,) A. H. 826 (A. D. 1422) Sultán Hoshang surprised the incautious army of Sultán Ahmed during the night. For sometime the uproar was considered as caused by the breaking loose of a mad elephant, till Malik Munír, aroused the Sultán, who mounted a kettle-drum horse, every one of his suite having horsed himself as best he could, and showed himself to the army. The first charge of Hoshang was directed on a number of Garásyás and Rajpúts who had encamped on the left, and five hundred of whom were killed in the first onset. Next they attacked another portion of the camp and killed many. Sultán Áhmed told Malik Khúban his equery to try and bring him information about Faríd Sultáni and Malik Mukarrab. Malik Khúban galloped away and saw both these nobles ready mounted and on their way to the royal tent. He informed them of the position, of the Sultán, and they, each of them, with a thousand horsemen, appeared before the Sultán, who in the height of his anger at this mishap reproached them grossly for their being more neglectful than himself. They asked the Sultán's permission to be allowed to attack Hoshang, but the Sultán very wisely restrained their ardour till daylight. The Sultán now ordered Malik Khúban to bring him further information, which he did, to the effect that Sultán Hoshang, fancying himself the master of the field, was standing near the royal tent of Sultán Ahmed and inspecting the horses and elephants which were being paraded before him. When the morning began to dawn Sultán Ahmed with his lion-like nobles and soldiers fell on the Málwá army. It was such a hotly contested field that both the Sultáns engaged personally in it till they were wounded. At last the elephant-drivers of Sultán Ahmed who were with the Málwá army took the opportunity of attacking Sultán Hoshang who, unable to oppose the force of their attack, turned his face and fled, and victory crowned the brow of Sultán Ahmed. So completely were the tables turned that the army of Sultán Hoshang left in the field the property of the Gujarát camp they had lately plundered in their hurry to escape with bare life. Sultán Ahmed rendered up prayers of thanksgiving for his dearly bought victory, and Sultán Hoshang with his broken army took shelter in the fort of Sárangpúr. Sultán Ahmed now returned to Gujarát, but halted midway when he heard Sultán Hoshang was picking himself up for one last effort to wipe out the shame of all his disasters. Sultán Hoshang approached suddenly and both the armies joined battle. They say that in this field Sultán Hoshang left four thousand men dead, and that a number of elephants of tremendous size and strength fell into Sultán Ahmed's hands. Sultán Ahmed returned victorious to Ahmedábád in A. H. 826 (A. C. 1422-23).

It is related that two months before this event Sultán Ahmed had written to Sheikh Ahmed Khattú, relating all the events of that time and expressing a fear that he would still for some time be detained in Málwá; the Sheikh in reply foretold the exact date on which the Sultán would return to Ahmedábád, saying "you shall in triumph and success return to your capital, God willing, in the year 826" and this date eventually fell true. How august the period which was graced by men with such purity of soul as the Saint Ahmed and the Saint Syad Burhánud-dín and his sons Sháh Alam and others, each of them qualified with such brilliant virtues.

For three years after this Sultán Ahmed remained peaceably at Ahmedábád.

In A. H. 829 (A. C. 1425) an army was sent against Ídar, and the Rájá fled to the hills and his country was plundered and laid waste. In A. H. 830 (A. C. 1426) Sultán Ahmed founded a city on the bank of the river Háthmati, eighteen miles from Ídar, and on the frontier, of Gujarát, and constructed a strong stonewall around it. He named it Ahmednagar[1] and proposed to pass much of his time in it. In A. H. 831 (A. C. 1427) the Sultán having sent out some men for bringing in hay, Púnjá, Rájá of Ídar, attacked the party and took away an elephant, but the party again collecting pursued Púnjá who made a stand at a place where there is a rock on one side and a deep chasm on the other, and the path along which does not admit of more than

---

[1] It now belongs to the Native State of Idar.

one horseman passing along it.   The royal elephant-driver, pushed
his elephant on, against the Rájá who was on horseback.   The Rájá's
horse taking fright, leaped into the chasm, destroying itself and its
rider, and Púnjá, Rájá of Ídar, was never heard of again.   The
second day after the event a wood-cutter brought to the royal Darbár
the head of Púnjá.   The Sultán asked if anybody knew Púnjá and
one of his followers who had for a short time served Púnjá came forth
and recognising the features of his late master, said :—" Ay, this is the
face of the Raoji !" [1]   Those present in the Darbár reproached the man
for naming an infidel so respectfully, but the Sultán stopped them
and added that the man was right in remembering his old master with
love and respect.   After this for two years the Sultán remained in his
own country and brought it into subjection and did not attack any
foreign land, and made laws for his army and the administration of his
kingdom.   He also settled the emoluments of the military in this manner
that half the pay of the soldiers should be defrayed by grants of land
and half by money ; because, if the pay were fixed to be all in money it
would not be lasting and the soldiers would be badly equipped and
careless in protecting the country ; but if half their pay were given by a
grant of land (jágir) from that grant they would obtain grass, firewood,
milk, and butter-milk, and if they engaged in agriculture and building
houses they would derive profit and would strive to protect the country
with their heart and life.   He also ordered that they should receive
the money portion of their pay monthly without delay or hindrance,
wherever they may be posted so that, wherever they might be, they would
have always to be be present, at their posts and if on any occasion they
should be called on active service they would not be obliged to borrow
money whether the expedition be a distant or a near one.   It was also
possible that on a distant expedition the income from the *jágir* would not
reach the soldiers on account of the roads being closed in time of war,
when they would draw the half share of their pay in money from the
Royal Treasury, or in case of the want of weapons of war   they
should not be in difficulties and obliged to borrow money, and would not
be anxious on account of their families as they would be maintained
from the produce of their *jágirs*.   It was also ordered that the treasurer
should be one of the royal slaves while the paymaster was a free man

---

[1] The expletive ' ji' is added to the name or designation of a person in respectful or
polite mode of address, as ' Ráo'—or Chief—and ' Raoji, Diván, and Divanji. My Lord,
or my dear Lord the Rao, and my dear Lord the minister.   Instance Akbar calling his
dying friend Faizi " Sheikhji ! will you not speak to me " ? Blochmann's, Ain-i-Akbari.

in order that they may not combine and stretch forward the hand of treachery and peculation. The same arrangements were made with regard to the Ámils or revenue officers of the districts. These arrangements lasted intact till the time of Sultán Muzaffar, the son of Sultán Mahmúd Begdá. In the time of Sultán Bahádur when a large number of foreigners joined the Gujarát army, economical administrators on taking account of the revenues of the kingdom found that they had in some Mahálls got up from one to ten, others from one to nine or eight or seven; but in no case was the increase less than double. After that changes and innovations were introduced and rules and regulations all laid aside. Abuses crept in and great disturbances arose as shall be mentioned in their proper place.

In A. H. 835 (A. C. 1431) news was received that Sultán Fírúz Bahmani, King of the Dakhan, had marched against the infidels of Bijánagar and had been defeated by them. Sultán Ahmed sent a large army to his assistance, as there was great and sincere friendship between them. When, however, the army reached the fort of Nánder,' Sultán Fírúz Bahmani was reported dead and was succeeded by his son Sultán Ahmed Bahmani who sent rich presents to Sultán Ahmed Gujaráti, and his army returned.

After that from the year A. H. 836 (A. C. 1432) to A. H. 845 (A. C. 1441) every year the Sultán used to send armies for the chastisement or correction of some Rájá or king. Some time it was to ravage the country of Ídar. Sometimes to awaken Nasír of Asírgadh to a sense of his position and duty. Sometimes to chastise Sultán Ahmed Bahmani, and sometimes to pillage Meywár. Sometimes he used to go out himself at the head of the army, but his armies always returned victorious. Never during the whole term of his reign was defeat met with by the Gujarát army.

At last in A. H. 845² (A. D. 1443) the messenger of death overtook Sultán Ahmed at Ahmedábád, and he was buried in the mausoleum at Mánek Chauk in that city. May God have mercy on him.

---

¹ This is probably Ránder on the northern bank of the Tapti near Surat. Sir Edward Clive Bayley calls it Thál-nér but is doubtful as to its correctness. See Bayley's Gujarat 114.

² The Miráti Sikandari omits the events of A. C. 1442-43, the flight of Kánha, Rájah of Jháláwar to Khándesh and the help given to him by Ahmed Bahmani. The reprisals by the Gujarát Sultán, the sending of his son with a large army and the defeat of the Dakhnis. Then follows the quarrel about the Island of Mahaim (Mahim) and Malik-ut-Tujjár's defeat. See Ferishtah (Pers. txt.) II. 369.

Sultán Ahmed was born on the nineteenth of Zil-hajj A. H. 793 (18th November A. C. 1391). It was in the twentieth year of his life that he mounted the throne, and he reigned thirty-two years, six months and twenty-two days, having lived fifty-two years and some months. It is said that from the time he reached the age of maturity to his death Sultán Ahmed never missed his morning prayer. He was the spiritual follower of Sheikh Rukn-ud-din Kán-i-Shakar, a grandson of Sheikh Farid-ud-din Ganj-i-Shakar, who lies enshrined in the city of Pattan in Gujarát. Sultán Ahmed had also great belief in Sheikh Ahmed Khattu, for whom he used to take a pride in performing even menial offices. Once on a dark night the Sheikh asked for a clod of earth for ceremonial purification and the Sultán handing him one, the Sheikh asked whether it was Saláhud-din (the Sheikh's servant). The Sultán answered—" No-'tis I." "Oh! the Virtuous Sultán!" exclaimed the Sheikh. And the Sheikh thenceforth always used to style him " Sultán Virtuous." The Sultán made his son a spiritual follower of the Sheikh. For virtue and probity and liberality the Sultán had no peer, and he ever strived in religious war.

Of his justice, it is related that having a son-in-law who from arrogance of youth, greatness, and close connection with the Sultán murdered an innocent person. The Sultán coming to know of this, ordered the young man to be sent before the Kázi bound and secured like a common criminal. The Kázi compromised the case with the relatives of the murdered man for a money compensation in the shape of two hundred camels. But the Sultán said that though the relatives of the dead man were satisfied with taking a price for blood, that he was not content with this sentence, which, lest others in power might be inclined to follow the example of the young man, should have been capital. In this case said the Sultán retaliation must take the place of blood fine. And he ordered the young man to be crucified in the midst of the market place, where after paying the penalty of his life he was buried the next day. The example of this summary justice of the Sultán was enough to restrain his other nobles and connections from acts of violence towards the poor. It is related that one day the Sultán was seated in a portico of the palace over-looking the river Sábar, which was inundated. He saw passing over its waters a black object. Ordering it out, he found that it was a big earthen jar for holding water. Ordering its mouth to be opened he saw within it the body of a murdered man. He collected all the wine-sellers, and asked them to identify the jar. One of them admitted it as his handicraft and said that he had sold it to a certain village headman. The headman was summoned and after investigation it was proved that he had killed a certain Baniá. The man was sentenced to death. These were the only two murders committed during his reign. The wholesome fear excited by his summary justice prevented others.

It is with certainty related that Sultán Ahmed had a poetical mind, and some of his verses in praise of Saint Sayad Burhánuddin are extant. The following is the first line of one of his odes:—

"As a pole star to guide us in our time, Burhan is sufficient,
His convincing proof for guidance being as well-known as his name."[1]

SULTÁN MUHAMMAD SHÁH, THE SON OF SULTÁN AHMED SHAH. A. H. 845 (A. D. 1443.)

On the third day of the death of Sultán Ahmed Shah, Sultán Muhammad Shah mounted the throne, and forthwith engaged himself in pleasures and luxuries, not caring for the affairs of state. In fact, he had not the capacity for them. He was, however, a great bestower of gold and his extreme liberality earned for him the name of "Gold Giver."

On the twentieth of the month of Ramazán, A. H. 849 (A. C. 1445) Heaven gave him a son of auspicious birth whom he named Fateh Khán, and in the same year he marched against the Rájá of Ídar, who, taking shelter in the hills, sent ambassadors to the Sultán asking forgiveness for past faults. His ambassadors were accompanied by his daughter, whose great beauty fascinated the Sultán who accepted her in marriage, and made her the means of conferring on her father the kingdom of Ídar.

Marching thence into Bágar (Wágad) he laid waste that territory and returned to his capital.

In this year the great Saint Shekh Ahmed Khattu[2] styled Ganj-Bakhsh bade farewell to this world for a better one. The numerical value of the word Ákhir-ul-aulia (آخرالاولیا) gives the Hejrá year of his demise. The Sheikh was a spiritual follower of Bábá Is-hák who sleeps

---

[1] The word "Burhan" means a demonstration or proof and Burhánud-din being the Saint's name, the play upon words loses force in the translation.

[2] Born A. H. 738 (A. C. 1337) and died at the age of 111 lunar years. He is also known by the name of Ganj-Baksh or Treasure-Giver. See Blochmann's Ain-i-Akbari, 507, Note 1.

his eternal sleep in the town of Khattu, in the district of Nagor, whence his title of Khattu.

In the year A. H. 855 (A. D. 1451), the Sultán marched out with the intention of taking Chánpáner. The Rájá of the place, Gangadáss, son of Trimbakdass gave battle and, being defeated, fled to the upper fortress which the Sultán besieged. When the garrison of the castle became straitened, the Rájá sent ambassadors to Sultán Mehmúd of Mándu offering to pay him a lakh of Tánkás[1] of gold for every march he should make to his assistance. Sultán Mehmúd without any regard for Islám in his venal greed for money, marched his army to Dohad which town was under Gujárát on the frontier of Málwá. On hearing of this, Sultán Muhammad Sháh raised the siege and came to the village of Kothra under Saonli (at present under Baroda) where falling ill, he returned to Ahmedábád and died on the twentieth of Muharram A. H. 855 (A. D. 1451-2), and was entombed near his father in the Royal Cemetery at Manek Chauk. He reigned nine years and some months.

The above is related on the authority of the Tárikh-i-Ahmed Sháhi.[2]

There are, however, authentic traditions coming down from father to son which are in vogue among the people of Gujárát, and one of which goes on to say that Sultán Mehmúd Khiljí of Málwá possessed right royal qualities. He took great care of his soldiery, and was very just to his subjects, and, with all this, was very kind to the poor and the saintly, and was a great believer in them. Wherever he heard of a man with saintly qualities, far or near, he used to send presents and gifts and by avowing to him the sincerity of his belief used to win his heart.

Having heard that in Gujárát there was a righteous person of the name of Sháh Kamál, (whose shrine is now situated behind the mosque of Khudáwand Khán, whose name was Sheikh Alím, in the Alímpura suburb of the city of Ahmedábád), Sultán Mehmúd who had formerly some connection and acquaintance with the Sheikh to whom he used always to send gifts and presents, asked of the Sheikh to pray for the gift to him of

---

[1] According to Ferishtah [Persian Text] I. 199—the weight of the Gold and the Silver tánkáh was one tolah. According to the present rates a tolah of gold costs Rs. 29-6 and a tolah of silver Re 1. According to Thomas's Chronicle of the Pathán Kings, (360) a Black (i.e., Copper) tánkah was equal to $\frac{1}{10}$th a Rupee.

[2] Sir Olive Bayley (p. 130) has Bahádur Sháhi.

the kingdom of Gujarát, stating that if he, by his prayers obtained it, he would construct for the Sheikh a monastic residence or refectory endowed with revenues equal to those of the shrine of Sheikh Ahmed Khattú which were three crores of Gujarát Tánkás annually. As earnest money he sent him five hundred Tánkás of gold. Somebody communicated to Sultán Muhammad of Gujarát the information that with all his pretence to purity and sanctity, Sheikh Kamál had such a sordid love for gold, that in spite of his show of holiness he had made his Kuráan-cover the repository of the impure pelf sent to him by Mehmúd Khilji. Sultán Mehmúd, on inquiry, finding the circumstances to accord with facts, wrested the money in anger from Sháh Kamál. The Sheikh, who in consequence of former friendship had a corner of his heart for Sultán Mehmúd Khilji, being now touched to the core by this high-handedness of the Gujarát, Sultán began openly to pray every day for the bestowal of the kingdom of Gujarát on his friend of Málwa. After a short while, according to the tradition of the Prophet (on whom be prayer and prayers!) "that the prayers of the oppressed are always granted though they be sinners," his prayers were granted by Heaven, and he wrote to Sultán Mehmúd to say that the kingdom of Gujarát was by the Great Bestower of rule fixed in his name, and even drew up an order purporting to emanate from the dread Presence of the Ruler of rulers to that effect, and asked him to set out forthwith.

Sultán Mehmúd immediately set out with an army of eighty-thousand horse for the invasion of Gujarát.

When Muhammad Sháh heard this he consulted a Wánia who was his associate. That light-minded man advised him to flee and dispose of his harem and treasure in ships, saying that the enemy like a dog getting into an empty house would find himself at a wrong scent and go away, and the king approving of his advice began to prepare vessels. When Sheikh Atá-ulláh who had the title of Kiwá-mul-mulk (and who resided in Syedpúr and populated this suburb, near the Asuria gate, and who was after his death buried there) heard that the affairs of the kingdom were going to the bad, the Sayad came to Ahmedabád, and seizing that Wánia took him in a corner, and having laid his hand on his dagger said: " Did you give the king this counsel to flee? I think before God that it is first necessary to slay you. " The Wánia replied, " As you are a man of discernment, it cannot be concealed from you why your king instead of consulting brave and gallant men like you, in such a difficulty, consults a mean, cowardly Wánia like me ! It is because he does not care to act upon and appreciate manly advice." The Sayad perceived that the Bania spoke the truth, and withdrawing his hand from his dagger for awhile, considered and thought he would now try the prince and gauge his mettle. Jalál Khán was at that time in the town of Neriád. The Sayad reached the place that very night, and said to Jalál Khán in consultation: "The king, your father, wishes to hand over to you the throne of the Sultánate that he with his women and treasure having embarked on boardships should go out fishing in the sea. If God should entrust you this kingdom, how would you act against Mehmúd Khilji who with a large army is coming to subdue Gujarát ? " Jalál Khán said: "If this kingdom should come into my hands I swear by God, the King of kings, that I would destroy the enemy or die." On hearing this speech, the Sayad was pleased and said: "Although the father is unworthy to act, the prince is a worthy youth." He then explained to him what was in his mind and said: "The chief nobles of the kingdom find that your father does not care for the kingdom of Gujarát, and as the ruler is departing from your family, they have determined to seat you on the throne and fight with Mehmúd Khilji." The prince agreed, and the Sayad secretly introduced the prince into Ahmedabád by the Mirku gate that night and poured the liquor of death in the Sultán's cup who died instantly. This happened in the month of Muharram H. 855 (A. C. 1451).

SULTÁN KUTBUD-DÍN.

Sultán Kutbud-dín mounted the throne A. H. 855 (13th February, A. C. 1451) and according to the custom of his ancestors he honoured his soldiers with rewards and dresses of honour.

The author of the Túríkh-i-Bahádur Sháhi writes that about this time Sultán Mehmúd of Málwá marched into Gujarát and besieged Sultánabád which was commanded by Malik Álá-ud-dín bin Sohráb on the part of Sultán Kutbud-dín. The Malik shut the gate of the fort in his face and commenced fighting with both cannons and muskets. Sultán Mehmúd besieged the fort for a week. Afterwards through the mediation of Mubárak Khán, son of Ahmed Sháh, and uncle of Sultán Kutbud-dín, who had left Gujarát in the time of Sultán Muhámmad, he came forth and met Sultán Mehmúd who made him swear allegiance on the Kurán. He, however, took an evasive and quibbling oath, saying : "If Álá-ud-din should turn against the Master, may the Word of God become an enemy of his life. " The Sultán listened to him and promoted the Malik and made him one of his chief Sirdárs, and marched from thence. And when he arrived at Sársá Palri, a village of the District of Broach, he sent a message to Malik Marján, the commandant of the Broach fort, pointing out to him how he had honoured Álá-ud-dín, and persuaded him to act in same manner and to come to him, bringing with him the chief merchants of Broach. Sídí Marján, however, gave a stern reply, and strengthening the fort commenced to fight. Sultán Mehmúd asked Álá-ud-dín, in how many days he would conquer the fort. He replied, that it would require six or seven months at least of mining and making trenches on all sides. The Sultán said, " I wish in six months to subdue the whole of Gujarát." Marching thence he crossed the river Narbadá and went towards Baroda. On the march, it so happened that one of his elephants became wild ("mast") and broke loose and at night entered Neriad, where the Brahmans slew it with swords. " When the Sultán came to Neriad and saw the elephant thus slain, and heard that the Brahmans had done this, he said : " The climate of Gujarát must be productive of bravery, that even the Brahmans of the place should dare to do such a deed." He then came to Baroda and looted that city.

Here the information was brought, that Sultán Kutbud-dín acting according to the advice of the saintly and holy men of the country had determined to oppose Sultán Mehmúd, and he advanced as far as Bánkáner Khán-púr on the river Mahi.

The advice given by the holy men of Gujarát to Sultan Kutbud-dín, under supernatural impulse, is omitted by the author of the Táríkh-i-Bahádur Sháhi. I, however, insert it here as I have heard it from such of the gentlemen of this country who have received the account as a tradition without break. Rumours of the numerical superiority of the Málwá army having reached Sultán Kutbud-dín, he was advised by his nobles to consult and ask for the benediction of Sayad Burhúnud-dín, the lineal descendant of the saint Makhdúm-i-Jahání, who was considered the tutelar patron of the Sultáns of Gujarát. The Saint assured the Sultán in the words of the Kuraán:—" Many a small party conquers a large one by God's behest."[1] So saying and regretting the conduct of the late Sultán in respect to Saint Kamál he asked his son

كُمْ مِنْ فِئَةٍ قَلِيلَةٍ غَلَبَتْ فِئَةً كَثِيرَةً بِاِذْنِ اللّٰهِ ٥

whom he used to style by the familiar diminutive of Manjhan[1] to go
and expostulate with the angry Saint by saying that the author of his
insult being dead it was not right to extend the ill-feeling to his son,
a sentiment which he had the Kuranic sanction in the verse. "No
carrier of weight beareth other than the weight of his own (actions)."[2]
Therefore that he was to forgive and forget, as in mercy there was a
luxury which revenge could not boast. He was to ask Sheikh Kamál
to write to Sultán Mehmúd to return to his territory and to save the
people of Gujarát from the evils of war.

Hazrat Sháh Alam went to the Sheikh, and word for word delivered
his message, but the Sheikh did not agree, and gave an unfavourable
reply which Sháh Alam communicating to his father, was desired by
him to repair again to the Saint and beseech him to forgive the past and
to entertain mercy and charity in accordance with his saintly exterior.
"Ask the Saint with my humble regards," said Sháh Alam's father " to
look to the safety of God's creatures and to practice forgiveness,
especially as in forgiveness lay the weal of men, that Dervishes who
hope most for Divine Mercy must act kind by according to the sacred
verse: Those subdue their anger and do good unto men, Allah loves
such doers of good." For (Poetry)—

> "How well hath the pure Firdausi observed!
> Mercy (of Allah) alight on his pure sepulchre
> Hurt not an emmet that draggeth a corngrain
> For it hath life, and sweet life is pleasant."!

Sháh Álam again carried this message to the Sheikh and made
repeated prayers for pardon, but the Sheikh descending from his first
position of apathy began to make use of angry and excited words. The
lord Sháh Álam again returned to his father and recapitulated all that
had passed, saying that the Sheikh did not leave his selfishness for
humanity, and that he did not like going to him any more. But the
Saint Kutbul-Aktáb said : " In this matter the safety of the people is
at stake, and we must not take offence for ourselves. Go you once more
and say : ' your slave Burhan-ud-dín kisses your feet and conjures
you by your love for Muhammad the Prophet of Allah to forgive this
fault for his sake. The people of Mandu are hard and without feeling,'
and the men of this country will not be able to live under them." '
Sháh Álam again went and gave his message to Sheikh Kamál, but

---

[1] Manjhan is the affectionate form of Manjhlá—a middle son, or daughter. He
was according to the Miráte Ahmedi the eleventh of the twelve sons of the Saint.

[2] Lá taziro wáziratun vizra ukhra.

the Sheikh who had not reached the perfection of the attainments and
qualities of a Derwísh, and had become vainly content with the little
of Divine Light that had shone on him, refused his prayer, roughly
saying: "It is now seven years that by fasts and prayers I have got
the kingdom of Gujarát transferred to the name of Mehmúd Khilji."
It is impossible for me now to turn back Mehmúd Khilji, who has
always showed belief in me and love for me, for the sake of the son of
the man who oppressed me. Go back young Sayad and tell Burhánud-dín with our loving prayers that I have let off the arrow from my
hand and it is hard to re-call it. The lord Sháh Álam smiled and
repeated the Persian couplet :

> "So near do saints in Allah's favour stand
> That shaft once sped, back they can call to hand."

On hearing these lines, the Sheikh flew into a rage and retorted :
"This is really no child's play that it may be subject to change
according to the fancy of the moment. Look you towards the Divine
Tablet on which the destinies of creation are indited and see.[1] Do you
not find that the kingdom of Gujarát hath passed from the rule of the
Tánk Dynasty to Mehmúd Khilji. So saying he raised his hand and lo !!
it held an order written on paper manufactured in Tús[2] and handing it
to Sháhi Álam continued : "Exaggeration in this matter is of no use.
Go ye back and recount the facts to your father." On hearing this
the blood of Háshim in the vein of Sháh Álam, waxed hot. He tore
to shreds the order or grant that the Sheikh had produced as coming
from Alláh and said : "This writ without the authentication of the
Kutb-ul-Aktáb (his father) is useless." Then came the Sheikh
to know his mistake and found that the Will of Alláh was otherwise
than what he believed it to be. The Sheikh at once fainted and saying :
"Young Sayad, thou hast used force ! " expired. When Sayad Burhánud-dín heard this, he said: " Manjhla ! thou hast acted hastily."

Sultán Mehmúd heard of this, but in proud self-assurance continued to advance. The people of Gujarát were scared and terrified.
Many determined to emigrate, and some prepared for death and
separation from home and family.

Sultán Kutbud-dín requested the Saint, to, either himself accompany
his army to the field or send his son whom he used to call Bápji (or dear
father) in respect for his sanctity ; and the old saint ordered Sháh

---

[1] According to the Musalman belief the destinies of all things created and to be
created, are recorded from the beginning of Eternity on a Tablet called the " Lauh,"

[2] The modern Meohéd, once famous for its paper manufacture.

Álam to go, considering that Sultán Mehmúd was the transgressor and Sultán Kutbud-dín the victim. On the second day's march a scarcity of water was felt, so that the Saint could not get water for the performance of his midnight ablutions. So the saint Sháh Álam asked leave of the Sultán to go, assuring him that victory was in his name. The Sultán, however, requested him to give him his sword as an instrument of good fortune, but the Saint said that he should content himself with the blessing, as the sword if not properly taken care of would do him harm instead of good. The king said it was impossible that he should intentionally give any slight to such a holy token. The Saint said that a day would come when such an event would certainly come to pass.[1] But the Sultán's eyes filled with tears, so he girded his sword round the waist of the king. It was at this time mentioned that the Málwá Sultán possessed an elephant as big as a mountain and as fierce as a giant. That its name was Ghálib Jang[2] and that the sound of the war kettle-drum always used to make it wild, in which condition no elephant could cope with it, and if by chance any did oppose it, the Málwá elephant never left it without ripping its belly open. For this reason this terrible animal was nick-named ' the butcher.' Sháh Álam having examined all the elephants of the Sultán's stables chose a middle-sized elephant who had not till then reached the age of *masti* or rutting, and rubbed his hand over his head saying, " Oh! Shudani![3] by Allah's help rip open the belly of the butcher." Then placing in his bow an unfeathered and blunt arrow he shot towards the supposed direction of Sultán Mehmúd's army saying, " This arrow reaches and breaks the umbrella stick of Mehmúd." He then returned to Ahmedábád.

Sultán Kutbud-dín marched towards the enemy, crossed the river Mahi, and halted at Khánpur Wákáner.

Rájá Gangádass of Chánpáner who had rebelled, and gone over to Sultán Mehmúd instigating him and guiding his steps, represented to Sultán Mehmúd that as the enemy had occupied the ford near Khánpur, he should go by the way of Itádi of the Bálásinor Pargana on to Kapadwanj.[4] The Sultán approving followed this direction. In this march Malik Imádúd-din bin Sohráb told the nobles who were his companions: "I have sworn not to desert my Master in this business. My Master

---

[1]. And the prophecy did prove true. See the account of the death of Sultan Kutbud-din, p. 40

[2] Ghálib Jang, the over-powering in battle.

[3] *Shudani*, a Persian word meaning literally ' promising.'

[4] The chief town of the sub-division of that name in the Kaira District.

is Kutbud-dín. I will therefore go to him, and you follow your Lord."
Hence they separated, and he joined Sultán Kutbud-dín, and told him
that the enemy was marching by way of Kapadwanj and requested
him to march in that direction, and Sultán Kutbud-dín accordingly
arrived and pitched his tents there before Sultán Mehmúd's arrival.
On the other side Sultán Mehmúd arrived, and encamped three
kos off. Sultán Mehmúd on the night of the 1st of Safar ·intend-
ed to make a night attack, but losing his way wandered about till
dawn. At sunrise Sultán Kutbud-dín drew up his army and placed'
Diláwar Khán, with a strong army and fierce elephants in
command of the right wing, and he entrusted the left wing
to Malik Nizám Mukhlisul-mulk. He himself with Khán Jahán
and Malik Munír Vazír, Mathá Khán son of Muzaffar Sháh and
Ziá-ul-mulk and Tu-ghán Sháh Khatri called Iftikhár Khán and
Sikandar Khán bin Sultán Muhammad bin Ahmed Sháh and Malik
Halím Aâzam Khán and Kádar Khán commanded the centre; in
the van he placed his brave and experienced veterans. On the other
side Sultán Mehmúd opposed his left opposite to his enemy's right
and his van to the enemy's van. It is related that when the battle
began to wage hotly, Sultán Mehmúd, riding on an elephant of
gigantic size and strength, Ghálib Jang, with a black umbrella on the
howdah refulgent in the light of the sun-like flame, took up a position
whence with the aid of his gigantic elephant at one onset he intended
to scatter the ranks of the enemy. He placed his elephant in front of
the ranks like a key with which to open the lock of the serried ranks
of the enemy. He little knew that the lock closed by Destiny cannot
be opened by the key of human device.

Sultán Kutbud-dín, on the other hand, was riding a roan horse and
had on a green umbrella. Each of the kings, standing in the centre of
his army, was on his side performing prodigies of valour, leading their
men on by courageous words and example, and promises of reward
and preferment. It is said that at first Muzaffar Khán, Governor of
Chanderi, with certain famous elephants, on behalf of Sultán Mehmúd
routed the left wing of Sultán Kutbud-dín, and plundering, penetrated
as far as the Sultán's treasure, which his men commenced loading on
beasts of burden. In the meantime the right of Sultán Kutbud-dín
defeated the left of Sultán Mehmúd. And van engaging with van,
the conflict reached the centre, and the elephants of Sultán Kutbud-
dín began to fight shy of the tremendous elephant "Ghálib Jang" of
the Málwá Sultán. Sultán Kutbud-dín said: "Bring 'Shudani" (the

elephant), which Sháh Álam had blessed and ordained as the destined instrument of the great elephant's death, "that it may rip up the belly of ' Kassáb,' as Bápji (the dear Father) has ordered." Shudani charged an engaged the Kassáb (butcher). At this moment a party of men, residents of Dholká, called Durwáziás, strong like elephants and brave like lions, dismounting from their horses, hamstrung the Kassáb like a cow, in a slaughter-house, and felled him to the ground, the Shudanis tusks having pierced its vitals and key-like opened out its entrails. About this time also an arrow flying from behind struck the umbrella-stick of Sultán Mehmud, and thus was wrought the miracle predicted by the Saint. The army of Sultán Mehmúd seeing this took to their heels. Muzaffar Khán, the life and soul of this invasion, was captured, and at the order of the Sultán his head was severed from his body and hung up on the gateway of Kapadwanj. These events happened on Friday, the first of Safár[1] A. H. 855 (March A. C. 1451). Sultán Mehmúd who had set his heart with pride on his army returned beaten and crestfallen ; and Sultán Kutbud-dín who had set his trust, according to the verse of the Holy Kurán: "When thou shootest (an arrow) it is not thou that shootest, but it is Allah,"[2] on the word of the holy men, returned triumphant and victorious.

It is related that Sháh Álam when departing from Sultán Kutbud-dín's camp, asked him to vow some offering to the souls of the Prophets. The Sultán offered one golden Tánká for each of the prophets. The Saint said it was too much and difficult for any worldly person to give. The Sultán insisted. The Saint said : "Make the Tánka one of silver instead of gold." The Sultán agreed. After the victory the Sultán sent 70,000 silver Tánkás to Sháh Álam for the offering, but the Saint returned them, saying that the number of the prophets was far greater than the number of the Tankás sent. The Sultán did not reply and neglected the agreement and Sháh Álam from his own treasury gave out one lakh and twenty-five thousand Tánkás of silver in charity to the poor. One day the Sultán suppressing all mention of the circumstances under which he had vowed the Tánkás, said to the Saint's father that he had sent so many Tánkás for charity to the young Saint which did not meet the honour of his acceptance and which he had returned. The Saint's father remonstrated with his son on the matter, saying that in charities there ought to be no haggling. But

---

[1]. The second month of the Musalmán Calendar.
[2]. Má ramaita is ramaita walákinnal Lába ramá.

Sháh Alam remained silent. This circumstance, however, was the root of a disagreement between the king and the Saint which ripened as time went on, and produced consequences which shall be mentioned in their proper place.

It is said that then Sultán Mehmúd of Málwá arrived on the confines of Gujarát, some Hindu clerks who had been dismissed by the late Sultán Muhammad of Gujarat, went and met Sultán Mehmúd. He asked them for a statement of the revenues of Gujarát, and they stated to him that two shares of the country were divided between the Jágirs of the military and Crown lands and one share went towards charitable assignments to religious persons and institutions. Thus it remained till the time of Sultán Kutbud-dín, and each king increased the religious share. Sultán Mehmúd said: " To conquer Gujarát would always be difficult ; for it has not only an army of soldiers to defend it, but an army of holy men to pray for its prosperity."

After Kutbud-dín returned to Ahmedabád victorious, he gave himself up to wine and women, and devoted his time to the giving of splendid entertainments and luxurious banquets. He built the Hauzi Kánkariáh, the ' Nagína' Bágh in the middle of the Kánkariáh tank and the Makadpur palace. Each one of these equals the mansions of Paradise and the gardens of Eden. Some years ago, this humble person saw all of them, but now except the abovementioned tank and garden (or the Kánkariá and Nagína Bagh), no trace of them remains.

In A. H. 855 (A. C. 1451) Sultán Mehmúd Khilji brought an army to conquer the Nágor country, and Sultán Kutbud-dín ordered Sayad Atá-ulláh (also styled Kiwámul-mulk) to proceed to the aid of the ruler of Nágor with a large army. They had nearly reached the confines of Sambhar[1] when Sultán Mehmúd hearing of their arrival retreated and returned to his own country. Kiwámul-mulk also returned to his own country.

After this Firúz Khán Dandáni, ruler of Nágor, died and Mujáhid Khán his brother having expelled Shams Khán, son of Firúz Khán usurped the rule over Nágor. Shams Khán going over to the Ráná obtained his protection, and with his assistance attacked Nágor. Mujáhid Khán being unable to resist fled, and went to Sultán Mehmúd Khilji. At this time the Ráná wished to break down the fortification

---

[1] A town in the province of Ajmeer about forty-one miles, north-east of the city of Ajmeer.

of Nágor.[1] Shams Khán objecting things came to such a pass that war
was declared between them. The Ráná returned vexed to his own
country and again marched on Nágor with an army. Shams Khán
strengthened the fort of Nágor, and himself came to Sultán Kutbud-dín
to demand aid and gave his daughter in marriage to the Sultán who sent
Rái Amichand Mának aud Malik Gadái and others to relieve the
garrison of Núgor, and kept Shams Khán with him. The above mentioned Amírs fought with the Ráná near Nágor, a severe conflict, in
which though many Musalman and numerous Hindus were killed
success inclined to neither side. The Ráná after laying waste, the
neighbourhood of Nágor returned to his own city. In A. H. 360 (A. C.
1456) Sultán Kutbud-dín marched an army into the Ráná's country
to revenge his raid on Nágor. On his way thither Krishna Deorá[2]
Rájá of Sirohi, was admitted to an audience and petitioned the
Sultán that the Ráná had wrested from him the fort of Ábu which had
been the residence of his ancestors, and requested redress. The Sultán
ordered Malik Shaábán Imádul-mulk to take the fort of Ábu from
the servants of the Ráná and hand it over to Krishna Deorá. The Malik
unacquainted with warfare in a mountainous country, got entangled
with his army in the defiles near the fort. The enemy closed
all the passes, and coming on them from all sides of the hill
defeated the Malik, and very many of whose men were slain. The
news of this reverse reached the Sultán at Kombhalmer. About this
time the Ráná sallied out of the fort and being defeated returned to it.
The Sultán invested Kombhalmer and sent strong detachments to
ravage to the Ráná's country. They say that these forays so
impoverished the Ráná's country that not a head of cattle was left in
any Hindu's house, and innumerable male and female slaves fell into
the hands of the Muhammadans. Ráná Kumbha being helpless asked
pardon and subscribed to strong covenants never again to attack

---

[1]   This is an error.   It was only a part of the fortifications that the Ráná wished
to destroy. Ferishtah (II. 379) is more accurate. He says that the Chitor Ráná, Kúmbha
had agreed to help Shams Khán on condition of Shams Khán allowing him to permanently
dismantle three of the battlements of the fort of Nágor. He was anxious to place this
lasting humiliation on the fort to transmit to posterity a sign of his having avenged the
crushing defeats and reverses inflicted by Shams Khán's father on Ráná Mokal, the Ráná's
father. Though Shams Khán had at first no option but to accede to this stipulation, he
was afterwards so taunted and put to shame by his kinsmen that he said : " Our heads
must fall before these battlements go down."

[2]   The name is very unintelligibly written in all the MSS. Sir Clive Bayley writes
it Khátia. My MS. has Kanha-Kanahiya or Kashna. The Bombay Gazetteer History of
Gujarát, however, has Krishna (p. 33, Note 3).

Nágor or any Muhammadan territory. The Sultán returned to his country and rewarded his army and re-commenced his career of enjoyment. After some time ambassadors of Mehmúd Khilji arrived with a message to the effect that the quarrels between believers were the cause of security and peace to the evil-minded infidels, that the better course would be for all Muhammadans, being brethren, to unite, and having made agreements of friendship, combine to expel the wrong headed infidels, especially this turbulent Ráná Kúmbha who had so frequently harassed the Musalmáns. "Let the Sultán," said he, "march against him from that side, and I will march from this, until between us we shall destroy him and take his country in equal shares." The Sultán consenting made firm agreements regarding this, and in A. H. 861 (A. C. 1457) led an army against the Ráná Kúmbhá. On the other side Sultán Mehmúd marched against him until he reached the Kasbá of Mandisúr. Sultán Kutbud-dín first reduced the fort of Ábu and handed it over to Krishna Deorá and marched thence to Kombhalmer and plundered its vicinity. At this time Ráná Kumbhá was in the fortress of Chitor. The Sultán turned in the direction of Chitor. The Ráná with 40,000 horsemen and 200 picked elephants issued from Chitor and having occupied narrow defiles and taken up a difficult position commenced the battle. They say that the battle lasted for five days and a cup of water sold for five *phadiáhs*, which is equivalent in value to twelve *tánkahs* of the Muradi currency. On the fifth day the Muslims were victorious and the Ráná defeated and crestfallen with grieved heart and pale face returned to Chitor. The end of this affair was that the Ráná Kambhá sent envoys, who, with great humility and a thousand apologies and prayers for pardon, agreed to pay tribute and never to harass the Nágor country again. The petition was granted and the Sultán returned to his own country, the Ráná having pacified Sultán Mehmúd by the cession of Mandisúr and some other Parganás which were contiguous to the Málwá frontier. Three months after this Ráná Kumbhá broke his engagement and marched to plunder Nágor.[1] The news reached Malik Shaábán Imádul-mulk, the vazír at midnight. The Malik at once went to the palace, enquired for the king, and was told that he was asleep. The Malik said, "Awake him?" The slave girls said, "We dare not." The Malik then himself entered the sleeping apartment and commenced to shampoo the king's foot. The Sultán awoke and asked, "Who is it?" The Malik replied, "Your slave

---

[1] Sir Clive Bayley says it was six months after this.

Shaâbán." He asked, " Is it good news!" He replied, "All is well."
The Sultán said, "Then explain." The Malik said, "News has
arrived that the accursed Kumbhá has again broken his treaty, and has
marched againts Nágor. If the Sultán will at once beat the drums for
a march and himself issue forth from the city, the Rána on hearing
of it will turn back and retire, and not act in a similar manner
again; if not. complications will arise. We must, therefore, give the
matter prompt consideration." The Sultán said, "My head is heavy
with the fumes of wine and I am unable to mount." The Malik said,
"Let the king come in a palanqin." The king at once ordered the
drums to be sounded for a march and sitting in a *pálki* came outside
the city on the Kumbhalmer side. The spies of the Rána at once
communicated to him the state of affairs and the Rána immediately
urned and went to his own country. After this in A. H. 862 (A. C.
1458) Sultán Kutbud-dín led an army by way of Sirohi and thence
entering the Rána's country laid it waste and returned on the third
Rajab[1] to his capital. In A. H. 863 (A. C. 1461) Sultán Kutbud-dín's
cup of life having filled he cried ' Adsum ' to the call of Alláh. The
length of his reign was eight years six months and thirteen days.

It is related that when Sultán Kutbud-dín mounted the throne, the
mother of Fateh Khán, his step-brother (the future Mehmúd Begdá,
the most renowned of the Gujarát Sultáns) Bíbí Mughli, took shelter
with her sister Bíbí Mirghi, the wife of the great saint Sháh Álam, the
mother of Sháh Bhíkan another son of Sháh Alam's and the daughter of
Jám Júná[2], ruler of Sindh. Sháh Alam assured her to be satisfied, and
live in peace in his house with her sister, and that she would be out of
reach of danger. The mother of Fateh Khán with the greatest of care
used to live with her son in that house, but she was so afraid for the life
of her son that she was always on the alert. One day while in intoxication Sultán Kutbud-dín called Fateh Khán to mind, and asked
where he was. He was informed that Fateh Khán was with his aunt in
Sháh Alam's house and was a prime favourite of the Sháh. This
kindled the jealous rage of the Sultán who determined to take the life
of the young man, ignorant of the fact that this determination of his
would ultimately prove his own ruin and destruction.

One day he sent a message, which gave forth the evil intentions he
arboured against his brother, to Sháh Alam insisting on his giving

it K
Guja.
---
[1]   The seventh month of the Musalman Calendar.
[2]   One of the Jáms of Thatta in Sindh.

up Fateh Khán to himself whether the Saint wished it or not. The Sháh returned word saying that the young man had, for fear of his life, taken refuge with him, under which circumstances it would be highly improper to send him back. That he was the ruler, and might seize him wherever he could lay hands on him. The Sultán hereupon moving from the city, took up his residence in palaces of Khedpúr, near Rasulábád, where the Saint used to live, and sent out spies with orders to give immediate information in case they saw Fateh Khán that he may be captured. One day the Sultán sent his chief Queen Ráni Rupmanjri, who was a disciple of the Saint, accompanied by a large party of eunuchs to the house of Sháh Alam with orders to search out, seize, and bring Fateh Khán. The Ráni saw Fateh Khán sitting near the Saint, and caught his hand and began to drag him away. The Saint smiled and said, "You take Fateh Khán's hand to-day, but a day will surely come when he will take yours." And as predicted, it came to pass that Fateh Khán, as Mehmud Begdá, married this very queen after the death of Sultán Kutbud-dín. On hearing these words, the Ráni desisted and dropping his hand apologised and asked the pardon of Sháh Alam, and returning told her husband that, however much she searched, she could not find Fateh Khán.

One day the Sultán heard that Fateh Khán was at his lessons with Sháh Alam. The Sultán at once riding a fleet horse reached the mansion of the Saint, and began unannounced to push in. The porter whose name was Mukbil resisting, the Sultán said, "Do you oppose my going to the Bápjí (dear father) by his orders?" When he heard the voice of the Sultán, the Saint cried out to the porter to give entry to the Sultán, saying at the same time to Fateh Khán, "Read on 'old fellow';"[1] and the ten-year-old Fateh Khán assumed to the sight of the Sultán the appearance of an old man with gray hair and brows and bent back. The Sultán sat for a while in the room, but besides the Saint and the old man he could not see any one in it, though he looked very attentively about. He at last got up ashamed and went away venting his disappointed wrath on his spies.

Sultán Mehmúd used to say: "In those days they used to dress me in female garb to guard against the possible contingency of my being recognized by the Sultán's spies. One day while on the balcone

---

[1] The words used in the text: "Padh dokrí!" supply an interesting insta the strange mixture of Sindhi-Hindi, and Gujaráti in vogue in those days am Ahmedábád Bukháris.

with my nurse, a spy gave this information to the Sultán who dashed into the place; my nurse on seeing him lost her senses, and somebody informing Sháh Alam of it, he said, 'Fear not, how can he take a tiger?' When the Sultán caught my hand, my nurse cried out, 'Oh, this is the daughter of such a one!' naming some man or other of the Saint's kin. The Sultán examined me closely and found also, to my surprise, that I was organically as well as externally a woman! He went away, and told his companions the circumstance. They said: 'At any rate you should have brought the person downstairs.' He again came up, and again taking my hand was so terrified to see in it a tiger's paw that he ran away, and never again repeated an attempt on my life."

The rancour of the Sultán towards Sháh Álam gathered force every day, and at that period Bíbí Mirghi, the wife of Sháh Alam, died. Sháh Alam now considered himself bound by religion as well as propriety to tell Bíbí Mughli, the mother of Fateh Khán and the sister of his deceased wife, to now look out for herself a separate residence, as the death of her sister removed, according to law, the sisterly connection hitherto existing between her and the Saint, and admitted of the possibility of marriage. Bíbí Mughli was plunged into profound grief at these words of the Sháh. It was at this time that Jám Firúz, the uncle of the ladies, told Sháh Alam of a matter which, till then, was a secret.

The fact was, that Jám Júna, the king of Thatta in Sindh, had two daughters, Bíbí Mirghi and Bíbí Mughli, the first of whom he affianced to Sultán Muhammad and the second to Sháh Alam. But the Sultán, hearing of the greater beauty of Bíbí Mughli, partly by force and partly by gold, persuaded the ministers of the Jám to marry Bíbí Mughli to him and Bíbí Mirghi to Sháh-i-Alam.

It is related that when Sháh Alam, with a sad heart, related the story of the ruse to his father, Kutbi-Alam, the old Saint, gave vent to the prophetic words: "My son, you are fated to posses both the cow and the calf" [1]; told him not to grieve, as he was destined to have both the ladies. This saying of his father's Sháh Alam remembered, and observing the great inclination towards him of Bíbí Mughli, he married her, and the Bíbí also used night and day to serve him like a true lover and a handmaid in the great love that she bore for him, a love which

<hr/>

[1] The words in the text are: "Bete! tusádh nasíb-dheun wa bachchah." The v indicated the lady coming to the young Saint with her son at a future date.

the Sháh also looking to the great beauty and virtues of the lady to as great an extent reciprocated. One night the Sháh saw his wife, in the devoted love and homage that she had for him, sweeping his room with her long hair. Sháh Alam, coming to know of and enchanted with her devotion, asked her to request something of him, saying, that the gates of Heaven's mercy were open. She said that, as he had prophesied that Fateh Khán would ascend the throne of his ancestors, she prayed him to be as kind to Fateh Khán after he mounted the throne as he was during his boyhood; and that he must not be offended with any of Fateh Khán's forwardnesses or insolences if any appeared from him. Sháh Alam said, " It is destined that Fateh Khán is, in a short period, to mount the throne of Gujarát, and it is also destined that after doing so he will often be insolent towards me, and I shall, for thy sake, pass over his conduct."

One day the Sháh sportively placed an empty basket of fruit on Fateh Khán's head. His mother, always alive to the interests of her son, requested the Sháh to place the basket upside down, and when he did so, she fondly drew from it the omen of his being one day covered by a royal umbrella.

The marraige of Sháh Alam with his father's widow was the cause of Sultán Kutbud-dín's openly expressing his displeasure with the Saint. One day, in intoxication, he mounted and made for the suburb of Rasulábád and gave orders for its destruction. The men, ordered on this duty, went about demoralized with an indescribable fear, running from one to another, until the Sultán himself rode up to them, pressing them angrily onwards by hand and tongue; at this time, by the ordainment of Heaven, a mad camel appeared on the scene. He attacked the Sultán, who drawing his sword, aimed a blow at its head, but missing, hit himself on the knee. The Sultán fell down from his horse, and was taken to the place in a *pálkhi* where he died after three days in the year A. H. 863 (A. C. 1458). People say it was not a camel, but the Angel of Death himself in that form, and that the common and popular metaphor likening the camel to the Angel dates from that period.[1] They say that it was the self-same sword which was presented by Sháh Alam to Sultán Kutbud-dín at the opening of the

---

[1] In Persian and Urdu poetry the camel is usually likened to an angel.

war with Sultán Mehmúd Khilji with which he now struck himself
this blow.

   Some people relate the circumstance of his death otherwise.
They say that one day the Sultán ordered the male population of city
of Ahmedabád, not to go out of their houses, and to keep their
windows closed, as he wanted to go about, showing the city to his
harem. While promenading the streets of the city with his harem,
a man suddenly emerged out of a back-alley. In a transport of
rage, the Sultán struck him a blow with his sword which, the
man at once disappearing, fell on his knee. God knows the truth.

   It is related that when in his last illness one day, when in great
suffering while seated in one of the projecting windows of the palace
overlooking the river, the Sultán observed a wood-cutter with great
labour fording the river with a great load of wood from the other
bank of the river Sábarmati. After crossing the stream the man,
unfolding his girdle-cloth, took out some thick loaves of millet, and, with
no other condiment but three onions and a huge appetite, consumed the
whole with great gusto. He then went to the river bank and took a
hearty drink, and coming to the shade of the wall below the window,
lay himself down to enjoy a sound sleep. The Sultán overhead,
heaved a deep sigh, wishing it were possible for him to change places
with the sturdy, but poor wood-cutter !

   The author of the " Bahádur Sháhi" says that Sultán Kutbud-dín
was poisoned by his wife, who was the daughter of Shams Khán, with
a view to make her father the successor of her husband to the throne
of Gujarát. When the Sultán was in the last agony Shams Khán was
put to death by Sultán Kutbud-dín's nobles, and the Sultán's mother
ordered her slave girls to cut the lady to pieces. It is possible that
poison was administrated when the Sultán was confined to bed on
account of his wound. But God knows best.

ACCOUNT OF THE ACCESSION OF DÁÚD, UNCLE
OF SULTÁN KUTBUD-DÍN.

   On the third day after Sultán Kutbud-dín's death Dáúd Khán, son
of Sultán Ahmed, was selected by the great and powerful vazírs
and amírs of Gujarát. On the third of Rajab, A. H. 863 (A. D.
1458-59) he was deposed from the throne on the fifteenth of the same
month. They say that while yet he was not properly invested with the
powers of a ruler, he gave a sweeper,[1] who was his neighbour during the

---

[1] The word used in the text is *farrásh*, or carpet-spreader.

days he was a Khán, hopes of promotion to the title of Imádul-mulk, while the great noble of that name was alive. In the same way he promised another low man the title of Burhánul-mulk, while the noble of that name, the chief of Sultán Kutbud-dín's nobles, was alive. These matters becoming public from the talk of these base men, the great nobles and vazírs of the Kingdom said among themselves :— "This man passes such orders while yet his orders have no force, what will he do when they become conclusive? Let us remedy the evil before it happens." Then again he began to do mean actions, taking accounts of the royal clothes and ornaments, at the time of Sultán Ahmed I. (may he be given high place in Heaven !) and taking away the ornaments of the ladies of Sultán Muzaffar's harem and sending them to the treasury. His first order was to reduce the grain thrown to pigeons in charity, and reducing the number of lights in the palace. The nobles pronounced him unworthy the Sultánic throne of Gujarát, and proposed Fateh Khán to succeed him, sending Imádul-mulk, the son of Sohráb, to Bíbí Mughli, who, in the first instance, declined to put her son in the dangers and temptations of the throne. The nobles, however, insisted, and, in the end, brought Fateh Khán to the Bhadar with right royal pomp and circumstance. The nobles made him royal obeisance, and named him Sultán Mehmúd Sháh. They say when the noise of Sultán Mehmúd's progress to the Bhadar fell on the ear of Sultán Dáúd, he asked what it all was, and being told the fact, he betook himself by a back door to the river Sábarmati, and made himself an example of the truth of the Kuránic verse : "Thou givest the rule unto him thou willest and deprivest him of it thou wishest." After some days he joined the fakírs of the monastery of Shekh Adham Rúmi, in which position he, in a short while, made great progress, and died shortly after. He reigned twenty-seven days.

SULTÁN MEHMÚD BEGDA ASCENDS THE THRONE OF GUJARÁT IN THE MONTH OF SHAÂBÁN A. H. 863 (A. C. 1459).

The Defender of the Faith, Mehmúd Sháh Begda, put his foot on the throne of the Sultánate on Sunday, the 1st of the glorious month of Shabaán H. 863 (A. C. 18th June 1459) in the great city of Ahmedábád, and by his accession he conferred grace and lustre on the country of Gujarát. The origin and cause of the surname Begdá are said by some to be the following :—

Begda, in the Gujaráti language, is the name for a bullock whose horns stretch horizontally forward in the manner of a person extending his arms to embrace another, the moustaches of the Sultán being so thick and long that they resembled the horns of such a bullock. Others say, that Begdá is derived from *"bě"* two, and *"gadh,"* a castle, from the fact of his having taken the two rock-fortresses of Júnágad and Chámpáner; and hence he was called Begdá. God best knows the truth.

May it not remain secret that this Sultán was the best of the Gujarát Sultáns as a ruler, as a warrior, and a dispenser of justice. He was never exceeded in worth by any of the dynasty, either by those that preceded, or by those that followed, him. His love for Islám, and his sound sense in his youth as well as manhood, were great. His physical strength as well as courage were enormous, as was, notwithstanding that he was a king, his appetite. The quantity of food he used to eat was one Gujaráti maund, the seer of which consisted of fifteen *"Behlúlis."*[1] After taking his regular meal, he used to eat five seers of parched rice as dessert, and at the time of retiring to rest he used to order two plates of *"Samosás"* (triangular minced-meat sausages) to be placed on each side of his bed, of which he used to sup whenever he used to get up from his sleep (which he did several times) during the night. Immediately on getting up and saying his prayers, he used to breakfast on a cup of Mecca honey, a cup of *ghi* or clarified butter and a hundred and fifty golden-plantains. And he used often to say : " Oh God Almighty ! if thou hadst not given thy slave Mehmúd the blessing of dominion, who could have filled his belly ?"

The virile powers and cravings of the Sultán were in proportion to his appetite and digestion. The women of his country were too weak for him ; and, after cohabitation with his several of his wives, he used to derive satisfaction only from a young and strapping Abyssinian lass. He was thirteen years, two months, and three days old, when he ascended the throne ; and, according to ancestral usage, he gave the military gifts and presents, and conferred titles of distinction on some persons.

Some months after this, some misguided nobles, of the names of Kabíruddin Sultáni, surnamed Burhánul-mulk, Mauláná Khizr, surnamed Seiful-mulk, and Chánd, the son of Ismáil, surnamed Azud-ul-mulk and Khájá Muhammad Hisámul-mulk, having quarrelled with the vazír Malik Shaábán Imádul-mulk, set themselves to work the ruin of

---

[1] A maund of forty seers, the seer being fifteen *Bahlúli* The *Bahlúli* according to Elliot's History of India (v. 115, note 2) being $\frac{1}{70}$ the rupee.

his wealth and position. Going one day to the Sultán's ante-chamber before the time of Imádul Mulk's arrival, they represented to the Sultán that the vazír contemplated treason and wished to set up his son Shahábuddín on the throne and become independent. That they were true to their salt and could not close their eyes to this, and asked the Sultán to take immediate action. " And what, " asked the Sultán, "could that be ?" They suggested that the vazír should either be killed or imprisoned. The Sultán became silent. When the vazír came to the ante-chamber, the nobles seizing him put a collar round his neck, and fetters on his legs, and placed over him five hundred of their own trusted guards, and sent him up to the Bhadhar for imprisonment. They then went away well pleased to their houses, and engaged themselves in pursuits of pleasure. When night fell, Abdullah, the chief of the elephants' stables, represented to the Sultán that it was not advisable to have imprisoned Imádul-mulk, that the nobles, who were of the Malik's party, were preparing to flee the country, and that the refractory nobles who were the secret partisans of Habíb Khán, the son of Ahmed Sháh, the uncle of the Sultán, had taken him to their house where they were keeping him, waiting for the first opportunity to set him up as king. On hearing these words, the Sultán went and consulted his mother, who, summoning Abdulláh and administering heavy oaths to him, asked him to state the whole truth to her, which he repeated. The Sultán on his part consulted his devoted and faithful servants, Muhammad Háji and Malik Isá. They were of opinion to immediately release Imádul-mulk and surprise the malcontent and treacherous nobles, and to give up their houses to plunder. The Sultán ordered Abdulláh to bring out all the royal elephants in full armour and draw them up before the Darbár, and, having seated himself on the throne, said to Sharful-mulk : " Bring out that faithless Imádul-mulk that I may wreak my vengeance on him, and make an example of him." Sharful-mulk, going to execute the royal orders, was not obeyed by the guards of the rebellious nobles, and returned, and reported to the Sultán how matters stood ; the Sultan himself going to the Bhadhar called aloud to "bring out Shaábán." When the guards heard the voice of the Sultán they could not but obey, and brought their prisoner forward. When they had done so, the Sultán said to them : " Bring the traitor up to me that I may ask him how he entertained such designs and had no thought of the royal wrath." When the guards did so, he ordered his fetters off. When the guards saw this, some of them ran away to their masters, but some of them stood up, with folded arms, and told the Sultán that they were his servants, that they had imprisoned the vazír at what they deemed to be the royal command, and now released him under the same.

In the morning the Sultán went up to the Bhadhar, and sat there, and when the nobles heard of it they, with their supporters and men all armed and equipped, set out for the Darbár. At that time there were, in attendance on the Sultán, of slaves and servants, only three hundred persons. Some of them proposed that the Sultán should go out by the Sábarmati postern, and having conveyed himself to a place of safety assemble the army and come back, but the Sultán did not give ear to these craven counsels and stood his ground firmly. When the nobles drew near the Bhadhar, the Maliks Shaúbán, Háji and Kálú asked leave to order the elephants to be made to charge against the approaching rebellious nobles, who, they said, would be sure to take to flight. The Sultán consenting, about six hundred elephants were made to rush at the nobles, who dispersed and ran away, and their soldiers threw up their arms and concealed themselves as best they could in the city. The nobles betook themselves out of the city and wandered about in every direction. Hisámul-mulk went towards Pattan where his brother Rukn-ud-dín was police officer. Kabíruddín Azdul-mulk fled to the Sábharkanthá, where a Rajpút, whose brother he had killed, beheaded him, and brought his head to the Sultán who hung it up at the city gateway. Burhánul-mulk was an extremely fat man and could not run. He could only ride as far as Sarkhez, where a eunuch of the Sultán, who had gone on a religious visit to the shrine of Sheikh Ahmed Khattú, found him having let his horse loose, sitting in a corner at a spot where at present the village Fatehpur is situated. He was caught, and brought to the Sultán, who ordered him to be thrown below an elephant's foot. Mauláná Khizr Sei-ful-mulk was deported to Díu for imprisonment, whence he was re-called afterwards through the kind mediation of Malik Shaábán and a jágir given to him.

At the time of these events the Sultán was fourteen years old ; yet he showed such strength of mind and mature judgment, that he destroyed the rebels and gave redress to the wronged, and from these days till his death his word was so effective that it was never disobeyed. For the services they performed at this period, the Sultán gave the titles of Azdul-mulk to Malik Háji and appointed him Master of Requests and Petitions of the kingdom, of Ikhtiárul-mulk to Malik Baháuddín, of Farhatul-mulk to Malik Túghá, of

Nizámul-mulk to Malik Ísá, of Burhánul-mulk to Malik Saûdulláh, of Imádul-mulk to Malik Kálú, and of Mukhlisul-mulk to Malik Sárang, whom he sometime after distinguished with the still higher title of Kiwámul-mulk. He, also on this occasion, ennobled with jágírs and titles fifty of his other officers and in a short time an army equal in every way to that of Sultán Kutbud-dín's was formed in Gujarát. Now followed a period of such peace and prosperity that no eye had seen nor ear heard; the soldier was independent and in comfort, the dervish careless of all but the worship of the Almighty, the merchant happy in his trade and profit, and the whole country full of peace and tranquillity, and free from anxiety and danger.

The Sultán ruled that the jágir of every Amír or soldier, who was slain in battle or who died a natural death, was continued to his son; if he had no son, half the jágir was continued to his daughter; and if he had no daughter, he settled certain allowances on the dependants of the deceased that they should have no cause of complaint against the Government. They say that, on a certain occasion, some one represented that the son of a certain deceased Amír was not fit for his jágir. The Sultan replied, "Never mind, the jágir will make him fit." After this no one ever made such objections, and, in truth, the secret of the content of his subjects was that he never confiscated jágirs, except for oppression, and he never departed from the rules of Government. During the reign of Mehmúd Shah the Martyr [1] certain of his economical ministers in checking the accounts of the revenues of the kingdom found them to have increased ten-fold, the income of no village being less than double or treble its former revenue; and the merchants also benefited by the safety of the roads throughout his entire dominions. The cause of the comfort of the religious orders in his time was that the Sultán himself respected that holy class, and caused the greatest regularity to be observed in the remission to them of their yearly stipends. He also constructed for the comfort of his of subjects, refectories and lofty saráis for travellers, and imposing collegiate structures and mosques like Paradise; and the reason of the thriving condition of the cultivators was that the Sultán besides being very just and impartial, tolerated neither oppression nor injury. Great and poor are agreed in this that, among the Sultáns of of Gujarát either before or after him, there was no one like Mehmúd Begdá. He conquered the fort of Júnágad and the country of

---

[1] The author probably means Mehmúd III. of Gujarát.

Sorath and the fort of Chánpáner and its neighbourhood, and, having abolished the customs of the infidels, he introduced in those countries the laws of Islám. The merits of all the good actions that will be done up to the Day of Judgment by those he converted to Islám will be laid to the credit of his account, as says the tradition of the Prophet : " He who establishes a virtuous practice, to him is due its reward as also the rewards of those that follow it after him." Although Sultán Bahádur, his grandson, was a greater conqueror, he was not so masterful an administrator as Sultán Mehmúd Begdá, who was unrivalled for excellence in both.

Praise be to Allah ! the period in which Sultán Mehmúd lived was an epoch singularly fertile in the production of great men. In Khurásán, contemporaneously, with him ruled the great Husein Mirzá with the unrivalled Amír Ali Shér as his minister, and the poet Mauláná Jámí[1] as the most brilliant of men of letters. The throne of Delhi was graced by Sikandar, the son of Bahlúl Lódi, with the gifted Miyán Bahlu Khán as his vazír. Mándu had a ruler like Sultán Giyásuddín, the son of Mehmúd Khilji, and the Dakhan, a king like Mehmúd Bahmani, with Khájá Jahán as his minister. To say that the soul of the great belligerent Sultán Mehmúd of Ghazni had sought a second habitation in the body of Sultán Mehmúd Begdá, would not be an exaggeration, as all the deeds and actions of the latter bore a striking resemblance with those of the former. They say that on the day of his coronation Khudáwand Khán Malik Álím, who was much attached to the Sultán and was a man of a high order of scholarship, handed over to the Sultán a copy of the poems of Háfiz (a book which is consulted for auguries and omens) which the Sultán opening at hap hazard found that it had opened at the page containing the ode beginning with the following verses :—

" Thou whose proud form adorns the kingly gown,[2]
Whose pearls refulgent grace the imperial crown;"

being a eulogy on a great, brave, and virtuous king, whose deeds would throw into the shade those of Alexander the Great. After the recital of these verses the Debír or a Secretary of the Sultán got up and read verses ; the last of which complained of the emptiness of his wine cup and called to witness the Mohtasíb (a censor morum whose

---

[1] Sir Clive Bayley (Gujarát 168) calls him Maulana Háji.

اى قباى پادشاهى راست بربالاى تو .. تاج شاهى را فروغ از لولوى لالاى تو [2]

offensive office furnishes a source of endless merriment to the bacchanal Súfi in the Poetry of Musalman countries). As the Mohtasib of the city was also present and the reciter unwittingly extending his hand pointed him out the felicitousness of the recital was much welcomed, and drew applause and dresses of honour from many of the nobles especially Illadáw and Khan and his son who were men of an elegant scholarly taste. All the royal and the faithful nobles present were much gratified at this highly auspicious prophecy, and were presented with valuable dresses of honour and gifts.

It is said that corn has never been so cheap in Gujarát as it was during the reign of Sultán Muhmúd. Like the armies of Jenghíz the Moghal, his army never suffered defeat. He ordered that none of his soldiers should ever borrow money at interest, and he appointed a separate treasurer who should make advances to whoever was in need, and should recover them according to agreement, and owing to this the money-lenders were rather straitened; further, his men thought less of them than dogs, and the king used to say : " If the Musalmáns borrow money at interest, how shall they be able to fight ? "

The great abundance of fruit trees, such as pomegranates, khirnis (*Momusops-Indica*), Jámbus (*Eugenia-jambolana*), Gúlars (*Ficus-glomerata*), cocoa-nuts (*Cocos-mucifera*), and Bels (*Ægle-marmelos*), and Mhowras (*Bassia-latifolia*), and Banyans (*Ficus-bengalensis*), Áonlas (the shrubby Phyllanthus or Phyllanthus Emblica) which are to be found in Gujarát, arose from the attention and fostering efforts of this Sultán. He had such a consideration for roadside trees, that he used to encourage their plantation by giving prizes to the planters, and that whenever he used to see any shade-tree such as a Banyan (*Ficus bengalensi*), a Ním (*Elia azadirachta*), a Pípal (*Ficus religiosa*), he used to pull in rein there, call for its owner, and talk to him for a while with great condecension and kindness, and ask him whence he watered the tree. If the owner said that water was distant and he was put to trouble in carrying it a long way, he used to get a well or a step-well built there, out of the State Treasury. He used also to promise that the planters might be sure of reward in proportion to the number of trees they planted. The " Paradise Garden," which is five *kós* in length and one in breadth, was built, and the Shaában garden was founded by the Sultán. In the same way, if he saw any shop or house empty or in ruins, he used to send for the owners and ask the reason of their being in that condition, and giving pecuniary assistance, if required, used to order its construction. The whole country of Gujarát was such that, the Koranic verse, "he who enters it is safe," descriptive of Mecca, applied to it. [1]

In the latter part of his life, the Sultán used to devote the greater part of his time to devotion and penitence, and tears of mortification and the prayers,[2] called the "Impregnable Fort," were ever on his lips. One day Malik Sárang, the founder of the suburb of that name near Ahmedábád, asked him : "Why, with the proud possession of such a kingdom as that of Gujarát, do you wail and cry ?" The Sultán said : "Oh insensate, my patron Sháh Álam used to tell me that the end of Mehmúd would be " Mehmúd" (محمود a play upon words, meaning " good"). Now, however, much I strive for such an end I do not see in myself any worthiness for it. The stream of my life floweth on fast, and what hath flowed returneth not; hinc illiæ lacrimææ ! alas, I knew not the Master's worth when he was by! At last the Sultán joined himself with Sheikh Sirájud-din, who was a perfect Saint of the age and was by his teaching and direction saved from this delirious and repining condition of the mind.

One day the Sultán hearing the praises of tha saint Sheikh Sirájud-din, the apostle of Kutbe Álam and a great reclaimer of the misguided from Amínul-mulk asked that nobleman to meet him that night at the palace postern on the river Sábarmati. Amínul-mulk did so, and the Sultán issuing asked him to lead him to the monastery of the Saint which he did, the Sultán following alone, with only a sword under his arm, and on foot. Reaching the monastery of the Sheikh, Aminul-mulk went in to announce the Sultán, who was called in, and going in saw the saint seated on a crazy old cot on which, in obedience to his invitation, after saluting the Sheikh and shaking hands with him, the Sultán took his seat at the foot. After a while, he with great sincerity of heart asked him to show him the way to rectitude and the favour of God, and freedom from the passions. The Dervish told him it was extremely difficult for a layman, especially for a king, to devote his heart and soul to heaven. But the Sultán with honest singleness of purpose said he was ready even to give up his royal dignity for his soul's good ; and the Dervish assured of his earnestness said that though one hour of his righteous life as a king was equal to an year of devotion as a Dervish,[3] he would send him his advice in the course of the following day on which he was to act without doubt or question. The

---

[1] Mandakhalahú Kána Ámins. Kuraan chap.
[2] These prayers consist of a repetition of wishes for peace of the soul of the Prophet together with some other stereotyped words.
[3] The Saint here repeats the famous lines of Sa'ádi expressive of the proverb : " the cowl does not make the monk."

Sultán entrusted the duty of conveying this message to Amínul-mulk, and went away. The message with which the Dervish charged that nobleman, with his subsequent conduct, was of a nature to put to the severest test the devotion and faith of the Sultán for holy men : He asked for a high place in the royal service near the Sultán's person, the place of the chief officer of Revenue and Accounts. The Sultán without his belief being in the least shaken gave him the place and next day the Sheikh girding a sword and mounting a horse went to court and was formally invested with the dress of honour. After performing his duties for sometime the Sheikh requested the Sultan to be given quarters near him, and this also being done he came and lived near the Sultan's private apartments. The people of Ahmedabád lost all faith in the Saint and began to speak of him openly as a designing imposter, but the Sheikh made light of it. The real motive of the Sheikh in all this was to at once try the Sultán's faith as well as to give him spiritual teaching, unobserved by the world. In a short time when he thought the Sultan had made himself perfect, he asked his leave with a request never to seek him again and disappeared. Mercy of Allah on such dervishes! The Sultán was the spiritual follower of Sheikh Rehmatulláh, the son of Sheikh Azizulláh, the Resigner in God, and the mausoleum of this Saint is in the suburb of Sheikhpura which is said to have been founded by him.

Though illiterate, the Sultán's mind from his constant association with learned men was stored with such a rich stock of useful knowledge, colloquial and historical (both sacred and profane) legal, poetical and biographical that, except scholars, nobody in speaking with him could say he was unlettered. His notes and queries on learned matters were highly ingenious. Ibni Afras, the translator of the book " Shifa," has mentioned several instances of the Sultan's quickness in deciding difficult points of law. This is one of them copied verbatim. There is a tradition to the effect that the Prophet (on whom be peace !) cursed a boy who passed before him during his prayers and thereby vitiated the prayers. The boy at once became a cripple and could not move a foot. Some people consider this tradition weak, other authorities do not. Those who lay it down to be unsound argue that the passing of a boy before the Prophet could not vitiate his prayers, and that the Prophet would never curse a child in non-age. Those that consider the tradition valid corroborate it by the testimony of Zeid, the son of Òmar, who stated that

7 M

he saw in Tábúc (in Syria) a cripple who said his name was Yezíd, the son of Mehrán, and admitted having become a cripple by the curse of the Prophet for having passed before the Prophet while in prayers in his boyhood. The Sultan, stating that the curse of the Prophet, like the destruction by the Prophet Elias of the boat, was, by Divine inspiration and command, laid the tradition down as valid. This was admitted by all the learned men as a just decision and has found place in the book Shafá.

In A. H. 864 (A. C. 1460) the Sultán went with a force to hunt at Kapadwanj, and in the adjoining plain reviewed his army and prayed and after the reading of the Fátihá,[1] said: " If God wills in the ensuing year I will found a new city." As at the time of the reading of the Fátihá the face of the Sultán was turned in the direction of Sorath, the wise men of the time guessed that the Sultán desired the conquest of Fort Girnár, and after this he returned from Kapadwanj to Ahmedábád. In A. H. 865 (A. D. 1461) he marched from Ahmedábád and encamped on the bank of the river Khári. At this camp a letter arrived from Nizám Sháh, son of Humáyun Sháh Dakhni, to the effect that Sultán Mehmúd Khilji at the instigation of Nizámul-mulk Ghori, who, in the time of Humáyun Sháh, had fled to Mehmúd Khilji, with a numerous army had entered and commenced to ravage the Dakhan. That he had, therefore, advanced forty kós from his city, and was awaiting him at the Gháts, and besought aid from Sultán Mehmúd. The Sultán receiving the letter from the Dakhan started and reached the country of Nazarbár ; at this camp he received another letter from Nizám Sháh to the effect that, though the Sultán Mehmúd Khilji had shown great activity in his operations, he on his part had not spared fighting, had defeated the enemy's army and had captured 50 of his elephants. But that the Dakhan army became engaged in plunder, when Sultán Mehmúd attacked them with 12,000 horses. At this time, said Nizam Shah, he had but few men, still he fought bravely, but that at length Sikandar Khán withdrew him from the field to Bídar from the battle, and brought him into the city of Nazarbár. He added that Sultán Mehmúd had besieged the city of Bídar, and that now without the aid of the Sultán there was no mode of escape. He, therefore, trusted the Sultán would cast his glance like the rising sun in his direction, and dispel the darkness of oppression. On Sultán Mehmúd, king of Gujarát, marching

---

[1] The repetition of the first 'Sura,' or Chapter of the Kuraan, as a requiem of peace for the soul of the Prophet.

with a large army to the aid of Nizám Sháh by the way of Burhánpur, the Khilji raised the siege of Bídar and returned to his own country by way of Gondwánáh. At this time the Rájáh of Gondwánáh, who was with him, said : " This road is one where there is little water, and the jungle is very dense, and the passes are narrow ;" but the Sultán Mehmúd Khilji through fear of Sultán Mehmúd Gujaráti chose this road, and at once marched performing two days' march in one day, They say that he came to such a place that from want of water 6,000 of his men became food for jackals and vultures, and when he entered the Gondwúnáh passes, the Gonds rose against him, and plundered his baggage. Thus after a hundred misfortunes he issued from the mountains and reached his own country. He now caught, and slew the Gond Rájáh, though the Rájáh pleaded that he had warned him. At length when Sultán Mehmúd Gujaráti reached Thánesar which is under Burhánpúr, he reviewed his army. It is related from authentic sources, that in the time of no king of Gujarát was there so large and well equipped an army, nor had any of the kings of his time ever sent such forces in any direction. He had in this expedition seventy-three nobles and had devoted the whole revenue of Gujarát to the pay of his army, and had given up his own crown villages for four years as a contribution to the enlarged expenses of the army, defraying his personal expenses from the treasure left by former kings. Of this treasure also it is related that he spent two-thirds in rewards and food supplies for the army during these four years.

When Mehmúd Khilji returned to his own country, Nizám Sháh sent his Vakils to the Sultán, and they spared nothing in thanking and praising him for his aid and requested him to return to his own country. The Sultán marched thence for his own country.

Afterwards in A. H. 867 (A. C. 1463) Sultán Mehmúd Khilji with 90,000 horse marched to the Dakhan and ravaged and laid the country waste as far as Daulatábád. Nizám Sháh again asked for aid, and the Gujarát Sultán acceding marched to Nazurbár. Sultán Mehmúd Khilji hearing this, returned to his own country by the way he had come; and the Sultán also returned to his capital, and thence wrote to Sultán Mehmúd Khilji that it was not the part of good men to harass the lands of Islám—" You should," he added, "therefore dismiss such ideas from your mind for the future, but if you again invade the Dakhan, I will on this side attack Mándu, take therefore your choice." After this Sultán Mehmúd Khilji gave up attacking

the Dakhan." Afterwards in A. H. 868 (A. C. 1464) Sultán Mehmúd
Gujaráti sent for a large number of damascened swords from Telingán
for war, and in A. H. 869 (A. C. 1465) he marched against the Bárodar [1]
mountains, conquered the rock fortress and returned to his own country.
In A. H. 870 (A. C. 1466) he went to Ahmednagar for hunting, and
on the road Bahaúl-mulk-bin Alaf Khán, also called Aládáud-dín-bin
Sohráb, killed without cause, Adam the armour-bearer of the Sultán
and fled, and hid himself. Malik Háji Imádul-mulk and Malik Kálú
Azdul-mulk were ordered to go and capture, and bring him wherever
he might be. Malik Háji and Malik Kúlu, being helpless, captured
Bahául-mulk and persuaded two of his followers to go to the Sultán and
say they were guilty and Bahául-Mulk innocent, promising that they
would only be imprisoned and afterwards released. They did so, and
the Sultán at once ordered them to be killed. When, however, he
found out the deceit which had been practised upon him, he caused both
the Maliks to be put to death, and after this no causeless murders were
committed during his reign. He conferred on Malik Bahá-ud-dín
Ikhtiyar-ul-Mulk the title of Imád-ul-Mulk and honoured him with the
post of vazír.

In A. H. 877 (A. C. 1472) Mehmúd Sháh conquers Girnar,
and converts Ráo Mandlik, the fist attack being made
in A. H. 871 (A. C. 1466).

It is so related that in the time of Sultán Mehmúd Begdá the Rájá,
Ráo Mandlik of Girnár and Junágadh, had become so haughty and
insolent with the Musalmán Sovereign of Gujarát that he did not consider
himself in any way inferior to that potentate. He considered his rock-
castle of Girnár and his fort of Junágadh impregnable, and he had under
him a country like that of Sorath in which centre all the beauties and
merits of Málwá, Khandesh and Gujarát. The ports of Gujarát receive
many products that are first imported by the ports of Sorath. Purity
of God! It is the same, once prosperous country that now, on account
of the constant change of its governors, has become the land of
marauding free-booters, swindling merchants, charlatanic priests,
grasping land-owners, and ragged soldiers. The free-booters of
Sorath used always to harry the frontiers of Gujarát. Sultán Ahmed
I., the founder of Ahmedábád, had unsuccessfully attempted the conquest

---

1. So my MS. Sir Clive Bayley has "Báwar." Ferishtah—[Persian text II. 385]
calls it Bárúd, and places it between Gujarát and the Konkan, and describes as a strong
hill-fort. The Bombay Gasetteer History of Gujarát (35), correctly, calls it Barúr. Sir
Clive Bayley's note (Gujarát 178) on this fortress is interesting.

of Sorath. For this reason the Súltán always felt a great longing to conquer Sorath, but with great deliberation on account of the great strength of its fortresses and their great capacities of storage, &c. At last, he after consulting the omens, in A. H. 871 (A.C. 1467), undertook the expedition.

Be it known that there is a mountain surrounding Girnár on all sides but the northern. On the south there is a pass (a valley?) between two mountains, twelve *kós* in extent, and in this valley there is a jungle so dense that a horse cannot pass through it; it has numerous caves and it is uninhabitable, except for birds and beasts and a tribe of infidels, called Khánts, who bear a greater resemblance to wild beasts than men. They dwell on the sides of the mountain, and, if any army march against them, they run away and hide themselves in the caverns. In the forest there are such trees that few know their names. There are also many fruit-trees in the mountains: like the Mango (*Mangifera Indica*); the Khirni (*Mimusops Indica*), the Jámbúl (*Eugenia jámbolúná*), the Gúlar (*Ficus glomerata*), the Imli (*Tamarendus Indica*), and the Áonla (*Phyllanthus emblica*), &c. Near the foot of the mountain westwards, about three arrows-throw runs the Wanthali[1] road, leading to the castle of Junágadh, constructed wholly of stone. There are three gates to the castle, one facing the east, the other the west, and the third the north. As one enters the gate, facing the north, he has to enter another gate facing the west. The derivation of the name of Junágadh is so given by the people of Sorath, that in former times the capital of the country of Sorath was the village of Wanthali, five *kós* to the west of Junágadh. The country between Junágadh and this place was so densely wooded that neither horse nor man could pass through it. Many of that Rájáh's ancestors had ruled there, when one day a wood-cutter crossed the distance by accident with the greatest difficulty, and reached a place where he saw a stone-well with an old gateway. He went back, and reported to the Rájáh what he had seen. The Rájáh ordered a clearance of the wood between the city and the gate, and asked of the architects and historians of his time to ascertain the name of the old city, but all of them expressed their inability to do so, and the place was called Junágadh, the old fortress (city), as nobody could say the date of its building or the name of its founder. There are two wells in the old

---

[1] A village about eight miles south-west of the town of Júnágadh.

fort called Noḳhan and Angoliá, and two step-wells, one called Ari and another Brájári.

The Rájáh of the land was called Rao Mandlik, and it is noted in Hindu histories that his ancestors had ruled over the country from father to son for nineteen hundred years. In this long period the city was once taken by Sultán Muhammad Tughlak, emperor of Delhi, and once by Sultán Ahmed, the son of Muhammad Sháh Sultán of Gujarát, but the Hindus subsequently gathering force re-took the place from the deputies of these two Muslim powers.

It is said that when Sultán Mehmúd determined to take the fortresses of Girnár and Junágadh he ordered his treasurer to take stores of ready money in gold with him to the amount of fifty millions and ordered his Kúrbegi (or keeper of the royal armoury) to take with him one thousand seven hundred swords of Egypt and Yemen and Maghrebi and Khurásáni and Alleymand on whose handles was from four to six *sers* of gold; and three thousand and three hundred Ahmedábád swords with silver hilts, weighing from four to five *sers*, and seventeen hundred daggers (Khanjár) and double-edged daggers (Jámdhar), with gold on their handles, weighing from two *sers* and a half to three *sers*, and he ordered his master of the horse (Akhtahbegi) to take with him two thousand Arabian and Turkish horses with gold trappings. In short, when the Sultán besieged the fort of Junágadh, the infidels of those parts placed their families and provisions in a defile, called Maháilah (Muhá-bala!) which was very strong position and determined to fight to the death. One day Tughlak Khán, a prince of Sindh, said to the Sultán:" The Maháilah is a very impregnable place, and no army has ever penetrated it, and conquered it." The Sultán replied, " If God wills I will conquer it." One day the Sultán, mounted as if for hunting, went in the direction of the Maháiláh. When the Hindus saw but a small party, they were careless and thought it would not attack them. Suddenly, the Sultán came upon them, and the infidels after a short fight fled and went into the jungle. When the army heard that the Sultán was engaged, they followed him, and leaving their horses outside the defile, they entered it on foot, and the great part of the families and provisions of the Hindus fell into the hands of the army, and the Sultán returned victorious to his quarters, and occupied himself in furthering the siege. They say that in the next four days' siege the Sultán distributed the fifty millions of ready money in gold and the swords and daggers, in presents to the soldiers, so that they should strive strenuously to conquer the fortress and should dismiss laziness and carelessness from their minds. He also sent out powerful detachments to ravage the country of Sorath, and countless plunder fell into their hands. Ráo Mandlik now sent his agents and showed great humility. The Sultán thought it best to suspend the operations of the siege of the fortress for that year and returned to his own country. In A. H. 872 (A. C. 1468) the Sultán heard that the Ráo Mandlik, when he visited his idol temples did so in great state and splendour and with a golden umbrella over him. The Sultán was seized with kingly jealousy and he caused to be got ready 40,000 horses and many elephants, and ordered them to take from him his umbrella and regalia and if he refused to give them up, to lay waste his country with fire and sword. As soon as Rájá Mandlik heard this, he sent the umbrella and ornaments with fitting submission to the Sultán. The army returned and were honoured with kissing the Sultán's feet. The Sultán bestowed these ornaments on his musicians. After this in A. H. 873 (A. C. 1469) news was received of the death of Sultán Mehmúd Khilji and of the accession of his eldest son Gheíasud-dín to the throne. Several of the Amírs represented to the Sultán that after the death of Sultán Ahmed, Sultán Mehmúd Khilji had endeavoured to conquer Gujarát, and that now if the Sultán wished to conquer Málwá it would fall easily into his hands. But the Sultán said, "To covet the country of a brother Muhammadan, whether he be alive or dead, does not befit a Musalman."

In A. H. 874 (A. C. 1469) the Sultán again sent an army to Sorath, and having plundered and ravaged the country it returned. Afterwards the Sultán resolved to conquer Girnár and turning his face towards the country of Sorath, started thither by rapid marches. On hearing this the Ráo Mandlik without being sent for, and without any message, came into the presence of the Sultán and said, " Whatever service the Sultán may command, this slave will be ready to perform with his life. Without my having committed any fault why do you endeavour to ruin me." The Sultán said, " What crime is greater than infidelity ! If you desire safety acknowledge the unity of God, and become a Musalmán with a true heart that I may entrust to you other dominions in addition to your own, else I will destroy you." When the Ráo Mandlik saw how the case stood, he fled that very night and entered the fort. While he was absent with the Sultán, his officers had collected provisions and strengthened the forts of Junágadh and Girnár. One day the Sultán reached the foot of the mountain, and the infidels poured forth as numerous as ants and locusts from the fort and commenced to fight. After much fighting they were defeated, and entered the lofty fortress of Girnár. In this way the fight went on for two days. On the third day the Sultán went himself to the battle, and fought from morn till eve with the infidels with both sword and spear. That day the soldiers of the Sultán were more successful, the infidels fled, and re-entered the lofty fortress. The Sultán divided the trenches amongst his men, and appointed each Amír to a place. The infidels every day came from one quarter or another, and fought. One day some Hindus came suddenly into the trench of Álam Khán Fárúki, one of the famous nobles, slew him and departed. The Sultán made great efforts in being on the alert, and the Hindus became straitened. A Waniá, named Withal, Ráo Mandlik's minister, consulting with the garrison of the fortress, said : "This time Sultán Mehmúd will not depart without conquering. It is better for us to go to the higher fortress of Girnár than to remain in Junágadh, because it is stronger than this one, and has plenty of provisions." The garrison agreed with him, and they sent ambassadors to the Sultán, and said : "If the Sultán of the world will spare our lives and will not hinder our families, we will take our families and stores, and come out of the fort, and surrender it to the Sultán's servants." The Sultán replied, "Be it welcome to you." They then taking their families and stores, made for the lofty fort of Girnár. The Sultán coming to know of this, ordered his army to plunder them.[1] The army ran in pursuit and reaching the middle of the mountain commenced the fight. That day many Muhammadans became martyrs, and they sent many Hindus to their last account, but the Hindus managed to convey their families into the lofty fortress, and every day issuing thence, they gave battle. After a long time when their stores ran short, and they were reduced to extremities of privation, they prayed for quarter. The Sultán agreed to their prayers on condition of their adopting the faith of Islám. Ráo Mandlik now issued forth from the fort, received the honour of kissing the Sultán's feet, and

---

[1] Sultán Mehmúd's conduct was not singular. Deliberate and systematic breach of faith with unbelievers was accounted a virtue by Muslim rulers of Mohmud's ilk, and has given birth to the Gujarati proverb : "It is foolish to trust the word of one whose stomach contains another's flesh! (meaning a flesh-eater). Jena-pet-mán parko-más, Ténosho-vishvás." The Muslim rulers justified their conduct by the tradition of the Prophet : "Al harbs Khadatun—War is fraud."

handed over the keys of the fort to the Sultán's servants. This happened in A. H. 877 (A. C. 1472). The Sultán recited the creed[1] of Islám, the Ráo repeated it and saved himself from the flame of the Sultán's wrath which was like the fire of hell. After his conversion the Ráo used to say : " Before I met the king Sháh Shamsuddín Bukhári" (who lies buried, in the neighbourhood of the town of Unáh,) "had attracted me towards Islám. Now by the kindness of the Sultán I am exalted by the profession of the faith with the tongue while believing in it with the heart." But they say that whenever he remembered Girnár and his former kingly state, he used to weep copiously.

This is what the author of the Táríkhi Bahádur-Sháhi says, but I have heard from reliable men of Gujarát that the cause of the Sultán being induced to make this last conquest of Jùnágadh and Girnár was different. It was this: The Wánia Witthal was the vazír of Ráo Mandlik, and the adminstration of all the affairs of the Ráo was in his hands, and he turned against him. The cause was that the Wánia had a wife of the name of Mohini who for peerless beauty was renowned in her time. One day Ráo Mandlik saw the sun of her beauty and became excessively enamoured of her. The end of the matter was that after much endeavour he obtained possession of her. This infamous intrigue being discovered by her husband he placed the saw at the root of the power and kingdom of the Ráo. Repressing the mortification of his heart, he represented with great show of zealous concern to the Ráo, that the provisions in the fort were old and had become unfit for consumption. He asked orders to replace the old provisions with fresh ones. The Ráo said, " Why do you not do so?" Beginning to remove the provisions, he secretly sent a man to the Sultán to tell him that the fortress was emptied of stores, and that if the Sultán would now make an attempt to conquer the fort, he could easily capture it. The Sultán was delighted and started at once for Jùnágadh and Girnár, and having arrived by forced marches conquered both the forts. God knows the truth of the affair.

Some say that the cause of Ráo Mandlik adopting Islám was that when he descended from the fortress, and came to the Sultán, the Sultán took him with him to Ahmedábád. One day he went to Rasúlábád which was the residence and is now the place of burial of Sháh-i-Alam. He saw that many elephants, horses and men were

---

[1] The creed is : Lá-iláha illal-láh, Muhammad-ur-rasúl-ulláh. There is no God but Alláh, Muhammad is his Prophet.

8

collected before his house, and he asked what amír dwelt there? They replied it was the Darbár of the Shǎh-i-Álampanǎh, the king who was the refuge of the world. He asked, whose servant was he, and who paid him ? They replied : " He was a dependent of Allǎh alone." He asked, " whence then has he obtained all these things of royal state?" They replied, "God gave them to him." He asked if he could have an interview with him and went and saw him. As soon as his eyes fell on the face of Shǎh Alam he said, " Tell me what is necessary to be said by one who wishes to become a Muhammadan. The Hazrǎt Shǎh recited the creed. The Rǎo repeated it with the tongue and admitted the truth of it with his heart. In short from his visit to the house of that good man he obtained the honour of admission into Islǎm.

At the time of Sultǎn Mehmúd's siege of Júnǎgad there were but few cannon and muskets in the higher fort. The garrison fought sometimes with stones and sometimes with arrows and muskets. Fighting for a long time in this manner with great vigour and energy, the Sultǎn's sustained efforts to conquer the fort failing to open the door of victory, he became much grieved, and wrote to Khudǎwand Khǎn, who was the adept of his day in the science of astrology and who having resigned the post of vazír, had retired to his own house, in Ahmedǎbǎd : " Although I don't fail in fighting strenuously, yet up to the present time I see no hope of victory, though I am determined either to clasp the bride of Victory in my arms or die a martyr." Khudǎwand Khǎn wrote in reply, " Send me an account of the mode of your attack, and where your trenches are, and who is in command over each." This was sent accordingly. The Khǎn altered the position of the trenches and wrote the names of the amírs who should be placed in ommand in each, and requested the Sultǎn to make an attack on the fortress on a certain day. The Sultǎn acted according to the writing of the Khǎn, and on the appointed day God opened the door of victory to him.

After this victory the Sultǎn sent to the cities and towns of Gujarǎt for great sayads and noted wise men and kǎzis, and officers acquainted with the Muhammadan faith to enforce the laws of Islǎm, and settled them in Júnǎgadh, and in the towns under it and he himself remained there, and commenced to populate the town, and to repair the city-walls of Jahǎnpanǎh, and built lofty palaces, and ordered his amírs to each of them build a residence for himself. In the course of time a city was built that was a twin to Ahmedǎbǎd. The Sultǎn named it Mustafǎbǎd. Thus was Sorath brought without any opposition under his rule, and all the

Hindu chiefs and land holders with humility and submission and without demand or importunity brought and paid him the tribute due from them.

News was now received that Jeysingh, son of Gangdás, Rájá of Chámpáner, harboured the discontented men of the Baroda and Dabhoi *sarkárs* and purposed to rebel, and having made friendship with the king of Mándu expected assistance from him. The discontented about Ahmedábád, as a melon takes colour from another melon[1] became also ready to rebel. The king appointed Malik Jamálud-din his armour-bearer as *faujdar* over the great city of Ahmedábád, and its dependencies with the title of Muháfiz Khán. The above mentioned Malik made such excellent arrangements that theiving and high-way robbery became extinct, and the citizens and villagers slept with open doors, and the merchants opened their loads on the roads and stages. Fortune smiled on Muháfiz Khán. His son[2] took tribute from those turbulent people who had never paid it before. After some days the Sultán entrusted to him the entire government of the city of Ahmedábád. This service also he performed in a manner which met with approval. After a few days he became viceroy, and performed these duties also well. He was now invested with the office of vazír of the kingdom and was allowed to retain his old posts and dignities of which the agents of the Malik performed the necessary work. This Muháfiz Khán was grand-father of the author of the " Táríkh-i-Bahádur Sháhi." In short, the Sultán also appointed an amír to bring into order the country of Baroda, and he appointed Malik Bahául-mulk styled Imád-ul-mulk to the thánedári of Sankheda, and he entrusted to Malik Sárang Kiwámul-mulk the Thánedári of Norkha, and that of Dákhna to Táj Khán, son of Sálár. The appointment of these posts prevented Jeysingh from rebellion. In A. H. 876 (A. C. 1471) Ráo Mandlik was dignified with the title of Khán Jahán and a *jágír* was bestowed on him, and the golden idols which had been taken from his temples were sold and their proceeds distributed among the soldiers.

After this the Sultán made an incursion into Sindh, and in one day marched sixty-one *kos*, and plundered the countries of the zamíndárs, adjacent to Sindh. The land in these parts is salt and in the rain it remains under water. One portion of the country is an arm of the salt sea and the tides of the sea flow over it. Its breadth in some

---

[1] All growing ripe at once.—An Urdu proverb.
[2] Ferishtah (Persian text-II. 390) calls him Malik Khizr and says he exacted tribute from the Rájás of Vágad, Idar and Sirohi.

places is six kos and in others greater or less. Its water is always salt and the land is not fit for cultivation, and except fish and salt, produces nothing. They say that in this foray there were only six hundred horse with the Sultán. The *zamindárs* of these parts of Sindh, the Sumrás and the Sodhás[1] on hearing of the Sultán's arrival, at the head of twenty-four thousand horse, took up a strong position. But on seeing the Sultán's army, they sent their agents to him agreeing to become Muhammadans. The Sultán refrained from their slaughter, and said if they wished to become Muhammadans they should act according to the precepts of Islám, and give up inter-marriage with the Hindus, and send some of their chiefs to attend on the Sultán ; that their chiefs should accompany the Sultán to Júnágadh, where, having learned the precepts of Islám, they might return to their families and instruct them. They agreed with fervour, and came with fitting presents, and were allowed to kiss the Sultán's feet, and accompanied the victorious return of the Sultán to Júnágadh. The Sultán handed them over to the learned in religion for instruction. Some of them after they had acquired knowledge of Islám returned to their country, others being charmed with the Sultán's favour remained with him, giving up their homes and families and becoming in course of time worthy of confidence and advancement.

In A. H. 877 (A. C. 1472) the Sultán marched with a strong army to chastise the lawless tribes of Sindh, with 900 horsemen, each with two horses. He reached Sarpalah, and there fought with, and conquered 40,000 Hindu *zamindárs* of Sindh who were skilled archers, and having captured their wives and children brought them to Júnágadh.

In this year (A. C. 1472) Sultán Mehmúd conquered Jagat and Sankhodwárá.[2] The cause of this conquest was that Mauláná Mehmúd of Samarkand who was distinguished for his great scientific and poetic attainments had embarked from the coast of the Dakhan to go to Samarkand. He was on his way captured with his property and family by the pirates of Sankhodwárá who brought him and his two sons to the shore, and set them adrift keeping with them his women and property. The Mulla after a hundred dangers and misfortunes betook himself to the

[1]. According to Ferishtah (Persian text II. 390-91) these people (more probably Jádejas) lived in Katchh which Ferishtah, erroneously places in the limits of Sindh. He represents the people as wild and worshippers of the elements. The next expedition was against the Jats and Baluchis of Sindh proper. The author erroneously calls them Hindu *zamindars* of Sindh.

[2]. Dwárka (north latitude 22°15', east longitude 69°) on the north-western shore of Káthiawar, famous for its temple of Krishna.

Court of Sultán Mehmúd. They say that the sons of the Mulla were so very young, that they were unable to travel on foot. The Mulla was not strong enough to carry both of them at once on his shoulder or his hip. He therefore used to carry one of the boys on his shoulder for a short distance, and then to set him down, and returning, he used to carry the other and bring him along. In this manner in several days he travelled seventy *kos* and arrived in the presence of the Sultán with grieved heart and flowing eyes, and so repeated his tale of wrong and oppression that the recital touched with pain the heart of the Sultán, and of all present. The Sultán asked for all the details, and with tearful eyes and a thousand sighs the Mulla related all his sufferings. Although previous to this the Sultán had felt a desire to conquer Jagat and the island of Sankhodwár, the most famous places of Hindu worship the difficulty of the road to Jagat and the wildness of the neighbourhood and the strength of the Island of Sankhodwár, used to make him hesitate. The Sultán was considering about it, and was thinking how it might be managed, when this occurrence happened, and the new desire strengthened the old one. The Sultán became restless and said, "As long, God willing, as I do not punish these Hindus, I shall feel averse to take rest." He consoled Mulla Mehmúd, and showed great pity for his misfortunes, and sent him to Ahmedábád. On the 17th of the month of Zilhajj, he marched against Jagat, and reached it by forced marches. The Hindus fled to the Island of Sànkhodwárá. He then plundered Jagat and cast down the buildings thereof, and destroyed the idol temples, and broke the idols to pieces, and thence he pitched his camp at Adhámrá, which is about ten *kos* from Jagat on the sea-shore opposite the Island of Sánkhodwárá. The author of the Mehamúd Sháhí writes that the place was an abode of snakes, so that no one in the army slept that night for fear of them, and there was no tent in which a snake was not found. It is said that they killed seven hundred snakes in the suite of tents belonging to the Sultán alone. One of the marvels of this country is this, that on the 9th of the month of Asádh, which is the commencement of the monsoon, from the eleventh to the fourteenth, which the Hindus called the *Igiaras, Báras, Teras, Chawdas,* and *Púranmashi,* birds as big as *Mainás* of a special appearance, come from the sea and perch on the top of the idol temple which is in the village of Mádhupur on the sea-shore in the Mángrol district. Many of them die and the survivors take to wing after about two hours. When these have flown away, the dwellers there pick up the dead ones, and guess from their feathers whether or not their monsoon will be favourable. If they see that the black feathers preponderate in the head and tail and there is a white patch in the middle of the bird's body they guess that there will be more rain at the commencement and end of the monsoon, and less in the middle, and if it be black in the middle, and white at the two extremities, they guess that there will be more rain in the middle of the season and less at the beginning and end; and thus when black preponderates, excess of rain, and where white, want of it, is prognosticated. If the whole of the bird's body be black,[1] continuous rain, and if all white, total absence of rain is foretold. It has never happened, but that these birds came on the days of the months named, and they say also that birds of this sort used also at that time of the year to come and perch on the idol temples of Patan, Diú, and Jagat, which are situated on the sea-shore, and the inhabitants of those places similarly drew omens from them.

In short the Hindus of the country of Jagat strengthened themselves in the Island of Sánkhodwár. The Island of Sankhodwár is three *kos* from the shore, the sea around it being very deep. The pirates under the Rájá of Jagat were the inhabitants thereof and plundered all travellers by sea. When the Sultán saw that the Hindus of these parts had entered this island, he sent for boats from his ports and embarking in them well equipped and armed soldiers, he set out with his own special troops to conquer that island. On every side the warriors of the faith embarked in boats, and having arrived close to the island, commenced to fight. The Hindus did not fail in sending a rain of arrows and bullets and in fighting with sword and spear. At length the warriors of Islám were victorious from their superior strength, and killed the greater part of the Hindus, but some of them embarking on their ships took to flight. The Sultán entered the island and prepared boats with good seamen to chase and capture the vessels of the enemy, and the Musalman, who had scaled the temple, began, with a loud voice, to give the call to prayers, and they demolished the temple, and broke its idols. The Sultán praised God in a prayer of two *rekaáts*,[2] and the family of the Mulla who were in the prison were released. They say that great plunder in rubies and pearls of fine water and costly clothes fell into the

---

[1] The bird called, *Maina* in Hindustáni, is the starling (Gracula religiosa). The only other bird resembling it is the *Tiliar*, commonly called a Bajri bird (Pastor rosens) by Gujarat sportsmen. It has the closest resemblance to the description given here.

[2] Literally genuflexion. The Prayers for thanksgiving are not long.

hands of the Musalmáns; and the Sultán remaining some time built a mosque, and collecting a large quantity of provisions and having handed over charge of Sánkhodwár and Jagat to Malik Túghá who had the title of Farhat-ul-mulk, himself returned to Junágadh. The conquest of Jagat and Sankhodwár happened in A. H. 878 (A. C. 1473). The island had not been previously conquered by any king, and it s conquest was now effected through the effort of the arm of Sultán Mehmúd, the Champion of the Faith.

Two years after this, in A. H. 880 (A. C. 1475) Hazrat Sháh Alam, the great Saint, died. The date of his demise is gatherable from the numerical value of the letters in the word *Fakhr* " Glory," as also from the words *A'khir-ul-Auliya*—the last of the Saints.

On Friday, the tenth of Jamádul-Awwal of the above year (A. C. 1475) the Sultán arrived at Mustufá-bád, Júnágádh. By chance some of the warriors of the faith who had embarked in boats in pursuit of Bhím, son of Súgar the Rájá of Jagat, having captured the said Bhím and put fetters on him, and a collar round his neck, brought him to Mustufá-bád. The Sultán bestowed on each of his captors handsome reward, and ordered that they should bring Mulla Mehmúd of Samarkand from Ahmedábád. When Mulla Mehmúd came from Ahmedábád to Júnágadh and had an audience of the Sultán, the Sultán ordered that Bhím should be handed over to Mulla Mehmúd that he should take his revenge on him. They brought Bhím with a collar round his neck and fetters on his legs. The Mulla rose, and praised the king and his zeal for Islám and said, " By the good fortune of the king I have attained my object." Afterwards the Sultán ordered that they should take Bhím to Muháfiz Khán at Ahmedábád, that having hewed him into pieces he should affix a piece to every gate of the city as a warning to other lawless people. When they brought Bhím to Ahmedábád Muháfiz Khán acted according to this order.

After the Sultán had satisfied himself in bringing the affairs of Sorath into good order, the desire of conquering the fortress of Chámpáner which had remained dormant in his heart was re-kindled and he marched from Mustufábád to Ahmedábád. On the way he received tidings that certain Malabar pirates having fitted up several ships were harassing the ports of Gujarát. The Sultán accordingly turned to Ghogha and sent skilled sailors on vessels properly equipped to punish the Malabáris, and himself came from Ghoghá to Cambay and thence marched to Sarkhej. Paying a visit to the tomb of Sheikh

Ahmed Khattu, he halted three days, and fixed the *jágirs* and allowances to the sons of those who had fallen or died natural deaths in this
campaign. Whoever had a jágir it was confirmed to his son and he
who left no son, half of his jágir was given to his daughter, and he who
left no daughter had his dependants provided for in a fitting manner.
During these three days the Sultán's eyes were constantly filled with
tears, and he was in great grief. On seeing these signs one of his attendants said to his Majesty, "After many years the Sultán through his
good fortune having conquered, forts like those of Junágadh and Girnár,
is returning to his capital. What then is the reason of thus halting at
three *kos* from the capital, and what is the cause of this grief, while
the people of Gujarát are all awaiting the arrival of the Sultán, and
the families of the soldiers are anxiously expecting their arrival.
This is surely an occasion for joy and gladness, and not a time for
sorrow and lamentation." The Sultán replied, "I should indeed be
a thoughtless and unworthy man if after arriving here in safety and
comfort I do not enquire after and make provision to assuage
the grief of the widows and families of those who have for ever
marched away from this transitory world. It matters little if we
delay for two or three days to enter the city, but to enter it without
enquiring after and comforting and cooling the ardour of the grief of
those whose dear ones have not returned, would be far from
considerate or humane." They say that during those days Kázi
Najmuddin, ruler of the religious ordinances in the city of Ahmedábád,
came out to congratulate the Sultán. The Sultán heaved a pitious
sigh and said: "Ah Kázi you congratulate me, but you should tell me,
how those fare, whose sons and brothers have become martyrs or
have died during these last five years? Had they remained in
their houses how many offspring would they not have had. Just
consider the sacrifice at which I have purchased my victories."

     In short, after satisfying the distressed and the suffering, in the
month of Shâabán the Sultán entered the great city of Ahmedábád, and in
the month of Ramazán he took his army against Chámpáner. When he
arrived at the village of Morámli which is of the Sáonli *parganah* and
situated on the banks of the Mahi, he ordered a halt, and thence sent a
strong force to lay waste the Chámpáner country. The army after
ravaging the country returned, and when the rainy season had arrived
the Sultán returned to his capital, and having passed the rains in
Ahmedábád, he went in the direction of Mustafábád, and after

spending sometime near Mustafábád in hunting and the chase, he returned to Ahmedábád. But the desire of the conquest of Chámpáner was
never absent from his mind, and each time he left Ahmedábád for
hunting, his thoughts were occupied with Chámpáner. By chance one
day while hunting, he arrived on the banks of the river Wátrak, which
is twelve *kos* from Ahmedábád in a south-easterly direction, when he
heard that sometimes in that place highway robberies took place.
He ordered a city to be founded on that spot named Mehmúdábád, and
from that day the building of the city commenced. He ordered a strong
stone-embankment to be made on the river and lofty palaces were erected
on it. The building of this city bears witness to the excellence of his
judgment and the quickness of his understanding, and the water of that
river is very sweet and wholesome, and, in fact, were one to say that of
all places in the world for beauty of climate and site none comes up to
this, he would be right.

When in A. H. 885 (A. C. 1480) the Sultán went to Júnágad,
he left his eldest son Ahmed Sháh in Ahmedábád, and placed
Khudáwand Khán in charge of the young prince. As the army had
wearied of the continual expeditions of the Sultán, some rebellious persons incited Khudáwand Khán to set up Ahmed Sháh on the throne and
act treacherously to the Sultán.[1] Imádul-mulk, one of chief nobles
whom they took into confidence, was a true servant and upset
all their plans, by advising the nobles to beware lest this flame
should become too strong. The end of this was that the Sultán
became acquainted with the plot, and coming from Mustufábád to
Ahmedábád he severely punished Khudáwand Khán and his like.

In A. H. 887 (A. C. 1482) except in the territory of Chámpáner
there was no rain in Gujarát. Malik Asad, chief equerry[2] of the Sultán,
who was posted at the *thanah* of Morámli called also Rásúlabád,
began to plunder the Chámpáner territory. When he reached the neighbourhood of the fort of Chámpáner, the Ráwal Patái, Rájá of Chámpáner,
issuing from the fortress, joined battle. The Malik fought bravely, but
was defeated, and most of his followers were slain and two of the
Sultán's elephants with several horses which were with the Malik

---

[1] Ferishtah (Persian text, II. 395) relates this attempt of the nobles to depose
Sultán Mehmúd at greater length. Mehmúd tested the loyalty of his nobles by giving
out that he was determined to proceed on a pilgrimage to Maccah. When, however, he
came to know that the chief part in the conspiracy was borne by Khudá-wand Khán, the
only punishment he dealt out to him was to name one of his pigeons after that nobleman.

[2] Or it may be, one of the chosen and exalted slave officers of the Sultán.

9

were seized with all their equipments by the Ráwal. On hearing this news, the Sultán was enraged and the desire of the conquest of Chámpáner became fixedly engraved on his heart.

When the Sultán set out from Ahmedábád for the conquest of the Chámpáner fortress, and arrived at Baroda the Ráwál Patái became alarmed, and sent his agents to the Sultán, and made most humble submission, but, however humbly his *vakils* begged for pardon, their request was not acceded to, and the Sultán said, "Except the sword and dagger no other message shall pass between you and me." His agents returned to him sad and sorrowful, and related the state of affairs. The Ráwál now made up his mind to die, strengthened his fort, and prepared for the final conflict. The Sultán having arrived, laid siege to the fortress, and each day, from morn till eve battle raged between the army of Islám and the ill-fated Hindus. When some days had passed in this way, the Sultán ordered covered approaches to be constructed and engineers versed in the art, commenced to construct them. They say that they used to buy a bundle of poles for one gold *ashrafi*[1], and used it in the construction of approaches. The Ráwal Patái now sent his minister Súr to Sultán Ghiásuddín Mehmúd Khilji, requesting aid, and promising that he would give one *lákh* of *tánkáhs*,[2] each *tánkáh* being worth eight Akbari *tánkáhs* for every march that the Sultán should make from Mándu in the direction of Chámpáner. When Sultán Ghiásuddín understood this matter, he marched from Mándu to Naálchah, a village three *kos* from Mándu, and became occupied in reviewing and organizing his army. When Sultán Mehmúd heard this, he entrusted the conduct of the siege to some of his nobles, and himself marched towards Mándu and making forced marches arrived at Dohad, which is situated on the frontier of Gujarát and Málwa, and encamped there.

Sultán Ghiásuddín, apprehensive of what might happen, devised a stratagem to give up the expedition : Having assembled learned men and Kázis, he informed them how Sultán Mehmúd was besieging the fortress of Chámpáner, how the Rájá of Chámpáner had sought aid from him,

---

[1] A gold coin from Rs. 16 to 24 in value.

[2] About two rupees of the present currency, a small gold or silver coin.

and he asked their opinion in the matter of helping him. They unanimously replied, "It does not behove a Muslim potentate to aid an unbeliever at such a time." Sultán Ghiásuddín on hearing this returned to
his own capital, and Sultán Mehmúd also returning, came to Chámpáner.
The Ráwál Patái now became hopeless of succour. The approaches had
by this time been completed, and the garrison were in great straits.
They burned all their property and families, and issuing from the
fortress commenced to fight.[1] They say that all the garrison were
slain, except the Ráwal Patái and his minister Dúngarsi, who were
wounded and fell into the Sultán's hands. The Sultán caused them to be
imprisoned in charge of Nizám Khán. They say that in this
interview, although the Ráwal Patái was ordered to observe the
ceremonial of the Sultán's court, he refused to conform to it. After
five months when his wounds were healed, he was brought to the
Sultán who ordered him to embrace Islám, but he refused. Finally by
the order of the learned men and Kázis his head was struck off, and was
exposed on a stake. His minister Dúngarsi, who was brought to a place
near this stake, managed with sudden activity and resolution to snatch a
sword from the hand of Sheikhan bin Kabír, one of the attendants of the
Sultán, and inflicted on him a fatal blow. In the end they killed him
also. They say that two daughters and one son remained of the Ráwal's
family, when they brought them to the Sultán; he sent his daughters
to his harem, and gave his son to Seiful-mulk to adopt as a son, and
he grew up in the care of the Malik, and ultimately in the time of Sultán
Muzaffar bin Mehmúd he was ennobled with the title of Nizámul-
mulk, and became one of his chief nobles. The conquest of the fort of
Chámpáner took place in A. H. 889 (24th November A. C. 1483-84).

The climate of Chámpáner was very pleasing to the Sultán, and
he made it his capital, and built there a large city which was
named Muhammadábád, and a lofty mosque was constructed, and the
Sultán also erected a fort round Chámpáner and called it Jahánpanáh,
and the amírs, vazírs, merchants, and wánias, each one, built for
himself lofty dwellings. In A. H. 890 (A. C. 1485) he caused to be laid
out gardens like paradise round the city, and thus in a short time the
city of Muhammadábád was so adorned and beautified that the inhabitants of Gujarát wrote the plan of Ahmedábád on the paper of forget-
fulness, and agreed on Muhammadábád being without an equal. The

---

[1] Ferishtah (Persian text, II. 396-97) gives a more detailed account of the taking of
Pávágadh.

city of Muhammadàbàd full of lofty dwellings, with its suburbs pleasing
and free from all unpleasantness, was the residence of the great men
and the dwelling of the beautiful of the time.   Its gardens[1] were filled
with flowers of different colours and fruit of every kind, mangoes with
rich flavour, and melons of famed sweetness, and pomegranates, and
grapes, and almonds of delicate flavour, and apples and the sugar-cane
the mother of all sweets, fine figs and plantains and custard apples,
and the *Khirni* (Mimusops indica) like pale gold, with flavour like
milk and sugar, being equally wholesome, and the *tád* (Brab palm)
with its juice like milk, and its tender fruit of which *sharbat* is made
like *fáludah* (a kind of flummerry), and the cocoanut (Cocos nucifera)
whose pulp is like *halwa* and its juice most agreeable and delicious,
also the Jack and the *Ramphal* (Annona reticulata) and *Kamrakh*
(Averrhoa carambola) and the *Phálsá* (Grevia Asiatica) and the *Aonla*
(Phyllanthus emblica), each of which has its own peculiar flavour and
refreshes and comforts the heart and soul.   Let it not be concealed that
some physicians prefer the water-melon to the sugar-cane and some say
the opposite.   The best kinds of sugar-canes are better than common
mangoes, but the best mangoes, are better than all kinds of sugar-cane.

There were also sweet-smelling flowers like red roses and *serti*,
the dog or China rose (Rosa glandulifera) the *Chamli* (Jassemine) and
Champá (Michelia champaca) and *Bel* (Eaglæ marmelos) and *Moghrai*
(Jasminum zambac) and *Jáijúi* (Jasmínum auriculatum), and *Borsal*
(Mimusops elengi), *Kewrá* and *Ketki* (Pandanus odoratissimus), each
blossom of which is like the perfumer's box and on each
Narcissus is a navel as of the musk gazelle of Tártary.   There
are other flowers of different colours from looking at which the
rust of the heart would be removed, and the eyes of the beholders
would be enlightened.   They say that with the fruit-trees and flowers
in such plenty there was so much sandalwood to be found in the
neighbourhood of Chámpáner that the people used it in house-building
and it sufficed them.   Blessed be Alláh! was it this Chámpáner—
now is the abode of the tiger and lion?   Its buildings are ruined, its
inhabitants have given their property to the winds of destruction, even
its waters are poisoned, and its air such that it deprives the human
frame of its strength.   Thorns grow now where flowers bloomed, and
where gardens smiled there is jungle, dense and frowning, and there

---

[1] The whole description of the gardens and fruits is a tissue of poetical puns, and has
been translated as closely as possible without the floweriness of the text interfering with the
accuracy of the English.

is neither name nor trace of Sandalwood trees. Of a truth the Koranic saying has here been realized: "Every thing on earth shall perish except the Face of thy Glorious and Gracious Lord."

They say that a man from Khurásan petitioned to the Sultán saying, " I am perfectly skilled in laying out gardens and in designing buildings. If a place be allotted to me I will lay out a garden that will gladden the Sultán's heart." The Sultán said, "Choose in the neighbourhood of the city such a place as may suit your purpose," and he ordered his officers to give him whatsoever he might require. The man laid out a nice garden, and built a small pretty fountain in it, and he contrived fountains and water-falls, an art previously unknown in Gujarát. The Sultán was very delighted on visiting it, and rewarded and was kind to its builder. At this time a Gujarati carpenter named Hálú, petitioned saying, " I also will build a garden as good as that opposite to it if you give the order." The Sultán said, " Why not if you can do it ?" and Hálú in a certain time laid out a garden better than the first one. On seeing this other the Sultán was much delighted, and asked him: "The people of Gujarát are not acquainted with this art. Whence then did you learn it ?" He said: " I disguised myself as an ignorant labourer and worked for the man from Khurásán, and partly by watching what he did and partly by my own skill, I acquired the knowledge." The Sultán was pleased, and praised him for his work and intelligence and perseverance, and gave him large presents with a handsome dress of honour. Several of those buildings remain to this day and that garden is well known and famous, and the people of Gujarát call this garden Hálól. [1]

In short most of the elegant arts and crafts that are now common in Gujarát were copied from men of skill and genius from other countries, and Gujarát like an accomplished person became a collection of merits gathered from different sources. It was in the time of this great Sultán that the people of Gujarát learned arts and wit, else before his time they were very simple, homely folk indeed. A soldier of the Sultán's army who held office near the person of the Sultán after some considerable sojourn at court, obtained leave to spend some time at home in his country. He lived there a certain time, and at the time of returning to the Sultán he looked

---

[1] Hálol, at present, for administrative purposes a subdivision of the Panch Maháls, is four miles from the hill of Pává Gadh. The ruins of old Chámpáner are described by Major Miles as extending as far as Hálol. See Asiatic Researches (Bombay) II., 151.

about himself to choose a present suitable enough to take to
the Sultán from his country. At last, thinking what a fine crop
of vetches his estate had produced that season he determined
upon them as the best rarity to present to the Sultán. He forthwith
packed up some hampers of fresh-green-vetches. Round all these
hampers he wrapped a pretty red cloth, and made a present of
them to him. The Sultán asked him what it was. He said, it was some
particularly fine vetches which he had brought for the Sultán's
favourite horse. The Sultán smiled his thanks, encouraged whereby
the unsophisticated countryman proceeded to give an account of a
koli woman in his village, who, he said, used to bear a son every year.
This year, said he, her husband was dead, and if the Sultán was so
inclined, she was worth translation to the royal harem to multiply heirs
for the throne. The Sultán laughed, and the more he did so, the
more the yokel began to assert the truth of his story swearing that the
woman had given birth to seven sons in seven years.

The existence of the Sultán was, one would say, for the happiness
of his people. There was not a man who had the load of an injustice
or injury on his heart, and everyone was blessed with happiness and
liberty; no one ever dreamed of infringing the Muhammadan law,
seeing that the Sultán himself was so obedient to it. It was a matter
of "like king like subjects," as the adage goes.

It is related that once a goldsmith while on his way to present a
beautifully set and ornamented *rubáb*[1] to the Sultán, was met
by Kázi Najm-ud-din, who was at that time the ruler of religious
ordinances in the city of Ahmedábád. The Kázi asked him what it
was he was carrying, and to whom it belonged. He said it was a
"*rubab*," and that it belonged to the Sultán. The Kázi ordered
his men, who ran and snatching the instrument from the goldsmith's
hand returned with it to him. The Kázi dashed it to the ground
scattering its gold and precious stones into pieces. The goldsmith
ran wailing and weeping to the Sultán and said how he had for months
been preparing and setting jewels on the *rubáb* ordered by the king,
how the Kázi Najm-ud-din had snatched it from his hands while he was
bringing it to the Sultán, and destroyed it. The Sultán uttered not a
word, but, after getting up from the Darbár when in his private apartments, he exclaimed (in the words of the Urdu proverb),[2] " *Níchí Bèrí-*

---

[1] The *rubáb* is the Arab guitar, a wire or stringed instrument. It is like the
Indian *sitár*, save that it's face is covered by parchment.

[2] Literally a lowly or low-growing *Bèr* (Jujube) is shaken by all.

sab ne jhèri!" All gladly turn to shake a lowly tree, meaning all hands turn readily to harm the small in consequence or the lowly. "Why," added he, "does the Kázi not go to Rasúlábád, and fulminate his legal decrees against Miyán Manjhlá? (the familiar name by which the saint Sháh Álam was known). He, contrary to the law, dresses in silk and hears music!" The Kázi on hearing of this, with the intention of reforming the Saint also, having looked up and noted down his authorities on a piece of paper, put the paper by way of a note or memorandum into the folds of his turban with the intention of giving it to Sháhi Alam when he met him next. He hoped to elicit from the Saint a favourable reply which would at once reform the learned though mistaken Saint. The next Friday then the Kázi went to Rasúlábád. Sháh Álam used to keep himself aloof and in strict privacy for six days, worshipping God, and contemplating the Divine Existence. On every seventh day or Friday, in obedience to the command (of the Prophet): " Be kind unto Alláh's creatures," he used to come out, and mix with the people, and inculcate on them the ways of God, and satisfy the demands of the needy, and direct the foot-steps of the straying, till the time of the *Asr* or second afternoon-prayers, when again he used to return to his privacy and not come out even if the king of the period called on him. In short, when the Kázi went to Rasúlábád, he was granted an interview by the Saint, immediately on seeing whom the fierce flame of the Kázi's bigotry became extinguished. He made his obeisance very respectfully, and sat down before the Saint. A carpenter was working before the Saint, who happened that day to be in a black, rough woollen cap and cloak. No sooner had the Kázi taken his seat, the Saint asked him what paper he had in the folds of his turban. The Kázi said, "They are some traditions." The Saint asked on what subject. The Kázi, too embarassed to repeat them, handed the paper to the Saint, who, when he unfolded it, found, and observed to the Kázi, it was blank. The Kázi was lost in astonishment and confusion, and however much he searched his turban, he found no other piece. At that time a stick lying in the chamber attracted the alchemistic glance of the Saint, and turned into an ingot of pure gold. The Saint asked the Kázi to appropriate it, as he had a large family. The Kázi said, "I do not want gold, but union with the Lord, which I can obtain from no other but you. It was now the time for the Saint to retort : "But I love music and musical instruments and silken attire," objected the Saint, "and he who accepts those could only be my friend." The Kázi,

said, he accepted all, and was ashamed of his past conduct. Sháh Alam
now got up. At that time as has been observed he had on a dress of
rough wool. He took up a piece of common rope that was lying before
the carpenter who was working in the room and tied it round his waist,
and stuck a small stick dagger-wise under it, and went out with the Kázi
towards the mosque. As soon as he came out of the room, the rope
assumed the form of a golden girdle, the piece of stick, of a poniard
with jewelled hilt, and the rough woollens appeared of the texture and
stuff of fine cloth of gold. He asked the Kázi to bear witness that the
dress of Manjhan (a humble diminutive of his name Miyán Manjhlá),
was the same that he had seen, but if it was the will of Alláh that he
should appear in gold cloth and brocade in the eyes of the people of the
world, who was poor Manjhan to stand between it? Saying so he
turned to pray. After the prayers the Kázi entered the number of
the Saint's followers, became by degrees one of the elect, and received
the honour of becoming the Saint's deputy.[1]

In A. H. 891 (A. C. 1486) the Sultán entrusted the great city
of Ahmedábád to Muháfiz Khán, and started in the direction of Mustafábád, and after a certain time spent in settling difficulties there, he
returned to Muhammadábád. Again in A. H. 892 (A. C. 1486-87) he
went in the direction of Mustafábád, and when he arrived at the
town of Dhandhuká which is on the frontier between Gujarát and
Sorath, he there entrusted the country of Sorath with the fortress of
Junágadh to prince Khalíl Khán, and returned to Ahmedábád. In this
year a party of merchants petitioned that while they were bringing
four hundred Iráki and Turki horses from the countries of Khurásán
and Irák together with certain Indian stuffs with the intention of
selling them in the Sultán's territories, when they reached the fort
of Mount Abu, the Rájá of Sirohi seized their property, not even
sparing the old clothes they were wearing. "To whom," said they
should we complain but to the King, the Champion of the Faith to give us
redress." The Sultán caused them to give him a statement of the price
of the horses and other property, and having seen it, he ordered that
the sum should be paid to the merchants from the imperial treasury saying, "I can recover it from the Rájá of Sirohi." They brought the gold

---

[1] Another anecdote of the miraculous powers of Saint Sháhi Álam is given in the text
on the authority of Sayad Mehmúd Bukhári, the author of the history called "Sham-í
Jalál, to the effect that in a celebration of the Saint's anniversary of death that took place
during the administration of Khán-i-Aâzam Mírza Azíz Kokah (A. C. 1588-1592 and
1600-1606) a certain *muhtasib* or censor of morals who had whipped a singer for singing
songs near the Saint's grave, himself began to dance and sing on entering the shrine.

and counting it in the Sultán's presence gave it to the merchants.[1] The Sultán sounding the drums for a march took an army in the direction of Sirohi and sent a threatening order to the Sirohi Rájá to this effect. "Immediately on the receipt of this order, hand over the horses and property taken from the merchants to the servants of the Presence, if not, consider the Royal army as arrived." The Sirohi Rájá when he understood the purport of the exalted order, sent the horses and property together with a fitting present to the Sultán, and with much humility begged for pardon. The Sultán returned to Muhammadábád, and for four years led a life of pleasure and ease at Muhammadábád, going during the hot season, when the melons were ripe, to Ahmedábád, and after a sojourn of three months in that city, returning to Muhammadábád.

In A. H. 896 (A. C. 1490) the Sultán heard that Sultán Muhammad Lashkari, king of the Dakhan had killed Khwájah Mehmúd,[2] called Khwájah Jahán, who was a matchless vazír, and that Bahádur Gíláni who had been brought up by the Khwájah had rebelled at the port of Dábhol.[3] Sultán Muhammad Lashkari dying at this juncture, his son Sultán Mehmúd Bahmani, a boy of tender years, was placed on the throne. It was also reported that many of the nobles of the Dakhan had, with the intention of obtaining independence, broken out into rebellion, and that disorder had come over the affairs of the Kingdom of the Dakhan ; that during this interval Bahádur Gíláni, an adherent of the Khwájah's, had taken the opportunity of obtaining possession of several districts of the Dakhan, and having collected many ships was committing piracies on the Gujarát coast and that fear of his depredations had paralyzed the trade of the ports of Gujarát. The reason of his vexing the Gujarát ports was that Malik-ut-Tujjár Dakhani after the murder of Khwájah Jahán fleeing from the Dakhan came to the port of Khambáyat. Bahádur sent a person from Dábhol to ask for the hand of his daughter in marriage. At this juncture Malik-ut-Tujjár died, and his *wakil*, one Muhammad Hayát, rejected with contempt Bahádur's offer of marriage, and addressed to Bahadur the message: "What power has a slave

---

[1] This is interesting as the first case mentioned of the form of compensation which under the name of *Valtar* was until very lately in vogue in Gujarát.

[2] Otherwise called Khájah Mehmúd Gáwán.

[3] On the north bank of the river Vashishti (called Halewacko and Kalewacko by the early navigators), in the Ratnagiri District. About this time, according to Athanasius Nikitin, Dabhol was the great mart for all nations living along the coast of India and Ethiopia.

purchased for six pice to offer to marry the daughter of Malik-ut-Tujjàr ?" When Bahádur's agent returned and explained his message, Bahádur sent certain assassins who killed Muhammad Hayát. After all by the assistance and influence of the people of Khambúyat, the girl was not sent to Bahádur, and that ill-starred man commenced to plunder the ports of Gujarát. They say that for several years ships neither came nor went from or to the ports of Gujarát, and that the sea-borne trade of Gujarát was so crippled that the people were reduced to eat coriander seed with their *pán* in place of their betel-nut or *supári*.

On hearing this the Sultán became exceedingly enraged, and sent Malik Sárang Kiwám-ul-Mulk by land against Dábhol with a powerful army and elephants like mountains, and sent three hundred boats with well-armed men furnished with both cannons and muskets against Dábhol by sea. When the land army reached Agási and Bassein, which are situated on the frontier of Gujarát and the Dakhan, the ministers of Sultán Mehmúd Bahmani thinking that Sultán Mehmúd of Gujarát being a patron of theirs who had several times helped them and secured them from the hands of Sultán Mehmúd Khilji, of Mándu, that they should in return for his kindness anticipate him, and having cut off Bahádur's head sent it to him before the arrival of his army against Bahádur. Lest, also should this foreign army enter their territory, and the disturbance should increase and attain unforeseen proportions, the best course was thus to turn it back. They sent, therefore, a letter to Sultán Mehmúd Begada to the effect that the army of the Dakhan also belonged to his friends, if he gave the order the Sultán's army might remain where it was and it should be their duty to punish Bahádur, and if they failed in this, the Sultán could then act as he chose. After this the whole army of the Dakhan assembled and marched against Bahádur who issuing, fought with them, and his army was defeated, and Bahádur himself fell alive into their hands. His head was struck off, and brought to Sultán Mehmúd Bahmani, and he wrote of it to Sultán Mehmúd Begda and the Sultán re-called his army.

After this in A. H. 899 (A. C. 1493) the Sultán led an army in the direction of Morasá, on account of the rebellion of [1] Alif Khán, one of

---

[1] The word used in the text is ' *Maula-zádáh.*' The word *Maula* in Arabic means both a master and slvae ; and ' Zádáh' means born. This Alif Khan was a son of Alá-ud-din bin Sohráb, who distinguished himself in the reign of Sultán Kutb-ud-din for his faithfulness to his master at the cost of his breach of faith with Mehmúd Khilji.

the exalted slave born nobles of the Sultán, who held Morùsa as *jagir*. When he heard of the pomp of the Sultán's arrival he fled, and entered the city of Meimún, also called Káreth, which is situated in the neighbourhood of the mountains of Lúnáwárá, and remained there a short time, and then went to Sultán Ghiásuddín Khilji. Ghiásuddín Khilji gave him no shelter because his father Aláuddin-bin Sohráb had behaved treacherously (to his ancestor Mehmúd Khilji of Málwa) of which mention has been made above. He, therefore, went thence to Sultánpúr, when, finally, the Sultán forgave his fault, and in A. H. 901, (A. C. 1496) he again entered the Sultán's service.

After this in A. H. 904 (A. C. 1499) the Sultán took an army against Asír, because Ádil Khán Fárúkhi, ruler of Asír and Burhánpúr, had delayed sending the fixed tribute. When he reached the bank of the river Tápti, Ádil Khán sent the tribute with many apologies. The Sultán returning sent his army by road of Nazarbár, and himself with his force went to see the forts of Thálner and Dharmál, which Imád-ul-Mulk, Asas had conquered, and having seen them returned to Nazarbár and joining his army, returned to Muhammadábád.

In A. H. 906 (A. C. 1501) he heard that Sultán Násiruddin, son of Sultan Ghiásuddin, having slain his father had ascended the throne of the Sultánate. The Sultán desired to take his army in the direction of Mándu. In the end, however, on Sultán Násiruddín making submission he refrained from the purpose and for seven years did not make an expedition.

In A. H. 913 (A. C. 1507-8) he took an army against Chauls (Cheval) and thence marched against Bassein and Maháim on account of the disturbances created by the *Firangis*.[1] When he arrived at Dún (Dáhánu ?) he received news that Malik Ayáz, a slave of the Sultán and Governor of Diu, with ten Turkish ships, manned by Turkish troops, had gone to the port of Chaul, and having fought with the seditious *Firangis*, and having killed many of them, had with his guns sunk one of their big ships, which contained very valuable property. In this battle four hundred of the Malik's men with some Turks had become martyrs. The Malik being victorious, returned to Diu and the Sultán was greatly pleased and caused Malik Ayáz to be rewarded and sent him a dress of honour, and himself returned to Bassein, and having stayed there for six days,

---

[1] The Franks or Europeans, and in a narrower sense the Portuguese.

on the 9th of the month of Moharram A. H. 914 (A. C. 1508) returned to his capital.

After this Álam Khán bin Ahsan Khán, grandson of[1] the Sultán whose father had been the ruler of Asír and Burhánpur, requested his mother to petition the Sultán that seven years had elapsed since the death of Ádil Khán bin Mubárak, who had died without male issue, and that the amírs had raised to the throne one of the family of Malik Rájáh, having named him Ádil Khán, and had become masters of the country and were making free with its revenues. If the Sultán would raise the petitioner from the dust and exalt him to the throne of his ancestors, this act of kindness would be of-a-piece with the gracious protection of the lowly which had always been the distinguished trait of his royal line. When the mother of Álam Khán, the son of Ahsan Khán, made this petition to His Majesty, the Sultán consented, and in the month of Rajab (the seventh Musalmán month) of the abovementioned year, he handed over Asír to Álam Khán, and himself set out for Nazarbár. He spent the month of Ramazán (the ninth or fasting month) at the village of Sábli on the bank of the river Máhi, and sending for Prince Khalil Khán from Baroda took him with him.[2] When the Sultán arrived at Nazarbár, Malik Hisámuddin Mughal, in whose possession was half the country of Burhánpur, and who had written secret letters to Álam Khán offering to invite the Sultán to his aid if he joined him, on learning that Sultán Mehmúd himself was marching in that direction, departed from the agreement he had made, and having made an alliance with Nizámul-mulk Bahri, the ruler of Ahmednagar, brought him to his assistance and seated Álam Khán Khánzádah on the throne of Burhánpur.[3] Malik Ládan Khilji who possessed the other half of the country of Burhánpur on account of the enmity he had with Hisámuddin, went to the skirts of the hill of Asír. At length when the Sultán arrived at the fort of Thálner Nizámul-mulk placing 4,000 horse of his army at the disposal of Hisámuddin himself returned to his capital. Having halted some days at Thálner owing

---

[1] A son of his daughter or niece.

[2] The translation by Sir Clive Bayley places the village of Sábli on the Narbadá. This portion of the text, however, is confusing and vague. The Tabakát-i-Akbari (Persian text) seems to be more accurate. It says the Sultán issued orders to collect the army in Rajab (the seventh Musalmán month), and set out for Burhánpur in Shaábán (the following month), and spent the Fasting month (Ramazán, the ninth month), in camp at Sábli.

[3] Álam Khan (which was also the name of the pretender) was the protege of Ahmednagar. The title of Khán-Zádah is enjoyed by younger sons of royal families.

to a slight indisposition the Sultán ordered Sayad Ásaf Khán who was unequalled for intelligence in his day with Azízul mulk, the fief-holder of Sultánpur and Nazarbár, to march against Hisámuddin and drive him out of the country, and to gain over Ládan Khiljí and appoint him in Hisámuddin's place. When Sayad Ásaf Khán arrived at Ránobar, which is a dependency of Burhánpúr, the army of Nizám-ul-Mulk-Bahri with Álam Khán Khánzádah, fled towards the Dakhan, and Hisámuddin avoiding an engagement came to Thálner by another route and paid his respects to the Sultán. Malik Ládan Khilji also came and made his obeisance. After the Id-ud-duhá (the sacrifice festival following the pilgrimage in the twelfth month of the Musalmán calendar) Álamkhán, the son of Ahsan Khán, was ennobled by the title of Ádil Khán and four elephants and three lákhs of *tankas* were given to him, and he was placed in the government of Ásír and Burhánpúr. The Sultán also promoted Malik Ládan Khilji to the title of Khán Jahán and gave him the village of Banás or Biyás under Sultánpur and Nazarbár which was the birthplace of the said Malik, and nominated him to assist Álam Khán. He also made peace between Hisámuddin and Khán Jahán and brought them together, and he dignified Malik Muhammad Mákhá, or Bákhá, son of Imádul-mulk Asírí with the title of Gházi Khán, and Malik Álam Sháh, the thánedar of Thálner, was granted the title of Fateh Khán and his brother Malik Yúsuf the title of Saif Khán, and the eldest son of Malik Ládan the title of Mujáhid Khán. All these amírs with Nasrat Khán and Mujáhidul-mulk Gujaráti were attached to the service of Ádil Khán, who, pleased and joyful with much pomp, started for Asir. The Sultán returned to his own country, and Malik Hisámuddin for two marches accompanied the Sultán. When he took leave, the village of Dhanúra or Dhantra under Sultánpur and Nazarbár was bestowed on him. When the Sultán arrived at Muhammadabád, he granted leave to Prince Khalíl Khán and directed him to return to his own appointment at Baroda. He sent Sikandar Khán and Latíf Khán, the sons of Khalíl Khán, with him and retained their younger brother Bahádur Khán with himself and showed towards him the love of a father and the affection of a grandfather. He often used to say: "This son of mine will be a great king." It is related that one day he took Bahádur Khán and seated him on his knee and said to him with great affection, "Oh! Bahádur Khán! I have prayed God to bestow on thee the Kingdom of Gujarát and God has accepted my prayer!"

In the month of Zilhaj, the twelfth Musalmán month, A. H. 916 (A. C. 1510) the Sultán went to Pattan. This was the last expedition of the Sultàn. He assembled the great and learned men of Pattan like Maulaná Moínuddin Kázrúni and Tájuddin Suyúti, and said to them, " this time I have come to take leave of you all, I think that the measure of my life is full !" All invoked blessings on him. The Sultán visited all the tombs of the saints at Pattan and on the fourth day he left Pattan on his return to Ahmedábád. When he arrived at Sarkhej he visited the tomb of [1]Sheikh Ahmed Khattú, and looking earnestly at his own tomb which he had built in his life time at the foot of the Sheikh's, said : " This is the future home of Mehmúd ! In a short time he will descend hither !"

After this he came to Ahmedábád and fell sick and remained ill for three months, and he sent for Prince Khalíl Khán from Baroda, and told him that he was about to die, and gave him fatherly advice. It so chanced, however, that he recovered, and gave leave to Khalíl Khán, but on account of a number of ailments combined with an impaired stomach and the weakness of old age the illness returned after three months. He ordered that Khalíl Khán should again be sent for, but before his arrival, at the time of the second afternoon prayers on Monday, in the blessed month of Ramazán in A. H. 917 (A. C. 1511), he departed from this transient life for the Eternal Abode. They carried his sacred coffin to Sarkhej and in the above mentioned place committed it to the dust—may the mercy of God be on him !

The period of his reign was fifty-four years and one month, and his honoured age sixty-seven years and three months. The Sultán was a disciple of Sheikh Rahmat-ulláh-bin Sheikh Ázízullah, the Resigner in Alláh, who sleeps his eternal sleep in Sheikhpurá, a suburb of Ahmedábád, which was populated by him. The Sheikh was of a high stage of mystic attainments and was an excellent man.

Darya Khán was the first of the three friends and companions of the Sultán's youth. It was Daryá Khán who built the great dome to the north of the city, and this dome is so lofty that there is not another built of brick of such dimensions in all Gujarát. Another associate of the Sultán's was Alaf Khán Bhokai, who built a lofty mosque near Dholka to the west of the fort, and travellers both by sea and land

---

[1] The name of the Saint is in the text prefaced by the words in Arabic : " The Ful[l] Moon of the Truthful, and the Argument of the Knowers of God."

agree in stating that no brick-built mosque in this country equals it in size.

Malik Muhammed Ikhtiár was the third of his companions. When the Sultán ascended the throne, he conferred on each of his companions the rank of a *panj-hazári*, or leader of five thousand horse, and the title of Khán. Malik Muhammad, however, did not accept the title, saying that his name was Muhammad, a name so sacred that no title or appendage could add to its worth ; all the others, however, accepted their gifts. One day the Malik was passing in a palanquin through a suburb of Ahmedabád of the name of Mithápúr. There was a very shady tamarind tree on the road, the cool shade of which tempted the nobleman to shelter himself under it from the scorching rays of a noon-day sun. He stopped there and gave himself up to sleep, and in the cool of the shade slept long. When he awoke he saw that in a mosque in the corner of the shady nook a *mullah* was teaching children. His name was Mulláh Kabír, and he was one of the followers of the great saint Sheikh Hamíduddin Nágori, one of the most famous of saints. The Mulláh was passing his time in worship, retirement and obscurity. The nobleman on awakening from his siesta, made his ablutions, and said his prayers in the following of the Mulláh. After the prayers, the Mulláh cast a searching glance and for a time gazed steadfastly at the nobleman in such a way that he was attracted towards the Mulláh, and felt such a rapture in the attraction, as to lose sense of everything else. When after a time he regained consciousness, he got up, and went home. Though his house had everything in it of comfort and luxury he was restless. The next morning he again went to that tamarind tree. When he reached the Mulláh, he sat respectfully in his presence for some hours, and again went home. For some days he continued to do so. One day the Mulláh told him in privacy that he was of the world worldly, and asked why he came there so often to the detriment of his own affairs. If he was for the worship of God, he should give up all else and should devote himself wholly to God's service; if not, he should not take the trouble as that was a very difficult life in which success was by no means easy. The Malik said he wanted a day to consider and deliberate with his own mind, and see which why his mind was inclined to follow, and which to abstain from. The Mulláh said, "So be it." The Malik went home, and summoning before him all his servants he paid them all their dues, giving each a sum of money

over and above his claim to obviate the possibility of want, should
any of them be long in getting work. He then collected his female slaves
round him and offered those their emancipation who wished for it,
and offered those marriage who wished for a husband. He gratified
the desires of them all. In fine, the Malik having got ready an inventory of all his valuable 8 horses, elephants, cash, and ornaments with
his estates, &c., went to the king, and placing before him the inventory,
told him to give away the property to whomsoever he wished, as it
was his (the Sultán's), and was no longer required by him (the Malik).
The Sultán thought he was speaking in displeasure and with great
concern inquired the reason, and showed great kindness and sympathy,
assuring him of visiting his vengeance upon anybody that may have
wronged him. But the Malik said he had the whole of his life been
serving the Sultán, but that he now wanted to serve Him who had
placed the cap of servitude on the head of the Sultán himself.
He said these words and got up and returned home. The Sultán
called Darya Khán and Alif Khán, who were sincere friends of the
Malik, and recounted to them the words of the Malik, and showed
them the inventory. They said, through their great friendship for
the Malik, that he was gone mad to say such words. They asked for
the inventory and requested leave to go to the man and to restore him
to his senses. The Sultán gave up the papers to them. When they
reached the Malik's house he guessed their errand and sent them word
to wait awhile as he would shortly meet them. In the meanwhile he
sent for a barber, and taking up his sword[1] ordered him to at once shave
his head. He then ordered him to shave off his beard and mustaches
and eye-brows, in the belief that these hair had grown up by food
and amidst passions and desires unhallowed and ungodly. He then
sent for his wife and told her that whatever was then in the house
was hers and it was enough to last her a life-time. He gave her leave
to go to her father's house, adding that if she had a desire for another
husband that he gave up in the name of God all his marital rights
upon her, and that she was welcome to marry any one she list. That
faithful lady, however, said, if the way to God imperatively required
all this that she was silent, if not, she would follow him like his shadow.

---

1 The Malik had to enforce his order with a threat of the sword, as his order to
shave his head included the shaving of the "four-eyebrows" (chahár abrú), the Musalman
devotees tonsure, and he was sure the barber would out of love and regard for his former
state hesitate to carry out orders of which his master might afterwards have cause to
repent. The barber also like the Sultán possibly took the same view, i. e., the Malik was
giving up the world in anger.

She said it was not meet that she should be the sharer of his love and his happiness in the days of prosperity and not be allowed to share his adversity also. He said if she cared for his companionship he was agreeable to bear her company. The good wife having got her wish, collected all her ornaments and jewels, threw them away before her slave girls, and adopting the dress of one of them, and taking the hand of her husband accompanied him in broad light of day, and came with him before Darya Khán and Alif Khán who were waiting and passed by them. The friends astounded at what they saw, got up and going to the Sultán represented to him all that had occurred, saying that their friend was, alas! spirit possessed. The Malik betook himself to the Sheikh. The Sheikh got up, and taking the hand of the Malik's wife said to her, "Sister, go thou within to thy sisters," and so saying led her into his *zenána*; when inside, he asked his women, if they knew that the lady was no less than the wife of the Ibráhím Ad-ham[1] of the day, "Consider her society a boon and lose not an opportunity of serving her." Saying this to his women, the Sheikh came out, and initiated her husband into his order. It is related that the Malik rendered himself so humble in his penitence that he used bare-footed to carry on his head the water for the Sheikh from the river Bábarmati by way of the Three Gates Market to the Sheikh's place, a distance of over a mile. People at first used to taunt him with madness, but he earnestly adhered to his humble mode of life. One day the Sultán saw him in this plight, and remarked to Daryá Khán, "Do you see Malik Muhammad? If he puts himself to this trouble for the sake of his faith, he must be in a wonderful state of mind." Daryá Khán said, "It seems to me from the present conduct of this man that he will ere long become the object of general veneration.' People flocked to him with a thousand objects in numbers, and what was more, gained their aspirations, and obtained their wishes. The Sheikh used to say, he wanted the Malik to obtain higher spiritual distinction, but that he had stopped short in the middle of his course. The Malik on hearing this became ashamed and regretful and from that moment he began to follow a course which ultimately made him as shunned of the people as he was yet awhile sought after. He began by making himself so free with people's property taking from one

---

[1] Ibráhím Ad-ham was a famous Saint who, from being one of the richest men of Balkh, became a *darrísh* for love of God. He ranks amongst the highest of Islám's Saints. According to Abul Mahásins *Nujúm*, his death took place in H. 160 (A.D. 776-77), but Abul Fida places the event a year later.

and giving away to another, that though he never kept anything to himself, people began to shun him. In the end the Malik got the title of Muhammad Ikhtiár from the court of the Forgiving King of Kings and died in the highest odour of sanctity, even Sháh Álam admitting it.

Another of the Sultán's religious nobles was Abdul Latíf Malik Mehmúd Dáwarul-Mulk. He was of Koreish[1] origin. Though rich in matters worldly he was devoted to religion, and thus it was that he was styled Dáwarul-Mulk. Lest the concourse of men, horses, soldiers, and elephants at his door, should hurt any of his neighbours, he sold his mansions in the city, and constructed houses outside the city for himself. They say that he charged the cultivators of his estates only the small rates sanctioned by the Muhammadan Law, and not an iota above. People used to flock to his *jágirs* which became so prosperous that one of them excited the covetous desire of the Sultán's son-in-law. He asked of his father-in-law to be allowed to take the Malik's *jágirs*, saying that any other *jágir* that would be given to the Malik, would, in his hands, become as prosperous. The Sultán declining this proposal, this misguided young man attempted the Malik's life. But the Malik could not be harmed. The bravoes were captured, and when asked by the Malik who had set them to the deed they had attempted, they replied they had not the wherewithal to marry their grown-up daughters, and that the Sultan's son-in-law had promised them help had they succeeded in taking his life. The Malik said, "Ay, want is a bitter thing, and drives men to such bad actions"; and ordered them to be given the necessary sums, and to be set free.

The Malik was a believer in the saintliness of Sháhi Álam, and by his guidance had attained to the position of a saint. They say that a prince of the Dakhan being afflicted with white leprosy[2] was brought before Sháh Álam, while the Malik was pouring water on his hands (duties the honour of which appertained permanently to the Malik) while making ablutions and repeating the prayers for that ceremony. So engaged, Sháh Alam did not make any reply to the entreaties of the people of the diseased prince. After ablutions he ordered the water remaining in the ewer to be administered to the prince, who, no sooner he drank

---

[1] The tribe from which the prophet was descended. As according to a tradition of the Prophet stating that every convert to Islám was of himself, many converted Hindus took the surname of Kureishi, the surname has lost much of its original sense of nobility in India, where every new convert calls himself a Koreishi.

[2] Leucoderma.

it, than he was, by the grace of God, cured of the unseemly tailment. As Khwájáh Moínud-din of Ajmere had Sálár Masúúd his almoner, so Malik Mehmúd was Sháh Álam's. Crowds of people from the Dakhan used to come and return with heart's content having gained their desires.

The Malik was appointed by the Sultán thánedár of Amrún ten *kos* from Morvi in the district of Jhálawár. He used [1]often to engage in warfare with the unbelievers. In one of hi expeditions against Bhuj, the capital of the Rájá of Katch, having crossed a part of the Ran, which is an arm of the salt sea, and having on the third day returned to the habitable part of the country, he went to sleep under the cool shade of a tree, and saw on waking that some of his men were grazing their horses in a cultivated field of *Jawár* (Sorghum vulgare). He remonstrated with them as to the justice of such a proceeding, but having suffered from three days' want of food and fodder, they replied that they themselves could well appreciate equity in the midst of want, but that it was a virtue their horses did not understand. The Malik said he was sure if their forbearance and patience proceeded from the fear Divine, their horses also would surely share their patience; saying so, he let loose his own horse near a very green and inviting field. The horse did not move an inch and stood as if he were standing in obedience to the bit. Finally the Hindus of Amrún rendered obedience to him. One of the land-holders of those parts, however, who used to regularly wait on the Malik, was a man of mischief and evil nature. He told the Malik that a certain *Garásiá* (a land-holding Rajput) of his fraternity had a sword of unrivalled temper. "When he comes to you," said he, "do draw it from the scabbard and see of what famous metal is the blade." On the other hand, he warned the *Garásiá* that the Malik was so displeased with him that he had determined to kill him at the first opportunity, and that he had arranged that his men should fall on him (the *Garásia*) at a pre-arranged signal, which was to be the drawing by the Malik the *Garásia's* sword from the scabbard. The *Garásiá* told his servants that the Malik had preconcerted his death. "When the Malik draws the sword," said the land-holder to his men, "do you be the first to fall on him and kill him." The Malik, unaware of the treachery, took the sword from the hand of the *Garásiá* when he came to the audience. He had not well grasped the handle when the Hindus fell on him, and killed him. From that day to this the fame of the Malik as a martyr attracts numbers of believers from far and near to his shrine, and his miracles, after martyrdom, have been numerous. The blind are given eye-sight, the lame return whole, the barren are gladdened by the birth of children and few return disappointed from his shrine. Others having some desires to be obtained, put fetters on their legs with locks of iron joining the fetters. It has often happened that, when one of these has gained his desire, the lock has opened of itself, and the fetters have dropped. Some people wishing for gold are given it by the saint by being directed to apply to a particular person at a given address for a certain sum. The man referred to as the giver is also directed in a dream to pay the sum on appearance to the person described. From the date of his martyrdom H. 915 (A. D. 1509) up to now, H. 1020 (A. D. 1611) one hundred and five years have passed, still men continue to believe in him.

They say that another of the great nobles of the Sultán was Malik Ayáz. Although he was a slave bought with gold, yet he was fit to govern a kingdom, and lived in and maintained a marvellously high state. They say that besides menial servants there were a thousand water-carriers on his establishment. He had a large tank made of leather, and when his army was on the march they took water from that, and gave the horses and elephants to drink. Several memorable works still remain in Gujarát which were executed by him. For instance, he built the fort of Díu which the *Firangis* have now[1] destroyed; and have built another fort in its place. He constructed a bastion in the sea, called *Sankal Koth* (or the Chain Bastion) and connected it with the shore by means of an iron chain that the ships of the *Firangis* should not be able to pass over it, and that tower is still standing. After the martyrdom of Sultán Bahádur, Mehmúd's grandson, this fortress, city and port fell into the hands of the Portuguese. Malik Ayáz constructed gardens in the island of Díu, and of the two arms of the sea which coming from either side of the island of Díu, curve to the north, he built a stone bridge, which at present the Portuguese have broken down. During the government of the Malik, the *Firangi* was unable to enter the Gujarát ports. Now, however, by degrees, things have come to such a

---

[1] A. C. 1611 (A. H. 1020) the time in which the Historian flourished.

pass that without a permit from the *Firangi*, a vessel dare not leave any of the ports of Gujarát, except Surat, and this also is owing solely to the gallantry and bravery of those entrusted with the government of the city of Surat.

It is related that at the time of taking his meals, the Malik's orders were that his servants should blow a trumpet which was the signal for everybody who was hungry to present himself at the table-cloth. From head to foot the table was served in an impartially equal style. Immediately on taking his seat the Malik used to glance over from right to left, and woe to the steward who should have made any the least difference in serving the guests. His table-cloth used to be stocked with the delicacies of Persia, Turkey and India. After dinner the plates of each guest used to be scrupulously handed over to his servants with the same impartiality. After that they used to bring *átr* and *pán*. His table was always so served. His army also was the best clad in the kingdom. The lowest of his servants were well-dressed, and his soldiers most completely armed and equipped. The soldiers of his army, up to the veriest scavanger, used to be clad in velvet and brocade, and silk embroidery and scarlet, and to bear swords and quivers and poniards with gold and silver bars and rivets. They say that in the days of Sultán Muzaffar, son of Mehmúd, Ráná Sángá having collected an army of nearly 100,000 horse, suddenly swept down on the Gujarát frontier near Ahmednagar which is situated about 10 *kos* from Ídar. The army of Sultán Muzaffar was dispersed about the country, and it took time to collect. Nizám Khán Bahmani and the patrollers of the roads of that *Súbáh* having issued from Ahmednagar with 4,000 horse joined battle and defeated the greater part of the Ráná's forces. In the end, however, 3,000 men of his party became martyrs, and he himself with many others, came wounded from the battle, though nearly 7,000 of the Rajpúts were slain. When this news reached the Sultán, he sent for Malik Ayáz from Sorath. The Malik came with his army by forced marches. The Sultán placing some *amirs* and a large army under Malik Ayáz appointed him to carry on operations against the Ráná. The Ráná turned back. The Malik pursued him. They say that in spite of the forced marches and the daily expectation of battle, the principal amírs used to come and dine at the table of the Malik, and who-ever of them was unable to come, the Malik's servants sent food to him. Several of the amírs who considered themselves of equal rank with the Malik took umbrage at these arrangements, and they told their servants not to return the copper trays and china vessels, so that food might not again be sent to them, and their servants did so. When this had gone on three days, the Malik's steward of the kitchen went to the presence of the Malik, and represented the matter to him saying that the vessels in which food had been sent to the tents of the amírs were not returned. The Malik replied, "Never mind keep you on sending food in the same manner as you have hitherto done." They say that they went on sending food in this manner for one month, and did not ask for their vessels back. After one month the amírs struck with admiration at the generosity and vast stores of the Malik, returned his vessels, and acknowledged his greatness. In short, the Malik pursued the Rána as far as Mandisúr. At night the Rajpúts made a night attack on the camp of the Malik, and after slaying many horses departed. The Malik ordered that they should bury the slain horses, and that they should replace each horse killed by a horse of the same colour from the Malik's private stables. Seven of the most broken down and infirm horses of the number killed were allowed to remain ; when in the morning the spies of the Rána having counted them, told him that in the night attack only seven of the Malik's horses were killed, the Rána much chagrined, reproached his Rájpúts for seeking to magnify the number of the horses they had killed while in truth they had slain only seven sorry beasts.

The Malik had three sons: Is-hák, who received the title of Changís Khán, Malik Túghá, and Eliás. Is-hák was very fat, with a frame like an elephant, and he used to generally ride on a camel because no horse could be found up to his weight; nevertheless he was a very good marksman, and an excellent wrestler, and no athlete could escape from his grasp. Eventually, Sultán Bahádur the son of Sultán Muzaffar, the son of Sultán Mehmúd, at the instigation of Rúmi Khán, put to death the three sons of the Malik. If it please God, I will hereafter relate in detail, each in its proper place, the cause of the coming of the Rána in the time of Sultán Muzaffar, and the cause of the deaths of these sons of the Malik in the reign of Sultán Bahádur. Is-hák had a hundred wives, married and concubines. His virile powers were extraordinary, and it is said that his wives loved him so much and that he kept them all so happy, that at his death many of them committed suicide. Malik Ayáz himself died in the time of Sultán Muzaffar, son of Sultán Mehmúd.

Another of the great amírs of the Sultán was Malik Shaâbán who had the title of Malik Shark.[1] He had been bought with gold by Sultán Muhammad son of Sultán Ahmed, and he attained greatness during the time of Sultán Mehmúd, and reached the rank of a minister. He was a man of great wit and generosity. They say that at this time there was neither in the East nor West a *vazír* like him, and all the people of God were happy during his administration. He constructed a garden in the suburbs of Ahmedábád with a lofty mosque on the east of the city called the Bagh-i-Shaâbán. Eventually, he turned his thoughts towards repentance and retirement, and sat in that garden in the service of God; and, although the Sultán pressed him to carry on the *vazarat*, he refused and said : " The rest and leisure that I experience during one day's retirement and quiet in this garden is such as I have never before enjoyed in my life." He never again left that garden and there ended his life, and he lies buried in the court of the mosque which is in that garden ; may God's mercy be on him.

Another celebrated amír was Khudávand Khán Âlím who populated Âlímpur to the south of the city of Ahmedabád, and built there a large mosque. The mosque is built of stone and paved with marble which was brought from a distance of two hundred *kos*. He was son-in-law of Sultán Muhammad, son of Sultán Ahmed. He was a man of noble character, ready of tongue, and conversant with many languages; in archery and the game of *Chaugan* (polo) he was without an equal. They say that it was he who introduced from Bijánagar and the country of the Dakhan the seeds of the *Kharbúzah* (melon) and saplings of the fig and of the solid bamboo. He several times rebelled against the Sultán. The Sultán forgave him and said : "If I slay Malik Âlím or exile him from the country, where in Gujarát can I find a man like him ? And in his extreme age, he also became a repentant man and a recluse occupying himself in the worship of God, passed the remainder of his life there in religious exercises.

Another celebrated amír was Alif Khán Bhukái who was of very exalted dignity and of a generous soul, and he was a friend and companion of the Sultán. The great mosque and stone-cistern behind the town of Dholka were built by him, and these buildings are witnesses to his exalted dignity and state. Travellers from all parts of the world agree that so large a brick mosque has not been built elsewhere in the world, as has previously been mentioned.

---

[1] Correctly Malik-ush-Shark, or the Lord of the East.

Another amír was Daryá Khán, the builder of Daryápur which is a celebrated suburb, north of Ahmedábád.

Another was Imádul-mulk Ásas who populated Ásaspúr[1] which lies between Rasulábád and Batwá. No suburb of Ahmedábád is so beautiful as this. The walls of its fortification are of burnt brick plastered with lime, and around it are gardens of ma ngoes and *khirnis* (*Mimusop, indica*) and Brab palms in great number. The flower of the Moghrá (*Jasminum Zambac*) which is the husband of perfumes, of all sweet smelling flowers reaches a perfection in Ásaspur such as it does in no other place. Hazarat Sháh Álam used to call this suburb " the *Karim-ut-tarafain*, or the gentle on both the sides, because to the south of it is Batwá where lies the tomb of Hazarat Kutbul-aktáb, and to the north of it is Rasúlábád formerly the residence, now the tomb, of Hazrat Sháh. From Batwá to Ásaspur, and from Rasúlábád to the above-mentioned suburb, are on both sides, gardens of mangoes and *khirnis*, whose grateful shade causes the traveller to call to mind the kindness of his mother and father. The tomb of the Malik is situated outside the suburb fortifications with a joy-giving mosque and built tank 10×10, or a hundred *gaz* square.

Another amír was Táj Khán Sálár, a generous man, of good disposition, so much so, that after his death no amír would accept his title, because no other was conscious of possesing his generosity and manliness. With the example of his liberality and generosity none of the nobles wished for his title, and rejected it. After some time, in the time of Sultán Muzaffar bin Mehmúd, Táj Khán Tariáni, the builder of the dome of Hazrat Sháh Álam Bukhári's tomb, accepted the title. He was Táj khán's equal in liberality, perhaps he even exceeded him, and he built Tájpúr which lies to the south within the city wall of Ahmedábád.

Another amír was Kiwámul-mulk Sárang who originally was the son of a Rájput, and his name was Sárang, and his brother's name was Múla. Both of them were captured by the Sultán, who caused them to adopt Islám. Malik Amín Kamál, the poet and companion of Sultán Bahádur, who was famous for his wit and repartee, was one of his descendants. An account of him in detail will be given in the reign of Sultán Bahádur—if God wills. In fine, both the brothers attained to great confidence in the time of the Sultán. They say that

---

[1] The village at present known as Isan-púr.

Malik Sárang was very bold in his expressions, and the Sultán used to permit it. The suburb of Sárangpur and a mosque outside the city to the east of Ahmedábád were founded by him.

Another noble Háji Kálú was a slave of the Sultán's. He populated Kálúpur to the east of the city. They say he was a learned man.

Then there were two brothers from Khurásán, Aázam and Moázzam, both skilful archers. They built the mosque between Ahmedábád and Sarkhej with a reservoir in which water does not stay. Near the mosque is a dome in which both the brothers lie buried. Some of the people of Gujarát relate a story of these two brothers which is not fit for repetition.

ACCESSION OF SULTAN MUZAFFAR II.

Sultán Mehmúd had four sons: of these, the first was Muhammad Kálá, and the name of his mother was Ráni Rúpmanjhari who formerly belonged to the harem of Sultán Kutb-uddin. After his death she came to Sultán Mehmúd. The above-mentioned prince and his mother died during the life-time of the Sultán. The tomb of Ráni Rúpmanjhari is well-known in the Mánek Chowk of Ahmedábád.

The second son was Apá Khán, and the name of his mother was Ráni Saráni. The Ráni's tomb is situated near the Asoria Gate. By the order of the Sultán poison was put into his cup, because he entered some one's house, and the master of the house came in and captured, and bound him. This news reached the Sultán who ordered that they should give him to drink poisoned sherbet.

Another son was Ahmed Khán who was given the title of Ahmed Sháh by Khudá-wand Khán, the mention of which has been previously made.

Another son was Khalíl Khán, the heir to the throne, who was afterwards styled Sultán Muzaffar, may the mercy of God be on him! It is said that the birth of Sultán Muzaffar happened after dawn on Wednesday the 6th of the month of Shaábán A. H. 880 (6th December A. C. 1475), and that the date is obtainable from the word فرخ Farrukh meaning the auspicious or happy. On account of his beauty he was named Khalíl Khán, and the name of his mother was Ráni Hirábái, daughter of Nága Ráná, a Rájpút chief of the banks of the river Mahí. About four or five days after his birth the Ráni quitted this transient abode for the eternal one, and her death caused the Sultán great grief. It is said that when Sultán Muzaffar was born, Sultán Mehmúd wrapping the new born babe in the clothes he was wearing, took him to Hans-Bái, his (Sultan Mehmúd's) step-mother. This lady had expressed a desire of bringing up one of her son's offspring. This old queen used to take greater care of the boy than perhaps even his mother would have done. The boy showed great promise so that though the heir-apparent Ápá Khán was then alive, Sultán Mehmúd and others also used to connect the hope of the throne with him and say : " It will be from this boy and his children that my line shall last."

Let it be known that at the close of Sultán Mehmúd's reign, Sayad Muhammad Jaunpuri, who claimed to be the promised Mehdi coming from Jaunpúr to Ahmedábád, put up at the mosque of Táj Khán Sálár, which is near the Jamálpúr Gate, where he used frequently to address and preach to the people. Crowds of people used to come to hear him. When Badrul-Árifín Hazrat Sayad Sháh Sheikh Jí, son of Sayad Mehmúd, son of Kutbul-Álam Sayad Burhánuddín, came to visit the Sayad, after shaking hands they sat in the above-mentioned mosque. The Sayad opened the conversation by repeating a verse from the Kuráán suited to the occasion, and Sheikh Jí also recited in answer another verse. The Sayad now read another verse, and Sháh Jí also read a verse in reply ; they repeated this three times.[1] After this the Hazrat Sheikh Jí took his leave, and on the way one of his disciples asked him concerning the Sayad. He replied, that Sayad Muhammad was a man possessing some degree of saintly or mystic ecstasy, who spoke to every one of the hidden things of God, and who did not talk to people according to their understandings. From what he had seen of him he thought that after his death there would arise great dissensions amongst his followers. They say that the words of the Sayad were very touching and had great effect, and whoever heard them used to devote himself to God's service. The Sultán also wished to hear the Sayad, but his ministers forbade him, " lest the eloquence of the Sayad

---

[1] This means that they carried on a short conversation in Kuranic verses, a very difficult thing to do, except for those who know the great Book by heart. The Sayad was the founder of the Mahdavi (now called the Ghair Mahdiya) sect whose followers can still be found in Pálanpur, the Dakhan and Hydarábád. He died at Farrah in Afghánistán in the year A.C. 1505.

should so touch the Sultán's heart as to bring disorder into the affairs of the State."[1]

One day the Sayad said, "I can show the Lord to the world with these eyes of the flesh." On hearing this speech, the *Ulamás* (learned men) of Ahmedábád took opinions regarding slaying him. All the Mullás signed *Fatwás* (orders) for his death, except Mauláná Muhammad Táj, who was the wisest of the Ulamás of the age and the teacher of teachers. He said to the Ulamás, " Have you learnt wisdom only to give your opinions for the death of this Sayad ?" After this occurrence the Sayad left Ahmedábád, and went to Pattan, and stayed at a village called Barli about three *kos* from Pattan, and there claimed to be the Mehdi. When the *Ulamás* of Pattan heard of his claim they hastened to slay him. The Sayad fled to Hindustán and thence went to Khurásán. When he arrived at a Kandahár village called Farrah, a party of men created a disturbance and slew him. But the Mehdiyás say that the Sayad died a natural death, and that no one killed him. God knows the truth. This happened in A. H. 910 (A.C. 1505).[2]

SULTAN MUZAFFAR II. MOUNTS THE THRONE.

Two days after the death of Sultán Mehmúd Sultán Muzaffar came from Baroda to Ahmedábád, and the ministers and nobles went to meet him, and were admitted to an audience. At the time of the Friday prayer, on the 7th of the blessed month of Ramazán, A. H. 917 (A. D. 1515) in the twenty-seventh year of his age Sultán Muzaffar sat on the throne of the kingdom. After the custom of his ancestors he bestowed on the soldiers and amírs many horses and dresses of honour fit for the rank of each. The list of the people who received titles that day is this :—Rashídul-mulk was distinguished by the title of Khudáwand Khán, and he was made *vazír*. Khush-kadam was made Mukhlis Khán, Malik Burhán was given the title of Mansúr Khán Malik Kutub of Azud-ul-mulk, Malik Mubárak was given the title of Iftikhárul-mulk, Nasírshádi of Mubárizul-mulk, Malik Sheikhji

---

[1] One anecdote is here omitted.

[2] About this date my MS. differs from that of Sir Olive Bayley, which gives the date H. 910 (A.D. 1505). My MS. gives the date H. 917 (A.D. 1515). Blochman (Áín-i-Akbari, p. v.) also gives the former date, so I have adopted it.

of Táídul-mulk, and Malik-Sháh, Ruknul-mulk. All these were
sons of noblemen who, during the minority of Khalíl Khán, were in his
service, and the amírs also of Mehmúd Sháh were exalted in rank
and emoluments. Learned and pious men also received fitting presents
and honours, and both the great and the small united in asking
God for blessings on the new Sultán.

Afterwards, in the month of Shawwál, the tenth month of the
Musalmán year, news was received that Mírzá Ibráhím Khán, envoy of
Ismáíl Sháh, King of the Irák and Khurásán, had arrived. The Sultán
ordered Malik Shark, Hamidul-mulk, Kutbul-mulk, and Khurásàn
Khán, with a number of other amírs to meet him, and conduct him
and his forty tall hat-wearers[1] with all honours to the foot of the throne.
The above-mentioned Mírzá presented to the Sultán, on behalf of his
sovereign, an extremely beautiful turquoise cup together with a small
box filled with jewels and valuable clothes and thirty Irák horses. The
Sultán received the Mirza with great cordiality and favour, and bestowed
on him and his followers dresses of honour suited to their rank and
kingly gifts, and ordered that they should be accommodated in a fitting
mansion, and that their daily supplies should be sent to them. After
some days the Sultán went in the direction of Baroda, and in that
district he founded a city which he named Daulatábád.[2]

At this time news was received that Khwájah-Jahán, a eunuch of
the household of Mehmúd Khilji the deceased king of Málwá and who was
one of his principal nobles, having made a sudden attack had deposed
Sultán Mehmúd, the son of Násiruddin, and had seated his younger
brother Sultán Muhammad on the throne. Sultán Mehmúd with a
large force came and laid siege to Mándu. For some time dissension
and conflict had raged between the two brothers. The end of it was
that Sultán Mehmúd was victorious and Sultán Muhammad fled and
sought protection with Sultán Muzaffar and encamped near Muhammadábád. At this time his humble petition, setting forth the above
cirumstances, arrived. The Sultán sent an order to Muhammad-
Muháfiz Khán, *Dároghák* (officer in charge) of Muhammadábád, to lead
Sultán Muhammad with due honours into the city, to provide him with
such things as he needed, and after he had rested from the fatigue

---

[1] According to the Tabakát-i-Akbari, the name of the envoy was Yád-gar Beg and
be and his forty men were Kazil-báshes or Shiah Turks, who wear tall red hats.

[2] The text is *dar-an-ziláah*, which literally rendered, means, in that district. The
Mir-ati Ahmedi has *dar-siláhi-án* which would mean 'by the side of it.' According to
Farishtah he gave Baroda the name of Daulatábád.

of his journey to send him to the presence. On receipt of the order Muháfiz omitted none of the duties of hospitality. When the Málwá Sultán came to the presence of Sultán Muzaffar, he regarded him with the eye of kindness and favour, and said, " If God wills, after the rainy season I will march against Mándu, and, having divided the kingdom of Málwá into two portions, I will bestow one on you, and one on Sultán Mehmúd." He directed Kaisar Khán to the thánedári of Dohad, which is situated on the Málwá frontier, to assemble the local chiefs and landholders, and to make himself acquainted with the roads and customs of Málwá. He ordered the principal paymasters and military officers to inform and prepare the troops for the expedition. The Sultán himself went to the village of Morámli which was the *Shikárgáh* (game preserve) of the late Sultán Mehmúd, for the sake of hunting and for some time remained in that village so occupied. At that camp Aâzam-Humáyún Ádil Khán of the exalted throne, ruler of Asír and Burhánpur, who was the Sultán's son-in-law, came with his sons and waited upon the Sultán, and after some days returned to his country. The Sultán went to Muhammadábád.

It so happened that one day the followers of Sultán Muhammad had a dispute with the men of the ambassador of Ismáil Sháh. Sultán Muhammad had an exceedingly valuable diamond and the ambassador Ibráhim wished to purchase it, but was unable to do so on account of the great price demanded. Some enmity sprang up on both sides. The prince, who was but an inexperienced youth, went one night with several men to the house of an old friend of his, and it so happened that this person lived in a part of the same *Sarái* in which Mír Ibráhim was residing. Some designing and evil disposed person told Mír Ibráhim that the prince intended to fly, and desired to loot the houses and property of the Persians. If, therefore, he could imprison him that night his act would to-morrow please the Sultán. The Mír not thinking of what might result, closed the *Sarái* door, and at midnight seized the prince and imprisoned him in his own quarters. The prince suffered much annoyance from this proceeding. In the morning he was released and his friends and followers assembling, proclaimed in the *bazaar* that an order had been issued to plunder the properties of the tall hat-wearers. As the confinement and annoyance suffered by the prince had caused much popular displeasure and excitement immediately on hearing this, a crowd collected at the gate of Mír Ibráhím's *Sarái*, and the red-hat-wearing Kazilbáshes stood ready to repulse them and protect their property. When overpowered by the numerical superiority of their assailants, the gate of the *Sarái* was burst open and the rioters having killed several of the Kazilbáshes, set fire to the houses and commenced to rob them. When the Sultán heard of this, he ordered Malik-ush-Shark-Imádul-mulk to go with the royal elephants, to stop the disturbance and take care that no harm should befall the Kazilbáshes, and to punish the ring-leaders of the affray. Imádul-mulk went, and suppressed the tumult, and having punished the rioters of low degree took care that Mír Ibráhím should sustain no injury, and brought him and his followers to the king's apartments. The king allotted a place for their residence in the palace. Mír Ibráhím now represented that he had been robbed of six *lákhs* of *tánkás* of money and property. At that time one Gujarát *tánká* was worth eight Murádi *tánkás*, as at this moment these *tánkás* are current in Khándesh and the Dakhan. The Sultán paid this sum from his treasury. On Friday, the 14th of the month of Ramazán, he dismissed the ambassador after presenting him with a *lákh* of *tánkás* in cash and a handsome dress of honour. He sent Khurásán Khán with him to escort him and to strengthen the loosened bonds of friendship and unity between him and the king of the Irák. He further sent seven huge elephants with wonderful trappings, a rhinoceros,[1] and wonderful birds and beasts and much handsome cloth and other presents for Ismáil Sháh with the abovementioned Khurásán Khán, and he provided two large ships for the embarkation of Mírza Ibráhím and his property. After this occurrence, the kindness that the Sultán entertained for Sultán Muhammad, underwent a slight change, and at the invitation of some of his amírs Sultán Muhammad left Gujarát without taking leave of the Sultán. Sultán Mehmúd, the son of Násiruddín discovering this, and that his amírs were discontented, assembled an army of Hindus, gave their chief the title of Medáni Rái, and entrusted the entire management of his kingdom to his hands. Medáni Rái collecting his relations and adherents raised a large army of unbelievers and fought a battle with Sultán Muhammad. Khwájáh Jahán

---

[1] My MS. has the Persian word *Karkdan* which means a rhinoceros and not *Gurg* or wolf as I find given in the other copies and the translation by Sir Olive Bayley. I think my copy is here correct, as sending a wolf to Persia would be no curiosity.

was slain, Sultán Muhammad defeated, and the entire Government of Mándu fell into the hands of Medáni Rái, to such an extent that he conferred all the chief posts about the court on his own relations and found occasion to slay the Musalmán nobles and leading men of the Sultán one after another. The Hindus commenced the oppression and violence natural to them, and introduced such evil customs and changes that the condition of the Musalmán dwellers in the capital and other cities of Mándu became unbearable. Sultán Muzaffar heard of these occurrences, and learned that after many years the rule of the Hindus had again returned to Málwá, and that no power remained to Sultán Mehmúd beyond the mere name of king, which also would shortly disappear. Sultán Muzaffar writhed with pain at all this and took upon himself the duty of removing these Hindus. He ordered an army to be collected and himself came from Muhammadábád to Ahmedábád, and visited the shrines of Ḳutbul-másháikh-Sheikh Ahmed Khattú and Hazrat Ḳutb-i-Álam and his sons, all saints of high degree, and visiting the tombs of his ancestors he besought them to give him resolution, grace and help, and after remaining a week in Ahmedábád he returned to Muhammadábád.

MARCH OF SULTÁN MUZAFFAR TO MÀLWÀ TO EXPEL THE HINDUS AND HIS ARRIVAL IN THE TOWN OF DHÁR AND HIS RETURN FROM THAT COUNTRY.

In the month of Shawwál A. H. 918 (A. D. 1512) having marched from Ahmedábád in the direction of Mándu, to drive away the unbelievers and aid the Musalmáns, he encamped some days in the town of Godhráh to concentrate the army. At this time news was received that Áinul-mulk, fief holder of Nehrwálá, otherwise called Pattan, was on his way to pay his respects to the Sultán when the Rájá of Ídar Bhím, son of Bhán, issued forth, and ravaged the country on the banks of the river Sábarmati. Áinul-mulk drew an army towards Ídar to repulse him and plundered and laid waste the Ídar country. When Áin-ul-Mulk arrived about three kos from Ídar, the Rájá of Ídar came with a large army and joined battle. Áhdul-mulk, brother of Áinul-mulk, together with many others, was slain. Áinul-mulk was defeated, and came to Pattan. The Sultán changed his intention of going to Málwá, and turned in the direction of Ídar, and arrived by forced marches to Morásá, and there prepared his forces against the Ídar Rájá and

ravaged and plundered his country. The Rájá of Ídar fled to the
mountains, and on the fourth day the Sultán marching from Morásá
pitched his camp near Ídar, and ordered that the houses, palaces and
temples of Ídar should be so destroyed, that neither their name nor sign
could remain. This happened in A. H. 919 (A. D. 1514). When the
Rájá of Idar heard of this he begged for the intercession of Malik
Gopi, who was originally a Brahman and one of the *vazírs* of the Sultán.
Malik Gopi obtained from the Sultán forgiveness of his fault.

As the Sultán was anxious to chastise the Hindus of Málwá, he
overlooked his fault and having levied from him the tribute
agreed on, he returned to Godhráh, and thence sent Prince Sikandar
Khán to Muhammadábád, and he himself went towards Málwá. When
he arrived at Dohad, he ordered the fort to be repaired, and marched
thence. When he passed the Deolah defile, which is very difficult, he
halted there for three days, and to keep open his communications
appointed Safdar Khán to be the thánedár of the place. At this camp
the son of the *mukaddam* (the head-man or chief citizen) of the town
of Dhár, which is a dependency of Málwá, came and having had an
audience of the Sultán asked for protection. The Sultán sent Kiwámul-mulk Sárang with several other nobles to convey his assurance of
protection to the inhabitants of Dhár. At this juncture news was
brought that Sultán Mehmúd Násiruddin and Medáni Rái had gone
in the direction of Chanderi, because Sultán Muhammad brother
of Sultán Mehmúd, who after the defeat above described had taken
refuge with Sultán Sikandar Lodi having obtained aid from him, had
come and had taken possession of certain territories of Chanderi.
Sultán Muzaffar said: "In bringing the army here it was not
my desire to take the country of Málwá from Sultán Mehmúd, a
Musalmán king. I only wished to expel Medáni Rái and others,
and to make peace between the two brothers. Sultán Mehmúd
is at present in great difficulty, and I will see how it ends, and
then do what the occasion demands." He then ordered Kiwámul-mulk
to come from Dhár. Kiwámul-mulk, on his return from Dhár, so
praised the deer park which had been constructed there according to the
orders of Ghiásuddín, that the Sultán desired to see it, and having left
Kiwámul-mulk at the camp and taking with him 12,000 fully equipped
horsemen and 150 elephants he started to see the deer park and encamped near the tank of Dhár. Some amírs now represented that it would
be a good thing to make an attack on Mándu. But the Sultán replied

that it was not well to visit a house in the absence of its master. On that day he performed the afternoon prayers at the shrines of Sheikh Kamál of Málwá and Sheikh Abdulláh Changál, who are buried in the vicinity of the town of Dhár. The people of the town, great and small coming out to meet the Sultán blessed and praised him. Next morning he gave Nizámul-mulk Sultáni and Razí-ul-mulk and Ikhtiárul-mulk and Malik Chaman, who had the title of Muzaffar Khán, and Saif Khán, leave to go and see the pleasant palaces of the the deer park and return the same day and report what sort of a place it was. He also himself got ready to set out to see the deer park. When evening came, and the amírs did not return, the Sultán said: "What is it? When they know that I am going to visit Diláwarah too". So saying, he started for Diláwarah, but did not find the nobles there. Alif Khán said: "Perhaps Nizámul-mulk has gone to Naálchah to see his brother Rái Singh, who lives there." The Sultán saw the Diláwaráh palaces, and returned to Dhár. After evening prayers news arrived that Nizámul-mulk was returning, having obtained a victory. The Sultán asked: "What victory?" They said that as Nizámul-mulk was coming from Naálchah, the Hindus who were in the fort of Mándu issuing, pursued and overtook him. Nizámul-mulk turning back, fought them. Forty of the Hindus were slain and the remainder escaped to the fortress, and Nizámul-mulk, triumphant and victorious, set out to join the Sultán. The Sultán was greatly enraged, and spoke harshly to Nizámul-mulk and said, "Wherefore did you go thither without orders? Had the battle ended in a reverse and had you been obliged to fly, whose would have been the disgrace?" On the third day the Sultán returned from Dhár to his camp, and thence set out to return to his capital. The author of the *Tárikh-i-Báhádur-Sháhi* says that being on personal attendance on the Sultán during this campaign, he was an eye-witness of the events he has recorded. In short, the Sultán returned to Muhammadábád.

In A. H. 920 (A. D. 1514) news came that Ráimal nephew of Ráo Bhím, Rájá of Idár, after the death of the aforesaid Rájá, encouraged by Ráná Sánga, Rájá of Chitor, had expelled Bhármal, son of Bhím from Idar, and had seized on the throne. The Sultán was not pleased at this and said, Bhím enjoyed the throne of Idar under his authority, and that he was surprised the Ráná had darod to help

13

Ráimal to oust Bhármal. He ordered Nizámul-mulk, fief-holder of Ahmednagar, to remove Ráimal from Idár and hand it over to Bhármal, son of Bhím. The Sultán then himself proceeded to Ahmednagar, eventually returning thence to Ahmedábád. Afterwards in A. H. 923 (A. D. 1515-16) Ráimal had many engagements with the army of the Sultán in which he was sometimes victorious, but more frequently defeated. While the Sultán was passing the rainy season at Ahmedábád in pleasure and enjoyment, the Málwá amírs Habíb Khán, Sheikh Chánd, and others flying from Medáni Rái, came to the Sultán, and related the oppression practised by the followers of Medáni Rái, and how the religion and precepts of Islám were being done away with at Mándu, how Medáni Rái had killed the principal men, while others having fled from their country were dispersed, how he meant shortly to kill Sultán Mehmúd or having drawn the hot iron over his eyes to blind him and imprison him. The Sultán hearing the overbearing conduct of the Hindus made a fixed determination saying, God willing, he would certainly march to Mándu after the rainy season and crush Medáni Rái and re-establish the rule of Islám in Málwá.

They say that when Sultán Mehmúd saw that all his country and treasure had passed into the hands of Medáni Rái, and that nothing remained to him, the Sultán, but the name, he desired to escape from Mándu. He went forth on the pretence of hunting and remained for some days occupied in that pursuit. One day he rode out from morning till evening. The Hindus who were placed over him as guards went to sleep from the fatigue of the hunting and except Medáni Rái's chosen men, no one remained with the Sultán. He was kept under a system of surveillance so jealous that if he drank water, it was a Hindu who gave him to drink, and if he desired to eat, no other than a Hindu brought him his food. Even the grooms and porters around him were Hindus. Amongst his Hindu guards was a Rájput of the name of Krishna, an inhabitant of the town of Kharal. As he was a land-holder of Málwá, he served the king with a more sincere fidelity than the other Rajputs. The Sultán said to him, " Krishna, I am weary of this life, and sore distressed. Could you not get two horses from the stables and show me the way to Gujarát that I may go to Sultán Muzaffar and get aid from him to punish these scoundrels. If you can do this, do it at once, and if God wills you will be abundantly rewarded." Krishna agreed, and at midnight brought two horses from the Sultán's stables. The Sultán mounted, one horse, and on the other he seated his favourite wife whose name was Ráni Kanákur.[1] Krishna leading the way took the road to Gujarát and travelling half the night and the whole of the following day they arrived at Bhánkorah, a village on the Gujarát frontier. As their horses were fatigued, they alighted under a tree near the village. Next day news of their arrival reached Kaisar Khán, the governor of Dohad, which is ten *kos* from Bhánkorah. Kaisar Khán came to attend on the Sultán and having paid him royal homage continued serving him and supplying the royal wants. He sent off a swift camel-rider informing Sultán Muzaffar of the arrival of Sultán Mehmúd as he had witnessed it. Sultán Muzaffar was pleased, and at once sent off good Arabian horses with gold saddles and bejewelled bridles, and elephants like mountains with housings of velvet, embroidered with gold, and kingly vestments, and well-trained slave-girls, and handsome slave-boys, together with treasure, and an establishment under the orders of renowned amírs, and wrote a letter of welcome expressive of his delight and the chagrin his enemies would experience at Sultán Mehmúd's arrival and requesting him to consider the Sultán's victorious army as arrived to escort him, God willing to destroy those treacherous Hindus and hand over Mándu and the country of Málwá to Sultán Mehmúd's servants.

When the Sultán's army approached Sultán Mehmúd, he went to meet it. All the amírs alighting from their horses kissed his feet. At the same time they pitched lofty regal tents with red walls and with all regal appurtenances. Sultán Mehmúd, glad and joyful, entered the tent, and the amírs alighted and took up quarters round the royal tent. When the spies of Medáni Rái saw and reported this to him, the hearts of the Hindus began to quake with terror. Two days after the sending of these amírs, on Thursday the 4th of the month of Zilkaád A. H. 923 (A. D. 1517), Sultán Muzaffar, with the intention of a religious war, placed his auspicious foot in the stirrup of good fortune. The author of the *Túrikh-i-Bahádur-Sháhi* says that when the Sultán resolved on the conquest of Mándu, the great men and nobles in obedience to the Sultán's wishes occupied themselves in reading the whole of the Kuraán. The Sultán sought the omen of victory by

---

[1] The word is either Kanak-Kuar or Kania or Kannya Kuar.

opening the holy book at random and drawing his omen from the last verse. The last verse on the page he thus opened was this :—[1]

" And they defeated them by God's will, and David slew Goliath and God gave him kingdom and wisdom and taught him what He willed. And if God had not prevented men, the one by the other, verily the earth had been corrupted : but God is beneficent towards his creatures."

After this consultation of the omen from the Kuraán, the Sultán, certain of victory, by confidence in that verse, marched from Muhammadábád on Thursday the 11th of Zilkaád. After three days' march he arrived at Godhra, and on Sunday the 21st of the above, he bade adieu to Prince Sikandar Khán on his departure for Muhammadábád, and taking Princes Latíf Khán and Bahádur Khán with him, he marched towards Muzaffarábád, and on Tuesday the 27th of the above month pitched his camp with good fortune and prosperity at the village of Bhánkorah. On Wednesday the 9th of Zilhajj while at this camp, news arrived that Sultán Sikandar king of Delhi had resigned his life unto his Creator, and that his son Sultán Ibráhím had ascended the throne. Sultan Muzaffar remained in that camp, and performed the third day ceremonies for the dead. On Friday the 11th of the above month he resumed his march and halted at Dhanigám, and on Monday the 14th of the above month he encamped at Deolah, and on Tuesday the 15th he met Sultán Mehmúd and gave him a right royal reception and so consoled him that Sultán Mehmúd found rest from the troubles of evil fortune, the privations of travel, and the treachery of his evil-disposed enemy. On Friday the 18th, he brought his victorious standards to Dhár. Medáni Rái who had remained in Dhár with the idea of opposing Sultán Muzaffar in battle fled to Ujjain and sent Rái Pithaura, Bhím-karan, Shád Khán, Budhan, Gángu, and Ugra·Sen who were the chief men of his army, to defend the fort of Mándu. On Sunday the 23rd, the Sultán with his army pitched his tents round Mándu, and prepared his batteries to invest the place. He appointed Kaisar Khán over the Dehli gate battery, and he nominated MalikImádul-mulk to command the battery at another gate. He surrounded the fortress on all sides. At this time Medáni Rái sent word to the garrison to negotiate and obtain a month's delay from the Sultán, pretending that they would surrender the fort after that period, and that in the meantime he would obtain such an army to their aid from the Ráná (of Chitor) that Sultán Muzaffar would have to leave the fort without

---

[1] The Kuráán. Chapter—The cow. See Sale's Translation of the Kuraán (chap. II., p. 30).

fighting and return to Gujarát. The Hindus began to use their vulpine wiles, and on Friday the 25th, the third day of the siege, Pithaura with several of his followers and relatives sent suitable presents to Kaisar Khán and Khudáwand Khán, and asked for quarter, and requested time for the besieged to bring out their families and hand over the fort to the Sultán's servants. Kaisar Khán and Khudáwand Khán brought them to the Sultán's presence. The Sultán granted them a safe reception and a truce for one month. The Hindus made a pretence of vacating the fort while they secretly wrote to Medáni Rái that they had accomplished his wish, asking him to do without fail what he could.

Medáni Rái went to the Ráná and said, "No one among us is greater than you in all India. If not nów when will you aid us who are of your race?" He agreed to give the Ráná on condition of his aid several fine elephants from the stables of Sultán Mehmúd, and several fine jewels from his treasury which were in his possession. The Ráná said, "I will come to Sárangpur and there take the jewels and elephants, and after that will act as may seem fit." The Ráná started accordingly for Sárangpur, a town under Málwá fifty kos from Mándu, with a great army. When this news reached the Sultán, the deceit and cunning of the garrison became apparent. He sent Ádil Khán Asiri and Malik Kiwámul-mulk Sárang with brave and intrepid amirs and picked fighting men against the Ráná, and ordered his own army to press the siege and put out their best efforts. The soldiers now made such strenuous efforts that on the third day, being the 2nd of the month of Safar they conquered the fortress, and put a large number of the unbelievers to the sword. They say that the number of the slain was 19,000. The author of the "Muzaffur Sháhi" says, that 40,000 were slain with 57 leaders of note.—God best knows the truth! The names of the Hindu leaders were these:—Pithaura, Udaikarán, Káhándeo and Ajáebdeo, Gházi Khán, and Shádi Khán, Ratanchand, Mánekchand, Bahádur Khán, Daulat Khán, Akhéchand, Kiratchand, Dúngarshi, and Gángu, Bikramsi and Mále Khán, Rái Jagat, Dharamsingh, Bhánsingh, Jetsingh, Fateh Khán and their sons and the sons of Thákarshi and Kákarha, and others. This occurred in A. H. 924 (A. D. 1518) as is gatherable from the last of the following verses :—

"Muzaffar Sháh conquered Mándu, the former capital of which was Dhár.
If you ask for the date of his victory,
It is the frustration of all unbelievers."

The date is also obtainable from the Arabic words : " Kad-fatahal. Mándu-Sultánunu." Our Sultán has, verily, conquered Màndu.

In the above lines, the word پریشانی : ' frustration ' supplies the numerical value from its letters.

Sayad Jaláluddín Munawwarul-mulk Bukhári and another eye-witness of these events record that in this conflict the Muslim army was helped by unseen and miraculous hosts. He says :—" After the defeat of the Hindus and after their opening the gates of the fortress to us, some of us agreed to go out for a stroll in the newly conquered city. We went up to the fort and were looking at the mansions and wherever we encountered a Hindu of the militant class we killed him, till we reached a mansion the doors of which were closed from within. We thought there must be Hindus within who must, for security, have closed the doors. With the name of Alláh we broke open the door and went in and found the house quite untenanted except the room of a sub-terranean, where forty Hindus were lying with their throats cut weltering in their blood. One of them had a little life left, and could reply to our questions. We asked him how it was he had been killed with closed doors. He said he and his companions had closed the doors for safety, but that a supernatural hand clenching a sword had appeared and killed them all."

In short the Sultán arrived victorious and triumphant in the lofty fortress, when some of his well-wishers represented that it would not be proper to hand over to Sultán Mehmúd the country of Málwá which was of greater extent than Gujarát, and which had only come into their hands after such troubles and hardships and the conquest of which had cost them the lives of 10,000 veterans.

Verse.

" No one can obtain a kingdom as ancestral property,
Until he shall have struck many blows with the double-bladed sword."

Immediately on hearing this speech the Sultán came down from the fortress, and said to Sultán Mehmúd, " Take care that none of my men remain up in the fortress."

Sultán Mehmúd said, " All the good fortune and happiness that
I now enjoy is through your favour. I have come by all, my kingdom
wealth and family, through your Majesty. If you will remain a few
days up here in the fortress, it will be a great honour to me." The
Sultán replied, "If God wills on the third day hence I will be your
guest. At present it is best as it is." Although Sultán Mehmúd tried
to force him much, he would not consent.

They say that after some time one of the Sultán's companions
asked the reason of his descending so quickly from the fort. He
replied : " People were endeavouring to persuade me not to hand
over the fortress to Sultán Mehmúd, and I had set out on this expedition
only as a religious war. I feared lest, God forbid, some temptation
should creep into my heart, and drive me to a conduct which neither
justice nor good faith could warrant. I therefore descended quickly,
and gave evil thoughts no place, and in this act I showed no
favour to Sultán Mehmúd. It was rather he who showed a favour
to me, as I have through him arrived at the good fortune of performing
a virtuous deed, and have been rewarded by the accomplishment of my
desires."

The history of the jewelled waist-belt is this :— When Sultán Kutbuddín, son of Sultán Muhammad, defeated Sultán Mehmúd Khilji at
the battle of Kapadwanj, there was such a slaughter as could not be
exceeded. By chance, in the heat of the fray, which resembled the
day of judgment, the ward-robe-keeper of Sultán Kutbuddín, in whose
charge was the jewelled belt, was by the restiveness of his horse carried
into the ranks of the enemy. The animal there became so violent that
the ward-robe-keeper fell from it and was captured by the enemy
and the jewelled belt was taken from him and given to Sultán
Mehmúd of Málwa. This jewelled waist-belt was in the Málwá treasury
at the time the Mándu fortress was taken by the strength of the arm
of Sultán Muzaffar. Sultán Mehmúd sent this belt together with
a fitting sword and horse, to Sultán Muzaffar by the hands of his
son who had been freed from imprisonment of the Hindus, on the day
the fort was conquered, and begged him to come and be his guest.
The Sultán agreeing gave his son leave with honour and presents.
Sultán Mehmud, by way of showing his joy, ordered the city to be
illuminated, and having adorned the palaces, he caused a kingly
banquet to be spread. They say that Sultán Mehmúd took such

trouble in this reception, that for magnificence it could not be exceeded. On the 11th Safar agreeably to his promise Sultán Muzaffar ascended the fortress. The great and small of Mándu, even the *pardáh* ladies and children, appeared on their walls and balconies to witness the procession, and blessed and praised the Sultán. Sultán Mehmúd behaved with great hospitality and showed great humility and after the banquet he showed the Sultán over the palaces. In the course of this they came to a mansion in the centro of which was a building in the form of a quadrangle, [1] carved and gilded, and round it were a number of apartments. When the Sultán placed his foot within the threshold of that building, the ladies of the harem of Sultán Mehmúd, having apparelled and ornamented themselves magnificently, all at once opened the doors of their chambers and burst into view like houris and fairies. They say that Sultán Mehmúd had one thousand beautiful women in his harem.

The Sultáns of Mándu had reached such a pitch of luxury and ease that it is impossible to imagine aught exceeding it. Among them especially Sultán Ghiásuddin was so famous for his luxurious habits that at present if any one exceeds in luxury and pleasure-seeking they say that he is a second Ghiásuddín. The orders of this Sultán were that no event of a painful nature or one in which there was any touch of sadness should be related to him. They say that during his entire reign news of a sad nature was only twice conveyed to him. Once, when his son-in-law died, and his daughter was brought before him clothed in white garments. On this occasion the Sultán is related to have simply said : " Perhaps her husband is dead." He said so because the custom of the people of India is that when the husband of a woman dies, she gives up wearing coloured clothes. The second occasion was, when the army of Sultán Bahlúl Lodi plundered several of the districts of Chanderi. Though it was necessary to report this to the Sultán, yet his ministers were unable to communicate it to him. They, therefore, asked a band of actors (*bhánds*) to assume the dress of Afghâns and mentioning the districts to act their being pillaged and laid waste. The actors did so. Sultán Ghiásuddin exclaimed in surprise : " But is the Governor of Chanderi

---

[1] The text has the words—Kaábah-wár–like the *Kaábah* or Temple of Makkah which is also quadrangular.

dead that he does not take vengeance on the country of the Afgháns for the injuries done to his districts?"

To resume, the '*harím*' of Sultán Mehmúd appeared like peacocks from Paradise with trays full of precious stones to scatter them over the head of the Sultán.[1] The recital of this verse is appropriate to that event.

COUPLET :—

> "Houris were drawn up in a line for a look at my love,
> The boys of Paradise in astonishment clapped their hands."

When the eyes of Sultán Muzaffár fell on their charms he bowed his head and said : "To look at other than one's own wives is a sin. Sultán Mehmúd said : "All these are my property and you have purchased me by your kindness. Now according to the dictum of law the slave and his property belong to his master, thus they are lawful for you, and they are all a present to you." The Sultán replied : "I wish you joy of them, let them retire to the *pardúh.*" At a single signal of Sultán Mehmúd they all vanished like fairies. The Sultán then came forth and all that day and night remained as a guest of Sultán Mehmúd. After the noon-prayers on the next day he took leave. Sultán Mehmúd presented magnificent presents, in the shape of Arab and Turkish horses, elephants like mountains, stuffs of different colour and jewels of different sorts. They say that from the time Sultán Mehmúd had left Mándu to solicit the help of Sultán Muzaffar, Medáni Rái had made no alteration in the allowances of the ladies of Sultán Mehmúd's *harím* in matters such as clothes, perfumes, and ready money ; that he used to supply them with these things without let or hindrance, and their gold and jewels remained in their own hands. Each day he used to come into the Durbár and send his respects to them and used to say : "I have not committed any treason that the Sultán has become aggrieved and has gone away. Please represent to the Sultán to come and take charge of his country and entrust the *vazarat* to another. I agree to always carry his shoes." With words of this kind he used to go, and the rules of looking after the Zenáná were carried on by the eunuchs just in the same way in which they used to be enforced when the Sultán was present.

---

[1] Scattering gold or silver coins or precious stones over the head of a bridegroom or conqueror is a form of sacrifice common in the East. The scattered coin is scrambled for by the crowd and with it pass away to the crowd the spirits of evil hovering over the head of the victor.

14

In short on the day the fortress was conquered, Shádi Kkán and Gángo who were amírs of the highest rank of the garrison were slain, and Hemkaran and Budhan issued alive from a wicket, and went to Medáni Rái.

They say that the garrison were so impressed with the terrors of the slaughter at the storming of the fort that Budhan after telling Medáni Rái some terrible accounts of the fate of the garrison asked for water, and immediately on drinking it fell down and died. On seeing this Medáni Rái and the Ráná became greatly alarmed. Medáni Rái said, "my relations and kinsmen have all been destroyed, my wife and children have fallen into the hands of the Musalmáns. Now of what use is life to me." Saying so he attempted to kill himself. The Ráná stopped him and took him with him to Chitor. They say that they travelled thirty-seven kos in one night. Ádil Khán of Asír, who was at Wabálpur, which is fifteen kos from Mándu, heard of the flight of the Ráná, informed the Sultán of it, and asked permission to pursue him. The Sultán saw no advantage in the pursuit, and sent for Ádil Khán to join him, and himself returned towards his capital. Sultán Mehmúd accompanied him as far as Deolah, and there Sultán Muzaffar gave him leave to depart after ordering Asaf Khan with several other amírs to go with Sultán Mehmúd and remain with him to help him. He also gave leave to Ádil Khán at this camp to return to Asír and Burhánpúr. He himself came thence with great pomp to Idar, and stayed there a few days for hunting, and thence came to Muhammadábád, and spent all the rains at this capital in pleasure and enjoyment. The soldiers rested from the fatigues and after the discomforts of a long campaign.

In A. H. 925 (A. D. 1520) news arrived that Sultán Mehmúd had marched on Karwan. Hemkaran, of whom mention has been made above, held that place. In the battle he fell by the Sultán's hands. On account of this it was reported that the Ráná collecting a large army advanced against Sultán Mehmúd, and a great battle was fought. The end of the matter was that Sultán Mehmúd fell wounded into the hands of the Ráná, his army was defeated, and many Muhammadans were killed. On hearing of this occurrence the Sultán was much concerned, and sent an army to protect the Mándu fortress. The Ráná on hearing this turned back, and went to Chitor, his capital.

They say that when Sultán Mehmúd fell wounded on the field, some men of the Ráná's army ran and informed him. The Ráná came in person, and having placed Sultán Mehmúd with all honour in a palanquin carried him away to Chitor, and from fear of the Musalmán kings who were round the Mándu territory such as Sultán Ibráhím Lodi, king of Delhi, Sultán Muzaffar, king of Gujarát, and others he treated Sultán Mehmúd with great courtesy.[1] When the Sultán's wounds were healed, he, with great honour, accompanied him for several stages, and then gave him leave: the Ráná kept the son of the Sultán with him as a hostage, so that the Sultán should not take his revenge. Sultán Mehmúd came to Mándu.

In the above year Sultán Muzaffar came from Muhammadábád to Ídar, and having for some time remained engaged in hunting in the game-preserves, appointed the son of the uncle of the vazír, Malík Húsain who had the title of Nizám Khán, and who was in bravery and courage the Rustam of the age, as thánedár of Idar in place of Nasratul-mulk, and then returned to Ahmedábád. The vazírs showed displeasure at this. The Sultán said, "I have selected this man as the best out of you all, and your grief now is of no avail." On account of this the vazírs were inimical to Nizám Khán and sought his ruin. In A. H. 926 (A. D. 1524) a *Bhát* or Rájput bard in Nizám Khan's assembly said, "At present there is not a Rájáh in Hindustán like the Ráná who assists Ráemal. How long so ever you may remain in Ídar, Ráemal is bound to take it." "What dog is he," returned Nizám Khán, "who shall dáre to aid Ráemal, while I am here; if he is a man why does he not come ?" The bard replied, "His arrival is near." Nizám Khán replied, "If he comes not, he is a dog ;" and he further took a dog and chained him and said, "If the Ráná does not come, he is like this dog." The bard departed, and went to the Ráná and related what had passed. The Ráná in anger coiled up like a snake, and at once pitched his tent outside the town, and came by forced marches to Sirohi. On hearing this news the Sultán desired to send aid to Idar, but the Sultán's ministers who were inimical to Nizám Khán said, "How dare the Ráná to fight with the Sultán's servants ?" In the meantime the couriers reported that the Ráná had returned to Chitor, and this information was at that time correct.

---

[1] It is a pity the author does not understand the chivalrous courtesy of the Sísodia Rájput who, though surrounded on all sides and even when hard pressed by the arms of Islám, maintained his independence and honour.

The Sultán placing Kiwámul-mulk in charge of Ahmedábád, himself went to Muhammadábád. The Ráná turned back and went towards the country of Wágadh which lies to the east of Idar. Nizám Khán sent to inform the Sultán that the Ráná with 40,000 horse had turned towards Wágadh intending to invade Ídar. He also reported that the usual strength of the contingent under his command at Idar, was 5,000 horse, of whom many had gone to Ahmedábád.

The vazírs in their enmity to Nizám Khán did not present this petition to the Sultán. Great men have said :—" What great fabrics of power have ministers malevolent of mind and crafty of counsel not brought to ruin and what heads have they not caused to roll. It behoves rulers to exercise judgment and discrimination not to appoint such men as ministers." In short, there was delay in sending aid, and the Ráná made a rapid descent upon Ídar. Nizám Khán who in those days had been ennobled by the title of Mubárizul-mulk, determined to join battle, the following day, but his followers restrained him saying that the Ráná had come to the attack with 40,000 horse, and that their 900 horse were nothing in comparison, and they added that his idea would not be pleasing to the Sultán, and that in the event of a defeat it would bring disgrace on the kingdom. Nizám Khán, how-ever, remained firm to his purpose, and after much discussion, it was settled that they should go to Ahmednagar, and, strengthening the fort, fight with cannons and muskets until assistance should arrive, when they would fight a pitched battle. They took Mubáriz Khán with them whether he would or no and went to Ahmednagar. There were some men however in Ídar who were the Sultán's own troopers (silehdárs). These men agreed among themselves to die martyrs and remained in Ídar in such a way that Mubáriz Khán did not become aware of it. When the Ráná came to Ídar, they issued forth and fought, and became martyrs. The chief of them was Malik Sajan or Sheikhan Utheria, and he was induced to take this course by the fact that the vazírs had said to him :—" The Malik will some day do such an act as will bring a load of shame on Mubáriz Khán."

. They say that a bard had composed some verses in praise of Mubáriz Khán in which he had compared the Ráná's army with cranes, and Mubáriz Khán's men with falcons. When the Ráná came near Idar, he said to the bard, " Where now are those falcons that you spoke of ?" At this time the men who were in the fortress issued forth, and the men who were in the front of the Ráná's army, fled. The

bard said, " Here come the falcons I spoke of." In short on his
way to Ahmednagar Mubáriz Khán met Khizr Khán, Asad Khán,
Gházi Khán, Shujá-úl-mulk and Saiful-Mulk who were coming from
Ahmednagar. They said to Mubáriz Khán, " You should have
stayed in Ídar, where we also were coming to fight the Ráná
together with you. For the idea that it may be said that we took
shelter within the walls of a fort for fear of this unbeliever cannot be
endured, in case he comes to Ahmednagar to-morrow. We shall fight
in the plain. Under these circumstances it would have been better
had we fought him at Ídar." Mubáriz Khán said, " My friends
counselled me that it was necessary to go to Ahmednagar though
I was not of their mind. Now the counsel is yours, and I also
am of your opinion." As they had met near Ahmednagar, they went
to Ahmednagar. In the morning arraying themselves, they came out
and drew up their army and stood ready. They were in all 1,200
horse and 1,000 foot armed with muskets. A day did not elapse
before the army of the Ráná appeared like a mountain on all sides,
and of the army (of Islám) 1,200 horse and 900 foot of the followers
of Mubáriz Khán and 400 cavalry belonging to the other amírs
determined to fight to the death. Advancing with the cry of Allah !
Allah ! they sought battle and attacked the enemy's van and routed it,
and attacked the centre, and dispersed it also, and thus they defeated
20,000 of the Ráná's cavalry, and killing and striking they thus advanced one *kos* till they were out of sight of the army that followed
them. The men in their rear thought that they must all have been slain.
They, therefore, showing their backs to the enemy, fled back to Ahmednagar. In short the death seeking *gházis* defeated the van and arrived
at the centre, and broke it also. Ibráhím Khán and Gházi Khán and
Sultán Shah who were the chiefs in this fight were killed with many
others. Others fell wounded in the field, but few remained without a
wound.

The followers of Mubáriz Khán saw that they were striking their
heads against a mountain, and that their heads would be broken, while
the mountain would receive no injury, so seizing him they drew
him from the battle by main force, and set their face towards the
fort of Ahmednagar, thinking that the fort was still in the hands of
the garrison. When, however, they came to the fort gate, they saw
that the garrison had left the fort before their arrival and fled.
Accordingly Mubáriz Khán and Safdar Khán made for the town of

Parántij, which lies about fifteen miles from Ahmednagar. Leaving the straight road, they went by another. But Asadul-mulk and others went by the straight road. The Hindus pursued and overtook Asadul-mulk. Asadul-mulk turning back gave battle, and was slain with his followers, and all his elephants and baggage fell into the enemy's hands. The Ránú encamped near Ahmednagar, plundered the city and imprisoned all the inhabitants. At night the Ráná assembled his advisers and took counsel. Some said that Ahmedábád was only fifty *kos* off that they would make a forced march and surprise it. The Ráná said: "Here were four hundred Muhammadans who have defeated twenty thousand and killed a thousand of your horse. If four thousand of their horse come against you, you would be no match for them. Besides none of my ancestors have ever come so far (even as this) or achieved such success. So for the present this must suffice." The Gujarát Garásiás who were with the Ráná, said, "If you do not choose to go to Ahmedábád, Wadnagar is near at hand, you should take it and return. The inhabitants of Wadnagar are merchants, and have much gold, so your army will return laden with booty." In the morning they marched accordingly to Wadnagar. Since the inhabitants of Wadnagar were all Brahmans, they came to the Ráná and said, "We have passed twenty-two generations here, and hitherto no one has either oppressed or persecuted us. Why do you, who are a Hindu sovereign, do so.?" The Ráná gave up his intention of plundering Wadnagar but taking from them some tribute he departed, and camped near Bísánagar. The officer in charge of that place took shelter in the citadel. The Ráná's men tried to take it, but they defended it till the time of evening prayer. In this turmoil and confusion the town of Visalnagar was also sacked. At night a report was spread in the Ráná's army that Ainul-mulk, and Fateh Khán, governor of Pattan, had arrived. The army of the Ráná remained all night under arms and in the dawn at once started in the direction of Ídar. From Ídar the Rána went to his own country.

On the day of the battle Kiwámul-mulk, governor of Ahmedábád, had started from the city to the aid of Mubárizul-mulk, and had camped at the village of Walád which is seven *kos* from Ahmedábád. Several of the refugees from the defeated army arrived there and said that Mubáriz-ul-mulk, Safdar Khán, and Gházi Khán were slain. Kiwámul-mulk halting in that place wrote of the above rumour to the Sultán. On the third day it was discovered that Mubárizul-mulk and

Safdar Khán were alive, and had alighted in the village of Rúpál which is in the district of Kari. The author of the *Tárikh-i-Bahádur Sháhi* writes that Kiwámul-mulk sent him to fetch Mubarizul-mulk in order that they might together pursue the Ráná. He says that he brought the Malik to Walád, and the Malik met Kiwámul-mulk when news arrived that the Ráná had marched from Idar by forced marches to Chitor. Mubárizul-mulk, and the writer of the *Bahádur Sháhi* left Kiwámul-mulk, and came to Ahmednagar. On the sixteenth day after the battle they buried the martyrs whose bodies were lying in the field and killed sixty of the Kántha Kolis who had come to Ahmednagar to purchase wheat. They remained one night in Ahmed-nagar, and in the morning as they could not get grain, they returned to the town of Burháni (Parántij ?). At this time they heard that Sultán Muzaffar had sent Ímádul-mulk and Kaisar Khán with a powerful army and several large and fierce war elephants to their aid. This army arrived at Ahmedábád, and thence reached Walád and having effected a junction with Kiwálmul-mulk, marched thence and arrived at the Kasba of Burháni (Parántij ?). A petition was from here written to the Sultán to the effect that the Ráná had gone to Chitor. If the Sultán gave the order, his slaves would proceed towards Chitor, and would endeavour to take their revenge. The Sultàn wrote in reply that as the rainy season had arrived they should remain for the present at Ahmednagar, and that after the close of the rains he would also come and chastise the Rána.

The amírs coming to Ahmednagar remained there. After the rains the Sultán having increased the pay of the army, and having advanced to each soldier a year's pay that every man should provide himself with equipments of war, in the month of Shawwál of the abovementioned year himself marching from Muhammadábád encamped at Hálol throe *kos* from Muhammadábád, and thence by forced marches came to Ahmedábád and put up in the Kehmdhrol palace near the Kánkarya Tank. At this time Malik Ayáz, gover-nor of Sorath, with 20,000 horse and many pieces of cannon, and artillery men, arrived and had an audience and represented, "If this business be entrusted to me, I will God-willing bring the Rána alive a captive into the presence, or will slay him." The petition of Malik Ayáz pleased the Sultán, and in the month of Muharram A. H. 927 (A. D. 1520) he marched from Kehmdhrol to Harsole, and having sent for the army of Ahmedábád he joined that also to the army.

Malik Ayáz again repeated his request, and the Sultán presented him with a handsome present and permitted him to go.

The author of the *Tárikh-i-Bahádur Sháhi* writes that nearly a hundred thousand horsemen were appointed with Malik Ayáz and a hundred elephants, and twenty thousand horse and twenty elephants with Malik Kiwámul-mulk; and the two armies were allowed to depart. Malik Ayáz and Kiwálmul-mulk went to Morása, and from Morása to the village of Rahmúlah which is under the country of Bágar.[1] Thence parties were appointed to ravage the entire country of Bágar as in the late disturbance the Rajá of Bágar had been an ally of the Rána, and Dúngarpúr, which was the place of residence of the Rája of Bágar, was burned and reduced to black ashes, and thence they went by way of Bánswára. By chance Shujá-úl-mulk, Safdar Khán, and Mujáhid Khán were once encamped with two hundred smart horsemen on the border of the camp, when a person came up to them and said, " The Rájá of Bánswálá together with Medáni Rái and his followers, have drawn up their forces and are standing on the hills about two *kos* from this. The aforesaid amírs with the men that were present mounted, and went in the direction of the hills. When the advanced guard of the Hindus saw from the heights that the Musalman army was coming with a few men, they opposed them and commenced to fight.

They say that like the noble companions of the Prophet, one footman engaged with eleven of the enemy. In the end the breeze of victory blew on the banners of Islám, and the faces of the unbelievers were covered with the dust of disgrace. In this fight eight Musalmáns and many Hindus fell beneath the sword. News of this engagement reached the camp and the army mounted to pursue the fugitive Hindus. By the time they met the army the amírs returned victorious and triumphant. On seeing the bravery of the Musalmáns, the Hindus were amazed and ashamed. The Most High made the army of the Musalmáns victorious according to the blessed Kuranic verse : " And how many a small body has defeated a great host by the aid of God."[2]

On hearing this news the Ráná was greatly alarmed. The Mahomedan General after this, having marched passed by the Kharji

---

[1] The orthography admits of the word being read Baksar as well as Wágar.
[2] See Sale's Translation of the Kuráán, Chap. II., p. 30.

or Kharkhi Ghát, arrived by forced marches before and invested Mandisúr which belonged to the Ráná on whose behalf Rajput Asúkmal was posted there. They say that this fort was very strong, and its wall was ten cubits thick. It was constructed from the foundations to half its height of sand-stone, and the upper half was of baked bricks. It was one of the constructions of Sultán Hushang of Mándu. The Rána came with a large army and alighted near the village of Nadisi, which is ten *kos* from Mandisur. Malik Ayáz, began at once to dig mines and construct covered approaches round the fort, but Kiwámul-Mulk and the other nobles of the army were inwardly on bad terms with him. At this juncture the Ráná sent his *vakil* or agent to Malik Ayáz admitting his fault and stating that he had by his conduct closed the road of apology. He offered if his fault was kindly overlooked to subscribe to a written compact agreeing never to act again save as behoved a servant of the Sultán, and to send all the elephants, horses and prisoners that had fallen into his hands at the battle of Ahmednagar, and expressed his willingness to give besides this whatever the Sultán might appoint. At this time Sultán Mehmúd Khilji also came from Mándu and joined the Gujarát army. Silehdi, the Rajput also was coming from Ráesen to see Malik Ayáz, but Medáni Rái came and dissuaded him and lured him away to the Ráná. By-and-bye all the Rájás of those parts came round the Ráná, but no battle took place as was expected by Sultán Muzaffar and the friends of his kingdom nor did the Fort of Mandisúr fall. Malik Ayáz, to disappoint Kiwámul-Mulk and his party, and against their wishes, agreed to peace. Kiwámul-Mulk sent word to Sultán Mehmúd that if the Sultán would join the project, he would fight with the Ráná under his auspices. Sultán Mehmúd agreed, but as the General of the Gujarát army, Malik Ayáz, was a born slave of Sultán Muzaffar, and Sultán Mehmúd secretly did not wish that he should give him honour over the others, he purposely connived coming to an issue. Sultán Mehmúd was, besides, not anxious to fight, because the Ráná had behaved in a friendly way to him, and, as has been mentioned, his son was a hostage with the Ráná, and the Ráná had released him, and he had even agreed to pay the Ráná a tribute. Malik Ayáz without consulting the Sultán or Kiwámul-Mulk made peace with the Ráná, and marched on ten *kos*, and encamped there. Sultán Mehmúd said to Kiwámul-Mulk, " I act according to the orders of Sultán

15

Muzaffar, nor would it become me to act contrary to his wishes." With these words Sultán Mehmúd marched for Mándu. The amírs, though they were very vexed and mortified, were powerless and the Malik turned towards Gujarát and came to Ahmedábád. The Sultán was very displeased and angry with the Malik and the people of Gujarát also condemned his conduct. The Sultán determined to march against the Ráná himself after the rainy season, and he gave Malik Ayáz leave to return to Sorath. The Sultán spent the rains at Muhammadábád and after the rainy season of A. H. 928 (A. D. 1521) left Muhammadábád, for the purpose of chastising the Ráná. When the Sultán reached Ahmedábád, the son of the Ráná came with the elephants, horses, and the tribute he had promised. The Sultán, therefore, stopped the expedition. After some time the Sultán went to hunt in Jháláwár, and after his return thence spent the hot season and the rains in Ahmedábád. After the rains, he dismissed the son of the Ráná. In this year Malik Ayáz died. When this news reached the Sultán he said, Malik Ayáz had reached the extremity of old age. Had he, he said, died in battle with the Ráná, he would have died a martyr. The Sultán conferred the post and rank of Malik Ayáz upon his eldest son and demanded the account and cash from the Sorath treasury. Malik Ishák sent the treasure with much valuable cloth stuffs, and the Sultán came to Muhammadábád from Ahmedábád by way of Kapadwanj and spent the rainy season there in pleasure and enjoyment.

In the beginning of A. H. 930 (A. D. 1523) he started for Morása, with a view of arranging the affairs of his own country, and thoroughly re-built that fort and arranged its defences. As the hot weather was near at hand he set out to return to Ahmedábád. On the road Bíbí Ráni, mother of Prince Sikandar Khán, passed away from this transitory world. She was one of the chief wives of Sultán Muzaffar. The Ráni was famed for her great good sense and for the motherly affection she showed to the ministers and officers of the state and to all gentle and simple. They buried her in the shrine of the mother of the Sultán which is near Khamdrole. The Sultán after halting three days came to Ahmedábád and suffered much grief and sorrow from the death of the Ráni, so much so that he fell ill. After recovery the Sultán came and passed the rainy season at Ahmedábád.

At this time Ádil Khán, the son of Sultán Behlul Lodi, who had come and taken up residence in this court in the time of Sultán

Mehmúd, represented that his nephew Sultán Ibráhím having killed certain great nobles and displeased the soldiery, the greater part of the amirs had dispersed and had sent an invitation to him. If leave was given him he would go to Dehli. The Sultán having ordered provisions to be made for his departure gave him leave to go to Dehli. Ádil Khán went towards Dehli. He took the title of Sultán Alá-uddín and fought with Sultán Ibráhím, but being eventually unable to gain his object fled to the court of Zahíruddin Muhammad Bábar Pádshah at Cábul and persuaded that powerful king to invade Hindustan, thus bringing ruin upon his house.

COUPLET.

" Dissension brings things to such a pass
That it brings ruin on old houses."

In A.H. 931 (A.D. 1524) Sultán Muzaffar marched from Muhammadábád to Ahmedábád and several times went hunting to Morasa and returned to Ahmedábád for the hot weather. At this time Prince Bahádur Khán petitioned that the revenue of his *jágír* was insufficient for his expenses and said that he trusted his *jágír* must not be allowed to be less than that of Sikandar Khán. His petition was not acceded to. Bahádur Khán was much grieved at this. In the latter part of the month of Rajab, the seventh month of the Muslin calendar, of the same year, he formed an expedition to go to Dúngarpúr. At first Raja Ráésingh of Dúngarpúr had the honour of an interview and after staying there sometime he went to Chitor and met Rána Sánga. Wha happened there shall be detailed in another place. Thence he went to the country of Mewát. Hasan Khán Mewáti who was the ruler of that place offered all his help. But he did not accept anything and went from thence to Sultán Ibráhím Lodi, while that Sultán was about to fight with Sultán Zahírudin Muhammad Bábar on the plain of Pánipat, 40 *kos* from Dehli. Sultán Ibráhím, sending for Bahádur Khán, received him with much honour and shewed him great kindness. On day a band of Mughals captured several men from the army of Sultán Ibráhím and were taking them away as prisoners. Bahádur Khán pursued and overtook them, and a conflict ensued which ended in Bahádur Khán's killing several Mughals and rescuing their prisoners and taking them back to Sultán Ibráhím's army. At this the people of Dehli praised and commended Bahádur Khán very highly. When Sultán Ibráhím heard of this, he became jealous of the popularity of Bahádur Khán, who on becoming aware of it left Sultán Ibráhím and set out for Jaunpur. Now, the nobles and people of Jaunpur were so discontended and weary of Sultán Ibráhím that they had sent a secret message to Bahádur Khán, that if ever he came to Jaunpur they would serve him heart and soul. While on his way to Jaunpur news came of the death of Sultán Muzaffar and he turned to go to Gujarát.

When Sultán Muzaffar came to know that Prince Bahádur Khán had gone away vexed to Baksar (Wágar?) he ordered his vazír Khudáwand Khán to write to him to return and that he would allot him a *jágír* equal to that of Sikandar Khán. Khudáwand Khán told the Sultán that Bahadur Khán had long left that place behind and had gone to Sultán Ibráhím Lodi. On hearing this, the Sultán was much pained and went from Ahmedábád to Muhammadábád. The above is on the authority of the *Tárikh-i-Bahádur Sháhi.* I shall, please God, relate on a future occasion what has come down by way of unbroken tradition from respectable Gujarát authorities.

In those days rain fell not, and people began to wail and lament, and the Sultán raised his hands in supplication to the Almighty, saying: "God Almighty! if thou art visiting on this land thy displeasure for poor Muzaffar's crimes and sins, take him away and save thy people from the calamity of famine, for the humble Muzaffar cannot bear any longer to witness the want and sufferings of the poor and the needy." As the Sultán was a saintly person whose prayers were for the most part efficacious the rain of mercy fell, but the Sultán lost his appetite and sickened. He was, one day, reading a commentary on the sacred Kuráán of the name of *Ma-álim-ut-tanzi* when he said he had read more in the days of his kingship than he did in those he was a prince. He had read half of that good book in this life, and hoped to be permitted to finish the other half in heaven. Those present began to praise him and pray for him, but he said, tha each of his organs was losing its life, and that he was conscious af it. At last in the same year A. H. 932 (A.D. 1525) he went from Ahmedábád to Baroda, and said, he had done so to bid farewell to Baroda, which was his beloved home. "Now," said he, "let me return to the shrine of my honoured parent at Ahmedábád," and he returned by unbroken marches to Khamdrole and stopped there. Each day his weakness increased, and he did not touch food for a month. He used often during this period to visit the royal palaces in the city. Khurram Khán, one of his favourite attendants, asked permission to spend some money in charity, to which the Sultan replied: "My dear friend I have during my life spent so much from the public treasury that I am thinking how difficult it will be for me to account for it before my Glorious Maker. Why should I now add to the load?" At length people despaired of the Sultán, and Prince Latíf Khán seeing that Sikandar Khán was heir to the throne and apprehensive of his life from his hands, on the new moon of Jamádil Awwal issued forth with his establishment and set out for Baroda. Some say this was in consequence of an intimation from the dying Sultán. At last on the second day of the above month, after morning prayers the Sultán summoning Sikandar Khán to his presence, gave him advice befitting his royal rank, and exhorted him not to harm his brothers, nor to be rash in injuring his nobles on suspicion, a proceeding which would throw into disorder the affairs of the kingdom. Prince Sikandar Khán began to weep, and the Sultán bade him farewell. He then sent for a palanquin, and went to his horse and elephant stables, saying he had taken his last farewell of all, and as that day was a Friday, he would take his last farewell of the men of all his establishments, and ask their pardon. Saying so he visited all the establishments the servants of which with tearful eyes and sad hearts pardoned him. He now went to his bedroom in the palace and asked his attendants to remove his bed from the throne which, he said, belonged to his ancestors, and ordered it to be made on a cot, which he said, belonged to his successor. They did so. In the meantime he heard the call to Friday prayers, nd on asking whether it was the time for prayers and on being told it was, he regretted he was not strong enough to attend the mosque, but sent some of his attendants to perform the Friday prayers. After an hour he made his ablutions and said his prayers, and with the greatest of unction and humility asked forgiveness for his sins, and having laid himself on his bed, he three times repeated the creed, and stretching forward his legs he rode the steed of his pure soul to Heaven. They consigned his mortal remains to the earth in the shrine of Saint Sheikh Ahmed Khattu, under the dome at the foot of the grave of Sultán Mehmúd. And this happened on Friday, the 2nd of the month of Jamád-ul-Awwal, A. H. 932. (A.D. 1525).

The period of his reign was fourteen years and nine months. The Sultán was the spiritual follower of Sháh Táhir, who sleeps the eternal sleep in Baroda. They say, that none of the Sultáns of Gujarát equalled him in piety, and knowledge and understanding. They say that during

the days of his dominion he had the honour of seeing the Holy Prophet
(on whom be peace!) in a dream, and the Prophet prayed to God to
save the Sultán from the fire (of hell). That same night a hundred
pious persons had the same dream (as if to attest the truth of the
Sultán's dream), and they all came in the morning to the Sultán and
related their dreams. Happy, and of fortunate destiny is he, who, in
his life enjoys a throne, and in the future is free from the wrath of the
Almighty and the tortures of hell! They say that one night the
Sultan was sitting in company with some wise and good men and conversation turned on many a topic of tradition and anecdote. In the
course of conversation a wise man said, that on the Day of Judgment
the Sun would come down as low as the length of a spear to burn
the souls of the wicked. On that day those who knew the Kuráán
by heart together with seven of their ancestors would be shaded
by umbrellas of Divine mercy and the heat of the Sun should be
as nought to them, by the grace of the word of God that they
would carry within their breasts. The Sultán heaved a heavy sigh
and deplored that none of his children had obtained the glory to
make him aspire to that mercy! And he set to commit the
Kuráán to memory after returning to Baroda, which was his *jagír*.
His hard study night and day harmed his eyes, which became sore
and red. His intimate friends now invited his attention to the verse
of the Kuraán :—

   " And God does not trouble his servants beyond their capacities."

They requested him to give his eyes a little more rest for some days.
But the Sultán continued in his course, taking pride in his ailment,
and in the period of one year and some months he finished the task, and
presenting himself before his father at Ahmedábád reported the circumstance to him, calling to mind the incident that gave it rise. The
Sultán embraced him and kissed him on the eyes and head, and
commenced to bless and praise him. They say that in the month of
Ramazán of that year—for sixteen nights, he recited the Kuráán at the
night prayers. The Sultán was very thankful and said: "With what
tongue shall I praise and thank the goodness of Khalíl Khán, who
has freed me and my ancestors on the Day of Resurrection from
the fierce heat of its Sun. How can I make a return for it? What
I possess is the kingdom. I will give him this, during my life-

---

¹ Sale's translation of the Kuráán, Chap : The Children of Imrán.

time, may it be a blessing to him!" He rose, and seated Khalíl Khán on
the throne, and himself sat on another. May God's blessing be on them
both, father and son! In the morning he invited all the officials,
nobles, and soldiers to a banquet in which such good dishes were
prepared that the men of that day said that they had never seen such
a feast given by any prince. After the dinner he related the events
of the previous night and his giving the kingdom to Khalil Khán as
a reward for his learning the Kuráán. All approved of it, and praised
both the king and the prince.

They say that the Sultán had a horse which was unequalled in
his galloping and his pleasant paces, and which was reserved for the
Sultán's riding. One day the horse had a colic, and though they
gave him a great many remedies they had no effect. An expert said,
" If they pour *Náb* or pure wine down his throat, it would benefit him ;"
and they did so, and the pain immediately departed. The Master
of the Sultan's Horse related the circumstance to the Sultán.
The Sultán bit his finger with grief and never after rode that
horse.

They say that the Sultán neither as a prince, nor afterwards
when he sat on the throne, took anything intoxicating. One day
Kiwámul-Mulk said, "Has the Sultán ever taken any intoxicating
thing ?" He said, "Yes, in the days of my childhood, when I
was but five years of age. My foot slipped off the balcony staircase,
and I fell to the ground, and received a severe bruise. At that time
Hansbái, who was my grand-mother and who had charge of my
bringing up, gave me two or three cups of wine to drink. I drank
them, but they made me very sick and I was at the point of death. The
Bái saw in a dream a person saying to her, ' Have you given Khalíl
Khán wine ?' She said, ' Yes.' He said, ' Repent and promise never
again to put wine to his lip, and he will recover.' Hansbái related that
she said, ' I have repented,' and her feet trembled, and she awoke, and
asked God for pardon, and I immediately recovered. I remember
that I drank wine on that day, after that God has watched over
me, and has guarded me from having anything to do—with this
impurity."

They say that Sultán Muzaffar rarely used even to mention intoxicating things, and when it was necessary to speak of them, he called
them all " pills," and therefore the people of Gujarát, have ever
since,—called intoxicating confections—" *goli*" or pills.

They say that the Sultán never gave up any good custom, and he always performed the prescribed ablutions, and took care to remain in a condition of ceremonial purity, and always acted up to the traditions and example of the Prophet, on whom be blessings and peace! He always remembered death, and his eyes were ever weeping and his heart grieved.[1] The Sultán took much trouble in serving and showing respect to men of learning, but he did not believe in *darvishes*, even as much as was necessary for the sake of decent appearance, but he rejected them as the learned object to *Súfis* or mystics. When the Sultán obtained the honour of knowing Sháh Sheikh Jí, son of Sayad Burhánuddin Bukhári, known as Kutbi Álam, his opinions in this respect underwent an entire change. Afterwards, in whatever place he heard of a *darvish*, he used to go to see him, and used to obtain what benefit he could from him; and the account of his meeting with that holy person, Sháh Sheikh Ji, I will hereafter relate—if God wills.

It must not be concealed that the wise men of Gujarát relate many miracles performed by the Sultán. This is one of them: Malik-ul-Hadyáh called Hurmuz-ul-mulk who was one of the Sultán's companions had no child, and on account of this was exceedingly vexed and grieved. He thought of going to the exalted Kaábah which is the place where all prayers are granted, to beseech Alláh the Granter of all wishes to give him a child. He came, therefore, to the Sultán and wept, and having shown his intention asked for leave. The Sultán felt compassion for him and said, "Malik-ul-Hadyah wait for this year, God will give you a son." The Malik waited. The Sultán left off animal food, spent his nights in prayer, and after the midnight prayers he lifted his hands in supplication before the Maker of the Morn, and begged for a son for Malik-ul-Hádyah. On the Friday night of that week he saw the Prophet in a dream, and besought him for a son for Malik-ul-Hadyah. The Prophet replied, that two sons should be born to Malik-ul-Hadyah, but that he should marry another wife. On hearing this message the Sultán awoke, and became happy, and performed a prayer of two *rakáats*, after fresh ablutions, and selecting a pretty Rájput virgin slave-girl of mature age from his daughter's attendants, he went to the house of Malik-

---

[1] In obedience to the Kuráánic ordinance : " And laugh ye little and weep ye more." Sale's Translation of the Kuráán, Chap. IX. The Declaration of Immunity.

ul-Hadyah, and gave the slave-girl to him saying : " From this maiden you will get two sons, but make a vow." The Malik did so. After some time the girl conceived, and when her days were accomplished a beautiful son was born. The Sultán himself walked to his house and repeated the *takbír* in the ear of the new-born babe, [1] and rejoiced with the parents, and after a week named him Lutfulláh. Sayad Muhammad, son of Sayad Jalál, says that he had seen that boy, and during the reign of Ahmed II., he was granted the title of Huzabrul-Mulk, and this miracle of the Sultán was well-known. After some time this slave-girl had another son who also eventually received a title. It is related by respectable people that the Sultán had a great regard and love for the Prophet, on whom be God's blessings and peace! He prayed much for blessings on him, and during the days of the Prophet's nativity he used to order food in his name, and feast the learned men. On these occasions he collected the wise men and the Sayads together, and himself served them, and after their finishing their dinner poured water on their hands, and at bidding them farewell on the 12th day of the nativity month he used to present each of them with cash and clothes sufficient for a year.

They say that one day, while reading the Holy Kuráán, the Sultán came to the verse about resurrection, and he could not restrain his tears. He said, " On that day what will be my fate ?" Mián-Sheikhji, who was his companion, said he thought the Sultán was never guilty of great sins, [2] and was generally occupied in devotion and prayer and that the people were pleased and thankful for his rule. On that day too the Sultán's honour would be great. But the Sultán said, " Sheikhji, on my shoulders there is a great load ; and my weeping and lamentations are on that account. Have you not heard the tradition of the Prophet, (on whom be peace !) 'Those bearing light weights of sin shall be saved, and the bearers of heavy loads shall be destroyed.,"

Sayad Jalál Munawwar-ul-Mulk says that when he was four years of age, his father Sayad Muhammad was slain in battle. On the third

---

[1] That the first mundane sound to reach the ears of a new-born infant should be the name of his Creator, Islám ordains—that the most honoured of a child's male relatives should repeat the *takbír* (the call to prayers) in both his ears.

[2] Sins are of two classes, صغيره small and كبيره great. The first consist of acts of common peccancy which no mortal born of woman can avoid ; the second include from crimes and delinquencies to the breaking of the commandment—" thou shalt not lie."

day Malik Asadul-mulk who was called Sheikhji Tamím, and who was one of the chief nobles of the Sultán, took him before the Sultán, and related the fate of his father to the king. The king directed him to approach and patted his head and face with his hands and said, " This boy will be very rich." From that day for ten years he says he remained in the Sultán's service, but never saw in all that time the Sultán scolding or behaving disrespectfully to any one. This the Sultán carried to such au extent that although he entertained a bad opinion of Kiwámul-mulk Sárang, and did not find in him the sincere regard a servant feels for his master, yet as he was a companion of his father Sultán Mehmúd who placed entire confidence in him after the death of Sultán Mehmúd, Sultán Muzaffar continued him, in the office of water-keeper (*ábdár*). From his exceeding goodness of heart Sultán Muzaffar did not transfer him from this important post though he was ever so suspicious of him that when Kiwámul-mulk, of Ramazán evenings, used to bring water to drink at the time of breaking the fast, the Sultán used to take the water from his hand, but before drinking it, to repeat certain verses of the Kuráán[1] as charms to avert the effects of the poison, he used always to suspect in the cup. At length the above-mentioned Malik became acquainted with the Sultán's mind, and said, " This slave has become old, and is unable to perform his duty of *ábdári*." The Sultán said, " Who, besides you, will be able to perform this duty ?" He said, " My nephew, who in the days you were a prince, was appointed your wine-bearer or water-bearer. He is fit for the service, so let your old slave be free." The Sultán acted accordingly. Duriug his whole life he never disgraced any of Alláh's creatures nor did he ever speak to any one contemptuously, but addressed every one with respect, nor was any one ever vexed with the Sultán. He used often to say, "If I were alone in the jungle, no one would harm me, because I have not injured, nor do I injure any one."

It is said that the Sultán was bathing one day before morning prayer, and the bath servants were pouring water on him. The king after washing his body asked for water, to pour on his head. By chance in the darkness of the night a rat had, through the neglect of the bath-servants, fallen into the vessel of warm water, and had been boiled therein. Its flesh, bones, and entrails had through the

---

[1] Chap. CVI. ending with the words, " the Lord of this House (the Kaâbah) who supplieth them with food and secureth them from fear," is believed to possess this virtue.

action of the heat become scattered in the water. The bath servants, ignorant of this, filled a small water-vessel from that large one and gave it to the Sultán, and the Sultán poured that water on his head, and all the entrails and flesh fell on his face and side. The Sultán horrified at this, leapt from the spot, and jumped in to the bathing tank, and cleaned his head, face, and side in it, and issuing, commenced to pray. After prayers he sent for the *áftáb-chís* or bath-servants. The bath servants having washed their hands of their lives approached. He asked, "How many of you are appointed on this service ?" They said, "One hundred men." " Cannot one hundred men," continued the Sultán, "discharge the service of one person and serve him decently ? I am old and forgive your fault, but my sons are young, and if you act towards my sons with such laziness and carelessness, how will you live in safety ? Oh, unfortunate men ! after this, do not again be careless and waste not my time in obliging me to speak to you again in a similar manner." How excellent are the words:

VERSES.

He is not a hero who in wrestling
Dashes down another hero.
But rather is he a hero who in a moment of anger
Subdues the cravings of his tempting heart.

And the words of the Sultán were prophetic. For in the time of Sultán Bahádur one of these very *áftáb-chís* poured boiling hot water on the hand of the Sultán. The Sultán ordered that boiling water should be poured on his testes that he might be a warning to others. They say that they poured boiling water on his privy parts and that they burst and he died immediately.

Sayad Jalál Bukhári relates that the Sultán used to write daily a chapter of the Kuráán in the *Naskh* character, and when the whole Kuráán was finished, he used to bestow it as a *waqf* or deodand to the Holy Makkah or Madínah that whosoever might desire to read it, might do so. One day he was occupied in writing, and wrote one page very well, and became very pleased, and said, "I have written that page very well ; " he wished that he might turn over the leaf. At this moment Latíful-mulk Soudha, the bearer of the royal insignia, who was standing behind him with his drawn sword, began to nod under the waning intoxication of his opium. The sword dropped from his hand, and fell on the Sultán's shoulder, the pen fell from the Sultán's hand, and blackened several lines of the page. The attendants pushed the man away

from the Sultán's presence. The Sultán did not say a word, but
taking a pen-knife erased the ink which had fallen on the page and
having rubbed in some chalk-powder he rubbed and glazed it over
again and commenced to write. When he had finished the chapter,
and replaced it in the writing-desk, he said, " Where is that fool
Latíful-mulk ?"   Sheikh Jí said by way of intercession for him, " My
Lord, he has thrown himself on the ground outside, and is weeping
bitterly, and is saying that he has committed a great fault, and deserves
that his head should be cut off or that he should be thrown under the
feet of an elephant." The Sultán replied: " Why should I cut off
his head, though, if he commits such careless acts again, his hands shall
be cut off, but tell him that he should never again appear before me."
Malik Sheikh Jí then said: " This is worse than cutting off his
head. What place is there for him in the world after that to go to ?"
" Miyán Sheikh Jí," said the Sultán, " tell him then not to eat
another *pill* " (meaning opium), " nor approach any thing intoxicating."
Malik Sheikh Jí said, " Your Majesty, he will not do so, he is repent-
ing."   The end of the affair was that Malik Sheikh Jí sent for him
and made him throw himself at the Sultán's feet. The Sultán forgave
him, and he, taking his sword, stood again behind the Sultán as
before. How excellent are the lines:—

> To punish evil with evil is easy
> If you are a man act well towards those who do you ill !

Sayad Jalúl Bukhári relates that there was a bath-servant, a
boy who was very clever and quick. Whenever the Sultán asked
him a question, he used to give an apt answer, at which the Sultán
used to be pleased and to smile. One day the Sultán was occupied
in his ablutions, and this pert boy was pouring the water. It
was the custom of the Sultán that when performing his ablutions, one of the servants used to lift up the turban from the
Sultán's head, and the Sultán used to wet the crown of his
head, and the servant used to replace the turban. After the
ablutions were performed, he used to place his hand on his
turban, and having unrolled and untwisted the end to the length
of two or three turns, used to wind it up again. One day while
thus engaged one of the attendants said, " Your Majesty, how
beautiful is the texture of the cloth of this turban ?" The Sultán
said, " It is not so very excellent, my servants wear even better
than this, but they do not bind it up in my style, but wind it
with a twist." The boy then said, " It does not look well, unless it is

done with a twist." The Sultán said, "Does then my way of binding the turban appear bad?" The boy said, "The style of the Sultán's turban is like that of *Mulláhs* and *Bohráhs*." Asadul-mulk gave the boy a slap on his cheek, and reproved him. The Sultán said, "Why do you strike him. He is but a child, he says what he hears from his parents. I am pleased that my turban should be compared with the turbans of *Mulláhs*. But why do they compare it, with the turban of *Bohráhs* who are *Ráfzis*,¹ while I am a *Sunni* and ask protection of God from them."

They say that a wine-seller once gave the Sultán a petition. An iron ring being on his hand, caught in the Sultán's sleeve and tore it. The Sultán opened the letter, and read it, and understood its purport, but he made an order that in future people wishing to petition should not give their petitions into his hand, but should tie it on the end of a stick, and so present it to him or his attendants who would take it from them, and give it to him."

Let it be known that the Sultán, who had the distinction of being a man of learning who acted upon his precepts, did not practise extravagance, whence those who cherished hopes without right, considered him to be a miser, and in meetings and assemblies used to decry him. This their opinion of the Sultán was the result of the excess of their avarice, not the Sultán's worldliness of nature. Had the Sultán been a world-lover, he would never have handed over to Sultán Mehmúd Khilji a country like Málwá and its treasures as well as the booty he had acquired from Medáni Rái with so much trouble, as has been abovementioned. Although other Sultáns of Gujarát gave away much gold like Sultán Muhammad bin Ahmed Sháh and like Sultán Muzaffar's son Sultán Bahádur, yet there is a great difference between the bestowing of gold and the bestowing of a kingdom. With money Sultán Muzaffar also was generous where there was need, but within bounds. It is said that Hujjatul-Mulk, the eunuch who, in the time of Sultán Bahádur Sháh, was ennobled by the title of Khán Jahán, was in the time of Sultán Muzaffar entrusted with the Police Magistracy over the city of Ahmedábád and he lived to a great age. They say that in police work he was unequalled. He could tell a thief from his face. It is said that one day he was walking in the *bazár*, and saw

¹ *Ráfzi* is an opprobrious term for '*Shíáh*,' meaning literally one who abandons, a heretic, just as the Roman Catholics used to style their Lutheran co-religionists.

a man sitting there. He stopped and said to Jívan, the nose-cut executioner, to seize the man. Men wondered thinking " this man has done no wrong, why does he arrest him without reason ? " When they seized, and brought him, and commenced to search his head-dress and waist-clothes, the keys of the hobbles usually put on the feet of Government horses dropped from his turban· It appeared that he was the leader of a band of thieves. At another time it struck Khán Jahàn in the course of his duties that four generations of the Gujarát kings had passed, and the allowances to religious persons stood as before, without change or alteration. Each king in his time had granted fresh grants ; he would, therefore, find out who of the grantees had died, who had gone away, and who were enjoying the grants. After enquiry and search he found that most of the original grantees were dead, and there was not a single instance of any of them having gone away or left the country. This last was owing to the country of Gujarát being in those times full of gold, and there was so much ease and comfort to be had in it that strangers who entered it never left it, and the natives of Gujarát would never think of leaving it for another place. In short the *jágírs* of the dead grantees were resumed, and Hujjat-ul-Mulk having realized the arrears on others brought them in gold to the Sultán. The Sultán said, " What and whose is this money ? " He said : "It is the Sultán's and the reason of its acquisition is that from the time of Sultán Muzaffar I. (may God have mercy on him !) these properties have been granted to religious persons, and thence till now their incomes have gone on increasing. When I made inquiry, I found that very many of the grantees were dead, so I collected the incomes of their properties and have brought them to the Sultán." The Sultán reproached him, and commenced to revile him, saying : "O fool, what shall I say to you ? If you were a man, I would have reviled you by calling you a coward ; if you were a woman, I would have called you unchaste. You are neither man nor woman, but the bad qualities of both are present in you. They who are dead, their sons must be alive, if no son yet a daughter, and if there be also no daughter, there must surely be a wife and slave-girls. If you have done this act of yourself, you have done ill. Do not again do such an act. Begone and return this gold to those from whom you have taken it and heal the broken hearts of those poor people with the ointment of apologies and excuses." After this he made an order, that an order should be issued to all the grantees of land on religious tenures in Gujarát to the effect that the *jágírs* of the deceased persons should be divided among their heirs according to the divinely ordained shares and that no person should be able to meddle with them now or in the future.

From that day the estates of deceased grantees have been divided according to the Divine ordinance, *viz.* :— "And for the male there shall be a share equal to that of two females."

It is related that when Sultán Mehmúd Khilji of Málwá made an expedition to conquer Gujarát, of which mention has been made above and when he reached the frontier of Gujarát, several clerks who had been turned out by the Gujarát Sultán, went over to and met Sultán Mehmúd Khilji, and showed him the revenue papers of Gujarát. The Sultán listened to the details one after another. Men said, "It is a good omen that the revenue records of Gujarát have fallen into our hands. It means that the country of Gujarát will also fall into our hands." Sultán Mehmúd said, "In this country much land is held on religious tenures. There is no district neither village in which there are not lands endowed on religious institutions or as pensions to religious men or officers, and this constitutes an army without horses and riders that like the stars is ever wakeful." Pensions were appointed for the poor at the sacred cities of Makkah and Madínah, which used to be sent to them annually without let or hindrance. A vessel was appointed to convey poor pilgrims thither without charge, the expenses of their trip to and from the holy cities being borne by Government.

The expenses of Sultán Muzaffar's private establishment were not extravagant, but in charity he was liberal. A great man has said: "Extravagance in expenses means niggardliness in good acts." Generosity opens the gates of high estate in the world to come and in this world brings a tenfold return. But it is not meet to patronise venal praise or to go in for the howlings of singers, acts which according to the sacred verse are sure to bring penury in this world and damnation in the next.

The Sultán was unequalled in soldierly accomplishments, and in swordsmanship had attained to such skill that he used to lift up an animal killed according to the order of the law, with his left hand and with one blow of the sword held in his right used to cleave its body intwain. With the spear he was such an adept that he used to carry off a ring on the point of his spear. It is related that the

Sultán to learn the true condition of the poor among his subjects, and to acquaint himself with their wants and opinions used to issue out of dark nights, and learning their grievances used to call them in the morning to do them justice, after listening to their complaint and wants in streets and market places during the night. It is said that one night he went into a mosque and found a sufferer crying in a corner. He asked of him the reason, but the man said, "Why do you ask, the reason is better unsaid." But the Sultán said, "Do say, perhaps the evil can be remedied." He said, "I am a poor man and a disappointed. Every night a rascal enters my house, and I can't prevent him. I am weary and wretched. To whom can I take this tale of mine and of whom ask its remedy?" The Sultán asked, "When does he come?" The man said, "Every night." The Sultán asked him to be of good cheer, for, said he, he vowed to consider food as forbidden and unlawful until he killed him. So saying, he asked the man to show the adulterer to him, and he followed the man to his house. It so happened, that the evil-doer did not come that night, nor the next, and on the third night the man came and occupied the same corner in the mosque weeping, and apprehensive, lest after his disappointment of the two fore-going nights, his champion should not come that night. In this condition the Sultán found him, and asking him, the man said his culprit had come that night. The Sultán asked him to lead the way and show. While on the way he asked him whether he wished the pair of the guilty ones to be killed or only the adulterer. The man said only the adulterer. On entering the man's house, the Sultán saw the rascal sitting with the poor man's wife. He called out to him to beware and receive the reward of his deeds. The man took up his sword and confronted the Sultán, and struck the first blow which was warded off by the Sultán, and such a blow dealt out in return that the man fell divided in two pieces and dead. The Sultán also sat down, as he had not eaten food since he had sworn the oath. He asked the owner of the house if he had any food in his house. He said he had a piece of *bájri* bread. He asked him to bring it, and ate of it and got up to go, when the victim told him: "To-morrow when the Kotewál hears of this he will confiscate my house and imprison me." The Sultán assured him saying, "That also I can remedy." He went to the palace and sent for the Kotewál and gave him the description of the house, and asked him to go there in such a way that the neighbours may not come to know to take the body of the man lying there and to bury it in the house and never to breathe to a man anything of it.

He was also a very skilful archer. It is related that while in Sorath, he went a-hunting and in pursuit of a deer he separated from his attendants and fell in with a band of dacoits. He attacked them with arrows and wounded several of them, while others flying escaped with difficulty. At this time his soldiers also, coming after him, reached him, and saw several Rajputs lying wounded by arrows, and the Sultán standing over them. They all alighted and kissed the hands and feet of the Sultán and praised his courage.

In wrestling the Sultán surpassed the teachers of this art. In all manner of shooting he was very clever and he was also accomplished in learning. In short he was so quick in learning anything new that when he once saw any art he became as if it were an old hand at it.

In conversation, wit and repartee, no one could approach him. He had a companion called Mulla Aiyúb, who was a scholar of respectable parts and a poet of elegance. He used to eat opium, and had written some lines in praise of that drug :

> Eat oh ! Sir, an atom of opium,
> That it may help thee in not giving way soon in copulation.
> Opium befits the learned,
> A learned man should act on his learning.[1]

Somebody carried this to the Sultán who smiled and said, " The Mulla has not written this to incite people to eat opium but to enlarge on its evil qualities. In truth the placing of ب (in بخور—) instead of مخور—م is a clerical error." The change, making the meaning of the word a negation instead of an imperative, i.e., " Do not eat " instead of " Do eat."

It is related that one day a man looking like a scholar came into the Sultán's assembly with the salutation " Peace be upon you!" pronounced أَلسَّلَامُ عَليكم—" Assalámun álaikum,'

---

[1] The beauty of the lines consists in the play upon the words عام and عمل tlm and pmal. Ámal has two meanings, practice or acting upon and an intoxicant. So the last line means both as translated above and : " Knowe'ge must be with an intoxicant" or " No knowledge without an intoxicant."

[2] After the article 'al' the Arabic Grammar forbids the 'nunuation' of the last syllable. Had the man dropped the article and said, السّلَام م عليكم it would have been correct. Whereas with the article it would mean something like :—" a, the salám (peace) be on you ! ''

instead of *assalámo áláikum* (which is correct). The Sultán replied at once :—

عليكم السلام يا جامع التنوين وَاللَّام

"And peace be on you, oh! joiner of the *nunnation* with the '*lám.*,'"

Again the Sultán was a great critic and connoisseur of music, and had an extremely pleasant voice. He could play on any instrument, be it the harp or the tambourine, or the lute, or the Jew's harp. Masters of this art used to boast being pupils of the Sultán. He was himself a composer in all branches of music, in '*Suramba*' and '*Dhya*,' and '*Náldhya*' and '*Barágít*' and '*Sawardálí*' and '*Chhand*' and '*Dohra*.'[1] They say in his youth he said to some masters of this art who were assembled before him, "Is there any dancing girl in the present day who could act the part of Sarasvati ?"[2] Now it is written in the books of the Hindus that a poetess of pleasant voice and unique sweetness of accent and modulation of voice, who is at the same time perfect as a performer of all sorts of instrumental music and an accomplished dancer could only be made by the favor of Sarasvati, and the personification of the part of Sarasvati could be undertaken by such a one alone who is acomplished in all these arts and who can, besides, equal the goddess in perfection of beauty and loveliness. The great musicians replied, "Peace be on the king, the personification of Sarasvati is extremely difficult. No one except Bái Champa, dancer of the Sultán, can take this part, for she is the peerless of her age in these arts." The Sultán ordered that preparations for the performance be made. They said every thing was ready except the swan, which (according to Hindu mythology) is the bird on which Sarasvati is said to ride. The King ordered all the goldsmiths of the city to be present and to be given the jewels they required. In six months they made it ready. The Sultán came and sat in the assembly and Bái Champa having dressed herself up as Sarasvati came in. On arriving she began to repeat poetry composed extemporely, separating line from line and then taking up the instruments, she played so that the professors of the art forgot the real Sarasvati. Then she began to sing and made those present in the assembly quite wild and entranced. Then she danced in the way in which that art should be practised, till the people present began to say that since the world began no body had acted so well.

---

[1] All these are the names of Indian rhythmic measures and musical modes.

[2] The Minerva of the Hindu Pantheon.

Historians have said that Sultán Muzaffar was so very humble and gentle that those who could be kept down with severity did not mind his authority and used to commit highway robberies and thefts with impunity. The roads were dangerous up to very near the city of Ahmedábád and rascals were fearless in sowing seeds of bloodshed in the midst of the city—just as some wise men have said :

VERSE.

If the king has no severity,
He takes an excuse from the hands of the audacious.
When the lion sheds his teeth and claws
He gets slaps even from cats and lame foxes.

The administrative powers were in the hands of Kiwámul-mulk Sárang and Malik Gobi or Gopi—the Brahmin. They were not influenced by the Sultán's orders, and they did what they liked whether the King was pleased or not. The Sultán never drew the hand of punishment from the sleeve of forbearance. Nor did he ever unsheath the dagger of wrath, and when he heard the complaints of the people he used to say : "I pray to God and you also beseech God that he may remove the oppression of the oppressor." The reason of this patience was that when Sultán Mehmúd (may God enlighten his fame!) departed this world, the nobles were divided as to who should succeed to the throne. Some said, " Khalíl Khán, that is to say Sultán Muzaffar, is like a priest (*mullah*) in disposition, has not the dignity befitting the kingly state, and the entrusting of this important matter to his son Bahádur Khán would be better. From Bahádur Khán's forehead the light of royalty is reflected. Others took the side of Khalíl Khán and wished to enthrone him. Among these were Kiwámul-mulk Sárang and Gobi or Gopi who said, "When the late Sultán seated Khalíl Khán on the throne in his life-time, we should not act in opposition to his wishes." All agreeing to this, they seated Khalíl Khán on the throne. Some say that this loyalty of theirs was the cause of his overlooking their faults until by their instigation the Rána attacked Nizám-ul-mulk as has been related above. Although the Sultán was aware of it, he forgave them, nor did he entirely turn away from them. His well-wishers said, "Slay him who desires ill to the State, for the death of such a graceless one is lawful." Just about this time a new event happened. Malik Gopi was a man of pleasure. They say that on the night of a banquet and dance at his house they used to take all the flowers of the gardens and the markets to his Durbár, and if any one that night wanted flowers, they could not be obtained. He had a celebrated and very pretty dancing-girl, called Dhár. A young man named Ahmed Khán, of the tribe of Tánk, a kinsman of the Sultán, without seeing her, simply from hearing accounts of her famed beauty, became enamoured of her. On one of the nights of her performances, having made an agreement with and disguised himself as a torch-bearer, he took a torch in his hand, and entered the place where she was performing. Although he was disguised as a torch-bearer, his countenance was recognized and the servants of the house seized him and kicked him nearly to death. When Malik Gopi saw that but little life was left in him, though knowing what was going on, he feigned ignorance and commenced to reprove his men and to make excuses to Ahmed Khán saying : " I was not aware of this. If you wished to see the dance, why did you not inform me. I should have invited you and shown you the performance." He sent for his palan-quin, and placed him in it, and sent him to his house. Next day Ahmed Khán died from the severity of the beating he had received that night and this circumstance reached the Sultán. The Sultán became very angry, and the relations of Ahmed Khán demanded blood revenge. The Sultán secretly gave them leave to take it. One night Malik Gopi was going to his house from the Sultán's Durbár, and they stopped him on the way and after inflicting on him several grievous wounds fled, but no wound was mortal. In the morning the eunuch Muhibbul-Mulk related to the Sultán what had taken place the previous night, and said that of the Malik's wounds none was mortal. Kiwámul-mulk said, " Malik Gopi the Brahman is a well-wisher of the king. The wounds of a well-wisher will never hurt him." The Sultán did not listen to him, but thought it not well to spare a wounded snake, and next day ordered an attack to be made on his house, that is, gave the people permission to plunder it. People ran and in the twinkling of the eye like a scramble at a wedding, they plundered his house and property, and having tied Malik Gopi's hands behind his back they brought him to the presence of the Sultán. It is at such times that the truth of the proverb:[1] " God spare us from the wrath of the gentle," is illustrated. The Sultán ordered him to be slain. Gopi said, " I am a Brahman, and was a beggar. I had arrived

---

[1] A tradition of the Prophet (on whom be peace !) which has become proverbial.

at this rank through your father's favour. Whatever I received from Government has been plundered from me and of all my possessions two were very precious. Had they been brought to the Sultán's Darbár, I should not have grieved. One was a slave-girl of great beauty, the equal of whom exists not, and the other were certain precious stones to be found in the treasuries of kings. Both are gone, and have been plundered from me." The Sultán repeated a couplet to the effect that, what comes lightly goes lightly. After this he said, "How much annoyance has been experienced by Musalmáns through this unbeliever. Slay him." The people were pleased at this order, and slew the unhappy man like a dog.[1]

ACCOUNT OF THE SELF-MORTIFICATION AND DEVOTION OF THE LORD SHÁH SHEIKHJI IN RESPECT OF BAHÁDUR KHÁN AND ITS RESULT.

It is related by the respectable people of Gujarát that when Sultán Mehmúd passed away from this transitory world to the everlasting one and Sultán Muzaffar ascended the throne, some of the faithful followers of his Holiness Hazrat Sháh Sheikhji represented to him, that the late khalífah[2] was dead, and the new khalífah had succeeded him. If the Saint went to pray for the departed and congratulate the living it would be but an act of kind courtesy. His Holiness said, "Our last meeting with his (meaning the king's) father was not good and this king is a youth and is besides a dry scholar, a kind of man who generally has neither any regard nor love for men of sanctity nor much belief in them. Therefore not to go is better." The followers then said that the kingdom of Gujarát was entrusted to the ancestors of the Sultán by his exalted house, and if he showed this courtesy it would be but acting on established precedent. That if his father did not appreciate this blessing, the present Sultán was wise and learned and knew these things. At last under pressure of their endeavours and entreaties the Saint went to Chámpáner. Most of the ministers and nobles being his spiritual followers went forth to receive him and brought him to the Sultán's residence and seated him near the royal apartments. The chamberlains ran and announced to the

---

[1] Here an anecdote descriptive of the knowledge of the Sultán as shown in the decision by him of a nice point of Muslim theology is omitted.

[2] A khalífah means literally a deputy, and is applied to a temporal ruler too on the principle of the first four rulers of Islám being so called on account of being the deputies of the Prophet.

Sultán the arrival of the Saint. The Sultán who was not aware of the Saint being in such close proximity said, "He pronounced against my father such a blighting curse, I wonder what he brings for me." These words having come plainly and directly to the ears of His Holiness he was hurt and got up and at once turned homewards without obtaining an interview with the Sultán. After some days the Sultán went to Ahmedábád. When on his way thither he reached the shrine of the Saint Kutbi Álam at Batwá he did not, as was the wont of the Sultáns of Gujarát, dismount to say his prayers at the grave of the Saint, but simply repeated his *Fátihah* (the first chapter of the Kuráán) on horseback and pushed on, on his way to the city. The Saint also did not care for the Sultán. After some days the Sultán fell sick, about the time of the anniversary of the death of Saint Kutbi Álam. He ordered the royal kitchen to be taken to Sarkhej on the night of the anniversary, and there to prepare food to feed the poor for the good of the soul of the departed Saint. He said he would himself follow the next morning. They did so. That night Saint Kutbi Álam appeared to the Sultán in a dream and said :—" Muzaffar Khán ! why don't you come to my house?" The Sultán asked, "Where is your noble house?" The Saint said, "At Batwá, the house of Sheikhji ; he who goes to Sheikhá's house goes to mine, and he who gladdens Sheikhá's heart gladdens mine. Go, therefore, to my house and the ailment that thou hast shall be changed into health." In the morning when the Sultán got up he ordered his palanquin and started for Batwá. That same night Kutbi Álam appeared to Sheikhji in a dream and informed him that Muzaffar Khán was coming to his house and that he was to receive him with kindness and place his hand on his head and back, so that Heaven may bless him with good health. In the morning, before the arrival of the Sultán, the Sheikhji told his companions that last night Saint Kutbi Álam had brought about a reconciliation between himself and the Sultán who was coming that day, and ordered the servants of his kitchen to cook the best of viands, and ordered that from each house in that town, he who was the best cook should come to his kitchen and cook the dish for which he was famous. After a few hours the Sultán arrived at Ásaspur, and sent a man to say that he was coming, and to ask the Saint to get some food ready for him as he was very hungry. The Sultán followed the man shortly. When he reached near the shrine of Kutbi Álam, he descended from the palanquin at some distance from the shrine, and walked on foot as far as the shrine and performing the ceremonies of prayers for the departed, he shook hands with His Holiness and the two great men smiled at each other. The Saint said: "As your Majesty was ordered to call on this darvísh, he also is in like manner ordered to meet you." The Sultán threw himself at the feet of the Saint, who having placed his hand on the head and back of the Sultán, took him into his arms, and afterwards took him to his own residence, and there the Saint, who was accomplished in secrets of religion and belief so expatiated on matters religous and divine before the Sultán, that he and all present went into an ecstacy and were beyond themselves.

VERSES.

The sure signs of a saint are these :
That no sooner you see his face than your heart yearns towards him.
The second is that his words lead you to ecstacy
And from the world of consciousness to that of pure unconsciousness.

After a while the Sheikh got up, went to his inner apartments, and sent out dinner for the Sultán. The Sultán, however, asked the Sheikh to join him at the table. At first the Sheikh asked to be excused saying he had a cough, but on being pressed by the Sultán he came out and they sat together and partook of the food. The Sultán ever and anon used to praise the delicious viands according to the Kurânic command: "And verily speak of the bounties of thy Lord." They then said their prayers together. The next morning the Sultán got up and said his prayers in the following of the Sheikh. After prayers they sat and the Sultán said to the Saint: "For some time past I was ailing and was losing my memory, but since yesterday I feel a comfort and a lightness, which makes me hope that the little that remains will also soon disappear." The Saint prayed for him and bade him adieu. On his way to Ahmedábád the Sultán told his companions: "Had I not seen the Saint I would have remained ignorant of the Knowledge of God." From that day the Sultán was a staunch believer in Saints and darvíshes ; and through their society obtained true knowledge. Allah be praised for that!

ACCOUNT OF THE REQUEST OF SULTÁN MUZAFFAR TO THE SAINT
SHEIKHJI FOR THE THRONE OF GUJARÁT FOR HIS
SON SIKANDAR KHÁN.

Sultán Muzaffar had eight sons. The eldest was Sikandar Khán, the second was Bahádur Khán, and Latif Khán, and Chánd Khán, and Nasír Khán, and others, and two daughters, one Rájé Rukaiyah whom he married to Ádil Sháh Burhánpuri, and Ráje Áyeshah who was married to Fateh Khán, son of the Pádsháh of Sindh.

Sikandar Khán, Rájé Rukaiyah, and Ráje Áyeshah were all from one mother whose name was Bíbi Ráni. The mother of Bahádur Khán was Lakshmi Bái, a Gohel Rájputáni, and the mother of Latíf Khán was Rájbái, the daughter of Ráná Mahipat who was a Rajput, and Chánd Khán, Nasír Khán, Ibráhím Khán, and two others were the sons of slave-girls. The authority over the palace and country and army was all in the hands of Bíbi Ráni, and 7,000 men drew pay from her establishment. The Sultán during his life-time had appointed Sikandar Khán his successor, and he placed no confidence in his other sons. He granted to each of them two or three villages that they should expend from their revenues what was necessary for their subsistence, and among these, two were granted in jágír to Bahádur Khán. These were the villages of Kaníj, ten kos from Ahmedábád, near Mehmudábád, and Gonah, ten kos from the above city near Tantah, near Batwá, which had been granted as estate to the offspring of Kutbul Aktáb. On this account Bahádur Sháh used chiefly to live at Batwá, and was included among the devotees of that holy man, and the Hazrat also was very fond of Bahádur Khán, and showed him much kindness.

It is stated that in the patent of discipleship granted to Bahádur Khán, the Hazrat wrote with his own pen " Sultán Bahádur." Some say that he wrote "Sultán Bahádur king of Gujarát." Besides this, one day he seated Bahádur Khán on his own couch and said to the people who were present, " In the end this is the king of Gujarát." All of them performed to him the kingly salutation and reverence. This circumstance became public, and went to the ears of Bíbi Ráni, who became disturbed, and thoughtful, and related the matter to Sultán Muzaffar and said, " Take Sikandar Khán also to meet the Hazrat and tell him you have made him your heir, and the Hazrat will then according to your desire bless Sikandar Khán, and be on his side." The king said, " Bahádur Khán has a jágír in Batwá and therefore is constantly there, and is constantly serving him, and these saints always bless those who go to them. Be satisfied since I have in my life-time made Sikandar Khán my heir, and the army and people all incline towards him, how will Bahádur arrive at the kingly state. The Hazrat is also aware of this, and in the mornïng I will go to him, and explain my intentions, and seek a blessing from him for Sikandar Khán."

The Bíbi brought large presents to the Sultán, and begged him to take them to the Saint that he might aid and bless Sikandar Khán. In the morning the Sultán, with all his children, went to attend on the Saint. He then first made Sikandar Khán, and then all the others in order his disciples. At this moment Bahádur Khán came, and having made a salutation, sat between the Sultán and Sikandar Khán. The king who was deep in conversation with the Saint did not notice his arrival and when the time to recommend Sikandar Khán arrived, said : " Your holiness knows that Sikandar Khán is the eldest of my sons, and is in every way decent and able, and I have made him my heir apparent." Saying this he stretched out his hand, and took the hand of Bahádur Khán, thinking it was the hand of Sikandar Khán, and said, " Your holiness will bless him that God may after me bestow the kingdom of Gujarát on him." The Sayad said, " Your prayer has been accepted by the Lord of the Kingdom, and He will vouchsafe the kingdom of Gujarát to him, and he will conquer another country besides Gujarát." The Sultán looked joyfully towards Sikandar Khán, and saw the hand of Bahádur Khán in his hand. He was sore troubled and astonished. The Sayad said, " Your desire shall be accomplished." The people of the assembly, who were men of sagacity and penetration, understood that the ball of fortune and victory had been carried away by Bahádur Khán, and that Sikandar Khán was not blessed with this good fortune. " To each one his fate." After this the Sultán took leave, and on the road he said to his companions, " Did you see what a shameless act this little beggar[1]," (meaning Bahádur Sháh), " committed. He came and sat above his elder brother." He said to Sikandar Khán, " Why did you let him sit above you." Sikandar Khán said nothing. Next day the Sultán collected all his nobles and ministers in a general darbár and said, "Know all of you and be beware that my successor is Sultán Sikandar Khán and it is incumbent and imperative on all of you to obey him." All willingly assented and paid him homage, and Bíbi Ráni and Sikandar Khán were satisfied. But they were forgetful of the

---

[1] The word used in the text is Kalandarah, a little calender or calender kin, a word of contempt for a darwísh. It is not inappropriately used for Bahádur, seeing that he used in those days to affect the society of darwíshes.

will of God, and they were not aware of the decrees of fate ; they also did not know for the fruition of whose desires the skies would eventually revolve and to whose wishes the times would accord.

In short, after this the soldiery and the subjects became confident that none other than Sikandar Khán would be, and was the successor of the Sultán. Though previously too they had hardly been doubtful, this became fixed and certain and every one began to place the saddle-cloth of submission to Sikandar Khán on his shoulders and to water the tree of hope from the fountain of his munificence. Sikandar Khán became jealous of his brother, and desirous of striking at the root of Bahádur Khán. Bahádur Khán fled to the shelter of the Saint, became hopeless of the protection of his father, and took up his residence in Batwá, and considering his good fortune in both the worlds to lie in the service of his spiritual guide and mentor, he remained in his society. The Saint also showed kindness to him and regarded him with special favour, but now and then Bahádur Khán used to break out in freaks of boyish thoughtlessness and youthful folly to the great annoyance of the people of Batwá. He sometimes used to knock off a man's turban, and at others to set his Georgian dogs at some poor wretch. The Saint had a door-keeper named Kábil, a Kokani, who used to break wind frequently. Bahádur Khán used to play tricks on him and afterwards used to conciliate him again by giving him presents, sweetmeats, and food. Oncehe directed his servants to undo the strings of the old man's drawers and tie up his hands and tie a string at the ends of his trousers and put a little bat inside them. On this being done, the terrified creature clawed his legs and hinder parts and tore his skin and blood flowed from the wounds, and in this state he went to the Saint and complained. Some of those present who aggrieved and offended with Bahádur bore a grudge against him said, "Bahádur Shah is constantly doing unbecoming things like this. He knocked off a man's turban the other day, and set his dog s at another man ; if he had not run, and taken shelter in the house, they would have torn his legs to pieces." The Saint became very angry and said, "The eaters of squirrels, that is, *Firangi* dogs, will tear him also to pieces, and his ruin will come from these dog-like people." Bahádur Khán on hearing of this repented, and at the intercession of some of the great friends of the Saint again presented himself before him. In the end Sultán Bahádur was slain by the *Firangis* (or Portuguese), and his honour was changed to dishonour. It is curious that some learned men found the date of his death to be contained in the words, " *Katili Kilábi Firang*," slaughtered by or the victim of *Firangi* dogs. Others find the date in the words, " *Katli Bahádur Khán akbar-i-shahíd-ul-bahr.*" The killing of Bahádur Khán, the great martyr at sea. These details will be hereafter related in the account of Sultán Bahádur—if God wills.

ACCOUNT OF THE DEPARTURE OF BAHÁDUR KHÁN FROM GUJARÁT TO HINDUSTAN ON ACCOUNT OF THE ENMITY OF SIKANDAR KHÁN.

It is said that on hearing the favourable prophecy of the Saint Sheikh Jí regarding the future greatness of Bahádur Khán, Sikandar Khán from envy and hatred, determined to slay him. Bahádur Khán understanding this, arranged with his trusted servants and partisans, and determined to flee. He explained the circumstances to the Saint, his protector, saying that when the Sultán his father also heard of the designs of Sikandar Khán he had said, " I am now grown old on account of this care, and physicians cannot cure my malady. ' Alláh's earth is wide,' why narrow it upon yourself, and not withdraw into some corner. On account of this I desire to go to Delhi, if your holiness give me leave." The Saint said :—

> " Let your heart repose in God, for He is the strongest of the strong,
> If your enemy is powerful your Guardian is yet more powerful."

The order for the kingdom of Gujarát has been confirmed in your name from the Darbár of the King of Kings ; only its time has not yet come. Until then let your travelling kit be loaded. Travel is lucky for you." At that moment Bahádur Khán made a mental vow to bestow the estate he enjoyed as a prince on the *fakírs* of the Saint Kutb-ul-aktáb if God ever made it his destiny to rule over the kingdom of Gujarát.

Bahádur Khán, with the leave of the Saint, his protector, started for Delhi. They say that at the moment of taking leave, the Saint said, "The kingdom of Gujarát has been confirmed in your name. If you have any other wish, express it that God may fulfil it." Bahádur Khán said, " Except the conquest of Chitor, I have no other wish, because the Ráná of Chitor has much harassed the Musalmáns of Ahmednagar, killing them, plundering their property, and taking them prisoners." The Saint hung down his head concentrating his thoughts in a trance like reverie. Bahádur Khán repeated his wish, but he replied not. On his repeating his wish the third time, the Saint said, " The conquest of Chitor depends upon the decline of your kingdom." Bahádur Khán said, " I agree to that a hundred times." The saint said, " If you will have it so who can alter the decree of fate ?" After sometime the Saint said, " This is our last meeting. You will return here speedily, but you will not see me. See that you never neglect pleasing Sayad Mehmúd *alias* Sháh Budha, as in this will be your advantage."

In short, Bahádur Khán went to Chámpáner, and having obtained some little money from the officers of those parts started for Delhi. This happened in A. H. 931 (A.D. 1524). This year Sháh Sheikh Jí whose name was Sayad Jalál, son of Sayad Mehmúd, son of Kutbi-Álam Sayad Burhánud-din died at the age of seventy-five years and six months as is gatherable from the word *Hazrat Sayad*.

They say that Bahádur Khán went from Chámpáner to Bánswálá, and from that place he went to the Ráná at Chitor, and stayed there some days. The Ráná came out to meet him with all honour and the mother of the Ráná called him her son, and was kind to him.

It is related that one day the nephew of the Ráná invited Bahádur Khan to dinner, and took him to his house. At night at a dancing entertainment one of the dancing girls, who was very beautiful, danced very well. Bahádur Khán gave much of his attention to her, and applauded her. The Ráná's nephew when he saw that Bahádur Khán was much inclined towards her, said out of jealousy : " Bahádur Khán, do you know who this dancing girl is ?" He said, " Please say." That ill-fated one said, " She is the daughter of one of the respectable families of Ahmednagar, which country the Ráná formerly plundered," and he then mentioned the name. Immediately on hearing this, Bahádur Khán gave him a sword-cut on the waist which cut that ill-fated one in twain, and killed him. An uproar arose. Bahádur Khán taking up his blood-dripping sword stood up. The Rájputs surrounded him and wished to slay him. This news reaching the ears of the Ráná's mother, she came running to the spot, a dagger in her hand and cried, " If any one kills Bahádur Khán I shall rip open my belly." The Ráná heard of this and said : " Why did that ill-fated man say such words to the son of the king of Gujarát ? He has only got the punishment for his folly. Now let no one kill Bahádur Khán or I shall ruin him." When affairs came to this pass

Bahádur Khán left that place and went to Mewát. The Kháns of that place offered to put him up and aid him, but he refused to accept their offers, and went to Sultán Ibráhim Lodi, son of Sultán Sikandar king of Dehli. At that time the Sultán was fighting with His Majesty, whose Abode is in Paradise, the emperor Bábar near the village of Pánipat. The Sutlán showed him much kindness, and what followed I will relate hereafter if God wills.

ACCOUNT OF THE ACCESSION TO THE THRONE OF SULTAN SIKANDAR, SON OF SULTAN MUZAFFAR, AND HIS ASSASSINATION IN THE COMMENCE-MENT OF HIS YOUTH AND REIGN.

On Friday, the twenty-second of the month of Jamádul Ákhir A. H. 932 (A. H. 1525 6), Sultán Muzaffar entered into the mercy of God as has been before related, and on the same day Sultán Sikandar, the son of Muzaffar, sat on the throne of the kingdom and shortly after-wards he went in the direction of Muhammadábád. They say that he passed by Batwá without visiting the shrine of the saints at that place. When he arrived near the tomb of Kutbi Álam Sayad Burhánuddín did not visit it and said, " Mián Sheikh Jí, the grandson of the Lord Kutbul Aktáb, was called by people the second Makhdúm Jahánián because forsooth, he prophesied that Bahádur Khán would be king of Gujarát, while Bahádur Khán himself seems to have vanished from the world !"

In short, when Sikandar Khán came to Muhammadábád on the twenty-fifth of the above month, he ascended the throne according to the custom of his ancestors, and to each of those who had served him in the days he was a prince he gave a title, and distributed 2,700 horses amongst his men. On seeing this the ministers and nobles of his father became disappointed. Even Imádul-Mulk, Khush Kadam, the Sultán's foster-brother, was grieved. The cause of this, I will relate hereafter if God wills.

At this time news arrived that Latif Khán had taken shelter with Bhím, Rájá of Munga,[1] in the hilly tracts of Sultánpur and Nazar-bár, and that several amirs were in correspondence with him. Sultán Sikandar, invested Malik Latíf with the title of Shirzah Khán, and, having given him 3,000 well equipped horses, sent him to expel

---

[1] Although the author places Munga in the hilly tracts of Nandurbár and Sultánpúr, there is reason to believe that the place is Mohangad or Chhota Udeipur. Rana Bhím of Munga and Rana Bhím of Pál seem to be the same person.

Latif Khán from the hills. When Shirzah Khán entered the defiles, the Rajputs and Kolis, occupying the heads of the narrow passes, commenced to fight, and Shirzah Khán with some famous nobles and 1,200 men were slain. When this news reached the Sultán, he appointed Ḳaisar Khán to take the field at the head of a large army. At this time several amirs joined Imádul-mulk and inspired him with the suspicion that the king contemplated his destruction, and enjoined him not to be neglectful or careless of this. The Malik said, "If the Sultán aims at my life, why should I not attempt his life before he deprives me of mine." They say that in these days Sultán Sikandar had a dream and saw the saints Kutbi Álam Makhdam Jahánián and Sháh Álam and Sheikh Jí, and Sultán Muzaffar also with them. The Sultán, his deceased father, said to him, " Sikandar Khán my boy, get up. Thou art destined to occupy the throne no longer." Sháh Sheikh Jí said, " Ay, it is so." Sultán Sikandár awoke from sleep, affrighted; he recounted the night's dream to Yákub who had the title of Darya Khán saying : " My heart also says that Bahádur Khán will come, and that there will be war between us." The author of the *Tárikh-i-Bahádur Sháhi* writes that Darya Khán related this dream to Yúsuf bin Lutfulláh, and Yúsuf told me, and so it passed until it became well known. In short, that day after an hour the Sultán went to play *chaugán* or polo from which he returned when one watch of the day was passed. After his return to the palace he took his food. When two watches of the day had passed, that is at mid-day, he slept, and his attendants went to their houses.

Sayad Jalál Munawwar-ul-mulk says : " When the Sultán returned from playing *chaugán*, I and my brother Sayad Burhán-ud-din were standing in the market, and we saw that there was no man nor woman who did not that day come out from their houses and shops to see the beautiful Sultán pass by with his cortége, for they say that the Sultán was very good-looking, and men called him the second Joseph." In short, the Sultán in royal state and magnificence passed through the market to his palace. The nobles and soldiers saluted him, and returned to their houses. After a short time Imádul-mulk, having wrapped a piece of cloth round his head and ears, and accompanied by forty or fifty blood-thirsty well-armed desperate men, passed from his house to the King's palace. When he was passing through the market, men remarked : " The Malik is going to-day after sixteen

days to pay respects to the Sultán." An hour had not elapsed when
an uproar arose that Imádul-mulk had assassinated the Sultán. It
seemed in the city as though the end of the world were come. Men
in great wonder and astonishment were weeping and wailing with
grief. " Oh God," said they, " what a terrible and sudden event
this is !" From that day it seemed as if the blood of Sultán Sikandar
washed away the words " tranquillity" and " prosperity" from the
tablet of the kingdom of Gujarát. The first of the Sultáns of
Gujarát, who was assassinated, was Sultán Sikandar, and, after this,
from him up to Muzaffar III. son of Mehmúd II, every Sultán became
a martyr. According to what the Prophet (on whom be peace) has
said :—" He who introduces a new custom, on him be the evil of it
and of the harm which is wrought in consequence of it ;" all
the wrongs that follow shall be written to the account of Imád-ul-
Mulk the evil-doer. They say that when that false one to his salt
entered the palace and drew near the king's sleeping apartment,
he saw two men outside the curtain at the door of the sleeping
chamber. One of these was Sayad Ílm-ud-din, son of Ahmed Bukhári,
grandson of Sháh Álam, son of Kutbi Álam, and the other Malik
Bairam bin Masûd. They were playing chess, and Malik Sondha,
the door-keeper, was standing holding a corner of the curtain and
Malik Pír Muhammad, a palace servant, was rubbing the feet of the
Sultán, and the Sultán was asleep. No one else was present. Imád-
ul-Mulk wished to pass through the curtain. Sondha, the door-keeper,
said that the Sultán was asleep, but he was unable to say anything
harsher to Imád-ul-Mulk, because the authority of the palace was in
the hands of that ill-starred slave. Imád-ul-Mulk gave no answer
to Malik Sondha, but taking Malik Bahár with him, he entered
within the curtain, and seizing Malik Bahár's hand said, " Have you
seen the crystal mirror that has come for the Sultán from Portugal ?"
This mirror was hanging at the lower side of the bed. The beauty of
it was that when a lamp was lit, the reflection of many lamps appeared
in it. It was a wonderful thing. The traitorous Bahár, said he had
not seen it, so taking his hand he drew him near the bed of the
Sultán. Bahár paused a moment. The wretch said, " Why do you
hesitate ? Strike !" Bahár, the unworthy, drew his sword. At this
moment the Sultán awoke and said, "What is this ?" Before
the others could come up, that evil one struck a blow, and cut that
tree of the garden of beauty and elegance in two pieces. After

that he killed Malik Pír Muhammud, the servant, with one blow
and grasping his naked blood-dripping sword, he and Imádul-
Mulk issued forth. When the Sayad saw the catastrophe, he drew
his sword on Imád-ul-Mulk. Imád-ul-Mulk said, " Do not be a rascal
Sayad." The Sayad said, " Oh mannikin, he is a rascal who is false
to his salt and who slays his king." The Sayad struck at him with
his sword, but his sword struck in the roof, and broke. The Sayad
advanced quickly, and struck with the broken blade on the head
of the Malik, and inflicted a slight wound, but they slew the
Sayad and Malik Bairam with their poniards. This happened on
the fourth of the month of Shaâbán A. H. 932 (A.D. 1526, about
the month of June). Praised be Alláh! not an hour had passed since
the time that Sultán Sikandar had passed through the bazár, and
had entered his palace in all the pomp and pageantry of royalty.

They say that they bore his body thence on a small broken cot,
the dangling legs of which had parted from their sockets. In this
manner they brought him to Hálol, which is ten *kos* from Chámpáner,
and there buried him.

COUPLET.

" The revolution of the spheres does not besprinkle the head of Parviz with blood,
   Yet in a moment it makes Kisra lose his head and gives Parviz his crown.

Two hours before this thousands were waiting in the polo-field
anxious to catch a glance of the Sultán's eye. Each one hovered
like a moth round a candle to pay his respects to the Sultán, and
if the Sultán returned the salutation by the meanest of his slaves,
its happy recepient was so overjoyed that he was ready to walk on
his head instead of his feet to receive it. And yet they say that at
the time the mortal remains of this idolized one were being carried to
Hálol, that from the fear and dread of that rascal of evil end, hardly
forty persons came round to perform the prayers for the dead over
the Sultán's bier.

In short, after he had made Sultán Sikandar a martyr, Imád-ul-
mulk entered the harem of the Sultán, and took Nasír Khán, the
youngest son of Sultán Muzaffar who was five or six years of age,
and placing him on his lap seated himself on the throne and named
the boy Mehmúd Sháh.[1] The army was also of the same mind with

---

[1] The placing the prince on his lap meant that he was to be his guardian and
regent over the kingdom during his minority.

him and all the nobles, soldiers and servants, and attendants came, and saluted him. Three of the nobles did not join them. One of these was Khudáwand Khán, who was the vazír of Sultán Muzaffar and whom Sultán Sikandar had confirmed in the post; another was the Sultán's cup-bearer, Fateh Khán Budhu, a prince of Sindh, who was son-in-law to Sultán Muzaffar, and the husband of Sikandar's own sister; the third was Táj Khán Tariáni, who built the shrine of the king of Saints, the lord Sháh Álam.

ACCOUNT OF THE FAITHLESSNESS OF IMADUL-MULK, THE BLIND OF HEART, IN CONNECTION WITH SULTÁN SIKANDAR, SON OF SULTÁN MUZAFFAR.

Reliable persons of Gujarát state that on the day of the accession of Sultán Sikandar to the throne, a slave of Bíbí Ráni, of the name of Khush Kadam, who later obtained the title of Imádul-mulk, with a baton in his hand, was seen giving himself the airs of a minister, because at her death Bíbí Ráni, the mother of Sultán Sikandar, had placed the young Sultán's hand[1] in the hand of the slave. From that day the idea had entered the evil mind of the wicked man that in the reign of Sultán Sikandar he would be the chief minister. Thus on the day of the Sultán's accession when the chief Hindu merchants of the city came to congratulate the Sultán, at the time of their taking leave, he asked for orders to bestow on them dresses of honour and titles. The Sultán said, " Let some one tell Khudáwand Khán," who was the chief vazír of the deceased Sultán, " to give each of them honours befitting his position." On hearing this order envy took possession of the mind of the traitorous slave, but he said nothing at that time. The Sultán sent for Khudáwand Khán. He came and stood outside the private curtain. Imádul-mulk though he saw him, disregarded his presence without announcing it to the Sultán. Khudáwand Khán contrary to custom, waited a long time outside the curtain. At length one of the Sultán's servants told the Sultán that Khudáward Khán was standing outside. The Sultán said "call him in." At that time Imádul-mulk pretended as if he was not aware of the Khán's arrival. The Sultán then called in a loud voice with much respect, " Khán Jí, be pleased to enter. " Khudáwand Khán entering placed his head at the Sultán's feet, and commenced to weep. The Sultán also wept, and embraced

---

[1] A dying person placing the hand of a dear one into that of a trusted friend means to ask the friend to extend the hand of help to the loved one through life.

19

the Khán and said, " May the post of minister, with all good luck, be with you as before." The Khán said, " This slave is old and prays for his emancipation, so that he may sit in a corner and remain occupied in praying for blessings on you." The Sultán said, " No one but you is fit for the office of minister." He bestowed on Khudá-wand Khán the ministerial dress of honour. Thus the fire of envy in the mind of that slave became more than ever inflamed.

It is related that after some days, Imádul-mulk of his own authority without obtaining the Sultán's permission and without consulting Khudáwand Khán invested an eunuch, who was the head of the police and city Magistrate of Ahmedábád with the title of Muhibbul-mulk, and granted him an increase of allowances, and brought him to the Sultán and said: " This eunuch does good service, therefore he has been invested with the title of Muhibbul-mulk, and his allowances also have been increased." The Sultán said, " Have you given him this title ? I am no child, I am both wise and capable and whosoever acts thus without my orders acts wrongly. The investiture and increasing the allowances pertain to the office of Khudáwand Khán who is the vazír of the Kingdom. Interference by another with his duties and powers shall be fruitless." So saying he rejected his petition. As this slave however was headstrong, and popular with the army, Khudáwand Khán for the sake of peace said to the Sultán, " Let the title be granted to him for the sake of Imádul-mulk, and you can increase his allowances at another time. " The Sultán remained silent and silence is half-consent. On this that ill-fated slave became very enraged and after that began to plot the death of the Sultán, and began to conspire with the amírs and soldiers who were on his side, and to win over to his side by gentleness and courtesy the hearts of those who were little inclined towards him. They say that he used to send for them one by one to his house and inquire into their circumstances, asking, for instance, " How many children have you ?" When the person asked gave him the number, he would ask : " Have you married them or not ?" If in giving a negation, want of money was given as the cause he would say, " Borrow from me and do the good deed by your children and marry them." In this way he distributed gold to men, making them write bonds for the amount he pretended to lend them which he afterwards tore up. He thus noosed the necks of men with the string of his obligation, and made with them contracts of partisanship. Sultán

Sikandar, ignorant of this, in the pride of youth, fortune and pleasure, passed his days like the days of *Id* and his nights like the nights of the *Shab-i-barát*.[1] Each day he devised a new pleasure. He devised and brought into fashion a new gown called after him the Sikandar Sháhi *jámah*. Whatever he desired he found ready at hand. He had a slave girl whose name was Názukleher, who was the object of his passionate attachment. They say that all the women of Gujarát agreed that a woman like Názukleher had never been in the harem of any of the kings of Gujarát, and further that in beauty and good qualities and virtue, Gujarát had never produced her equal. On the other hand, they said that there was not to be seen in that age a young man so pleasant and handsome as Sikandar Khán.

It is said that after the martyrdom of Sultán Sikandar, Názukleher went to the harem of Sultán Bahádur and Bahádur also was very fond of her. When Sultán Bahádur conquered Mándu, and brought the whole country of Málwá under his rule, he one day ordered that dancing girls of all classes, *Domnis*, *Pátars*, *Kumáchnis*, *Pari-sháns* and *Lolis* should be summoned to his presence. Band after band of women, dressed and jewelled in emulation of each other, to the number of about a thousand of every kind and from every country, presented themselves before the Sultán. They say that many among them were beautiful and some by universal suffrage of great beauty. Sultán Bahádur sent for them one by one, and bestowing on them presents, gave them leave to retire. Seeing this, Shujáát Khán, who was one of the principal amírs and a companion of the Sultán, said, " Of all these beauties who with eye-lashes like arrows, and eyebrows like bows, seeing every little thing and true of aim who have gathered before your Majesty, has not the arrow of the glance of any of them struck the mark of your Majesty's heart?" The Sultán said, " Shujáát Khán, I have in my harem a concubine before the Sun of whose beauty the loveliness of lesser stars like these fades and disappears. I will show her to you some day." They say that after a few days the Sultán while under the influence of wine became displeased with Názukleher for some little fault, and in a fit of uncontrollable passion drew his sword and clove her in two halves. At that moment he remem-

---

[1] The two *Ids* are Musalmán holidays, the festivities connected with which take place during the day. The *Shab-i-barát* which occurs in Shaábán, the eighth month of the Muslim year, is celebrated by illuminations and fireworks during the night.

bered the promise he had made to Shujáât Khán. Covering Názukleher
with a counterpane he sent for Shujáât Khán, and told him :
" Shujáât Khán, I had promised to show you the girl whose beauty
was like the refulgence of the Sun. To-day," said he, " by the
decree of God, she has expired. Living you never saw her. See her
dead, and observe what a paragon of beauty she was." So saying he
drew the quilt off from her face. Shujáât Khán looked at her. She
lay in her blood like the morning Sun in the midst of twilight, looking
pale like the Moon. He threw himself on the ground and said,
" Alas, what has happened? How has this come to pass." The Sultán
also became very grieved, and dashed his head against the ground,
but it was of no avail. Hence poets have said—

> " The son of man out from the root groweth not up again,
> Like the tree which struck at the root springeth up into new life."

They say that when Sultán Sikandar used to ride out all who saw
him, whether man or woman, admired him, but from respect for the
Sultán, no one could express his admiration. One day a man pretending to be a platonic lover said, " I am enamoured of the Sultán." This
news reached the Sultán who sent for him and said, " He is a good
man, but appears shameless. Tell him I will give him a hundred *Ashrafís*,[1]
but he must abstain from this thing, and never again show himself of
such mind. If he does, I shall order that his head and beard should be
shaved and I will have him placed on a donkey, and his shame shall be
published in every street and lane." The platonic lover agreed
to receive the gold. The Sultán sending for the gold, ordered it to
be put in a bag and tied it round his neck, and ordered that his head
and beard should be shaved and he mounted on an ass and paraded
through the streets and alleys that no one should again make such a
false claim. And in truth, had he shown himself pleased with the
disgrace in which a true lover glories, such a day would not have over-
taken him. He who flies from disgrace, Love ruins his honour.

It is related that when Sultán Sikandar sat on the throne all the
nobles and great men went to congratulate him except Sháh
Budha, son of Sháh Sheikhji Bukhári, who was then the chief of the
Sayads of Batwá. Sháh Budha did not go on account of the bad understanding between him and Sultán Sikandar. And that was as follows:

---

[1] The gold *Ashrafí* or Seraph, of which Hawkins (A.D. 1609–1611) says : " Seraffins
Ekberi which be ten rupees a piece." Thomas' Chron. Pathán Kíngs of Dehli, 425.

Some time after the death of Sháh Sheikhji Bahádur Khàn left Gujarát and went to Delhi. Some time after these events Sikandar Khán said to Sháh Budha, " Your saint is dead, and his disciples have become recluses " (a proverb expressive of the emptiness of curses or bless-ings). Sháh Budha said in reply, " The Saint is not dead. Rest assured that the friends of God die not, but move as it were from one house to another house, nor is the disciple wandering in a distressed condition, by this token that the prophecy concerning him will surely come to pass, and your kingdom is like a mirage or a bubble. It has no foundation and will not last." On hearing this speech the Sultán became more than ever displeased with Sháh Budha and withdrew the grant of Batwá which was enjoyed by the Sayads, and bestowed it on Sayad Muhammad Bukhári who had the title of Sádát Khán, and who was one of the sons of Sháh Alam, but he refused it. The end of it was that the truth of the prophecy soon became apparent. The whole duration of the reign of Sultán Sikandar was but two months and sixteen days, when the traitor Imádul-mulk Khushkadam slew the Sultán. Wise people have said : " Oh God, whomsoever thou wishest to cast down, thou throwest him amongst dervishes. We seek protection with God from it." The Sultán was the disciple of Sayad Mírán Jí the son of Sayad Sultán, the son of Hazrat Sháh Álam.

In short on the day of the accession of Nasír Khán to whom Imádul-mulk gave the title of Sultán Mehmúd as has been mentioned above, he distributed dresses of honour, horses and titles to the nobles and soldiery, but *jágirs* which are the results and supporters of titles he gave not. People said, " Titles without *jágirs* are things that bring shame." In the end the greater part of the nobles and soldiery became disgusted with him, and thirsty for his blood on ac-count of his atrocity, *i.e.*, the murder of Sultán Sikandar, but without a leader they were unable to do anything, so each of them retired to his estate. Disaffection, which was hitherto concentrated, began to spread forth. For the sake of doing something Imádul-mulk wrote to Imá dul-mulk of Elichpur by way of friendship to threaten the Sultán-pur and Nazarbár frontiers stating that he would pay him in gold for the expense of the march. And he wrote in like manner to Ráná Sánghá, and also assembled the zamindárs and sent a petition to the emperor Bábar and asked for aid.

The author of the *Tarikh-i-Bahádur-Sháhi* writes that he was at that time in Wadnagar, and that he sent a message to Táj Khán at

Dhandhúká that Imádul-mulk was seeking aid from the emperor Bábar, and that this would cause the downfall of the dynasty of the Sultáns of Gujarát. He requested Táj Khán to think well and to write a petition to Bahádur Khán also and start it off with a swift courier. At that time Bahádur Khán at the invitation of the nobles and leading men of Jaunpur had, without leave, left Sultán Ibráhím Lodi who was engaged with the emperor Bábar on the plain of Pán pat, and had started for Jaunpur and encamped in the garden of Pán pat. In that place Páyindah Khan Afghán who had come on behalf of the nobles of Jaunpur met Bahádur Khán. He said : " All the nobles of Jaunpur consider you their king, and are awaiting your arrival, and have sent me in your service that having presented this petition in your presence' I should lead you there. It is a welcome thing. You should not delay." The Sultán was willing to go, but at this moment the letter of Khurram Khán containing the news of the death of Sultán Muzaffar, and the accession of Sultán Sikandar, arrived, and it was also stated that the nobles and soldiers were all awaiting his arrival. If he should now arrive quickly, it was certain that the kingdom would pass into his hands, as the people and soldiers were also displeased with Sultán Sikandar. After the arrival of this letter Bahádur Khán remained for three days in that camp, and having performed the ceremonies of mourning, he gave Páyindah Khán his leave on the fourth day, and travelled in the direction of Gujarát with great speed. When he reached Chitor, Sayad Sher, son of Muínud-din Afghán, who, after the murder of Sultán Sikandar, had left Gujarát to seek Bahádur Khán explained to him one by one the news of the murder of Sultán Sikandar Khán and the treachery of Imádul-mulk and the enthronement of Nasír Khán. Bahádur Khán said, " If God wills, when I reach Muhammadábád, I will impale this traitor," and he started thence also. Prince Chánd Khán, who was with him, parted from him there, and went to Sultán Mehmúd, King of Málwá, and his brother Ibráhím Khan went with Bahádur Khán. Thence he came to Dungarpur. On hearing this news Táj Khán leaving Dhandhuká proceeded to meet him. At this time the Prince Latíf Khán coming to the neighbourhood of Dhandhúka, sent a message to Táj Khán, to the effect that if the Khán would join him, he would entrust the whole government of Gujarát to him. Táj Khán sent some money to Latíf Khán and stated : " Before this I have bound myself to Bahádur Khán, I cannot now make any arrangement to the contrary. It is better that you should at present retire."

On hearing of the return of Bahádur Khán the nobles who had identified themselves with Imádul-mulk and his partisans began to tremble. Imádul-mulk sent Azdul-mulk the leper with 300 horses from the Sultán's stables and fifty elephants from the elephant stables, and appointed him to the post of Morásá with orders to stay there and suffer no one to pass by that way to join Bahádur Khán. And Azdul-mulk started for Morásá, Razi-ul-mulk and Khurram Khán having come from Muhammadábád started with the view of meeting Bahádur Khán who arrived at Mángrech[1] otherwise called Muhammadnagar, and several other partisans of Bahádur Khán whose names were, Ázam Khán son of Píru or Badú, Malik Yúsuf bin Lutfulláh, Ráji Muhammad bin Faríd, Malik Masúd and others who, from fear of Imádul-mulk, had fled to remote places came and now met Bahádur Khán. Bahádur Khán went thence to Morásá, and thence to Harsol, and thence to Singúrgáon. At this time Khurram Khán, Razi-ul-mulk, and the greater number of Muzaffar Sháh's nobles came and kissed the Sultán's feet. The next day he pitched his royal tents at Nehrwálá.

ACCOUNT OF THE ACCESSION OF BAHÁDUR SHÁH AND THE REFULGENCE OF HIS FAME THROUGH GOD'S AID.

The author of the *Tárikh-i-Bahádur-Sháhi* writes, that on the 26th day of the month of Ramazán A. H. 932 (A. D. 1525) in that camp Táj Khán and Mujáhidul-Mulk and the writer of the Bahádur Sháhi, and the chief men of the great city of Ahmedábád obtained the honour of kissing the Sultán's carpet, and from that place with his kingly umbrella and with all pomp and state, the Sultán marched to Ahmedábád, and entered the city by the Kálúpúr gate. He went first to visit the tombs of his ancestors Mehmúd Sháh, Ahmed Sháh, and Sultán Kutbuddin, which are situated in the Mánek Chauk, and prayed over them, and he then went to put up in the royal palace in the city which is called the Bhadr saying according to the verse of the Kuráán: "O Lord, locate me in a good residence, for Thou art the best giver of residences."[2] On 27th night of Ramazán of the above year all the nobles of the king's party presented themselves. According to the rules of Sultán Muzaffar, he appointed to each of them his place, and, sitting with them, partook of food and each one of them thanked God with joy at the presence of the Sultán. The city of

---

[1] Another edition has Kapadvanj. [2] The Kuráán, Chap. "The True Believers."

Ahmedábád, acquired a new beauty and glory, and the country of
Gujarát which had become clouded by the absence of Bahádur.
Khán, gained lustre by the rising of the sun of his presence and the
phantom of unrest vanished from the hearts of the people of Gujarát
On hearing this news Imádul-mulk advanced to his followers one year's
pay in ready money from the imperial treasury and made them swear
straitly by the Kuráán that they would not desert Mehmúd Sháh. The
nobles used to take his gold, and used to leave Muhammadábád and
repair to Sultán Bahádur. Bahá-ul-Mulk and Dáwarul-Mulk, the two
greatest nobles attached to Imádul-mulk and who were concerned in
the murder of Sultán Sikandar, also came over to Sultán Bahádur.

The author of the *Tárikh-i-Bahádur-Sháhi* goes on to say that
on the morning of the day of the *Id* the Sultán ordered him to bring
the elephants arrayed and caparisoned to the Darbár. The Sultán,
having bathed and clothed himself in state robes, came out and
entered the Singár Mandap Palace the doors and walls of which were
gilded, and there took his seat. He ordered *khiláats*, or dresses of
honour to be presented to Táj Khán and other nobles. Thirty-two persons as below-mentioned received titles on that day : — (1) Khurram Khán
bin Sikander Khán was given the title of Khán-Khánán, (2) Safdar
Khán, the title of Alam Khán, (3) the son of Khán-Khánán, the title of
Nizám Khán, (4) Saádul-Mulk, the title of Shams Khán, (5) the son of
Nizám-ul-Mulk, the title of Mubári-zul-Mulk, (6) the son of Shams
Khán, the title of Saádul-Mulk, (7) Malik Táj Khán, the title of
Wajíh-ul-Mulk, (8) Malik Kutb Shamaáchi, the title of Ikbál Khán,
(9) Bahádur-ul-Mulk, the title of Alif Khán, (10) Mujá-hid-ul-Mulk,
the title of Mujá-hid-Khán, (11) Násirul-Mulk, the title of Katlak Khán,
(12) the son of Mujá-hid-Khán, the title of Majá-hid-ul-Mulk, (13)
the son of Katlak Khán, the title of Násir-ul-Mulk, (14) Maudúd-ul-
Mulk, the title of Taghlak Khán, (15) Malik Badruddin, the title
Maudud-ul-Mulk, (16) Malik Ráyat, son of Mujáhid-ul-Mulk, the title
of Nasír Khán, (17) Malik Sher, the title of Nasrat-ul-Mulk, (18)
Malik Mustufá, the title of Sher Andáz Khán, (19) Malik Muzaffar,
the title of Asad-ul-Mulk, (20) the son of Asad-ul-Mulk, the title of
Sháistah Khán, (21) the son of Malik Tagh-lak, the title of Seif Khán,
(22) Suleiman, son of Mujáhid-ul-Mulk, the title of Mansúr Khán,
(23) Abú, the son of Azhdar Khán, the title of Azhdar Khán, (24) the
son of Latíf Khán Báiwál, the title of Shirzáh Khán, (25) Shams
Khán, the title of Daryá Khán, (26) Shams Khán bin Taghlak Khán,

the title of Husein Khán, (27) Chánd Khán Bhandári, the title of
Huzabr Khán, (28) Kúmbhá Gohel, the title of Ráyán Ráo, (29)
Malik Sáhib bin Mujáhid-ul-mulk, the title of Habíb Khán.[1]

After this the Sultán mounted his elephant and went to the *Ídgáh*,
the place for the Íd prayers, and the people of the city delighted and
joyful, blessed and praised him. After this, on the second of Shawwál
he went to and alighted in his palace of Khamdhrol, and thence he
marched to Mehmúdábád. At that camp Muázzam Khán came with
some nobles and kissed his feet. Marching thence on the way to
Nadiád he had to halt two days at Sivanj owing to the river Sídhi
being in flood. Many men came from Muhammadábád to meet him,
and he pardoned all those who came after taking gold fromI mádul-
mulk. On the 11th of Shawwál, marching from Nadiád, he crossed
the river Mahi by the Khánpur ford. Imádul-mulk now sent Âzd-ul-
mulk to Baroda and appointed Muháfiz Khán Bakkál to the outpost
of Dhánej with the view that if these two great nobles who were chief
men, were separated from him, Sultán Bahádur would, on their account,
say nothing to him

> When the affairs of a man become troubled,
> Whatever he does avails him not.

Imádul-mulk also secretly sent for Prince Latíf Khán, because
Prince Latíf Khán was of age (and not a minor like the
prince he had set up), thinking that in case he was forced to fly he
would elevate the regal umbrella over his head, and fight with Sultán
Bahádur. Latíf Khán came to Dhánej. Imádul-mulk, however, became bewildered as to what to do. At this time Bahádur Khán entered
Ahmedábád.

They say that on the 11th of Shawwál Imádul-mulk severed his
connection with Prince Nasír Khán, went to his house, and never again
inquired about him. The head chamberlain of the royal palace kept
Nasír Khán in surveillance as a state prisoner.

They say that 5,000 men in Imádul-mulk's service assembled at
his house, and resolved to guard the life and honour of Imádul-mulk
with their own if Sultán Bahádur regarded him with anger. But
when the ensigns of Bahádur Khán entered the city, two or three
hundred men alone remained with Imádul-mulk, and the rest all fled

---

[1] Out of the thirty-two persons who are said to have received the distinction of
titles, twenty-nine only are enumerated in the text.

20

and concealed themselves in their houses, and the chief men among them left the city.   When the Sultán crossed the river Mahí he did not wait for his army, and the whole army had not yet crossed the river, when taking with him 400 horse and some elephants which had crossed the river, he pushed on to Hálol.   He first visited Sultán Sikandar's grave, and sent on Táj Khán with 300 horse to surround the house of the miscreant murderer of that Sultán.

They say that when the news of the arrival of Sultán Bahádur at Hálol reached Imádul-mulk, Khwájáh Mánek, the son of Jalál and Yúsuf, the son of Mubáriz-ul-mulk, said, " Imádul-mulk, to fly is better than to stay, for Sultán Bahádur will not leave you alive." He replied, " How shall I flee ?   I see naked swords on all sides of me, I cannot move hence, how then shall I run ?"   The murder of Sultán Sikandar had taken such a hold of his mind that he could not take even a step.

Some say that he said thus : " What injury have I done to Sultán Bahádur that I should fly ? Had I not slain Sikandar Khán, how could Sultán Bahádur have reached this high position ?"

Táj Khán with 300 Sawárs quickly arrived at, and surrounded the house of Imádul-mulk.

That wretch (Imádul-mulk) fled from his house and concealed himself in the house of Sháh Jí, son of Siddík, the executive officer of the ministers.   The people of the town attacked and plundered his house His wives, daughters, and female slaves were all carried off.   In the meantime the Sultán entered the city, arrived in front of the house of Khudáwand Khán Vazír, and admitted Khudáwand to the honour of kissing his feet.   Khudáwand Khán accompanied his victorious stirrup. As the Sultán placed his foot in the royal palace Táj Khán came and reported, " We have given up the house of that traitor to plunder, but we did not find him in it, perhaps he may be concealed somewhere in the city."   The Sultán commanded Kaisar Khán and Kabír-ul-mulk the police officer and magistrate, to search for and capture him, and with prosperity and good fortune alighted in the royal palace.   Half a ghadi (twelve minutes) had not elapsed, when a slave of Khudáwand Khán having captured Imádul-mulk dragged him into the Darbár, his head bare, his hands tied behind his shoulders and with a hundred indignities. An order was given to confine him in a small room of the Dil Kushá Palace.   The Sultán then ordered Táj Khán to ask the unhappy man why he had murdered the Sultán's brother. When Táj Khán asked him, he said, "What could I do, all the nobles had combined to kill Sikandar Khán." Táj Khán said, "You are a slave and were the slave of Sikandar Khán, why did you join the Sultán's enemies?" To this he gave no reply. All those who were present cursed him. The Sultán then went to see the room where Sultán Sikandar was murdered. The author of the *Tárikh-i-Bahádur Sháhi* states that the Sultán ordered him to send for Táj Khán from the Dil Khushá Palace, and that he brought him. Sultán Bahádur showed to Táj Khán the place of Sultán Sikandar's murder, and heaved a deep sigh and ordered that " *Bad Kadam*" (the Evil of Presence) meaning "*Khush Kadám*" (the Auspicious of Presence), which was the original name of Imádul-mulk, should be crucified on the morrow in front of the Darbár, and that they should tear to pieces Seifuddín and Ali who were his accomplices.

They say that when they were taking Imádul-mulk to the impaling stake some one said, "Repeat the creed." He said, "How shall I say it? My tongue will not utter the words." Alas! it is the fate of him who shall act thus with his master to be ruined both in this world, and in the next. They crucified Ímádul-mulk and Seifuddin and Ali on the 13th of the month of Shawwál, and on that day Muftih-ul-mulk, the son of Malik Tawakkul, a noble of Mehmúd Sháh's was ennobled with of the title of Imádul-mulk and was given the post of a minister.

In a short time all the ill-fated ones who were concerned in Sultán Sikandar's murder were killed in misery and pain, and Bahár, the villain, who was the actual perpetrator of the murder of Sultán Sikandar and was wounded on the day of the murder by Sayad Ilmuddín, remained concealed some days, but was eventually captured. The Sultán ordered him to be flayed and then crucified. Ázdul-mulk and Muháfiz Khán, who had fled to the mountains of Pál, joined Latíf Khán. They collected the Hindu chiefs of those parts and wished to raise a rebellion, but the good-fortune of Bahádur Sháh was daily on the ascendant, and they were unable to effect their purpose. The hand of Sultán Bahádur like a vernal rain cloud rained gold and jewels, and through hopes of receiving his largess the soldiers and nobles were not willing to go even to their houses, and all day remained present in his service. In those days there was a great famine. The Sultán ordered food to be prepared in certain places for all-comers, and when he went out riding, he never bestowed on any one anything less than an *Ashrafi* or gold coin in alms; and thus the rich and the poor of the city passed their days in ease and prosperity. The fame of the generosity of Sultán Bahádur became so great that it threw the name of Hátim[1] into the shade.

On the 14th of the month of Zulkaád A. H. 932 (A. D. 1525) according to the custom of his ancestors Sultán Bahádur ascended the royal throne, and gave the nobles and ministers valuable dresses of honour. He presented out of the treasury one year's pay to each soldier and hundred and fifty persons were ennobled by titles whose names for the sake of brevity I have omitted. He then retired to the private apartment and associated with the great and the noble, and after partaking of food with them he bestowed on each of them honours and rewards. Each one, glad and joyful, returned to his house, and praised and blessed the Sultán. He entrusted the place of minister to Táj Khán.

After some time news was received that Azd-ul-mulk and Muháfiz Khán, having joined Prince Latíf Khán, desired to excite a rebellion in Nazarbár. Táj Khán was, therefore, ordered to prepare an army to repulse them. Táj Khán represented that it would be proper to send Gházi Khán, the son of Ahmed Khán, for this work. The King said, " When I sat on the throne, I doubled his allowances. I now re-double them." He ordered Gházi Khán to go in the direction of Nadiád with a powerful army. After the Sacrifice Id Shujáát Khán, otherwise called Háji Muhammad, fled and went to Prince Latíf Khán ín Pál. The end of the business was that Táj Khán represented that the flight of Shujá-úl-mulk was at the instigation of Kaisar Khán. The Sultán said, " If the matter is so, Kaisar Khán must be captured." Táj Khán represented that not only Kaisar Khán, but Alif Khán and Dáwarul-mulk also who were accomplices of Imádul-mulk in the murder of Sultán Sikandar and were corresponding with Latíf Khán should be captured. When the King was convinced of this, he dismissed Alif Khán whom he was appointing to march against Latif Khán and arrested him with the other two nobles and they were all three beheaded. This happened in the year of his accession to the throne, that is, in A. H. 932 (A. D. 1525). After some time, Gházi Khán reported to the effect that Azd-ul-mulk and Muháfiz Khán and Bhím, Rájá of Pál, having joined Latíf Khán, had raided and sacked one of the villages of Sultánpur. That when Gházi Khán was informed of this, he marched against them. A great fight took place, but that through

---

[1] Hátim, commonly known as Hátim of Tai, was an Arab chief who flourished just before the Prophet. His unbounded liberality and chivalric generosity were so great that among a people so generous as the Arabs his name became immortal for them.

the good fortune of the King Azd-ul-mulk and Muháfiz Khán fled, and Rájá Bhím and his brother were slain in battle, and Latíf Khán fell wounded into their hands. Sultán Bahádur sent Muhibb-ul-mulk with speed to bring Latíf Khán. Muhibb-ul-mulk taking Latíf Khán returned to meet the Sultán. On the way Latíf Khán died at the village of Murghdarah and they buried him there, removing his body thence after a short time and committing it to the dust under the dome by the side of the dome on the tomb of Sultán Sikandar in the village of Hálol. After this Nasír Khán and three other princes were poisoned and killed by Bahádur Sháh, and were also buried near Sultán Sikandar's shrine. The news of the decapitation of Ḳaisar Khán and the above-mentioned nobles having reached the extremities of Gujarát, Rájá Ráisingh of Pál plundered the town of Dohad. When Sultán Bahádur came to know of this, he ordered Táj Khán to lay waste and pillage the whole country of Pál. About this time Ashraf-ul-mulk, servant of the king, who, in the time of Sikandar Khán, had been taken by Ikbál Khán and confined in the fort of Mándu, was brought thence.[1]

To resume, Táj Khán having entered the Pál mountains laid all Ráisingh's country even with the dust, and the fort of his refuge was dismantled. They say that in the month that Táj Khán remained in the country of Pál on this expedition, that no casualty occurred among Táj Khán's men save in respect of one man by name Hasan Muhammad, who was killed. All the rest of the army returned safe and laden with booty, and were admitted to the honour of kissing the Sultán's feet.

On the 15th of Rabí-ul-awwal, A. H. 933 (A. D. 1526), the Sultán went on a hunting expedition in the direction of Cambay. When he arrived at Cambay, one of the sons of Malik Ayáz named Ilyás, who has been mentioned, came and met the Sultán. He informed the Sultán that his elder brother Is-hák, had become a rebel, at the instigation of the Hindu chiefs of Sorath, and that ruining the good name of his house he had with 5000 horse advanced from Nawánagar and had come to the port of Dív. It was his intention by deceit and stratagem, to enter that island, and, after expelling all the Musalmán soldiers and merchants, to make it over to the *Firangis*. Mehmúd Áká the admiral, learning of this circumstance had filled ships with fighting

---

[1] The vagueness of the text here seems to be the result of some words being omitted.

men and cannon and muskets, and had opposed Is-hák, killing many
Hindus with his artillery. On hearing of these matters, Sultán
Bahádur started by forced marches from Cambay. On the first day he
camped at Manili, thence he marched to Gúndi, thence to Dhandhúka,
thence to Ránpur and from Ránpur to Jasdan. When Is-hák heard
that the Sultán had come in person he fled. He came to the Sorath
frontier, and started for the Ran, which is a creek of salt water.

.   The Sultán came from Jasdan to Wasáwar, and thence he came to
Deoli, a town situated fifteen *kos* from the fort of Júnágadh, and it
was here that news was received that Is-hak had fled in the direction
of the Ran and the Khán Khánán was ordered to pursue that rebel
They say that when Is-hák arrived near the Ran, Tughlak Khán,
who was the officer in charge of the district of Morbi, came quickly to
attack him. Is-hák turning joined battle. Tughlak Khán was defeated. At this time news arrived that the Khán Khánán was coming,
Is-hák crossed the Ran, and the Khán Khánán encamped on the shore
of the Ran.

Sultán Bahádur after parting with the Khán Khánán at Deoli,
remained ten days in that camp, and returning thence came to Mángrol.
From Mángrol he marched to the village of Chorwár, thence to the
town of Pátan in Delwárá, thence to the town of Korinár, and
thence to the town of Korbá or Korbud or Gorpur. He ordered his army
to encamp at Nawánagar or Delwárá and himself went to Dív.
Another son of Malik Ayúz, called Malik Túghá, who was in Dív, was
admitted to the honour of kissing the carpet. The Sultán remained
a month at Dív. After that having entrusted Div to the charge of
Kiwám-ul-mulk, and Júnágadh to Mujáhid Khán Bhíkam, he turned in
the direction of Ahmedábád. About this time he heard that the Ráná
had sent his son Vikramájít with suitable presents to him. From Dív
Sultán Bahádur marched to the town of Talájá, and thence to the port
of Ghoghá, whence by forced marches he went direct to the exalted
city of Ahmedábád halting no where in the way.

The son of Ráná Sángá was admitted to the honour of kissing his
feet, and the Sultán then remained in his capital for one month in
pleasure and enjoyment.

He then went to Cambay, and after a stay there of three days,
he returned to Ahmedábád. After a sojourn of some days in the
capital he went in the direction of Nándod for hunting. The

Rájá of Nándod came and kissed the carpet. Thence the Sultán went to the port of Súrat, and thence embarking in a boat, he went to Ránder, and returning to Súrat he marched in haste and arrived in one day and night at Muhammadábád, and spent the four months of the rains at Muhammadábád Chánpáner. After the rains he gave the son of the Ráná leave to return to Chittaur. In A. H. 934 (A. D. 1527), he again went to the island of Dív, and spent some days there in ease and pleasure. After that he rode one night and at sunrise arrived at Cambay. The rapidity of Sultán Bahádur's movements became proverbial. If any one travelled a long distance in a short time they used to say " he has travelled with the swiftness of Bahádur."

After remaining in Cambay for several days, he again embarked and sailed for the port of Ghogha and from Ghogha again sailed for Dív. He stayed at Dív for two days, and thence embarking on board a boat he returned to Cambay, and from Cambay set out for his capital. On his way thither he ordered the construction of the city walls of Broach. After this he took an army into the country of Wágar, and halted there for some days, and he marched thence, and encamped at Kapadwanj. Here the Rájá of Dúngarpur came, and met him. The Sultán now took his army to Dúngarpur and for some days he amused himself in fishing on the Dúngarpur lake, and sent his army to ravage the territories of certain Hindu chiefs of those parts. After this, the Sultán came to Ahmednagar, and from Ahmednagar he went to Patan to visit the tomb of his great ancestor Sultán Muzaffar, and he bestowed honours, riches and rewards on the learned and the devout of that town and returned to Ahmedábád. From Ahmedábád on the 1st of the month of Shaâbán, he went in one day to Muhammadábád Chámpáner and on the new moon of Ramazán of the above year having left all his army in the city, he himself with some special well-equipped followers went to see the city walls of Broach which had been newly built, and thence on the 9th of the above month he came to Cambay. Here, as one day he was walking on the seashore a ship came from Dív. The people of the vessel said that some *Firangi* ships had arrived at Dív and that Kiwám-ul-mulk had imprisoned all the *Firangis* and taken their property. The Sultán on hearing this went to Dív when Kiwám-ul-mulk produced the *Firangis* before him. The Sultán offered them the choice of Islám and all of them adopted the religion of Islám. After this the Sultán, with the intention of going to Muhammadábád, came to Cambay and thence went to the above city, and became

occupied in enjoyment and pleasure. At this time news arrived
that the Sultán's sister's son Muhammad Khán the son of Ádil
Khán with 2,500 horse had gone to the aid of Imád-ul-mulk of Káwel
which is a fort in the country of Birár. Nizámul-mulk with the
officers whose duty it was to protect the roads of the Dakhan, *viz.*,
Baríd ruler of Bídar and Khudáwand Khán Bantari and Ainul-mulk,
and others having united, fought with Imád-ul-mulk, and Imád-ul-
mulk was defeated. After that a petition of Adil Khán came to the
following effect : " Imád-ul-mulk from the time of the deceased Sultán
Muzaffar up to the time of our Sultán has been a devoted servant of
your kingdom and every year sends a tribute of elephants of war. The
nobles of the Dakhan having united, have expelled him from his
country, and he has no other refuge except your court." Imád-ul-mulk
also sent a petition and explained his condition. On hearing this the
Sultán said, " The nobles of the Dakhan are all oppressors. Imád-ul-
mulk is a victim of oppression and to succour the oppressed is
incumbent on religious kings." On the arrival of these petitions on
the 14th of Zilhajj of the above year in the middle of the rainy season
the Sultán marched and camped at Hálol, and sent orders in all
directions to collect troops. Another petition now came from Imád-ul-
mulk that his people were besieged in the fort of Banhari or Bathri and
that the fort had fallen into the hands of the enemy. On hearing this
the Sultán at once marched, and in the month of Muharram A. H. 935
(A. D. 1528), he arrived at Baroda, and halted there a month.

The author of the *Tárikh-Báhádur-Sháhi* writes that he was then
Dárogháh or superintendent of a department in Cambay, and an order
came also to him, and he joined the army. What he has written he
says he has written as an eyewitness : When the army was
assembled, the Sultán marched from Baroda. At this time Jaâfar
Khán son of Imád-ul-mulk arrived and kissed the Sultán's feet. The
Sultán showed him great kindness and consoled him. When the
victorious army reached Nazarbár, Imád-ul-mulk and Muhammad
Khán came and had an interview. The Sultán conferred favours on
them and bestowed on Imádul-mulk a girdle and a jewelled sword
with a gilt umbrella, and marching thence arrived at the fort of
Gálnah, and from Gálnah marched to Devgad also called Daultábád,
and on the 2nd of the month of Rabí-ul-Ákhir pitched his royal tent
in the vicinity of the fortress of Daultábád. They say that in this

expedition a hundred thousand horsemen and nine hundred elephants
like mountains accompanied the Sultán. When the garrison of Daultábád saw the army of Sultán Bahádur Sháh from their lofty citadel
they began to tremble with fear. Suddenly a part of the army of
Nizám-ul-mulk who lay in ambush behind the hill, commenced fighting
with the van of the Sultán's army. The army of Bahádur Sháh like
the waves of the boisterous sea received the attack of the enemy. The
Dakhanis were defeated. In this battle three noblemen were killed
on the Sultán's side. They were Mukhlis-ul-mulk, Muhib-bul-mulk,
and Muhib-bul-mulk's son. When the army of Nizám-ul-mulk was
defeated, Sultán Bahádur besieged Daulatábád. While so engaged the
ambassador of Nizám-ul-mulk came and told the Sultán that Nizám-
ul-mulk was willing to abide by the order and will of the Sultán. He
demanded an assurance from the Sultán for Nizám-ul-mulk's safety to
allow him to come and pay his respects. The Sultán gave his parole,
and the ambassador took leave stating that in ten days Nizám-ul-mulk
would do himself the honour of waiting upon the Sultán. When the ten
days had passed, another ambassador came and asked for ten days more
and as he showed much humility the Sultán again granted the
delay but said, "If he fails in his promise this time, I will lay
Daulatábád even with the dust, and will up-root its foundations."
When he did not again perform his promise, the Sultán was very
enraged, and ordered the soldiers to attack the fort on every
side, and war with cannons and muskets began, and for twenty days
there was constant fighting. From the extreme strength of
the fort however the chance of victory seemed remote, so the
Sultán marched thence towards Bídar. The ministers, that is, the
agents of Nizám-ul-mulk of Ahmednagar and Barid of Bídar and
Ádil Khán of Bíjápur and Khudáwand Khán Bathri, came to the
Sultán's presence with kingly gifts and after offering their tribute
stated that it appeared from evidence not to be the case that Nizám-
ul-mulk had oppressed Imád-ul-mulk. That Imád-ul-mulk was the
first aggressor inasmuch as he began the dispute by seizing the fort of
Máher from the officers of Nizám-ul-mulk, and that it was in
consequence of this that Nizám-ul-mulk took his revenge on him. Now
they were ready to abide by whatever the Sultán was pleased to
order. As in truth this was the case, the Sultán changed his
mind about punishing Nizám-ul-mulk and having made peace
between him and Imád-ul-mulk of Káwel, he returned towards his

own country and arrived at Muhammádábád on the last day of
Shaábán A. H. 935 (A. D. 1528). He fixed the salaries and allowances
of, and granted picked estates to, and ennobled with rank the numerous
Dakhanis who accompanied him and those that followed him, amounting, on their number being ascertained, to about 12,000 horse. In
the month of Ramzán he went to Ahmedábád to visit the shrines of
his ancestors, and then went to Cambay, and inspected the new ships
he had ordered to be built, and leaving that place on the Ramazán Íd
he went to Muhammadábád. In the month of Shawwál, he entertained and consoled Jám Firúz, King of Sindh, who had been
defeated by the Mughals, and had sought refuge with the Sultán, and
promised that he would restore his country to him. At this time
Narsingh Deva, nephew of Nársingh Rájá of Gwaliar, came to the
Sultán with an army of Rájputs. The Sultán gave him service and an
estate. Prathiráj, brother of Ráná Sángá, also came to the Sultán and
became enrolled among the vassals of the Sultán.

Afterwards in the month of Muharram A. H. 936 (A. D. 1529)
Jaáfar Khán,[1] son of Imád-ul-mulk-Káweli, brought and submitted the
petition of his father, stating that Nizám-ul-mulk had not acted according to his promise, and had neither restored his elephants, nor relinquished the town of Bathri which he took from him with its villages.
If, said he, the sun of Bahádur Sháh's presence once more rose in the
Dakhan, his object would be accomplished. The Sultán ordered the
military officers and paymasters to assemble the army for an expedition
against the Dakhan. On the 2nd of Muharram A. H. 936 (A. D.
1529), having marched from the great city of Muhammadábad, he
encamped at Dabhoi on his way to the Dakhan, and thence marched
on to Dháravli where Muhammad Khán Asiri came and met him.
When he had advanced a few marches Imád-ul-mulk-Káweli also came
and joined him. When the light of the sun of Bahádur Sháh fell on
the fort of Muler, Baharji Rájá of Bagláná was admitted to the
honour of kissing the carpet. The Sultán showed him much kindness, and gave him two magnificent ruby ear-rings. Baharji, by way
of showing his loyalty, gave one of his sisters in marriage to the Sultán,
and the next day at the Sultán's desire, he married another of his sisters
to Muhammad Khán Asíri and the Sultán marched thence. When he
passed the Bagláná frontier, and entered the confines of the Dakhan,
he bestowed on Baharji the title of Bahr Khán, and sent him against

---

1 Farishtah II. 427 says that this was Khizr Khán, the son of Alá-ud-din Imád Sháh.

the port of Chaul with orders to ravage and plunder that country. After that he pressed on by forced marches to Ahmednagar.

The Dhakhanis left the city and fled before the arrival of the Sultán. The Sultán ordered the principal buildings of the city to be levelled to the ground, and the gardens to be laid low. He halted there twelve days, and marched to the Báläghát, and thence sent Mujáhid Khán against the city of Áosá.[1] At this time Imád-ul-mulk said that there was a city in the territories of Khwájah Jahán, called Parinda, which was very prosperous and the greater part of the inhabitants thereof wealthy. The Sultan sent Malik Amín against that city. The Malik went off at once, and plundered Parinda and much property, and countless gold fell into the hands of the soldiery.

It was now reported that Nizám-ul-mulk Bahri, Baríd, Khwájah Jahán, and Khudáwand Khán had united their forces, and with a large army had marched against Asír and Burhánpur. Immediately on hearing this, the Sultán sent Kaisar Khán with a powerful force in pursuit of them. Next day he sent Muhammad Khán Asíri also to join Kaisar Khán with an invincible army and elephants like mountains. This army met the confederate forces of the Dakhan nobles in the country of Burhánpur and a great battle was fought. When the scales of the battle were equal the brave men of Bahádur Sháh's army called out, " Sultán Bahádur is coming." Immediately on hearing the name of the Sultán, the Dakhanis fled and dispersed and the army of the Sultán returned victorious and triumphant.

After the day of the battle, Baríd, ruler of Bídar, made peace with Imád-ul-mulk. Imád-ul-mulk asked for the hand of Baríd's daughter, and they made peace with each other. Imád-ul-mulk begged the Sultán to forgive Baríd, and the Sultán overlooked his fault. Baríd agreed to have the public prayers read and the coin struck in the name of the Sultán, and the Friday sermon was read in Sultán Bahádur's name in most of the cities of the Dakhan. The Sultán marched from Bír to the town of Bathri, and the Dakhan army entrenched themselves in the fort of Bathri. The Sultán ordered the army to be besieged. For some days battle and conflict raged. In the end, the Sultán left Imád-ul-mulk of Káwel there, with Alif Khán to help him and himself returned to his own country. On the last day of the month of Shaábán A. H. 936 (A. D. 1531), the Sultán with some of his chief followers reached by

---

[1] This seems to be a mistake. Farishtah II. 428 says that Bahádur Sháh sent his officers from the Báläghát to reduce the fort of Daulatábád.

forced marches the great city of Muhammadábúd, and on the 12th
of the same month his camp arrived after him. He spent the rainy
season in pleasure and enjoyment in his own capital.[1]

At the commencement of A. H. 937 (A. D. 1529), the Sultán
ordered an expedition to be organized to conquer Wághar. When he
arrived at Khánpur on the river Mahí, he ordered Khán Aázam, Ása
Khán, and Vazír Khudáwand Khán to march against Wághar. The
Sultán himself with a part of the army went to Cambay and Dív, and
on the 20th of the month of Muharram he arrived at Cambay, and
embarking thence on boardship he arrived at Dív, and purchased on
account of Government all the piece-goods and stuffs which had arrived
in the foreign vessels. They say that among that merchandise, besides
other articles, there were one thousand three hundred maunds (about
lbs. 59485)[2] of rose-water imported by the Turks. The Sultán showed
great kindness to the Turks who had come with Mustafa the Turk,
and he assinged them Dív as a place of residence, and having entrusted
Dív to the charge of Málik Túghá, the son of Ayáz, he returned to
Cambay and arrived there on the 5th of the month of Safar, and
halting there for one day, set out for Muhammadábád, and on the
27th of that month arrived in that city. Fateh Khán, Kutb Khán,
and Úmar Khán, Afgháns of the Lodi tribe, and relations of Sultán
Bahlúl, who, flying from the Mughals, had taken shelter in Gujarát,
were admitted to an audience. On the first day three hundred coats
embroidered with gold and fifty-five horses and some lákhs of Tánkáos
were given them as presents. After this the Sultán went towards
Waghar, and joined his camp near Morásá, and thence by forced
marches reached the country of Wághar. Prathiráj, Rájá of Dúngarpúr,
coming to Sambal, obtained the honour of kissing his feet, and the son of
the abovementioned Rájá, adopted the faith of Islám. Leaving his camp
in this place, the Sultán went to hunt alone in the direction of Bánswálá,
and hunted as far as Karji Ghát (east of the town of Bánswara). In this
camp Dúngarsí and Jájarsi, the emissaries of Rájá Ratansi, the Rájá
of Jeypur, came and kissed the Sultan's feet and presented tribute.
After this the Sultán returned to his camp, and bestowed Sambal on the

---

[1] Farishtah II. 428 says that the Gujarát Sultán was, to some extent, forced to leave
the Dakhan. The Dakhan army by occupying the passes had stopped the supplies
reaching the Gujarát camp and a famine began to be dreaded. In the meantime Nizám
Sháh agreed to give up the elephants, &c., captured from Mírán Muhammad Sháh, and as
the rains were near Bahádur left for Gujarát.

[2] A Gujarát maund is forty sers of forty tolas the ser.

new Musalmán, the son of Prathiráj, and gave one-half of Wághar to Prathiráj, and the other half to Changá.

They say that while in this place, one day the Sultán went out tiger hunting. A furious tiger appeared. The Sultán made a signal to Álam Khán. Álam Khán, with great bravery, attacked the tiger and slew him, but was also himself wounded. After four days Álam Khán died leaving four sons, Safdar Khán and three others. The Sultán conferred the estates of Álam Khán on his sons, and treated them very kindly. At this camp the agents of Rájá Ratansi petitioned that Sharzah Khán, with the son of Sultán Mehmúd Khíljí, had ravaged the Ráná's country. The Ráná also hearing this, ravaged and plundered the village of Sambal, a dependency of Málwá, near the city of Sárangpur, and that the Ráná was then engaged in fighting with Sultán Mehmúd Khilji near Ujjain. At this time news came that Sultán Mehmúd desired to slay Sikandar Khán, ruler of the country of Sinwás and Sílahdi (ruler of Ráesen). That both of them had fled to the Ráná, and that Sikandar Khán and Bhúpat Rái, son of Silahdi, were coming to Sultán Bahádur's presence. On the 27th of Jamádul-awwal both of them arrived, and were admitted to the honour of kissing the Sultán's feet and explaining their circumstances. At this moment Darya Khán and Kuraishi Khán, the agents of Sultán Mehmúd, having arrived and represented that Sultán Mehmúd Khilji desired a meeting and was only awaiting the orders of the Sután to approach him. The Sultán said, " Sultán Mehmúd has often written that he was coming, but has never come. Should he come it will be a cause of pleasure to both sides. I am now about to proceed by way of the Karji Ghát. Let him also come that way." The agents hereupon returned.

In short, on the day the Sultán passed the Karjí Ghát, Ráná Ratansi and Sílahdi came and were admitted to the honour of an interview, and thirty elephants and many horses and one thousand and five hundred handsome gold embroidered coats were bestowed on them both. After a few days Ráná Ratansi took his leave and returned to his capital, and Sikandar Khán and Sílehdi and Dalpat Rái and the Rájá of Idár and the Rája of Wághar and Dúngarsi and Jájarsi, the agents of Ráná Ratansi, all went in the retinue of the Sultán.

The Sultán said : " Sultán Mehmúd Khilji is also going to Sambal, so let us go there. We shall meet him there and come away." Muhammad Khán Asíri also was with him. The author of the *Tárikh-*

i-*Bahádur Sháhi* writes that he was present with the Sultán in this expedition, and that what he has written is from personal knowledge. When the Sultán came to the village of Sambal, he was in daily expectation of the arrival of Sultán Mehmúd. At that time an ambassador of Sultán Mehmúd Khilji came, and represented that Sultán Mehmúd had broken his arm by a fall from his horse while hunting in the country of Sanwás, and that his arrival would, in consequence, be delayed for some days. The Sultán said : " I will go to Mándu to enquire after his health, and there I will also see some one else." The ambassador then said that with regard to the demand of the Sultán fo the surrender of Chánd Khán[1] from Sultán Mehmúd that Sultán Mehmúd said that he considered Chánd Khán, the son of his sovereign who had taken shelter with him, and he could not commit such a base act as to hand him over. Sultán Bahádur said, " I do not want the surrender of Chánd Khán from Sultán Mehmúd, but tell him he should come." The ambassador returned, and the Sultán marching came to Dibálpur. News now came that Sultán Mehmúd had given his elder son the title of Sultán Ghiásuddin and sent him to Mándu to entrench himself within the fort of Mándu, intending himself to remain outside and ravage the country, thus refusing to perform his promise. This circumstance greatly enraged the Sultán. Shortly after this Fateh Khán Shirwáni and Álam Khán, nobles of Sultán Mehmúd, deserted their master, and joined Sultán Bahádur, and incited him to take Mándu. When the Sultán arrived at Dhár Sharzah Khán also came over to him from the fortress of Mándu. He said that Sultán Mehmúd wanted to kill him, and that he only saw his safety in flight, and had come under Sultán Bahádur's protection. The Sultán consoled him; and moved thence to the village of Diláwarah[2] and thence came and encamped at Naálchah. He appointed Muhammad Khán Asiri to erect his batteries at Sháhpur, which is on the west of the fort, and Alif Khán to command the batteries at Bahlúlpur, and the batteries of the Hindus who had accompanied him in this expedition, were placed at Bahlwárá or Bhílwárah. He himself with joy and good fortune, making a short march, alighted on the 20th of Rajab at Mehmúdpúr. Satisfactory arrangements

---

[1] This Chand Khán was the refugee half brother of Sultán Bahádur who first caused ill-feeling between Bahadúr Sháh and Mehmúd II. of Málwa, and who after the conquest of Mandu by Bahádur, betook himself to Goa and caused the breach between Bahádur and the Portuguese, which ultimately led to Bahádur's assassination.

[2] A village named probably after Diláwar Khán Ghori (A D. 1387-1405) fourteen miles north-west of Mándu.

for the blockade and siege of the fort were now completed and the brave men of both sides commenced to fight, and cannon and muskets were fired on both sides. Some time passed thus.

One day the Sultán sent brave and fearless men to reconnoitre the fort and see on which side the heights surrounding it were most lofty. After examination they reported that on the side of Songad-Chittauri the height is the greatest. The Sultán said, " If God wills, I will scale the fort on that side." Men in astonishment said, "This is the steepest of all ascents to the fort ; how will it be possible for the Sultán to succeed by that route ?" On the 29th of the month of Shaábán, the Sultán consulted with the Khán Khánán and some other of his special associates, and mounting early in the night went towards Songad-Chittauri. The main body of the army were ignorant of this enterprise of the Sultán. They say that as the Songad-Chittauri side of the fortress was very lofty, and ascent by that way very precipitous, the garrison convinced of the security of that side were careless of defence. The brave men of Bahádur Sháh's army ascended the fortress on that side during the night, and in the morning shouting ' Alláh! Alláh!' attacked the garrison in the courtyard of the fort and cried out that Sultán Bahádur had come. Immediately on hearing the name of Sultán Bahádur, the garrison fled. Sultán Bahádur with a body of his men scaled the citadel walls of Songad-Chittauri. When the army of Bahádur Sháh witnessed this they swarmed up like ants and locusts to occupy the fort. Habib Khán, who was one of Sultán Mehmúd's most distinguished nobles, commenced to fight, but was repulsed in the first assault. Sultán Mehmud with many elephants hastened to support him. But when he saw the regal umbrella of Sultán Bahádur he was unable to oppose him, and fleeing with 1,000 horsemen took shelter in his palace. For one hour the hand of slaughter and capture remained high. After that quarter and amnesty were proclaimed. This happened on the 29th of Shaábán A. H. 937 (A. D. 1529-30).

Sultán Mehmúd was besieged in his palace and saw that the only means of escape was by begging favour and forgiveness. So coming with his seven sons, he paid his respects to the Sultán. The Sultán entrusted Sultán Mehmúd and his sons to confidential keepers. On the 12th of the month of Muharram (H. 938 A.D. 1530-31) the Sultán made over the custody of Sultán Mehmúd and his sons to Alif Khán, Ikbál Khán and Ásaf Khán with orders to take them to Gujarát. When the abovementioned nobles arrived with them near Dohad, which is on the Gujarát frontier Ráisingh Rájá of Pál with his *Kolis* fell upon them with the intention of rescuing Sultán Mehmúd from their hands. The guards who were at that time round the Sultán's palanquin slew him in the tumult, and carrying his sons to Muhammadábád, confined them there.

All the country of Mándu fell into the hands of the Sultán Bahádur who showed kindness to the nobles of Mándu, and continued their estates to them. He appointed Malik Kálu, sister's son of Alif Khán their chief, and made him the military commander for the country to guard and protect it and strive in its prosperity.

On the 12th of Shawwál of the above year, *i.e.*, A. H. 938 (A. D. 1530-31) news arrived from Gujarát that Mánsingh, Rájá of Jhálúwár, which is a portion of the districts of Gujarát, comprising the town of Víramgúm, Mándal, Wadhwán, and others, had made an incursion and fought with Sháh Jíva, son of Sheikhan Saláhdár, and had slain Sháh Jíva. The Sultán ordered the Khán Khánán, as Jháláwár was under him, and as Mansingh had rendered himself liable to severe chastisement, to consider himself responsible for reprisal and to proceed to Gujarát. The Khán Khánán agreeably to the exalted order set out for Gujarát. On the 9th of the above month Muhammad Khán Asíri obtained leave, and in the month of Zilhajj, Salahdi also took leave to depart for Ráisen which was his residence. The rainy season now setting in, the Sultan with happiness and satisfaction spent it in the fort of Mándu, and at the close of the rains on the 9th of the month of Safar A. H. 938 (A. D. 1531), went in the direction of Burhánpur and Asír. When he reached Burhánpur, Sháh Táhir Dakhani, who was the most distinguished man of the Dakhan in poetry, and the elegant arts came on the part of Nizám-ul-mulk to the Sultán. At that time in the court of the Gujarát Sultán also, there were men of as high intellectual attainments as Sháh Táhir, like Sháh Mír, Sháh Kamáluddín Asláf and Sháh Abú Turáb, who possessed the privilege of seats in the Sultán's presence. Sháh Táhir also wished to be permitted the honour of a seat in the Sultán's presence. The Sultán through his minsiters and companions agreed to this on condition, that on the occasion of his first entry into the royal presence he should deliver the message of Nizám-ul-mulk standing, after which he was to take his seat; and Sháh Táhir did so.

The drift of the message brought by Sháh Táhir was that Nizám-ul-mulk was desirous of the title of Nizám Sháh. If granted this title,

would always accept the Gujarát Sultan's overlordship and would remain
over ready to render him liege-service. On the delivery of this message
the Sultán said, "If Nizám-ul-mulk is to be called Nizám Sháh, what
difference would there be between him and me?" Sháh Táhir said,
"There will still be a great difference; up to this moment Bahádur Sháh
has been the king of nobles, but now he will be known as king of kings."
The Sultán was pleased at this speech, and approved of Sháh Táhir's
endeavours, and bestowed on Nizám-ul-mulk the regal umbrella, and
from that day whoever sat on the throne of Ahmednagar was styled
Nizám Sháh.

It is said that when Sháh Táhir was admitted to the honour of
kissing the carpet, some merchants of Khurásán, who used to
trade in Gujarát, asked him to speak in their behalf to Malik
Túghá bin Ayáz, who was a slave of the Sultán, and the *Mír Bahr*
or lord high admiral of the Gujarát ports, to be pleased to remit the
customs dues amounting to Rs. 30,000 on the goods imported by
them. The Sháh said, "He is a haughty slave, and I do not like to go
to him." The merchants said, "If by your once going to him and
by one word of yours, our object can be attained, to delay would be far
from generous." The Sháh reluctantly went to his house. The Malik
without getting up to receive the Sháh made him a signal to sit down.
The Sháh saw in his appearance great haughtiness and dignity,
but he interceded for the merchants in a standing posture. The
Malik having granted his prayer said : " I will remit their customs duty
now and also hereafter, so that whenever in the future they bring any merchandise no one shall annoy them." He also gave the Sháh Rs. 60,000
as a present with many valuable pearls, each of which was considered
by pearl merchants fit for a king's ransom. They say that when
the news of this meeting reached the Sultán, he was angered with
Malik Túghá, and said, "Oh ill-fated one, why did you not
get up to receive Sháh Táhir." He replied, "Since that rebellious slave
Nizám-ul-mulk does not rise for him, I, who am a loyal slave of my
master, why should I get up to receive him?" The application of
the word ' rebellious ' to Nizám-ul-mulk was in allusion to the circumstance that Nizám-ul-mulk and his ancestors were slaves of Mahmúd
Bahmani, and had, by usurpation and violence, attained to royal rank.

To resume, afterwards Nizám-ul-mulk came and met the Sultán.
The Sultán received him with kindness, and bestowed on him the title
of Sháh. At this time he also bestowed on Muhammad Khán Asíri
the title of Muhammad Sháh, and he himself returned to Mándu, and

22

thence sent Malik Amín to Ráisen to fetch Silahdi. Although the
Malik pursuaded him much, Silahdi was unwilling to come. The Malik
wrote to the king, that although he had given him thirty millions of
tánkáhs as a present and bestowed on him a city like Ujjain and the
district of Ashta, and the estates of Bhílsah and besides these, elephants
and horses such as he had never seen before, yet Silahdi was behaving
traitorously and was not willing to come. He moreover entertained
thoughts of flying to Mewar. It was finally stated that this accursed
one in fact deserved death since he had wrested Muslim women from
their husbands and had kept them in his house as concubines. On
hearing this the flame of rage was lighted in the Sultán's bosom, and he
ordered Mukbil Khán, brother of the Vazír Ikhtiyár Khán, who was an
administrator as clever and wise as the famous Persian minister Amír
Ali Sher and to whom the rule of the capital was entrusted, to go by
forced marches to Muhammadabad, and start off thence with an army
and treasure to Sultán Bahádur's camp in Málwa. The Sultán himself
encamped at Naâlchah, and, by way of stratagem, gave out that he was
going to Gujarát lest Silahdi should awake from his dormouse sleep and
becoming aware of the destination of the Sultán's expedition flee the
country.

COUPLET.

"When Alexander the Great had to lead an army against the eastern nations
He used to pitch his tents facing the west."

Bhúpat Rái, the son of Silahdi, who was in the presence of
the Sultán, suspected the real design of the Sultán and mortally afraid
of the Sultán's anger, petitioned for leave to bring Silahdi. The
Sultán gave him leave, and leaving his army at Naâlchah, went himself
alone towards Dibálpur to hunt. Silahdi made certain that the Sultán
was going to Gujarát. He thought he would go to see the Sultán
and would obtain presents from him, and leaving his son in Ujjain,
he came to kiss the Sultán's feet. Malik Amín Nas said: "When
Silahdi became assured that the Sultán was going to Gujarát, and I
promised to get him from the Sultán one hundred thousand gold tánkás
and the revenues of Cambay with a hundred Arab horses, it was only then
that he started; had it not been so he would never have set out to come
to the Sultán." The Sultán said, "This wretch keeps Muhammadan
women in his house, and by the holy Law of the Prophet he deserves
death. I will never let him go alive unless he becomes a Musalmán."
Then marching from Naâlchah he came to Dhár, and on the 20th of

Rabí-ul-Akhir of the above year A. H. 938 (A. D. 1531). Ikhtiyár Khán with a numerous army, a train of artillery and much treasure arrived at Naálchah and was admitted to the honour of kissing the Sultán's feet, and on the 17th of Jamádul-awwal Silahdi and two of his men were imprisoned in one of the palaces of Naálchah. The army of Silahdi went to his son at Ujjain, and his camp was plundered by the people and the army and some few of his men killed and they brought all his elephants to the Sultán. At the sunset of that same day Imád-ul-mulk was sent against the son of Silahdi, and at the first watch on the night of the 17th of the above month the Sultán marched for Ujjain. When he reached Saádalpur, he ordered Khudá-wand Khán to bring the camp after him and himself pressing on reached Ujjain. Imád-ul-mulk accompanied the Sultán and represented that the son of Silahdi had fled, before the arrival of the army at Ujjain. On the 18th of that month the district of Ashta, which originally belonged to Hasan Khán of Mándu, was restored to him, and Ujjain was given in fief to Daryá Khán of Mándu. The Sultán marching rapidly came to Sárangpur, and halted there for two days until his camp overtook him. He gave the estate of Sárangpur to Mallú Khán as he, from the commencement of the Sultán's rule, had been in his service.

Afterwards he went towards Bhílsa which country had been converted to Islám by Sultán Shamsud-dín (Altamsh), king of Dehli. Since eighteen years the estate of Bhílsa had been subject to Silahdi, and the laws of Islám had been changed there for the customs of infidelity. When the Sultán reached the above place, he abrogated the ordinances of infidelity and introduced the laws of Islám, and slew the idolators and threw down their temples. On the 17th of Jamádul Ákhir he marched from Bhílsa and went in the direction of the fort of Ráisen and pitched his tents on the bank of a river which is two *kos* (four miles) from Ráisen, and leaving that camp also on the 18th, he encamped near a masonry tank close to the fort of Ráisen. At this moment an army was seen issuing from the fort. The Sultán mounted with a few chosen men and before the news of his having done so reached his army, he attacked the enemy, and it is said so wielded the sword that he cut those of the enemy he sabered in twain. The unbelievers fled, entered the fort, and the army attacked the fort on all sides, and a war with arrows and muskets and catapults and a fierce cannonade commenced. At sunset the Sultán ordered the belligerents

to retire to the camps, vowing destruction to the fort and its occupants
with the morrow's sunrise. In the morning the Sultán appointed his
nobles to the charge of the different batteries. Rúmi Khán, who, as an
artillery man was peerless of the age in an instant, threw down a bastion
of the fort by his well-directed fire, but the Hindus immediately repaired
the breach. The Sultán now sent a thousand of his Dakhani foot with
orders to root up a bastion by the foundations, and on every side orders
were given to dig mines and fill them with powder and spring
them. They say every one performed zealously the duty entrusted to
him, and they undermined and threw down the walls making a gap of
the length of an arrow's flight. When Silahdi saw this, he besought the
Sultán saying he was ready to embrace Islám and give up the
fort to the slaves of the Sultán. The Sultán agreed, and Silahdi
became a Musalmán, and Lakhman Sen, his brother, who was in the
fort, being sent for, also kissed the feet of the Sultán. After this,
these two brothers sat in consultation. Lakhman Sen objected to the
surrender of the fort, stating that Bhúpat had gone to the Rána
and was coming with the Rána's son Bikramájít, at the head of
40,000 horse and countless infantry to their help. That he, Silahdi,
had become a Muslim, and that the Sultán would on this account not
look upon their project with suspicion, while he, Lakhman Sen would
retain the fort until the arrival of the succour. Silahdi was pleased at
this proposal, and going to the Sultán, asked leave for the return of
Lakhman Sen to the fort, stating that he (Lakhman Sen) would give
up the fort to-morrow. The Sultán gave him leave. In the morning
they waited six hours for Lakhman Sen's return, but he came not.
Silahdi asked orders to go to the foot of the hill and ascertain the
cause of his brother's delay. The Sultán sent a troop with him, and
he went, but no one came to him from the garrison. Silahdi called out
from below:—"Oh! Rájputs, why will you be slain? The
Sultán's army will enter by this fallen bastion and kill you one by
one." By this he meant indirectly to convey the hint:— You
should repair and fortify this place, since this is the place whereby you
will meet with your death. He said other words akin to these, and
returned. They recounted the facts to the Sultán, and he was moved
to great anger. About this time, the younger son of Silahdi, with 2,000
horse, came and attacked the Sultán's outpost at Parsah or Birsáh.
Victory ultimately remained with the Musalmáns. On being defeated,
Silahdi's son repaired to Bikramájít and his elder brother Bhúpat.

Some of the chief men of his party were killed, and their heads were brought to the Sultán. At this time a report went round that Silahdi's younger son was slain, and it was his head that was sent to the Sultán. This threw Silahdi into great grief, and the Sultán's anger increased proportionately. He (the Sultán) said to Burhán-ul-mulk, "Had Silahdi not embraced Islám, I would have ordered him to be cut to pieces. Take him for the present to Mándu and keep him in imprisonment there, for we shall want him anon." As the Rána had given an army to Bhúpat and sent his son to his aid, the Sultán sent Muhammed Sháh Asíri and Itimád Khán against the Ráná's son, and also appointed another force to be sent against them. They marched quickly, and when they reached the town of Bersiá, news arrived that the son of the Rána was coming with an immense army. Next day, marching constantly, they arrived and encamped at the village of Kherad. Púranmal, son of Silahdi, who, with two thousand horse, was in this village fled without fighting. Imád-ul-mulk from his camp at Bersiá sent to the Sultán an account of the vastness of the Rána's army, and of its approach to aid the victims of the Sultán's wrath. On hearing this the Sultan said, " Though Muhammed Sháh and Imád-ul-mulk have sufficient forces to oppose the Rána, still it would be better if I were present in this engagement. I shall try if Alláh wills to capture these unbelievers alive. So thinking, he left Ikhtiyár Khán in charge of the siege of Ráisen and pressed on seventy *kos* by forced marches and in one day and night joined the army with thirty horse. The spies of the Rána informed him of this—and not daring to oppose Sultán Bahadur, the Rána retired one day's march from the camp in which he then was, and sent his agents as spies to the Sultán, with a message to the effect that he had heard that the guards who were in charge of Silahdi did not give him food and drink, and were otherwise harsh in their treatment of him. That he had sent his son Bikramájit to entreat the Sultán on his behalf, hoping to produce kindness in the Sultán's mind for him. If the Sultán ordered Bikramájit would seek the (Sultán's) presence. The Sultán said: "Let him come!" The agents returned to the Rána and said they had personally seen the Sultán and his army, and that his (the Rána's) army was no match for it. On hearing this the Rána fled the same night to his country.

At this time, news arrived that Alif Khán with 36,000 horse and cannon and innumerable elephants, had come from Gujarát and was near at hand. The Sultán sent a message to him that the Rána had disappeared like smoke, and that he was pursuing him with a powerful army and with great speed. He also with great haste joined in the pursuit. They say that in one day and night the Sultán traversed seventy *kos* and arrived at Chittaur. But before his arrival the Rána had entered the fortress. He then resolved to capture this fort after satisfactorily concluding the siege of Ráisen. He returned thence and came to Ráisen when the garrison despairing of succour expressed their readiness to surrender the fort if Silahdi were recalled from Mándu. The Sultán on his part desired to obtain the fort by treaty or surrender wishing to save the Muhammadan women who were believed to be in the fort, and whom he feared the Rájputs would burn alive in the " *Juhár*" (or ceremony of cremating the women alive) that they would celebrate, if it was taken by storm. In short, he sent for Silahdi from Mándu, in accordance with the request of the besieged. Silahdi came, and taking the Sultán's word for his brother Lakhmansen's safety sent for him from the fort, and he was admitted to the honour of kissing the feet of the Sultán. Then returning to the fort Lakhmansen quietly ordered the greater part of the Rájputs there to descend. He then represented that in Silahdi's zenána there were seven or eight hundred women, chief of whom was his wife Durgá, the mother of Bhúpat.[1] It was her request that he (Silahdi) should go over there and lead back the women below. The Sultán ordered Malik Ali Sher, the son of Kiwámul-mulk, to take Silahdi up and bring him gently back. Malik Ali Sher and Silahdi went up to the fort. The Malik saw that many Rájputs had assembled in the mansion of Silahdi. Silahdi went and sat amongst them in consultation. They asked him what the Sultán intended to give him. He said the Sultán had promised to give him the district of Baroda. They said, " Oh ! Silahdi, thou hast reached the end of thy life, why dost thou lose thy honour ? We have determined that our men should die sword in hand, and that the women should die in the *Juhár* flames by self-immolation. If you have any shame join us in this design." They then so worked upon his feelings by the relation of the traditions of their clan that Silahdi agreed to their wishes. He called Malik Ali Sher and showed him the grandeur of his house at which the Malik was struck with amaze. He told the Malik how all his

---

[1] According to Farishtah II. 436—37, this heroic lady, the mother, and not the wife, of Bhúpat was the daughter of the Rána Sánga of Chittaur. Farishtah calls her Durgávati.

wives and women had determined to die in the flames of the *Juhár* and how he was ashamed to survive them. He requested the Malik to return and say how he had resolved to die with them. The Malik did his best to persuade him, but he would not be shaken in his resolve. When Malik Ali Sher had reached the foot of the hill, the Hindus lighted the *Júhár*-fire and the men sallied out fighting desparately until they were all killed by the Dakhani and other soldiers who had ascended the fort. They say that the seven hundred wives of Silahdi, and the wives and daughters of the other Rájputs and the daughter of the Rána, the wife[1] of Bhúpat, the son of Silahdi, threw themselves together into the flames and were reduced to ashes. The casualty on the Muslim side was four killed. Many of the wives and daughters of the Rájputs were captured. This happened in the month of Ramazán A. H. 938 (A. D. 1531). It is related that Durga (the chief wife of Silahdi) forced all the Musalmán women kept by Silahdi to enter the pile, and they were all reduced to ashes except one whom Heaven saved from this Nimrodian holocaust and who came forth alive from the flames. The Sultán bestowed all the ornaments of the burned women on Burhán-ul-mulk Bunyáni, one of the famous nobles, and that nobleman accepted them. His acceptance was much condemned by generous-minded men of the day, who said it was not meet for an honourable man to accept such wealth. But the Malik deemed it lawful prize obtained in war.

Reliable people say that when Silahdi was imprisoned and asked to accept Islám, he would on no account agree, and it was with great difficulty that he did himself the honour of entering Islám, and was named Saláh-ud-din. It was ordered that Malik Burhán-ul-mulk Bunyáni, who was unequalled in probity and religious devotion, should attend to the religious instruction of the man and should inculcate on him the principles of the Sacred Law. It is said that when Silahdi first observed the fasts of the month of Ramazún, he was much pleased and said he had never found food and water taste so exquisitely delicious as they did after a fast. He used to say that while yet a Hindu he once asked a Brahman whether there was a way to forgiveness for the innumerable sins and short-comings of which he was guilty. The Brahman said there was none. He then asked a Musalmán Mulla the same question, and the Mulla said there certainly was hope of forgiveness for the worst of sinners, but the Mulla said he was afraid to say by what

---

[1] See note, preceding page.

way he could get salvation. Silahdi said that when he assured the
Mulla of his safety, he said that if a sinner entered Islám with a truly
penitent heart he would become as pure as a babe new-born. He
said he was really inclined towards Islám in the fullest sense of the term
from that day. They say that there were in his possession such vessels
and clothes and perfumes and things as were hardly owned by any
other king of the period. He had four troupes of dancing-girls, each
of whom was peerless in her own particular art. At the time when
these women gave their performances forty of them used to stand
holding lamps. Each one of these forty had two servants, one of whom
held betel leaves and the other scented oil (to feed the lamps). These
serving women also were decked with jewels and cloth of gold and other
ornaments. The wise men of the period used to verify in the luxury of
Silahdi the saying of the Prophet (on whom be peace): "The world
is a paradise for unbelievers and a prison for true believers." The
saying most appropriately applied to Silahdi. After the conquest of
Ráisen, together with all the cities that were under Silahdi's rule,
such as the districts of Bhilsah and Chanderi, &c., all these were
entrusted to Sultán Alam Lodi, who was a relative of Sultán Sikandar
Lodi who, about this time was expelled from Kálpi by Násiruddín
Humáyún Padsháh and had taken shelter with the Sultán with ten
thousand horse and numerous elephants. The reason of the expulsion
of Sultán Alam from Kalpi was as follows:—Mír Nizám-ud-dín Ali
Khalífah, the vazír of Bábar Pádsháh, had adopted Sultán Alam as a
son and took great interest in his welfare and had given him charge of
the district of Kálpi. Some years passed in this way and by the
Divine decree Bábar died, and the royal authority passed from his hands
to those of his son by Divine ordinance. The idea of rebellion now
entered the mind of Sultán Álam. When information of this
reached Humáyún, he ordered, Hindál Mírza with several other
famous nobles to chastise the impossible aspirations of Sultán Álam,
who gave battle to the Mírza at the village of Kánpúr in the vicinity
of Kálpi, and notwithstanding superiority in numbers, was defeated.
After that he came to Sultán Bahádur and entered his service.

After the conquest of Ráisen, Sultán Bahádur ordered Muhammad
Sháh Asíri to march against and capture Gágraon (where the Saint
Miyán Mítha lies enshrined) and which was taken by the Rána from
Sultán Mehmúd Khilji. · The Sultán himself went to Gondwánah to

hunt elephants. He caught many elephants and in one day captured the fort of Kánúr—which, during the reign of Sultán Násir-ud-dín, Emperor of. Dehli (A.D. 1316—1320) had gone into the hands of the Hindus, and which Silahdi also had often tried to subdue without success. He entrusted it to Alif Khán, and having subdued Islámábád, Hushangábád, and other territories of Málwa which were subordinate to those parts, and which had again passed into the hands of the local chiefs, he returned to the town of Sárangpur. He then went to the town of Akru, whence he went to Gágraon. This fort had held up to the time of the Sultán's arrival, but immediately on the Sultán's going, it gave in. The Sultán encamped four days in the neighbourhood of Gagraon and sent Malik Imád-ul-mulk from this place to Mandesúr, and after some days appointed Vazír Ikhtiár Khán also with Muhammad Sháh Asíri to that place. The Sultán himself returned to Mándu. Immediately on Imád-ul-mulk's going, Naku, the agent of the Rána, left Mandesúr, and Imád-ul-mulk took Mandesúr in the month of Shawwál. At this time the monsoons set in, and Muhammad Sháh, Ikhtiár Khán and Imád-ul-mulk having left Pír, the son of I'záz-ul-mulk, with a strong force at Mandesúr, left for Mándu which they reached in the month of Zilkaád and obtained the honor of kissing the royal feet. Muhammad Sháh now took leave for Asír and the Sultán departed for his capital, and on the 16th of the month of Safar arrived at Muhammadábád. After a few days, news came that the *Firangís*, with many ships, were coming to take Dív.[1] Immediately on hearing this the Sultán made a forced march and arrived at Cambay in one night. On hearing the news of the Sultán's arrival the *Firangís* fled, and the Sultán visited Dív and sent the great Egyptian cannon brought by Rúmi Khán with a hundred other pieces of ordnance, with the intention of the conquest of Chittaur to Muhammad-ábád. They say that besides many bullocks that they used to harness to this gun, 300 sailors used to be required to drag it along, and then only could it move.

After this the Sultán came to Cambay and from there to Ahmedá-bád to visit the shrines of his ancestors and went to visit the tomb of his Saint Sheikhji, the grandson of Kutb-ul-aktáb, at Batwah. Here he enlisted several thousand new men and made a large collection of arms

---

[1] This seems to have been the formidable expedition of 400 vessels and 15,600 men collected by the Portuguese Viceroy Nuno da Cunha at Bombay, which was repulsed off Dív on the 17th February 1531. Briggs' Muhammadan Power in India, IV. 132.

and sent them on to Mándu, and sent an order to Muhammad Sháh Asíri to start from Asír to join in the conquest of Chittaur. He ordered Vazír Khudáwand Khán with the army in Mándu to join Muhammad Sháh. When the artillery and arms had reached Mándu the Sultán on the 17th Rabí-ul-ákhir started by forced marches for Mándu and reached that city on the third day, and ordered Muhammad Sháh Asíri and Khudáwand Khán to march on to Chittaur. When the abovementioned persons reached Mandesúr, the Rána's emissaries came and petitioned that the Rána was willing to cede such portions of Málwa as were in his possession, to subscribe to any terms the Sultán might see fit to impose and further to acknowledge the suzerainty of the Sultán and perform any service demanded of him. Muhammad Sháh sent Shujáàt Khán to the Sultán to submit the petition of the Rána. The Sultán being excessively displeased at the reprehensible conduct of the Rána in coming to the aid of Silahdi, had made up his mind to conquer Chittaur and the petition of the Rána was not granted. Muhammad Sháh and Khudáwand Khán were instructed to order Tátár Khán, the son of Aláuddín, the son of Sultán Behlúl Lodi, to push on with a large body of Gujarátis, and take the initiative in laying siege to Chittaur, and to follow Tátár Khán with all the pieces of ordnance in their train. On getting the order Tátár Khán, taking the Gujarát army, pushed on to Chittaur. The historian of *The Bahádur Sháhi* says that he also was with the army. Tátár Khán expected that the Rána who had a large army would certainly give battle, but the Rána did not dare to take the offensive. On the 14th Rajjab A. H. 939 (A. D. 1532) Tátár Khán conquered and pillaged the lower portion of the fortifications. Next day he directed his attack to the portion called the Kotháh, and took it also carrying two out of the seven gates of the fort of Chittaur, and wrote his despatches to the Sultán. On the eighth day Muhammad Sháh and Khudáwand Khán arrived with the great cannon and artillery and besieged the fort on all four sides. After that the Sultán making a forced march pressed on at the head of 5,000 horse in one day and night from Mándu to Chittaur, and the army like a line of ants or a swarm of locusts poured in after him. The Sultán, ascending the hill of Chittaur, ordered the cannon to be brought up that they might be able thence to batter down the walls of the fort of Chittaur. At each discharge of the guns great masses of the masonry of the walls went rolling, and whole streets went crumbling down. They say

that the Sultán took personally such great pains in the siege of
Chittaur as exceeded the endeavours of even private soldiers. He
appointed Alif Khán to the battery on the side of the Lakhota gate,
Tátár Khán and Medáni Rái and most of the Afgháns to the batteries
against the Hanúmán gate, and he entrusted the White Bastion to
Mallú Khán and Sikandar Khán and several Málwa nobles and Dakhan
soldiers, and placed Bhúpatrái and Alif Khán in another quarter.

The author of *the Bahádur Sháhi* states that in this expedition
the Sultán had such a strong armament and munitions of war so ample
as would have sufficed for the simultaneous siege of four forts like
Chittaur with the certainty of success.

In short he laid siege to the fort and sent parties on all sides to
ravage the territories of the Rána.

They say that the scientific abilities displayed by Rùmi Khán in
the siege of Chittaur were unparalelled. His conveying his guns up
lofty hills opposite the fort, his adjusting of their aims, his mining and
running up of approaches so quickly was such as simply to render the
besieged helpless.

When the walls of Chittaur began to show breaches from the cannonade on all sides, the garrison perceived that the fort would soon
be conquered. The mother of Vikramájit, who was the chief wife of
the late Rána Şánga, sent emissaries and submitted that her son was an
old servant of the Sultán, and that he used to remain in Gujarát in
the Sultán's service. The old lady also stated with great humility
that the Sultán should overlook his fault, and by pardoning him grant
her a new lease of life. That he would ever after remain in his
service and never disobey his commands, considering the vassalage
an honour. That he would cede all that portion of Málwa which was
conquered from Sultán Mehmúd Khilji, and give the Sultán as tribute
the gold waistband, and crown and cap belonging to Sultán Mehmúd
Khilji, together with several jewels of which jewellers were unable
to compute the value, which had fallen into the hands of the Rána
on the day of the defeat of Sultán Mehmúd Khilji. Besides these
valuable stones, the Rána agreed to give ten millions of *tánkahs*, a
hundred horses and ten elephants.

As this petition from the mother of Vikiramájit was reasonable, the
Sultán agreed to it, and taking this tribute, on the 27th of Shaában

retired from Chittaur and halted a *kos* thence, and sent Burhán-ul-mulk and Mujáhid Khán with a strong army to conquer the fort of Ranthambor, and the towns under it.   He sent Malik Shamsher with twelve nobles against the fort of Ajmere, and himself on the 5th of the holy month of Ramazán, marched in the direction of Mandisúr, arriving in the town on the fourth day.   Halting there one day, on the 10th of the above month, he started off the camp for Màndu, and after two days making a forced march and travelling eighty miles in one day and night he reached Mándu, and on the 18th of that month, his camp followed him.   The Sultán sojourned some time in Mándu in happiness and enjoyment.   After some time he sent Muhammad Sháh Fárúki, with several celebrated nobles of Gujarát, against Nizám-ul-mulk Dakhni, with instructions to in co-operation with Imádul-mulk Kàwíli, expel Nizám-ul-mulk from his country and obtain possession of it.   Should he offer resistance, they were to stay and send for the Sultán, and he would hasten to them and capture this artful foe alive.   Muhammad Sháh started.   When he arrived at the village of Bír, Nizám-ul-mulk and Malik Baríd with a large army opposed him.   Muhammad Sháh sent this information by swift couriers to the Sultán.   Immediately on getting it the Sultán mounted a horse named " *Kúchak*," or the Little, who in fleetness equalled the wind, and with 12,000 picked horsemen from his powerful army set out with speed.   He arrived at Bír, in time to see the two armies drawn up against each other in line of battle with rock-like elephants in front, firing at each other.   At this time the sound of the drums of the advanced guard of the Sultán's army reached the combatants.   The Gujarátis began to hail one another, proclaiming the arrival of their Sultán.   As soon as the Dakhanis heard this, they fled, many of them falling victims to the destroying sword and spear of the Gujarát warriors.   Of the nobles of the Sultán's army the sons of Darya Khàn Bádhel fell wounded in the field.   They were taken up alive, and the Sultán showed them great kindness, and gave the eldest the titles of his father and doubled his wealth and estates, and said : " Whoever wishes to obtain the titles of his father, let him obtain them as these boys have done."

In short, after some days Nizám-ul-mulk came and saw the Sultán and wore the ear-ring of submission.   His territories were made over to him and he remained in Sultán Bahádur's retinue for some marches before he took leave.

The desire of conquering Chittaur again took possession of the Sultán's heart.   About this time Muhammad Zamán Mírza, grandson of

Sultán Husein Mírza Bábakra, King of Khurásán, who had married
Maásúmah Begam, one of the daughters of the emperor Bábar, and
sister of the emperor Humáyún, came and presented himself before
Sultán Bahádur. The fact was that this prince being of the blood royal
of the house of Timúr had aspirations to the throne, wherefore he was
confined in the citadel of Agra by Humáyún. When the emperor
Humáyún made his first expedition to the East to subdue Patna,
Báyazíd Afghán and Muhammad Zamán Mírza fleeing came and sought
shelter with Sultán Bahádur. This sowed the first seed of strife
between the Sultán and Humáyún. Then commenced a correspondence
between Sultán Bahádur and the emperor Humáyún which had for its
object the demand that Muhammad Zamán should not be given
refuge.[1] The style of the second letter from Humáyún to Sultán Bahádur is produced here verbatim :—

"After acting upon the laws of thanks to and praise of the
Almighty to Whom be glory for His bounties and after laudations to
the Prophet on whom be peace be it stated that when Kázi Abdul Kádir
and Muhammad Mukím reached this celestial threshold and gave
information of the ratification of the agreements and treaties (between
our governments) the hope of the restoration of good understanding
between ourselves which is the sure source of peace for the good of God's
creatures and the prosperity of towns and cities impressed itself on my
mind. It never occurred to me that you would after that trans-
gress the limits of the meaning of (the Kuráanic verse) ' Oh ye true believers perform your promises, ' and set at naught the behest of the
Prophet (on whom be peace). ' Verily the fulfilment of a promise is the
best form of faith.' Whereupon I sent Isláh-ul-mulk Maulána Kásim
Ali Sadr and Ghiás-ud-dín Kúrchi with the message that if your Sultánic
Majesty are with all that has passed still firm in the old and established
usage of amity, it would be proper that you should send to my court
that band of men who have chosen the road of baseness to our bounties
and have escaped to seek refuge with you, or drive them from your
presence and country. It was also desired that you may not in future
instigate the servants of this state to follow their example. It was expected that the persons above alluded to would bring back a definite
reply from your Majesty to these requests, so that the dust of ill-will
should be washed away by the waters of amity and the tree of friendship
again bear fruit. When the above-mentioned persons and Núr Muhammad

---

[1] Here the writer quotes some of the verses of the first and second letters of
Humáyun to Sultán Bahádur which are omitted.

Khalíl reached the foot of this lofty throne and delivered the agreement they were charged by you with, the contents of the above agreement did not seem to be as satisfactory as they were hoped to be. This caused great astonishment. You write about Muhammad Zamán Mirza that in spite of such treaties and engagements existing between the former emperors of Dehli and the late Sultán Muzaffar, that Sultán Sikandar, and Sultán Aláuddín and many other Sultáns have come to Gujarát, and have been received and provided for according to their conditions without thereby causing any breach of friendship between the ruler of Gujarát and the emperors of Dehli, and that in the same way if Mírza Muhammad remained with you, and was well received, it does not matter. This is not an argument in point. Let it not be concealed that the only mode of preserving friendship between us is that you concede to my wishes and send these misguided people to the lofty throne or refrain from protecting them, or keeping them in your country. If you act thus your faith will be clear as the sun in middle meridian. You will act thus if your thoughts go in accord with your professions and your acts agree with your words. If not, by what agreement can faith be placed in your treaty. It is probably known to your Sultánic Majesty that the World Conquering Lord (Tamerlane), may God enlighten the glory of his name, had several differences with the Sultán of Rúm, Ildarím Báyazíd (Bajazet), and though many signs of hostility appeared from that ruler, he did not think of laying waste the kingdom of Rúm, because Bajazet was engaged in fighting the Franks. When Fara Yúsuf Turkoman and Sultán Ahmed Jaldír fled from fear of the victorious army (of Timúr) and took refuge with Bajazet, the World Conqueror desired Bajazet not to give these men shelter, and intimated to him the advisability of expelling them from his territories. When Báyazíd Ildarím (Bajazet) turned his face from these friendly hints, what Fate had ordained, came about.

COUPLET.

If, in the house of virtue there is any one,
To him from Sa'adi's speech a word is enough
(Meaning Verbum sat sapienti.)

What more should I write. Peace on him who followeth the path of rectitude.

THE COMMUNICATION ADDRESSED BY SULTÁN BAHÁDUR TO HUMÁYUN.

After opening the words in the name of the Omniscient King, and perfuming the sense of smell with the praise of peace to and pray-

ers for the Best of the created (that is the Prophet) on whom be peace!
be it shown, that, what was sent by the chosen person of the sublime
court, Núr Muhammad Khalíl reached this court and obtained the
honour of kissing the edge of the carpet, and the letter of wonderful
contents, was also delivered and its proud meaning has been understood by this Sultánic Court. It is among other things, written that
Kásim Ali and Ghiásuddín were sent to represent to me that the
signs of truth and amity would appear, if the refugees to this court were
expelled from the guarded dominions of Gujarát. Verily this is a sheer
falsehood, for had your Majesty's delegates spoken to me even a word
on any subject except the general subject of amity and peace exsting
between us and of the treaties thereabout, matters would not have
reached this crisis—a crisis which has obliged your Majesty to
advance as far as Gwáliar. This is a bad idea and crude ambition.
It is known to all high and low that your Majesty had entered into
strong agreements and stringent treaties with that descendant of a
princely house, Sultán Muhammad Mírza, and had strongly ratified
them by oaths of friendship and brotherliness. When your
Majesty had the upper hand of him you broke the agreements and
turned your face from all truth and fidelity and hastened towards
hostility and enmity. The prince above alluded to, had heard
from the sons of the world, the fame of this house for bestowing
thrones and conquering dominions, and had heard how Sultán
Mehmúd Khilji after the treachery and tyranny of the Hindus had
taken refuge in this court, and how the late Sultán Muzaffar (may
Heaven be pleased with him and make paradise his lodging!) had
taken up his cause. In the same way I have also given merciful heed
to the complaints the Mírza has made of the evils he has had to suffer at
the hands of promise-breakers and considering the aid of a Muslim
in distress (in the words of the Prophet, on whom be peace, "Help
thy brother in distress") incumbent on me, I have thrown on him
the shadow of my patronage and protection in the hope that by the
favour of Alláh his hopes and my endeavours may bear abundant
fruit. Though the constancy of your agreements had become clear and
undoubted still in the presence of Kázi Abdul Kádir and Muátamin-
uz-Zamán, of Khurásán, I agreed to an oath on the Kuráan because of the
goodness of my own intentions, the purity of my motives and the charity of
my thoughts for every Muslim, and I considered that enough and binding.
In these days as the necessity of uprooting the foundations of the *Firangis*

appeared pressing I had to go to the port of Dív. Your Majesty, immediately on hearing of this, took opportunity to push on as far as Gwáliar dismissing from your mind the Kuráanic precept: "Break not your agreements after their ratification." It was not in the way of keeping agreements that your Majesty ordered the sermon of that place to be read in your name. Your Majesty who have not the grace to offer apologies for such a conduct consider yourself justified in dismissing my apologies unheard. Truly your Majesty's acts, as well as writings, savour of great intrepidity. I suppose your boasting of the exploits of your grand sire seven degrees removed (Tamerlane) is of a piece with it. Had you been able to write of a bit of your own achievements it would have been something. But it seems your Majesty's performances have not reached the stage of being spoken or written about? Probably the putting together of a long stringed narrative was all that your Majesty wished for. It is a pity your Majesty did not think of the smallest of my exploits—if only to edify yourself by taking an example therefrom.

COUPLET.

If thy sword has not the strength fit for prowess
  Wield not the sword of thy tongue !

If thou art diminutive in size
  Walk not on stilts to appear tall in the eyes of boys.

If thy falchion wants in mettle my boy
  Oppose not with it the wielder of a nobler blade.

By the help of God and by His grace it is known to all that as long as the throne (of this country) is graced by the occupation of this Presence (meaning himself) no ruler has had the strength or courage of opposing his powerful armies, whereas, your Majesty are engaged in contest with a low Afghán. Why do you inflict such a headache (as that of thinking of fighting with me) on yourself? According to the (Kuráanic) precept "Let not Satan mislead you" your Majesty should not permit pride to take possession of you. Surely in a few days whatever is the wish of the Creator shall appear.

COUPLET.

The devotee asked for a drink of the water of the Heavenly fountain
  Kausar, and Háfiz demanded a cup of wine,
  Let the result show what in respect of each is the wish of the Creator !

They say that the Sultán being illiterate ordered the despatch of this letter just as it was written by Munshi Mulla Mehmúd, without

becoming acquainted with its beauties or defects, and so it was sent.
It is said that this Mulla was formerly in the service of Humáyún
and had, by some act or other, earned his displeasure, which
effecting him to some extent he left the service of that monarch and
entered that of Sultán Bahádur. This stupid person with these motives
wrote the letter which became the cause of kindling this fire of
dissension. Every reverse that befell the Sultán was a chip from
the pen of this unpolished block and all the misfortunes that came
on the Sultán were of the inundation that formed itself from the
drippings of his pen.

It is so, related by men of gentility that when Mulla Mehmúd
brought this writing to the Sultán, the Sultán was in intoxication.
In that same condition this mischief-making treacherous person read it
over to the Sultán, and he, full of trust, without consulting or asking the
opinion of any minister, and without considering the merits or demerits
of the composition, ordered its despatch. When the nobles and
ministers heard of it in the morning and became acquainted with
its harsh verbiage, they struck the slap of anxiety on the thigh
of pain and represented to the Sultán the above facts. The
Sultán was much concerned and ordered Malik Amín Nas, who
was companion-vazír, to mount with all speed and recall the couriers
despatched with the objectionable communication. He also called
Abúji Náyik, who, afterwards, in the time of Sultán Ahmed II. reached
the dignity and position of obtaining the title of Wajih-ul-mulk and
the vazírship of Gujarát, and told him: "You are of my family (the
Tánk-tribe). It is necessary that you should travel with such speed
that you reach the Nirúr Pass before the courier does and turn him
back." Abúji mounting one of the fleet royal horses started with all
the speed he could and arriving at the Pass asked the guards if the
courier had passed. They said no couriers had passed till then.
So he sat for three nights and days and watched incessantly, but the
couriers did not appear and so he concluded they must have passed
another way. He, therefore, left the place, and going to Sultán
Bahádur related to him what had passed. Every one said nothing
could now be done and that what was destined would come to pass.

The Sultán again desired to conquer the fort of Chittaur and
entrusted the conduct of the business to Malik Rúmi Khán,
promising him the governorship of Chittaur after its conquest.
In his arrangements for the conquest of Chittaur Rúmi Khán
showed such wonders as the eyes of the world had never seen.

They say when Humáyún saw the letter of Sultán Bahádur, he was much hurt and he started from Agra for Chittaur with his armies. When he raised his victorious standards in the territories of Gwáliar, it occurred to him that if he engaged Sultán Bahádur while that monarch was besieging the fort of Chittaur, the act would be put down as indirectly helping the infidel against the Muslim, besides being contrary to the spirit of Islám. He, therefore, thought it best to await the result of the siege and halted at Gwáliar with these intentions. On hearing of the advance of Humáyún, Sultán Bahádur detached Tátár Khán Lodi with 30,000 well-equipped horse, and veteran soldiers to march upon Delhi, the capital city of India, by way of Biánu and subdue that country, so that Humáyún would have to return for the relief of his capital. If Humáyún did not fall back to oppose Tátár Khán, then it was as well if Tátár Khán became master of that country, and collected there a large army. And if Humáyún should come this way Tátár Khán would arrive from the other direction. It was thought that these tactics should at once give the Gujarát army heart, set apart for them a strong reserve-force and cause the dissipation of Humáyún's forces. If Humáyún Pádsháh marched or sent an army against him, Tátár Khán was instructed to entrench himself strongly and await the Sultan's arrival, but in no case to offer fight till the Sultán came to his aid, and. that on his part the Sultán would lose no time in going to his help.

They say that when Tátár Khán reached the territories of Biyána, Mírza Hindál, who with 5,000 valiant horsemen, had been despatched by Humáyún to engage him, came and opposed him. Tátár Khán, regardless of the prohibition expressed to him in such exaggerated terms by the Sultán, at once gave battle and was forthwith routed and his army dispersed. Tátár Khán, however, never placed foot outside the field of battle, and, as long as he had life in his body, performed acts of heroic manliness and valour. At last he was killed.

It is said by some authorities that his disobedience of the orders of Sultán Bahádur was due to the hopes he entertained to secure the throne of Dehli for himself, as he also came of a line of kings who had ruled over Delhi. He thought after winning this battle to assemble a large number of Afgháns round his standard, and calculated that after the engagement between Humáyúm and Sultán

Bahádur it would be easy for him to cope with one or both of the weakened combatants and assume the reins of the dominion of Delhi. This was why he disobeyed the strict injunctions of Sultán Bahádur and gave battle, and by his own treachery came to grief. The responsibility (of the truth or the reverse of this account) is on the head of the narrator.

They say that when the besieged Hindus of Chittaur were straitened, and Sultán Bahádur perceived that the prospect of the conquest of the fort was not remote, he said in a proud, boastful spirit, " Is there any one in this period who can fight with or oppose me ? " His Holiness the Maulavi Kázi-Mehmúd Jálandharpuri, who was present, fearlessly repeated the following :

Couplet.

"When no lion remains in a meadow
The lame fox begins to hunt there."

Sultán Bahádur was touched to the quick at these words and said that the Kázi should not remain within the limits of his territories. The Kázi (in the words of the Kuráan) said :— " The earth is God's ; neither of us remain in this country." He moved thence to Vírpúr[1] with the intention of proceeding to the pilgrimage and in the same year A. H. 941 (A. D. 1534) he passed away from this transitory world to the everlasting one. He was the spiritual follower of his father and received the gift of saintliness from his uncle, Kázi Ímád, and was the disciple of the lord Sháh Álam. He had great friendship with Sháh Sheikh Jí, the grandson of Kutbi Álam.

The Sultán was much embarrassed by the defeat of Tátár Khán and the heat of his arrogance and pride was chastened by the cold of misfortune and fear. At this time Chittaur fell. The Sultán wanted to fulfil the promise he had given to Rúmi Khán, but his vazírs advised that if he entrusted such an important place to such a person as Rúmi Khán that he would never obey him, so he changed his mind and did not perform his promise. Rúmi Khán was vexed at this and sent secret messages to

---

[1] A village on the Bávli river, eight or nine miles west of Lúnáwádá, in the Revákántha Agency (Bombay Gazettte, VI., 170). The Mir-ati Ahmedi (Persian Text II. 81) states that the grave of the saintly Kázi; like the shrine of Sultán Husbang of Mándu, possesses the power of sweating.

Humáyún, stating that if he came soon it would be easy to
defeat Sultán Bahádur, as the whole conduct of the war was
in his hands and that his advice, if followed by the emperor's army,
would make him victorious. So Humáyún turned from Gwáliar to
Chittaur. The Sultán asked Rúmi Khán how best to fight with
the emperor. He said, "we shall, like the King of Rúm (the Sultán of
Turkey), surround ourselves with gun-carriages, and when a large army
advances towards us I shall fire my cannon at them, so that if it is a
mountain of iron it will turn to ashes." The Sultán acted on the
advice of Rúmi Khán, and although the nobles said this mode of
warfare would not suit them, the Sultán did not give ear to them.
When they entered the ring fence of gun-carriages the courage of
the Sultán's soldiers began to cool and the emperor's troops were
encouraged. Rúmi Khán then wrote to the emperor that the Sultán
was confined by him in the enclosure of gun-carriages and that he
should order his soldiers to surround him with orders not to allow any
one to go out from within or come in from without. The emperor
gave the order and his Mughals formed a cordon round the Sultán's
camp and closed the roads, and grain became first scarce then unobtainable, and they began to live on oxen, horses and camels.
Several days passed thus, and at last the army of Sultán Bahádur
became so straitened that four horses could not feed two men to satisfaction. Clarified butter and such things became as rare as a phœnix.
The horses would chew one another's manes and tails and die. The
Sultán was bewildered. At this time a chief of the Banjhárás
or grain-carriers came and stated that he had brought a hundred
thousand bullock loads of grain, but from fear of the Mughal foragers
was unable to bring them in without convoy. If this was given him
he would bring the grain in and would afterwards bring more. The
Sultán secretly told off 5,000 horse for that duty, but Rúmi Khán
sent the information overnight to Humáyún with the message, that if
this grain reached the entrenched camp, matters would again be
prolonged. That monarch sent a strong force to cut off the supplies.
The intercepting Mughal force fought with the convoy, which was
defeated, and all the grain was carried off to the camp of Sultán
Humáyún. On hearing this, the army of the Sultán washed their
hands of life. The Sultán had still such confidence in Rúmi Khán that
he would not even drink water without consulting him, but now his
treachery became evident, and he also coming to know that he was
found out, fled and joined Humáyún. This event made the army

of Sultán Bahádur quake as if the day of judgment had dawned upon them. They say that one day ten or twenty horsemen from the Mughal camp with a little *howdáh* elephant in front approached the camp of Sultán Bahádur. A party from the army ran to attack them. The Mughal horsemen ran away without fighting, and the little elephant fell to the hands of the Gujarátis. When they brought the little elephant into the presence of the Sultán, two small boxes were found in the *howdáh*. All the nobles, ministers and wise men entreated the Sultán not to open the boxes saying, that the troops escorting them had fled away without showing the least fight and had left the elephant, and that this must surely be some ruse, and that therefore the boxes must not be opened. This, however, did not satisfy the Sultán and he insisted on their being opened. They were found to contain a small quantity of salt and some inches of indigo-dyed cloth. When the Sultán and his soldiers saw this (charm) an unaccountable feeling of craven fear took possession of their souls and the sight so scared the Sultán, that when night fell he ordered all the precious stones and rubies and valuables that were in his treasury to be burned, and the trunks of his huge war-elephants—that of all his possessions he held dearest, to be cut off. The eyes of the Sultán and of all those that were present in the assembly filled with tears. And he ordered a pair of immense mortars that he had, one of which was called Leila and the other Majnún, [1] to be charged with powder and burst. Then he ordered a horse and mounting it, without informing the army with some of his chief followers, turned his face towards Mándu. This happened on the 20th of the month of Ramazán A. H. 941 (A. D. 1534).

On the following morning a great commotion arose in the Sultán's camp. The Sultán having gone away, the army with neither the means of issuing out nor the possibility of remaining, lost heart. At this time, the powerful army of Humáyún came down on them, and the wise men of the army realized the truth of the Kuráanic verse :

" Thou vouchsafest dominion unto whomsoever thou willest
And taketh it away from whomsoever thou wishest ! "

---

[1] Leilah and Majnún are the Romeo and Juliet of the East. These Arab lovers flourished during the reign of the first Umawi Khalífah, Muáawiyah (A.D. 661-680 ; A. H. 41-61).—*Translator.*

and the meaning of the last hemistich of the Sultán's quotation from
Háfiz in the concluding portion of his letter to Humáyún was illustrated. The whole camp of the Sultán was plundered. Many soldiers
were killed, some taken prisoners and others escaped with bare heads
and feet.

They say that, when Humáyún saw the tent of the Sultán, which
was of uncommonly thick velvet down embroidered with gold, he
said it was evidently the property of a ruler possessing great
maritime power.

It is related that Sultán Sikandar, the son of Behlúl Lodi, used
often to say that the dependence of the kingdom of Delhi was on
wheat and jáwár (*Sorghum vulgare*) and that the greatness of the
income of the Sultánate of Gujarát, which had eighty-four ports
under its sway, was due to its revenues from corals and pearls.

The insignificant and humble person who writes this history has
heard from his father, that he was one of the chief officers, whose
duty it was to remain near the royal person of Humáyún in this
expedition. That he was the librarian, and the emperor was ever
engaged in reading and that (consequently) his services were always
required. On the day the emperor gained the victory, he sat on
the throne of pleasure and gave a general audience. All the nobles
and soldiers stood with folded arms each in his proper place. A
speaking parrot that had been taken in the spoils of Sultán Bahádur
was brought and its cage deposited at the foot of the emperor's
lofty throne. Its words excited general astonishment and wonder.
They say it was such a speaking parrot that if the famous parrot that
figures in the *Túti-Námah*[1] had been then alive, it would have taken
instruction from it. In sharpness of understanding, as in clearness
of articulation, it was so remarkable that it used to reproduce with
exactitude the words spoken by any one in any language. It is
related that when the cage of this clever parrot was brought and placed
before the emperor, Rúmi Khán was announced and the emperor
said : "Let him come." The moment the parrot heard the name of
Rúmi Khán, it began to say : " Fie on Rúmi Khán, fie on Rúmi
Khán the traitor, fie on Rúmi Khán the traitor." It probably repeated

---

[1] The *Túti Námah* is a famous work of imagination in Persian, wherein a parrot
gifted with wonderful wisdom and powers of speech is represented as telling certain
edifying stories.—*Translator.*

this no less than ten times. Rúmi Khán hung down his head in shame. When Humáyún ascertained the meaning of the words from an interpreter and saw Rúmi Khán ashamed, he said: "Rúmi Khán, if these words had been uttered by a human being, I would have ordered his tongue to be torn out from the back of his neck, but what can I do to an animal without understanding?" The people of the assembly guessed that when Rúmi Khán deserted the Sultán, the people there must have thus reproached him aloud and that the bird had repeated the words of those men now that the name of Rúmi Khán fell on its ears and recurred to its memory. The truth, however, was that God directed these words to fall from the animal for the warning of others in that assembly, for no one else in that assembly would have dared to address words so truthful in respect of Rúmi Khán to him.

To continue, Humáyún started thence and laid seige to Mándu. The Sultán was besieged and again the fire of disturbance and war and conflict was kindled. At this time Rúmi Khán wrote to Bhúpat-rái, son of Silehdi, reminding him of the Sultan's cruelty to his family, and stating that it would be foolish of him to give his sweet life for such a tyrant, on the contrary that it was the time for revenge and retaliation. Rúmi Khán suggested that Bhúpat should throw open the gate, that may be entrusted to him, to the followers of the emperor at the time of the attack, and that the emperor had agreed to give him his father's place, and, moreov r, do him many other kindnesses. Bhúpatrái, thus misled, opened the gate and took himself aloof, and the army entered the gates and ascended. When the Sultán heard of this, he said: "The saying of the wise: 'to kill the snake and bring up its young ones is not the act of the wise,' is not false. It always brings evil." Having made Malik Ráje his *locum tenens* and entrusted Songadh, the citadel of Mándu, to Sultán Álam Lodi, he went out by another gate and set out towards Gujarát. Some of the soldiers of Humáyún pursued and overtook him, but he turned back and fought them personally and so wielded the sword that he vanquished his opponents and went on. The fort was conquered. Sadr Khán was captured alive and killed. After this they assaulted the citadel and reduced the garrison to sore straits. Sultán Álam Lodi surrendered to the emperor, who ordered him with three hundred of his followers to be put to death. They say that on Tuesday, Humáyún donned the red garments (in token of royal anger and general massacre) and held a durbar, and ordered general slaughter. In one hour streams of blood flowed in every street and quarter of Mándu.

In the course of the massacre Manjhu, the musician of Sultán Bahádur, was captured by a Turkish Mughal. The Mughal wanted to kill him and had placed his hand on his sword hilt. The musician said : " What will you gain by killing me ? Save me, and I will give you my weight in gold. I am a companion of Sultán Bahádur and have no lack of money." The Mughal taking down his turban bound the hands of the musician and sat in a corner. Accidentally, one of the rájás in the following of Humáyún riding by, recognized Manjhú and at once alighting from his horse took Manjhu by the hand and led him along. The Mughal said his sword was drawn and the orders of the emperor were for a general slaughter, and that he would not let Manjhú go alive. As the Rajá also had a large following and the Mughal was alone, he was *nolens volens* dragged along with Manjhú till they reached the emperor's presence. They saw that he was so enraged that sparks of fire flew from his eyes wherever he cast them and except "slaughter" no other words issued from his lips. The Mughal complained : "This is my captive and he is a companion of Bahádur's, and this Hindu has by force brought him here." Khushál Beg Qúrchi, who had been sent on the mission to the Sultán previous to this war, had seen the rank and dignity enjoyed by Manjhú before Bahádur. He said : " Oh! my king, this Manjhú is the prince of singers." The emperor cast a sharp glance at him, but he repeated the same words and said again : " Health to your Majesty! such a musician does not perhaps exist in all Hindustán." The fire of the emperor's rage became extinguished and he ordered him there and then to sing something. Manjhú had not his peer in Persian song also. He sang so well that the mood of the emperor underwent a complete change and the ocean of his mercy began to boil. He at once changed his blood-red garments for green and gave a special reward to Manjhú and told him to ask for something, saying he would give him whatever he asked. Manjhú said : " Most of my companions are taken prisoners : I ask for their release." The emperor bound his royal quiver to the waist-band of Manjhú and gave him his own charger, and sent with him several of his chief men and told them : " Whomsoever Manjhu releases let no one hinder." They say that several people at that time complained to the emperor that Manjhú did not release his own relations only, but was setting free both relations and strangers. The emperor, however, said : " This is a very small matter. Had he asked for my kingdom to-day, I would not have turned my face but would have given it him most readily." Manjhu, it is said, became intimate with the emperor. They say whatever presents he received in the king's service he gave to that Mughal and used to say : " He has spared my life, how can I recompense him." The writer has received this account from his father, who was present in that assembly and who was honoured by holding a place about the person of the emperor. Ultimately, Manjhu fled and joined Sultán Bahádur. The emperor Humáyún used to say that it was Manjhu's misfortune had impelled him to take that step " Else I would have bestowed so much on him that he would never have remembered Sultán Bahádur." They say that when Manjhu reached Sultán Bahádur, the Sultan exclaimed : " To-day I regain whatever I have lost. My meeting with Manjhu has dispelled all my sorrow and rage, and I have no further desire ; what I was asking for, my God has given me."

When Sultán Bahádur came from Mándu to Chámpáner, a fort in the kingdom of Gujarát, he left vazír Ikhtiyár Khán and Rája Narsinghdeva who had the title of Khán Jehán in charge, and he himself going by Cambay to Sorath, took up his residence at Dív. Humáyún came from Mándu to Gujarát and besieged Chámpáner. The garrison had tried hard to take the large piece of ordnance called the *Bahádur Sháhi* up to the fort, but had only succeeded in taking it half way up the hill, when the army of Humáyún arrived. So the garrison spiked the mortar in three places and abandoned it. When Rúmi Khan saw it, he said he could repair it, and filled the holes with a mixture of seven metals. It could now take a smaller charge of powder and its range was somewhat reduced ; it was nevertheless a scourge of God and a terror. They say that the very first shot that Rúmi Khán fired from it, brought down the gate of the fort, and with the second, he felled a tree standing near the gate. The garrison, on seeing this, began to tremble. Now there was a *Firangi* in the fort, by the name of Sakta (Mesquita ?)[1] who was made a Musalmán by Sultán Bahádur, with the title of Firang Khán. He said to Ikhtiyár Khán : " What if I fire a ball down the

---

[1] Faria-e-Souza (quoted in Briggs' Muhammadan Power in India IV., 135-138) says that Firangi Khán was a Portuguese "apostate" of the name of John de St. Jago, who was in attendance on Sultán Bahádur at the time of that brave king's assassination by the Portuguese at Dív.

muzzle of that mortar and burst it?" And Ikhtiyár Khán replied:
" If you do so, I will enrich you beyond your wants !" Firang Khán
in the very first shot so directed the ball into the muzzle of the
mortar, as to shatter it to pieces. The people of the fort were
delighted. Ikhtiyár Khán gave the *Firangi* something less (than
he had promised), but Rája Narsinghdeva gave him seven maunds
of gold. They say that Rája Narsinghdeva was left behind in the
fort, because he was wounded. On account of the continuous cannonade, both from above and below, his wounds broke out afresh, and
he died. When the news of the Rájá's death reached Sultán Bahádur, he said, " Alas ! the fortress of Chámpáner is lost !" Afzal
Khán Vazír asked : " Has any news to that effect been received ?"
The Sultán said, " No, but Rája Narsinghdev is dead, and I despair of
this Mulla (or priest, meaning Ikhtiyár Khán) having the courage to
hold the fort !"

The favoured of God, Sayad Jalál-ud-dín Bukhári, surnamed
Munawwar-ul-mulk, used often to say that the fortress of Chámpáner
was such that if an old woman threw stones from above, the bravest
men in the world could not take it. Wonderful was the good fortune
of Humáyún that he conqured such a fort so easily. And the way in
which he won it was this :—One night the besieged sent down two
hundred Kolis from the fortress to bring grain, although provisions
were so plentiful that they would have sufficed for a ten years' siege.
But when good fortune forsakes men almost all their acts prove
ruinous mistakes. When the Kolis came below and arrived near the
batteries they were all captured and taken before the emperor who
ordered them to be killed. When seventy or eighty of them were
killed, one of the survivors said : " If you do not slay us, I shall take
you up by a way which none of the garrison are aware of." This
speech they reported to the emperor, who encouraged them and their
chief men and sent some of his brave men of tried valour with them.
The Kolis that very night took them up by such a path, as was not only
unknown to Humáyún's army, but even to the garrison. As soon as
the band arrived, they descended over the battlements of the fortress
and with the cries of "Allah ! Allah !" fell on the besieged, who were
astonished as to whence this calamity had dropped upon them. Some
threw themselves over the walls of the fortress, some were slain, and
others fleeing with Ikhtiyár Khán took shelter in the citadel known
as the Maulia, and the fort was won. This happened on the 7th of

the month of Safar, A.H. 942 (about the 8th of August, A.D. 1535). The Mughal army came up and after a while Ikhtiyár Khán also became helpless and begged for quarter, and the second day after the conquest of the fort, went into the presence of Humáyún. Since the Khán was a Mulla (a learned man) of pleasant manners, an astronomer and a poet, and was accomplished in all the arts, his company pleased Humáyún, who became extremely kind and favourable to him.

It is related that one day Sheikh Jamál Kambo who was styled the second Khusrao,[1] and who was the author of the following couplet:—

COUPLET.

Thy courtyard's dust the mantle I have worn,
The streaming tear in hundred rents hath torn.

The poet also was with the emperor in this expedition. He once told the Khán that he had heard he was very proficient in the art of enigmas, and asked him to find his name in the Kuráan. The Khán instantly replied, "Jama d, má lan,"[2] (i.e., he collected or heaped up wealth.) The Sheikh said: "My name is Jamál." The Khán read out the verse and showed that the numerical value of the letters in the part of the verse he had read out corresponded with that of Jamál and there was great applause.

They say that when once out riding Humáyún sent for Ikhtiyár Khán in a way expressive of great royal condescension. Ikhtiyar Khán failed to acknowledge his sense of the honour done to him in the manner prescribed by the elaborate etiquette of the Mughal Court. Those present showed an inclination to open the tongue of taunt and censure, but the emperor forbade them with a look of disapproval and said: "Ikhtiyár Khán do not be offended at my words." The Khán replied, "Your Majesty has the authority, do me the kindness." The emperor said: "It is the etiquette among the kings of my house that when a king does any one the honour (of thus calling him), that

---

[1] Amír Khusrao who flourished in the reign of Aláuddin (A.D. 1295-1315) is considered, and with justice, the Philip Sydney of the East.

[2] The original Persian lines are :

مارا ز گرد کوی تو پیراهن است برتن
آن هم ز آب دیده صد چاک تا بدامن

[3] The man's name was 'Jamál.' The Khán found out from the Kuráan two words جمع مالا Jamáa-málan, (vide Sale's Kuráan, Chap. civ "The slanderer") approaching the name Jamál in sound and furnishing a correct allusion, at once to the avarice of the person applying for the enigma and an opportunity for a safe and happy hit at a rival. This is justified by the context too, which says the bon-mot created a laugh at the expense of Jamál.

person should dismount to perform the royal obeisance, and then go back to his place, and if a man like you is done such an honour, he ought to rub his forehead with the royal stirrup, and that is enough for him. You must know (the Kuráanic verse) that 'When kings enter a town, they revolutionize it;' you know the rest."[1] Ikhtiyár Khán, alighting from his horse, and coming near the king, knelt down and kissed the stirrup, and said: "This slave of the Court has been born and bred in the Court of Gujarát and is ignorant of the manners of the Persian Courts and kings. The emperor should pardon him."

It is related that one day a Mulla entered into a discussion on a scientific point with Ikhtiyár Khán in the assembly of Humáyún. After some discussion, the argument of Ikhtiyár Khán prevailed, but the Mulla would not admit it. Humáyún observed that the argument of the Khán was the best, and that the Mulla should not enter into useless altercation. The Khán extemporised an enigma[2] on the name of Humáyún, which was much applauded by those present in the assembly, and praised by the king.

COUPLET.

No cheating quibbler can o'ercome my love's refulgent ray :
My Moon's bright-light leads hearts alone of those that prize fair play.

After the conquest of Chámpáner, Humáyún went to Cambay, and after having seen that district he arrived at Ahmedábád. The camp of the king was at a village of the name of Ghiáspúr, two miles to the south of the city of Ahmedábád. He went to visit the tomb of Hazrat Kutbul Aktáb Sayad Burhánuddín, the son of Sayad Mehmúd, the son of Sayad Jalál Bukhári Makhdúmi Jehúnián, at Batwa, two miles from Ahmedábád, and saw the *Lohlakkar*[3] stone and pronounced it a marvel such as he had never seen before. It is related about this stone, that one day Hazrat Kutbul Aktáb was at the time of the *'tahajjud'* or midnight prayers, walking out to answer the call of nature, when suddenly his foot struck against something and pained him. He uttered the following words: "Is it iron or stone,

---

[1] *Vide* Sale's Kurâan, Chap. xxvii : "Kings when they enter a city by force waste the same."

[2] The enigma consists in the Persian words of the couplet supplying also the numerical value of Humáyún's name. The couplet runs :—

کج باز بر نیاید نور جمال جانان
با ماه ماست روشن دلهای راستباران

[3] The *Loh lakkar* (meaning literally iron-wood) is still shown at Batwa. It consists of wood, stone, and iron, and hence the name.

or wood or what?" God in one night joined the three things in one.[1] In the morning a mob gathered to see it. The Saint ordered it to be concealed in some deep place and forbade its being dug up and said, "Whoever digs it up shall be issueless." After some years, a merchant dug it up, saying he was content to be issueless to make manifest the miracle of his saint. May God's mercy be on him! Since then they have placed it on a bench of wood, and high and low enjoy its sight. When Akbar Sháh (the Great) visited Ahmedábád, he took away half of it to Agra, and left the other half in its place, and this is preserved as an auspicious relic.

To continue, when the emperor heard of the rising of the Afghán, Sherkhán Súr, who afterwards became a great king and was called Shér Sháh, in Behar and Jaunpur, he left his half-brother Mírza Hindál[2] in Ahmedábád and Kásim Beg in Broach and Yádgar Násir Mírza in Pattan and Bábá Beg Jaldér, the father of Sháham Khán Jaldér, in the fort of Chámpaner, and went by way of Asír and Burhánpur to the capital of Agráh. At this time the nobles of Sultán Bahádur, of the names of Malik Amín Nas, who was governor of the fort of Ranthambhor, and Malik Burhán-ul-mulk Bunyáni, governor of Ajmer, and Malik Shamsher-ul Mulk, Governor of Chittaur, having effected a junction came near the city of Pattan with about 20,000 horse, and sent word to Sultán Bahádur, that if he gave them permission, they would engage with Yádgar Násir Mirza. The Sultán ordered them to delay the battle until he could join them. When the Sultán went to that part of the country, Yádgar Násir Mirza, avoided meeting him by going to Ahmedábád. The Sultán came to Pattan and thence marched to Ahmedábád. The enemy issuing thence encamped at Ghiáspur, which place has been mentioned above. The Sultán also pitched his camp on the bank of the river opposite. All night they were ready for battle and made sure that next day there would be a battle. The enemy lighted many lights and leaving them marched off during the night for Mehmúdábád. Near dawn Sultán Bahádur got intelligence of this and pursuing them that very day encamped at the village of Kaníj, which is about five miles from Mehmúdábád. At this time

[1]. The sense of the wood turning into stone and iron is this: The Saint as one of Alláh's elect—or in the words of the East, Alláh's beloved, was God. His words were the words of Alláh. As when "Alláh said be thou—and it was," so when the Saint called a piece of wood stone and iron, the Divine force of the words transformed the material into what the Saint fancied it to be.

[2]. This seems to be a mistake. According to Abul Fazl (Akbarnámah in Elliot VI. 15) Humáyun placed Gujarát in charge of his brother Mírza Askari. A little later the author rightly states it was Mirza Askari.

news arrived that the forces of the enemy that were stationed at
Broach had come and joined the main army at Mehmúdábád, and
that they intended to give battle on the morrow. Early in the
morning next day both the armies came into action and the brave
men of the armies began to fight. At first the Mughal army, like
a strong wind, scattered the clouds of the ranks of the Sultán, though
some of the brave chiefs of the Gujarát army—Mírán Sayad Mubárak
Bukhári, and Imád-ul-mulk and Malik Jí—stood their ground firm
as mountains though clouds of arrows poured on them and the lightnings
of swords flashed over their heads. At last the Mughal soldiery
fell to plundering, and the army of the Sultán that had dispersed
having rallied at the point where the nobles above-mentioned stood
their ground,   formed and attacked the enemy most gallantly,
and suddenly the zephyr of victory blew on the standards of
the Sultán. They say that the river Mahi became at that time
greatly swollen and many of the fugitives of the Mughal army met
their death by drowning. The Sultán went far in pursuit and drove
them out of the confines of Gujarát. He then went and stayed at
Chámpaner, and sent Muhammad Sháh Asíri, his sister's son, with a
large army in pursuit of the flying Mughals who were not allowed
to stop even in Málwa. Muhammad Sháh pressing forward passed
Mándu, and pushed on in pursuit as far as Ujjain, where he took breath
and encamped on the bank of the Káliáwah river, halting a night in the
palaces built by Násiruddin of Mándu on its bank.

Sultán Bahádur victorious and triumphant returned to Ahmedábád
and remained there a long time.

The period of the stay of Mírza Askari and the above-mentioned
Mughal nobles in Gujarát was nine months and some days.

The only anxiety that now weighed down the heart of the Sultán
was owing to the *Firangis* (Portuguese) having obtained a footing
and built a fort of their own in Dív. The Sultán was night and day
thinking of some means to get rid of these infidels.

ACCOUNT OF THE ENTRY OF THE PORTUGUESE IN THE PORT OF DIV
BY DECEIT AND ARTIFICE, AND THE MARTYRDOM OF SULTAN BAHADUR
IN THE PERFIDIOUS ASSEMBLY OF THEIR CAPTAIN.

When by the turn of the wheel of fortune, Sultán Bahádur was
defeated, as has been described above, and he came to Dív, the
Firangis offered to serve him and showed him sympathy, saying
that the ports of the seas were in their hands and that to whichever

port the Sultán wished to go they were ready to serve him in every
way. On his part the Sultán also began to treat them with mildness.[1]
One day they represented that the goods of the traders of their race
who came to Dív had to remain dispersed and in great insecurity, so
that if the Sultán gave them land equal only to a cow's hide in
extent, that they would enclose it within four walls, for the safety of
their goods. The Sultán granted their request. After this, when
the Sultán left Dív and went against the enemy, the *Firangis* got a
cow's hide and cutting it into thin ribands enclosed land according
to its measure and built a strong fort and mounted it with pieces
of ordnance and occupied it. When this news reached the Sultán
he became very anxious and began to think of dislodging these
infidels. But he wanted to gain his object by artifice and stratagem,
or by the easiest of means. He went from Ahmedábád to Cambay and
from that place set out for Dív. The *Firangis* thought that the arrival
of the Sultán meant some treachery, and though the Sultán adopted
the most amiable demeanour towards them, the *Firangis* took it to
signify the reverse. While encamped on the seaside near Ghoga
the Sultán sent one of his associates, Núr Muhammad Khalíl, to the
Firangi Captain instructing him to bring the latter to him by any
pretext or artifice he could devise. They say that when that fool
met the Captain he was so fascinated by his high courtesy and the
variety of his kindnesses that the Captain was able easily to elicit
from him the real motives and intentions of the Sultán, while Núr
Muhammad was intoxicated with wine. The responsibility for the
truth or falsehood of this story rests on the narrator. The night
passed in this wise. In the morning the Captain told Núr Muhammad that he was a loyal slave of the Sultán but could not go into the
presence owing to sickness. Núr Muhammad returned and related
this to the Sultán. The Sultán said he was afraid the Captain had
probably become apprehensive of something, and that he himself
would go to enquire after his health, and after removing his suspicions
bring him back with him. The Sultán took with him five or six of
his chief nobles. They were Malik Amín Nas Fárúki, Shujáat Khán
and Langar Khán, the son of Kádir Sháh (Mallú Khán) of Mándu,
Alif Khán, the sons of Sheikha Khatri, Sikandar Khán, Governor

---

[1] Bahádur followed this temporising policy with the Portuguese as he dreaded
Humayun's pursuit of him even as far as Dív, and, as a matter of fact, the Mughal
Monarch had advanced as far as Dhandúka, when owing to Sher Khán Súr's rising he
had to retrace his way to Upper India. (See Abul Fazl's Akbarnamah Elliot VI. 15).

of the province of Sanwás, Ganeshráo, brother of Medáni Rái.[1]
The Sultán ordered them not to carry their arms. It was in vain
that ministers and nobles counselled that it was not becoming the
royal dignity of the Sultán to go it booted not and according
to the holy verse : "When their hour cometh they tarry not an hour
nor do they hasten," the Sultán sped to his own destruction.

VERSES.

To work his fateful stern emprise,
Grim Death has fingers five,
With two he shuts his victim's eyes,
With two to close his ears doth strive,
And with the fifth upon his lips,
Cries hush for ever more !

He stepped into the boat. The Portuguese Captain came to
receive the Sultán as far as the shore and took him to his quarters
(on boardship) and began to show him the most deceitful respect.
The Sultán also talked in the same fashion, but as Fate did not
favour his designs it was of no avail. After some conversation
the *Firangis* began to make signs among themselves. The
Sultán now understood that matters had gone beyond his power
and that the tide of good fortune had turned against him. The
nobles said : "Had we not warned you and foretold that you would
cause our ruin ?" He said : "It was thus ordained by destiny." The
Sultán got up and the *Firangis* poured in from all sides. They say
that Sultán Bahádur had already reached the boat when a *Firangi*
came from behind and by a blow of the sword made the Sultan
a martyr, and threw him into the sea. All his companions also
attained the rank of martyrs.[1]

---

[1] Abul Fazl mentions Rúmi Khán to have been one of the party stating that he was
saved from drowning by a friendly Portuguese. But the author does not give his name
among the nobles enumerated. (Elliot VI. 18).

[2] Of the various accounts given of Bahádur's death both by Persian and Portuguese
historians, the narrative given by Abul Fazl (Akbarnámah in Elliot VI. 19) seems the
most natural and in keeping with Bahádur's impetuous vigour and bravery. Abul-Fazl
says that when on reaching the Viceroy's ship Bahádur found the Viceroy's sickness to
be feigned he sought at once to return. The Portuguese were unwilling that such a prize
so nearly secured should so easily slip out of their hands. So the Viceroy asked the
Sultán to tarry a while and inspect some curiosities he had brought for him. Bahádur
saying they might be sent after him turned quickly to regain his boat. A European
Kázi or priest placed himself in the Sultán's way, seeking to stop him. Bahádur cut
him down and leaped into his own boat. The Portuguese vessels surrounded the Sultán's
boat and a fight ensued. Bahádur with another noble threw himself overboard. The
noble was saved by a friendly Portuguese. The Sultán perished in the waves.

It seems from a comparison of all the accounts that the Portuguese did not con-
template Bahádur's death at that time, but that each party hoped to seize the
person of the other. Mutual suspicion turned into a fatal affray, a meeting which
both parties intended to be peaceful. (See Appendix I. Gazetteer History of Gujarát
contributed by the translator).

COUPLET.

" Fie on the trickery of fool-favouring fate,
That makes the lion quarry for the cur. "

This event happened on the 3rd of the blessed month of Ramazán A. H. 943 (about February 12th, A. D. 1536). This date can be gathered from a date-script composed by the vazír Ikhtiár Khán :— سلطان البر و شهيد البحر Sultán-ul-barri-wa-Shahíd-ul-bahr, or the Sultán of the land and the Martyr of the sea. The date can also be obtained from the phrase قتل سلطان بهادر Katli-Sultán-Bahádur, i. e., the assassination of Sultán Bahádur. The Sultán was twenty years of age when he ascended the throne, and reigned eleven years. He was thirty-one years of age when he attained martyrdom.

Let it not be concealed that most of the people of Gujarát say that the *Firangi* General, that is to say, the chief of their ports, had come to Tarak Bandar with one hundred and fifty ships and had anchored off Sankalcote. The Sultán to show his sincere cordiality (to the *Firangis*) went to see their ships. When the Sultán's barges came among the vessels of the *Firangis* they surrounded them and striking with lances, killed the Sultán and his companions, and threw their bodies overboard. This, the people of Gujarát say, is the true account. They say that the enmity of the *Firangis* against the Sultán owed its origin to his writing to the Sultáns of the Dakhan, to co-operate with him in attacking the Portuguese with a view to the re-capture of the Gujarát and the Dakhan ports that had fallen into the hands of the *Firangis*. This communication fell into the hands of the Portuguese and was the cause of their action. God knows best.

They say that when on this visit of his to Dív, Sultán Bahádur reached Mángalore[1] (which is sixty miles from Dív), Kázi Mehmúd who was the ruler of the religious ordinances of that town stated to the Sultán that there was in that town a schismatic called Sheikh Yásín Suwari, who had a habit of refusing to repeat the creed when called upon to do so.[2] The Sultán said : " Call him." He

---

[1] The modern Mángrol, north latitude 21° 8′ east longitude 70° 10′ is a seaport town on the South Coast of Kathiawar. It it supposed to be the Monoglossum emporium of Ptolemy (A. D. 150).

[2] For a Mussalmán to refuse to repeat the creed when called upon to do so, is heresy.

was brought to the presence. The Sultán sent him word to repeat the creed.[1] He said he would not. The Sultán asked the reason. He said: "I know—and my God—who are you to ask me to repeat it, and why should I repeat it before you?" The Sultán ordered him to be taken out, saying that he might be allowed to go if he repeated the creed, if not, that he should be beheaded. However much people persuaded the half-witted man to repeat the creed, he persisted in refusal. They reported this to the Sultán and he repeated the order to kill him. When the executioner drew h sword the man asked him to convey his last words to the Sultán. They were: "Tell the Sultán that from my death to thy destruction more than a week shall not elapse." By the ordainment of God, what the Sheikh had foretold exactly came to pass.

COUPLET.

"Who knows that in this depthless sea,
The pebble or jewel more precious be."

To continue, after this event the high dignitaries, ministers and nobles of the state such as Imád-ul-mulk, Malikji and Daryákhán Husein and Ikhtiyár Khán Khánji and others, sent the bad tidings of the martyrdom of Sultán Bahádur to Muhammad Sháh Fárúki, who was the sister's son of the Sultán and the ruler of the country of Asír and Burhánpúr, and who at the head of some sixty or seventy thousand horse was then encamped in the city of Ujjain under Málwa, and nvited him to Gujarát. They said that the late Sultán had during his life appointed him his heir apparent, having one day seated him on the throne and ordered the nobles and ministers of the state to do him honour, and that they had all obeyed. The Sultán had taken the course to publish the wish and desire that after him the rule and the kingdom may descend to him. It was with this intention that he had nominated Muhammad Sháh to the command of the Dakhan (forces) and had appointed most of the famous nobles under him, some of whom were his equals, and others who like Mallú Khán, the ruler of Málwa and Sikandar Khán Governor of Satwás and Silehdi, the Rájpút Governor of Ráisen, considered themselves superior to him

---

[1] The first tenet of the creed is called "the good word" the 'Kalimah-i-Tay-yibah.' It is this:—"There is no God but Alláh, and Muhammad is His Prophet"—a tenet which the great free-thinker, Gibbon, has immortalized by his well-known epigram: 'An eternal truth and a necessary fiction.'

in rank. These did not like to submit to the command of Muhammed Sháh. The Sultán, having learnt of their scruples, had, with a view to remove, them, seated Mirán Muhammud Sháh on the throne and had himself saluted him that no one might object to serve under him.

When Sultán Bahádur attained martyrdom, Ikhtiyár Khán and Afzal Khán were at Ahmedábád. Imád-ul-Mulk and Malik Jívan Tawakkul who was the head of the royal Slave-nobles and the first in bravery and valour, being then at Baroda and having there heard of this event, also went to Ahmedábád. At this time news came that Mírza Muhammad Zamán, the son of Bad-í-úz-Zamán, the son od Sultán Husein Bábakara, the king of Khurásán who has been mentioned above, was at Úna, a town twelve miles from Dív, and that he was entertaining thoughts of laying claim to the Sultánate. That he had been to the chief wife of the late Sultán, and with great humility and mildness had said that the late Sultán (may he be forgiven) had no son and had called him brother, and that if the lady adopted him as a son and supported him he would conduct the affairs of the kingdom in the best way; he said he was by descent the most deserving of this. His object was, if the ladies consented, to take their gold and ornaments and spend them in raising an army. The ladies replied that he was mistaken if he thought that they had as great a right of interference in affairs of state as the ladies of Persia had. That their incomes and maintenances were fixed and that they had nothing to do with state affairs. That he had best represent the matter to the ministers and nobles and consult them.

When the ministers and nobles heard of the designs of Mírza Muhammad Zamán, they considered the duty of removing this evil foremost in importance and they said the fittest person to do this was Imád-ul-Mulk, who, they suggested, should in person go there. Vazír Ikhtiyár Khán especially talked in a manner very complimentary to Imád-ul-Mulk to induce him to go. He went so far as to say that they were men of the pen, but Malik Imád-ul-Mulk was a man of the sword like whom at that time there was nobody in Gujarát. This speech did not please Vazír Afzal Khán who said : " Yes the Khán is right. No one of the chief nobles of the Sultán is equal to Imád-ul-Mulk in rank, only he has never fought a battle nor broken a hostile rank." From these words Imád-ul-Mulk turned away his face and ultimately left for Sorath with a strong force for the expulsion of Mírza Muhammad Zamán. He reached the vicinity of the town of Únah by forced marches. Mírza Muhammad Zamán came forward and gave battle and was defeated. When the news of the martyrdom of Sultán Bahádur and the prompt endeavours of Mírza Muhammad Zamán to obtain the throne of Gujarát reached Humáyún, he is reported to have observed :—" If that black slave (meaning Imád-ul-Mulk) is alive, the designs of Mírza Muhammád Zamán will not succeed."

Imád-ul-Mulk after his victory returned triumphant and victorious to the capital city of Ahmedábád. Afzal Khán and Ikhtiyár Khán both of whom were wise, prudent and accomplished men said to one another, " The head of this slave had turned, even before he had gained this victory—how will he now act upon our advice and wishes? We had better throw up the office of vazír and retire from the turmoil of business, and refrain from saying a word about state affairs. For if we keep up our connection with affairs it may one day happen that you or I may have to give advice and it may be disregarded and create ill-feeling. It is therefore better that we should act so as to avoid a cause of difference."

VERSES.

" The moth that to the candle flies,
   Though drawn by Love gets scorched and dies,
What though Love's union be his aim,
   He is no less burnt by his flame."

Ikhtiyár Khán said, " There has never hitherto appeared any difference of opinion between him and me and he also will not run counter to my wishes." Afzal Khán said, " However much we may try to agree with him, our very presence will be irksome to him." But the words of Afzal Khán made no impression on the mind of Ikhtiyár Khán, and Afzal Khán said to himself : " The Khán has become old and his dotage has weakened his brain ; let me mind my own business, he surely knows his own best." He went to his house and laid aside all the worldly appurtenances and detached himself from all mundane matters, and placing a padlock on his door and tying the key to his trouser-string, he entered his house. He kept only one servant to cook and serve his meals to him. They say that on the day that Sultán Mehmúd ordered the house of Álam Khán to be plundered by the public, and himself rode to the house of Alam Khán (to witness the execution of the order) he passed by Afzal Khán's house which was on the way to Álam Khán's house. When the Sultán passed by his house Afzal Khán came forth and made his obeisance to him. Up to that time, he had not set foot out of that house, nor received any visitors except a dervish in whom he had faith and to receive whom he used himself to open the padlock and admit him to his house. After enjoying the company of the dervish when the dervish used to go away the Khán would retire into his usual solitude.

What happened to Ikhtiyár Khán, together with the account of the sack and plunder of Álam Khán's house shall, God willing, be stated in its proper place.

Take we up now the thread of our narrative from where we dropped it. They say that when the letter of the nobles and ministers, conveying the tidings of the death of Sultán Bahádur and inviting Muhammad Sháh to come over to Gujarát reached Muhammad Sháh, that from the excess of the love Muhammad Sháh bore for his uncle, the broad world became narrow in his eyes. From that day he bade adieu to all worldly pomp and bodily pleasures. He began to fast every day and break his fast at sunset with a little whey and pass the whole day in prayers. He did not communicate the news of the demise of his august relative to any one of his soldiers. He never talked to any one, but if he ever opened his lips it was to utter the words I am burnt! I am burnt!" They say that at this time there were about sixty or seventy thousand horsemen with Muhammad Sháh. One of his nobles congratulated him on his accession to the throne of Gujarát, but Muhammad Sháh said: "If they gave me dominion over the fourth (or) habitable (part of this) world, without my uncle Sultán Bahádur, it would be nothing to me." On the seventieth day after the martyrdom of Sultán Bahádur, Muhammad Sháh also resigned this life.

When the news of the death of Muhammad Sháh reached the ministers and nobles (of Gujarát), they said, no other heir to the kingdom now remained except Mahmúd Khán the son of Latíf Khán, the brother of Sultán Bahádur. At this time this Mahmúd Khán and Mubárak Khán, the brother of Muhammad Sháh, were both in confinement in the town of Biáwal in the province of Khándesh. They say that when Sultán Bahádur jealously slew all his brothers,

except Mahmúd Sháh, who was then an infant at the breast, no near
relative of his remained. One day, he sent for the infant also
with the intention of killing him. When however his eyes fell on
the little Khán he was moved with compassion and took the infant
up in his arms. The hand of the little Khán while he was throwing
it up and moving his little limbs and kicking as children are wont to
do, fell and closed upon the beard of the Sultán. Bahádur Sháh, struck
with pity by the innocent unconcern and helplessness of the child
said :—" Thou conjurest us by our beard[1] to give thee protection. We
grant thee thy life and give up the thought of thy destruction." He
handed him over to his guardians to keep him and bring him up in
confinement. After the lapse of some days he again sent for Mehmúd
Khán. Those who had charge of him took him to the Sultán from his
schoolroom in the clothes he happened to be then in. When the
Sultán saw the soiled and untidy condition of the little prince's
apparel, he was displeased with the custodians and said, " Is this the
way you take care of a prince ? Is this meet dress for princes and
is this the proper state in which you should bring him before
me ? If you act so with him to-day and if to-morrow perchance
he becomes a king, he will surely avenge these wrongs on you."
Muhammad Sháh also happened to be present in that assembly
so after saying this, when the Sultán looked at Muhammad
Sháh he added (having as has been mentioned above previously
appointed Muhammad Sháh his heir), " It is settled that after me
Muhammad Sháh will be king." He then said to Muhammad Sháh,
" Muhammad Sháh ! I entrust Mehmúd Khán to your care. Treat
him as you think best having due regard to your own circumstances."
Muhammad Sháh made over both Mehmúd Khán and Mubárak Khán
his own younger brother, to the charge of Malik Shamsuddín with
orders to keep them in confinement in Biáwal, a town under Burhánpur. Mehmúd Khán and Mubárak Khán used to live in the same
house at Biáwal. After the death of Muhammad Sháh his son, who
was of tender years, ascended the throne of Khándesh. The chief nobles
and ministers thought that Mubárak Khán, the brother of Muhammad
Sháh, was both young and clever. Lest he should raise a disturbance,
they thought it would be better to wipe his name off the page of
existence. So they sent a number of people to bring him to Burhán-

---

[1] To put one's hand to the beard of another is a gesture of humble entreaty and
supplication. It possibly means " by the honour of this beard save me."

púr the capital of Khándesh, and there to kill him. But, God willing, this shall be detailed in its proper place.

When the news of Muhammad Shah's demise reached the nobles and ministers (at Ahmedábád) they said there was no heir to the Kingdom except Mehmúd Khán. They wrote to Malik Shamsuddín, the governor of Biáwal, that after the martyrdom of Sultán Bahádur the people of Gujarát hoped to make Muhammad Sháh their king, but God's intentions with regard to him were different. There remained now no heir to the throne besides Mehmúd Khán. It was proper that he should be sent soon, to take charge of the kingdom of his ancestors. They sent Muḳbil, the brother of Ikhtiyár Khán, to proceed by forced marches and bring the prince. Malik Shamsuddín made over the prince to Muḳbil Khán, who started on his return to Gujarát, and sent Mubárak Khán to Burhánpur. They say that the nobles and ministers (of Khándesh) made over Mubárak Khán to nobleman of the name of Íbrat Khán to take care of him for the night intending to do with him as should be resolved upon on the morrow. Íbrat Khán took Mubárak Khán to his house and told him to demand whatever his heart wished for that night, for, said he, " to-morrow you know well, what will come to pass." Mubárak Khán, with tearful eyes told him :—"To night remove the fetters from my hands and feet and co-operate with me and see what I do. If I am killed my name and yours shall live for aye ; if I live and Heaven protects me, I shall give you a reward the memory of which shall ever remain indelible on the page of time." God softened the heart of Íbrat Khán and he removed the fetters from Mubárak Khán's feet and rose to help him. Mubárak Khán and Íbrat Khán with some of the latter's slaves and followers went near dawn to the royal palace and commenced to kill and to take prisoners. The guards at that time had gone away to their houses. There was nobody except menial servants, some of whom were killed and others ran away. Mubárak Khán taking his nephew on his lap ascended the throne and sent a message to the nobles that the regency of the kingdom during his nephew's minority pertained to him, and that the nobles should remain on their fidelity and loyalty well assured of their safety. All of them submitted. That day passed thus. At night he slew his nephew and in the morning, issuing forth, he sat on the throne by himself. The nobles came and did him homage, and with folded arms stood, each in his proper place. They struck coin in the name of Mubárak.

Sháh and his title of Khán became changed into that of Sháh. The Disposer of all dominion gave the land to Mubárak Sháh and sent his nephew to the kingdom of non-existence.

COUPLET.

All night he wept besides the sick man's bed,
At dawn the sick was whole the mourner dead.

ACCOUNT OF THE ACCESSION OF SULTAN MEHMÚD II. ON THE THRONE OF THE KINGDOM. THE OPPRESSION OF THE NOBLES OVER HIM IN THE COMMENCEMENT OF HIS YOUTH AND THE SULTAN'S VICTORY OVER THEM AFTERWARDS BY GOD'S HELP.

Those acquainted with events relate, that in the year A. H. 943 (A. D. 1536) Sultán Mehmúd II. ascended the throne of Gujarát, in the eleventh year of his age. His mother was the daughter of Behrám Khán, prince of Sindh, who was a descendant of Tamím Ansári,[1] may God be pleased with him! Sultán Mehmúd was born in Sorath in A. H. 932 (A. D. 1525), in the life time of Sultán Muzaffar II. They say that on his birth Sultán Muzaffar consulted the astrologers as to his future. The astrologers said his fortune showed signs of his becoming the lord of a kingdom, but that there was one Constellation which threatened a certain period of his life with misfortune. As the measure of Sultán Muzaffar's life was nearly full, and as he knew that it was difficult to recover from the disease he was suffering from he had grave apprehensions as to the safety of his other children after his death. So he made over the throne in his life-time to Sultán Sikandar, and gave Latíf Khán (a younger son of Sultán Muzaffar and the father of Sultán Mehmúd II.) a hint saying, '' God's world is wide, betake yourself to a safe corner and throw not away the opportunity of enjoying the few days of this fleeting life in happiness.'' He sent some money to Latíf Khán for expenses adding that if he stayed his brother from kingly jealousy would kill him. Latíf Khán set out travelling.

---

[1] The Ansáris or Helpers were those of the people of Madínah who gave shelter to and helped the Prophet on his flight from Makkah, the event which in History is designated, the Hijrah or Flight. The title has become one of honor and is retained by their descenedants to this day. The Sumras of Sindh claimed descent from the Ansári here mentioned, though the claim does not appear to be well-founded. Sir Henry Eilliot, (History of India. I., 483, 490), believes the Sumrás to be of the Pramára subdivision of the Agni-kula race of Rájputs.

The public Friday sermon was read and coin was struck in the name of Sultán Mehmúd and the post of minister was conferred on Imád-ul-Mulk, whose name was Malik Jíwan bin Tawakkul, and Darya Khán whose name was Husein was styled the "*Majlis-i-Girámi*" or (member of the) Exalted Assembly or High Councillor. Imád-ul-Mulk and Darya Khán in concert carried on the Ministry and the revenue affairs of the State. They appointed Ikhtiyár Khán, vazír of the late Sultán Bahádur, and brother of Mukbil Khán and Diláwar Khán son of Mukbil Khán, to wait upon and watch the Sultán whom they kept in a kind of surveillance, not permitting any one to approach him with the exception of certain servants who were in their confidence. The Sultán had to eat what food they sent him and wear what clothes they provided him with. The Sultán chafed under this treatment, but from his great sagacity and sharp intelligence he never showed his annoyance. He absorbed himself to such an extent in amusement and sport that he never showed any the least concern for his kingdom or his army. He used to take every opportunity of saying both in public and private: "A king who has ministers like Daryá Khán and Imád-ul-Mulk has no business to bother himself with affairs of state, the chief object of being a king is leisure and ease; these I am able to secure and enjoy to an eminent degree; what care I for affairs civil or military? My ministers and statesmen know the wants of the kingdom, and will surely do that which is best for it." He used sometimes to make inquiries about Makkah and Madínah, "For," he would say: "my desire to visit those holy places has taken the form of a resolution." Speeches like these used to lull his ministers into happiness and security, and they used with the greatest satisfaction to administer the affairs of the kingdom. One day Lád Khán, the son of Mukbil Khán, said, "If the Sultán orders I shall kill both Darya Khán and Imád-ul-Mulk." The Sultán judging that these words would not remain secret, all the attendants then present being the confidential partisans of the ministers, at once mounted, and went to the house of Imád-ul-Mulk and communicated to him what the son of Mukbil Khán had proposed. Imád-ul-Mulk called Daryá Khán to his house and repeated to him what the Sultán had said, and they both went to the Sultán's palace. They sent for Ikhtiyár Khán and Mukbil Khán and Lád Khán, Mukbil Khán's son and strangled them in full Durbár. This happened in A. H. 944 (A. D. 1537). The words: *Ba-náhakk kushtah,* unjustly killed, form the chronogram of the year of their death. They say that when they were adjusting the rope round the neck of Ikhtíyár Khán, he raised his hands to Heaven and said, " God Almighty ! thou knowest that I am innocent. I know nothing of all whereof they suspect me, and they are murdering me unjustly." He had begun to repeat the creed when the executioner tightened the rope. After he died and became cold they got him down and loosened the rope from his neck ; his eyes which had started from the sockets went back to their original condition and his tongue finished the words of the last half of the creed—" Muhammad is the Prophet of Alláh," and he died. That Ikhtiyár Khán should have had such a Godly end is not to be wondered at. He was a pious, devout and innocent man. They say that when Imád-ul-Mulk saw this occurrence he said : "Oh Darya Khán ! the last moments of this man argue that he was innocent, and if it was so we have killed him unjustly and tyrannically. His blood will surely bring evil on us." And ultimately it proved so and Imád-ul-Mulk was tortured to death in a most painful manner by the Sultán and Darya Khán had to leave his wife and children and fly for his life to Dehli and died there in exile in great misery, and not a trace of these men remained as shall be detailed hereafter, God willing.

After some time it occurred to Darya Khán to overthrow Imád-ul-Mulk and enjoy the power of the ministry alone by himself. He took counsel with Fattúji surnamed Muháfiz Khán, who was his intimate friend and depositary of his secrets and took the Sultán outside the city on pretence of hunting and brought him hunting as far as the banks of the Mahi, some forty-five miles from Ahmedábád. Here he collected an army from every direction. The greater part of the nobles except the followers of Imád-ul-Mulk came to the service of the Malik. He then sent a message to Imád-ul-Mulk ordering him in the Sultán's name to leave Ahmedábád and retire to his estates. Imád-ul-Mulk seeing that affairs had assumed an unfavourable aspect, tried to assemble an army and take the Sultán away from Daryá Khán's hands. He spent much money from the royal treasury to raise an army, but none of the great nobles would join him. Failing in his endeavours he went to his estate which was Jháláwár. The Sultán came to Ahmedábád. After five or six months, Daryá Khán taking the Sultán with him led an army against Imád-ul-Mulk who gave battle near Pátri, a village of Víramgám, and was defeated. Sadr Khán Zubairi, who was the chief of his army, was slain, and Sharzat-ul-Mulk captured alive. Imád-ul-Mulk went to Mubárak Sháh, the king of Burhánpúr. Daryá Khán took the Sultán in pursuit as far as the Burhánpúr frontier, and sent a message to Mubáraksháh asking him to capture and send the traitor Imád-ul-Mulk and in case he did not, that his harbouring him would not bear good fruit. Mubáraksháh replied that Imád-ul-Mulk was something like his adopted son as he had taken refuge with him, and that he would never cease to protect him. He collected his army and gave Daryá Khán and the Gujarát Sultán battle at the village of Dángri, a dependency of Burhánpúr, but being defeated withdrew to the lofty fortress of Asír. The famous elephants of Mubáraksháh fell into the Sultán's hands. These elephants the names of the best of whom were *Báwan Bír*, *Bát Singár* and *Singhdulan* were animals famed for their enormous size and great courage. Thence the Sultán went to Burhánpur, and Imád-ul-Mulk fled and sought shelter with Ḳádir Sháh at Mándu,[1] the ruler of Málwa. The Sultán remained for some time at Burhánpúr, and eventually made peace, stipulating that the public sermon should be read and the coins struck in his name. After the return of the Sultán to Gujarát, all the power fell into Daryá Khán's hands, and only the name of royalty remained with the Sultán. Daryá Khán carried on the administration in such a way that there was no one in Gujarát either gentle or simple, who did not bless his rule and was not pleased and grateful for it. The people said that the time of Sultán Mehmúd Begda, which was the best period of the sway of the Sultáns of Gujarát, had returned. Every one lived in pleasure and happiness according to his means. They found in the word *Khush-hál* (meaning happy) an apt chronogram for the begin-

---

[1] This was the Mallú Khán of Sultán Bahádur's reign. Mallú Khán became the subject of the following poetical epigram improvised by Sher Sháh Súr when in A. C. 1542, he was dragged down from the throne of Mándu by the weight of that monarch's displeasure and when shortly afterwards Mallú escaped from his captivity :—

باما چه کرد دیدي ٠٠ مآو غلام گیدي

See how this slave base-born,
Mallú treats us with scorn.

To which one of Sher Sháh's courtiers as promptly replied :—

قول رسول برحق ٠٠ لاخیو فیا العبیدي

The words of the Prophet are true,
A slave, ne'er weal can do !
Farishtah, Persian Text II. 533-34.

ning of his administration. The letters forming this word yield the numerical value of the Hijrah year 945 (A. D. 1538). They say that Daryá Khán gave an exceedingly large number of grants of land (*wazifáhs*) in Gujarát. There were few pious men to whom Daryá Khán did not give grants. Many soldiers with large families who held estates on military tenure were given additional lands in reward. They say that he used to keep with him numerous blank forms of grants ready made out with the King's seals attached, wanting only the name of the donee and the extent of the land to be given to be inserted, lest deserving people should be kept waiting or should have to experience the bitterness of dancing attendance on clerks and place-men. Whenever he heard of a recluse engaged in God's service or of a deserving person in want, he used to fill in one of those forms the name of the person, the extent of the land yielding revenue proportionate to his wants or deserts, and to send him the grant duly completed. It is related that one day having in this way filled in an order he sent it together with some ready money by one of his servants to a certain pious man. The man by mistak gave the money and the order to another man of the same name. When the Khán heard that the person he meant had not received his donation he inquired of his servant who said he had given it to a certain person, but that if the Khán wished he would take it back from him and make it over to the man the Khán meant to be the real recipient. The Khán said he did not mean the man, but that God had given it to him and that the taking back would change the pleasure it had given into pain and it would not be right. He filled in another *firmán* for a larger area of land and sent it together with some gold to the right man thinking that as he and the accidental recipient of his bounty bore the same name it would be better if the land given to each was not equal in extent, and also that the *firmán* or one of the grantees might not in future be considered a forgery. With all these good qualities Daryá Khán was a man of pleasure. He gave up affairs of State to the management of Álam Khán Lodi, and himself fell to the enjoyment of music and sensuality. They say that during the administration of Daryá Khán, every house and mansion, every alley and market-place, echoed with the sound of music and song, of carousal and revelry. He had famous and talented musicians in his service like Náyak Abhú and Náyak Husaini, the son of Náyak Bakhshú, and Rang Khán and Malhaí, the sons of Náik Chatar, and Khem Harman, who had such magic in their song as to bring down and enthrall Venus from the height of the Heavens[1] and whose soul-stirring melody breathed life into the bones of the long departed (famous professor) Náik Gopál. He employed many other singers besides these, each of whom was unsurpassed in his particular branch of the art. Of dancing girls and professors of the Terpsichorean art there were people like Mohanrao and Rang Ráo and Desi Ráo and Kanhúráo[2] at whose dancing the Heavens suspended their revolution and the Moon looked pale for envy. Sayad Mehmúd Bukhári used to say that he remembered from his father the following anecdote on the authority of Bái Champa, the concubine of Sultán Muzaffar whose mention has gone before. The Bái used to say: "One day Daryá Khán came to pay his respects to me and invited me to one of his parties. As soon as I placed my foot in his hall of entertainment the clouds of perfume that arose overpowered me and the sight of the colours and patterns of his carpets and the elegance and beauty of the painting and gilding of his halls struck me with bewilderment. Though I belong to the *harím* of Sultán Muzaffar who also had an elegant taste for and was not a little fond of such things, yet even in his time I do not remember having seen such an entertainment."

At last, however, all this state and pomp of his came to an end, and in this wise :—Although accounts of the extremities to which the Khán indulged in and carried his voluptuous and luxurious habits often reached the Sultán, he invariably disregarded and left unheeded the reports. Nor did the Sultán in public or private display any disgust or dislike. Daryá Khán, however, could never catch a word from which the Sultán's inner thoughts could be understood. He was always trying to find out the real state of the Sultán's mind, and had ordered the attendants to let him know his daily and hourly thoughts. They say he one night sent to the Sultán a girl of the girls of his house in whose intelligence and sharpness of wit he had full confidence. He instructed her, when in privacy with the Sultán, to try and lead the conversation to himself and to speak complainingly and with apparent ill-will of him and to hear what he said. He also told her to say that the Sultán

---

[1] Venus in the ancient Persian Pantheon holds the place of Terpsichore in the Greek, and is called the dancer of the celestial regions رقّاصِ فلک Rakkási falak.

[2] This word is illegible in my edition of the text. Sir Clive Bayley omits this anecdote altogether. See his History of Gujarat 411, Note 1.

was King only in name and that the enjoyment of virtual power was
in the hand of Daryá Khán and that this was far from the jealousy
with which kings should guard the royal prerogative.   He asked
her to communicate to him the reply the Sultán should give her by
a certain eunuch early in the morning.   The girl went and had the
honour of being admitted to the bed of the Sultán.   However much
she talked of the treachery of Daryá Khán the Sultán did not give ear,
and when in the morning the Sultán awoke, he got up and standing
on a corner of his cot he voided water[1].   When the girl saw this she
sent word to Daryá Khán by the eunuch early in the morning
relating this circumstance and stating that the poor monarch was
crazed and did not know whether to make water sitting or standing.
When Daryá Khán heard this, he exclaimed : " My friends, I do not
know what to think of this young man ! The more I try to fathom him
the more I fail.   This much I can say that he is either the greatest
of all fools or the shrewdest of the wise !"   It so happened that one
day Alam Khán Lodi and Alíf Khán and Wajíh-ul-Mulk Tánk
and Alp Khán Khatri who were intimate friends of one another
and of Daryá Khán asked Daryá Khán's leave to go to their estates
He said : " With pleasure ! But it strikes me that I should first show
you a performance of my dancing girls and then give you leave."
It was fixed that this entertainment should take place the following
night.   All of them with light and happy hearts went to their homes.
When the light of the day changed into the darkness of the night
Latíf-ul-mulk, another of the intimate friends of Daryá Khán, went
to the house of Alam Khán.   Latíf-ul-mulk was famed for his great
beauty, and for that reason, Daryá Khán did not admit him to his
entertainments.   Latíf-ul-mulk used on this account to feel much
chagrined and mortified.   Going to Alam Khán's house Latíf-ul-mulk
by way of mischief told him : " I feel great pity for you and have come
to acquaint you with the truth.   Be it known to you then that Daryá
Khán has so arranged that having got up an entertainment and plied
you with wine he may kill all four of you."   On hearing this they
became much concerned and alarmed as to what remedy to adopt to
escape from this calamity.   Their connection with Daryá Khán was
of such a close nature that they could, on the one hand, hardly believe

---

[1] To void the urine in a standing position is in the East a breach of propriety
so egregious that the person guilty of it is considered either a reprobate whose
evidence the Law of Islám rejects against a respectable Muslim, or a maniac who is
not responsible for his actions.

he would entertain such a design against them without cause or reason; while, on the other hand, they could not doubt Latif Khán's veracity. They passed the night in great care and anxiety and passed the following morning also in the same restless deliberation. When night came Daryá Khán made his preparations for the reception and sent men to fetch the above nobles, who having prepared for death presented themselves. Daryá Khán, ignorant of the supicions that troubled his friends, his object in giving the entertainment being to promote intimacy, tried to make the reception pleasant by expressing happiness and taking infinite pains to put his friends at ease. His endeavours, however, failed to dispel the cloud of anxiety from their brows. All the guests having arrived the time now came for the cup to circulate. As often as these nobles drank they intimated by signs to one another that the cup they were quaffing was the cup of death, when they glanced at the dancers they began already to imagine them Houris of Paradise. The spirits of the melancholy friends drooped in proportion to the pitch to which rose the hilarity of the mirthful Darya Khán. When Daryá Khán, instead of seeing signs of gratified enjoyment in the faces of his friends, saw them shadowed with anxiety and apprehension, he said : "Friends, what is the matter? Why do I not see you merry and joyous in such an entertainment?" They hung down their heads. When he pressed them much for an explanation, Álam Khán said : "It is the fear of losing our lives makes us so !" "How?" asked Daryá Khán. "It came to our ears from Latif Khán," returned Álam Khán, "that you would kill us to-night. Having heard such a thing how could our faces beam with happiness?" At these words the fire of indignation began to rage in Daryá Khán's heart and he broke up the party and sent for the Kuráan and swore on it that what they had heard from Latif-ul-mulk was not in his farthest thoughts. He comforted them and dismissed them, and in the morning they left for their respective seats in the country. Daryá Khán then sent for Latif-ul-mulk and told him : "Thou wretch ! why didst thou invent this lie against me ?" And he ordered his head and beard to be shaved and sent him round the streets of the city astride on a donkey and then committed him to prison. The friends and relatives of Latif-ul-mulk went to the chief men of the city and supplicated them to mediate with Daryá Khán for his release, and his release was obtained. The unhappy man remained for some time concealed in his house till his hair and beard grew again. He then went to Álam Khán and said to him: "Was it becoming of you to bring such a disgrace on one who out of sympathy said a word of warning to you?" Álam Khan was ashamed and told him: "Wait, I give up my claim to the titles of gentility and manliness till I avenge these wrongs on Daryá Khán."

Imád-ul-mulk leaving Burhánpur went to Málwa. Mallú Khán was the ruler of that country. Mallú Khán was one of the house-born slaves of the Sultáns of Málwa. When Sultán Bahádur conquered Málwa Mallú Khán entered his service. The Sultán was kind to him and kept his son Langar Khán in his presence and sent him with Muhammad Sháh in pursuit of the fugitive Mughal army when it was driven out of Gujarát. Langar Khán was killed at Diu with Sultán Bahádur, as has been related above, when Muhammad Sháh also tasted the cup of Death. Mallú Khán remained at Mándu, and consolidating his power by degrees brought all the territories of Mándu under his rule. Mallú and Imád-ul-mulk were close friends and Imád-ul-mulk, while he was in power during the commencement of the reign of Mehmúd Sháh, sent the umbrella of royalty with permission to strike coin in his name and to adopt the title of Kádir Sháh to Mallú Khán. Mallú Khán ordered the public Friday sermon to be read and the coin to be struck in his name, and styled himself Kádir Sháh, and his intimacy with Imád-ul-mulk increased apace. When evil days came upon Imád-ul-mulk, as has been above related, he took shelter with his friend Mallú Khán. Darya Khán, displeased at this, got a royal order to be written to Kádir Sháh in the name of the Sultán to the following effect:—"Though the bonds of friendship and loyalty of Kádir Sháh with the Gujarát House are strong, it was a matter of great surprise to hear that Kádir Sháh had given harbour to Imád-ul-mulk, who, preferring disobedience to duty, had first gone to Mubárak Sháh. Kádir Shah must have heard what misfortunes his ill-omened advent had brought on Mubárak Sháh. Now that it was heard that Imád-ul-mulk had gone to him (i.e., to Kádir Sháh), it was fit that he should capture him and send him to the foot of the throne or expel him from Málwa and renew his former friendly connection with this kingdom." Kádir Sháh wrote in reply that "Imád-ul-mulk had given up the profession of arms and had become a darwísh. That as he, Imád-ul-mulk, was an old slave of the throne of Gujarát he had bestowed a village upon Imád-ul-mulk, thinking it not meet to allow him to carry his suit to foreign courts. That

Sultán Mehmúd might rest assured that Imád-ul-mulk had given up all claims to and ideas of politics, adopted silence and retired to the corner of seclusion and obscurity." Darya Khán was afraid lest his enemy should gain the help of some powerful auxiliary. The possible descent of Imád-ul-mulk even by himself upon Gujarát was to Darya Khán the source of constant dread and disturbance of mind. He was much hurt at these words, ordered a march, and directed the advance equipage of the Sultán to be taken to the palace of Khamdrol, which is situated near the Kánkaria tank outside the city of Ahmedábád. He sent orders to the nobles and military officers to come up with their forces as an expedition against Kádir Sháh was resolved upon. The nobles with their forces came pouring in from all sides. After some time he took the Sultán also to the camp quarters but himself remained in the city. He used to spend about two hours of his time every day at the camp in the Sultán's service, and then returning to the city used to spend the rest of his day in pleasure and enjoyment. The whole of the army too used to return to the city in his following, and only a limited number of guards used to remain with the Sultán and these also after performing their turns of duty used, on being relieved by others, to return to the city.

So long as the Sultán was of tender years he bore all this, allowing things to take their course, but now he had reached the period when he began to step from boyhood into the prime of youth, and his desires began to assert themselves. He began to sigh and be grieved, for what his heart yearned for was enjoyed by Daryá Khán. It is related that, one day Daryá Khán took the Sultán, with Mírán Sayad Mubárak Bukhári, to his house to show them one of his entertainments. When the Sultán entered the mansion, and saw the sylph-like forms of the dancing-girls he well nigh lost his senses. Some of these girls especially so charmed him, that, the large number of valuable jewels that he had brought to present them with, appeared quite trifling in his eyes. The Sultán sat up till late in the night. Daryá Khán then got up from the assembly, retired into privacy with one of those fair-faced ones and with her in his arms sank to sleep. The Sultán was left alone. He could not brook this, and whispered into Sayad Mubárak's ear :—" Míránji ! do you see the insolence of the slave ? He has left us alone, and is drunk, and has presumed fearlessly to retire

28

with that girl ! " The Mírán said :—" Never mind Sire ! All these
that you have seen, shall before long, be the servants of your Majesty.
It is only a question of time ! "

VERSES.

> There is a time for every thing,
> A season for each tree,
> *Tamúz* does not the violets bring,
> Nor roses the month of *Dí*.[1]

And the sequel did so turn out that all the harem, treasure,
circumstance and state of Daryá Khán fell into the hands of the
Sultán, as shall be mentioned hereafter.

When Álam Khán heard that the Sultán lived outside the city,
that Daryá Khán, with the army, passed the nights in the city, and
that the Sultán was much vexed and pained at this treatment, he
sent a petition secretly to the Sultán from Dhandúka, which is about
forty-five miles from Ahmedábád and which formed a part of Álam
Khán's estates, stating that he was an ancient and faithful vassal of the
Sultán's house, and could not bear to see Darya Khán lording it over his
king in such luxury and pleasure, and his king passing his days in
such pitiful privation and penury. That he had therefore retired in
silence to his estates, but that if the Sultán had any desire of dominion
he might go to Álam Khán's estate and then his servants would remove
the oppressor. The Sultán sent Charji, the bird-catcher, whom he
afterwards ennobled with the title of Muháfiz Khán, on pretence of
bringing some hawks from Júnágadh, to meet Álam Khán at the town
of Dhandúka, which was on the way to Júnágadh, and on his return,
to take from Álam Khán the oath of allegiance and fealty. Charji
went to Álam Khán, and returned with the most satisfactory
professions and assurances from him to the Sultán, and it was arranged
that two hundred horsemen should march by night from Dhandúka, and present themselves under the Khamdrol-Palace walls,
and that the Sultán, joining them, should be conveyed towards
Dhandúka to Álam Khán. On the appointed night the horsemen
brought a horse-carriage below the palace walls. The Sultán
grasping a rope, alighted, and seating himself in the carriage began
to traverse space with the miraculous speed of a saint (flitting
through it). In the morning he reached Jámbwa, a village under

---

[1] Tamúz, is the month corresponding with July, as Dí is the first month of the
winter corresponding with December, of the Syrián and Pahlavi calendar.

Jhálawár, about thirty-nine miles from Ahmedábád. Wajíh-ul-Mulk, the holder of that fief, came forward to meet him and had an interview. The Sultán stayed a little while and again departed, and reached Dhandúka. Álam Khán came, and doing himself the honour of kissing the Sultán's feet, said " May the arrival of the Sultán be auspicious! God willing matters will take the course hoped for by his loyal followers. "

When Daryá Khán, after sunrise, according to his custom, went from his house to the Darbár, he heard that the Sultán had gone away to Álam Khán. Daryá Khán asked Fattúji Muháfiz Khán, who was his intimate friend, and confidant, what was to be done. The latter said : "However much I enjoined thee before this, to blind this youth and put such another in his place as would remain submissive to thy control, thou didst not regard my counsel; still, before he has gained power, set up another king, assemble an army, and we shall yet capture him alive."

Daryá Khán, having produced one of the grandsons of Ahmed Sháh from Ahmedábád, caused the public sermon to be read, and the coin to be struck in his name, and giving him the title of Sultán Muzaffar, collected fifty or sixty thousand horse, and advanced on Dhandúka. From the other side, the Sultán, with Álam Khán, at the head of ten or twelve thousand horse, opposed him in the vicinity of the village of Dáhor under Dholka, about forty miles from Ahmedábád. They say that though Daryá Khán took infinite pains to try and win the hearts of his soldiery, that they still deserted him and went over to the Sultán.[1] They say that, in this engagement Álam Khán was posted on the right[2] of the Sultán's forces, and that on the side of Daryá Khán opposite to Álam Khán was Fattúji-Muháfiz Khán, a brave man, one of whose constant sayings was :— "God Almighty! it always surprises me why one man should flee from another!"—On the left side of the Sultán, were Mujáhid Khán Behlím, who was known by his title of Mújahid-ul-mulk and his brothers and on the side of the enemy, opposite to them was Shamsher-ul-mulk,

---

[1] A longish piece of poetry omitted.

[2] My translation does not agree here with Sir Clive Bayley's in more than one point. According to my MS. Álam Khán was posted on the Sultan's right and not on left, and it is more likely that the Sultán would at such an important juncture honour him by posting him on the right. Also, according to my MS. Mujáhid-ul-mulk was Mujáhid Khán's title and not the name of his brother. But this, as will be seen further on, is an error.

brother of Fattúji Muháfiz Khán. Wájíh-ul-mulk and Táj Khán and
Alaf Khán Durráni, the Afghán, and Alp Khán Khatri were ˙in the
centre with Sultán Mehmúd. Against the Sultán, on the opposite side,
was Daryá Khán and the new king he had set up with the name of Sultán
Muzaffar and some other Kháns such as Sultán Aláuddín, brother of
Sikandar Lodi, king of Dehli, who had come and entered the Gujarát
service in the time of Sultán Bahádur. In the van on both sides were
men of tried valour and experience, veterans who had seen war.
They say before van dashed against van in hand to hand combat
Álam Khán from the Sultán's side and Fattúji Muháfiz Khán from
the other, advanced and engaged in a personal encounter. The
conflict lasted for the greater part of an hour and waxed so hot
that sparks of fire flashed forth from the cuirasses and helmets
of the combatants. In the end Fattúji was defeated and he retired
to the centre of Daryá Khán's army. With this part of Daryá Khán's
army he again attacked the centre of Sultán Mehmúd. The Sultán
unable to withstand the shock was routed and retired to Ránpúr, a
town, about fifteen miles, to the west of Dhandúkhá. From Ránpur
he went to the village of Kot Pálliád, nearly eight miles from Ránpúr
in the district of Saroha, under the province of Sorath. Álam Khán,
on being defeated, went to Sádra, a place on the bank of the
Sábarmati, about twenty-six miles north of Ahmedábád. Daryá
Khán returned in triumph and victory, and encamped near
Dholka. But the fortune of Sultán Mehmúd was on the ascendant.
In spite of the Sultán's reverses on the field, the men of Daryá
Khán's army came pouring in to him, deserting Daryá Khán
and joining either Alam Khán or the Sultán, so that in three
or four days Álam Khán could again muster 12,000 horse. He
wrote to the Sultán to join him, saying, that, this time, God willing,
they would beat the rebels and capture their leaders alive. When
Daryá Khán saw his ranks deserting him and thinning daily and
going over to the Sultán, he did not think proper to remain at
Dhandúká, and marched towards Ahmedábád, thinking that he was
after all master of the treasury, and that his gold would again bring
him about a large army. But when he appeared before the city, the
citizens closed the gates in his face and opened a musketry fire
upon him, and would not give him admission, saying he was a traitor.
He left the gates, and gained entrance into the city by breaking open
the Vírampur wicket. He was daily cheering his men by open-

handed gifts of gold, but they went out at nights and joined the Sultán. The Sultán now marched towards Ahmedábád, and Darya Khàn fearing lest the citizens should capture him and make him over to the Sultán, sent his women and treasures on with Fattúji to Chàmpáner, instructing him to establish himself firmly there, and that he would proceed to Mubárakshàh at Burhánpúr, and bring him to their aid. With this arrangement he left for Burhánpúr. This took place in A. H. 950 (A. D. 1543).

The Sultán made his triumphal entry into Ahmedábád with good fortune and left for Chámpáner and going up to that place by forced marches besieged it. Fattúji did not flinch from opposition and fighting, but eventually experienced, what the great and the good have said:—

> " Thy liege lord's power attempt not to defy,
> Thou'lt surely fall though thou art heaven high."

The Sultán by might of arm took the fort by storm. They say that on the day the fort was taken people saw the Sultán performing such prodigies of valour, as have not been exceeded. The sharp-shooters from the fort brought down six or seven persons standing close to the Sultán, but the Sultán did not budge an inch to right or left, nor did he cause the umbrella to be removed from over his head. However much the Vazír Afzal Khán insisted on the umbrella-bearer moving away the Sultán did not like it, and made signs to the umbrella-bearer to remain where he was, and kept on advancing, until the soldiers scaled the fort on every side, and Fattúji fled and ascended the citadel called Manliya, whence he was ultimately captured and brought before the Sultán. The Sultán ordered that he should be confined in the fort of Súrat. All the treasure and harem of Darya Khán, numbering nearly four or five hundred fair damsels fell into the Sultán's hands, and his heart was pleased, and he said to Mírán-Mubárak :—" Mírán Jí! Your words have passed from the curtain of the Unseen into the field of Entity !" The Mírán replied:

> " However long he may in freedom roam,
> The deer is destined for the lion's maw,"

Is a well-known proverb.

To continue: The Sultán remained victorious and triumphant at Chámpáner, absorbed for three months in the pleasures of youth. The post of minister was conferred on Ashraf Humáyún Burhán-ul-Mulk Bunyáni, a religious and pious man. They say Burhán-ul-Mulk once saw the Prophet, (on whom be peace) in a dream, and asked him whether what he had heard about the red-rose having been created from the Prophet's sweat was true? The Prophet of God, (on whom be peace) wiped his brow, on which there then happened to be beads of perspiration and threw them down, and lo! they were fresh red-roses. Alám Khán was given the post of Chief of the nobles and Commander-in-Chief of the army. One day, Alám Khán submitted to the Sultán, that Imád-ul-Mulk was an ancient slave of his house and that Daryá Khán had banished him for his own evil ends. If the Sultán issued a *farmán* of recall to him he would come and kiss the royal threshold. The Sultán issued a *farmán* for Imád-ul-Mulk's recall.

To continue: After his successes, the Sultán, fancying himself secure from the fickleness of fortune, began to incline towards and show kindness to the base born. He ennobled Charji, the bird-catcher with the title of Muháfiz Khán, and gave him a place about his exalted person.

That mean, narrow-minded wretch, used to drink wine, carry disreputable tales of the nobles and ministers to the Sultán and represent himself his loyal counsellor. The great men and ministers were dissatisfied on this account. About this time Imád-ul-Mulk came from Mándú. The Sultán gave him great respect, and conferring the district of Broach with the port of Súrat on him in fief, dismissed him to his seat.

Charji, the bird-catcher, one day, said to the Sultán at a wine-party: " Health and long life to your Majesty, a new tent wants new-ropes ! These old coils will be of no use, their non-existence is better than their existence. But before thinking how to rid ourselves of the others, two men should be killed forthwith : one of them is Sultán Alá-ud-dín, who was with Daryá Khán in the battle that took place near the village of Dáhor; the other is Malikji Shujá-át-Khán, who is also one of those (that joined in taking up arms against their sovereign). The killing of these two shall serve as an example for the others." The Sultán immediately, without consulting any of the ministers or nobles, ordered these two noblemen to be beheaded, and their bodies drawn on the impaling stake, and betook himself to privacy, and allowed no one admittance for three days. Hereupon Álam Khán Lodi said to Imád-ul-Mulk : " Sultán Alá-ud-dín was a brother of Sultán Sikandar Lodi, and this is the third day that his body is lying below the scaffold; tell the Sultán to permit us to take down his body, and give it decent burial." The Malik said: "I have taken leave to depart to my seat." Álam Khán insisted, saying "It does not matter." Imád-ul-Mulk went to the court. As soon as he entered the palace Charji coming out from the Sultán's chamber asked him: "Malik! you were given leave to repair to your seat, why have you returned?" The Malik said: "This is the third day that the body of Sultán Alá-ud-dín is lying under the scaffold, go and submit to the Sultán our request to be permitted to bury him. This mean wretch laughed a sardonic laugh and observed with malicious meaning:—"Malik! we have only killed two traitors to-day, we shall ere long kill more, it is no business of yours, go you to your estates." "These words kindled the fire of indignation in the breast of Imád-ul-Mulk, and he said: "My dear Khán! those others are not birds for you to kill so easily!"[1] With these words he got up, and left and went to Alam Khán and related to him all that had occurred, saying: "If you wish to live awhile, kill this wretch of a Charji, and send this Sultán out of the city." Saying so he went to his own quarters, and proceeded to his estates. Álam Khàn and Wajíh-ul-Mulk, and Alp Khán Khatri, and the whole army except Burhán-ul-Mulk, the Vazír, united together and resolved not to pay their respects to the Sultàn till they had killed Charji. Álam Khán with all the nobles armed themselves and mounted and first took the bodies of the two victims and interred them. They then came and posted themselves at the grand mosque in the palace. The Sultán prepared to undergo a seige, and for three days matters went on thus. At last water becoming scarce in the palace, and the Sultán being reduced to extremities, sent Burhán-ul-mulk to them to make enquiries as to their object. They said they were the slaves of the Sultán, and had no complaint to make against him, but that they wanted Charji to be sent over to them, as he was not fit for royal service, and was ever misleading the Sultán. The matter was much discussed, but the Sultán did not agree to give up Charji. At last Burhán-ul-mulk and Afzal Khán suggested to Alam Khán the propriety of their giving in for the present, and not pressing the point further, adding that the Sultán would accept, afterwards, whatever they would say. They said they were not rebels, and desired to be led to the Sultán, that they might pay their respects and return. The Sultán gave them audience. One of the confederate nobles was a secret friend of Charji's. He advised

---

[1] This was a covert allusion to Charji's former avocation.

him not to show himsef at this audience, as they would surely kill
him. But this ill-starred and doomed wretch, disregarding the advice
with usual perversity and vain of the royal favour, swaggered
in, drunk, and stood behind the Sultán with his hand on the
throne. When the nobles came, and each one having made his
respects, stood in his respective place. When Álam Khán's glance
fell on Charji his anger flamed up, and he gave a signal to
his men to despatch the ill-fated wretch. The followers of Álam Khán,
Sayad Chánd of Mándú, and Sáleh Muhammad Aláh-diyá and Malik
Ládan, having drawn their swords, fell on Charji, who ran and hid
himself under the throne, but they seized him by the hair of his head,
and dragging him out, cut him to pieces. However loudly he cried
for help, and the Sultán ordered his assailants to desist, it availed not.
The Sultán in impotent wrath drew out his dagger, and struck at
his abdomen, but Alp Khán caught and held his hand. Still the point
pierced the surface, and a great uproar arose. They took Charji
outside and buried him, and bandaged the Sultán's wound, and
placed him under a guard. The rule of the Sultán again ceased from
that day, and he fell in the confinement of the nobles. They kept him
under surveillance as he used formerly to be, and they left nothing to
the Sultán's discretion or power. His favour to the mean bore him
this fruit, and his patronage of low persons placed fetters on the feet
of his desires as some great man has observed:—

COUPLET.

"He's not a king who cherishes the vile,
You can't with kingship meanness reconcile."

The king who makes the promotion of low persons his rule of
conduct is sure to bring about his own ruin.

They say that the day the Sultán gave Charji the title of Muháfiz
Khán, Afzal Khán Vazír, by way of affected ignorance, asked whether
anybody knew to what tribe or class Muháfiz Khán belonged. Malik
Amín Kamál, who was a poet and a man of wit, said : " I know to
what tribe Muháfiz Khán belongs, he is a *Parmár*[1] by tribe, and holds
Nariád in fief. " Parmár is the name of a tribe of Rájputs, and Nariád
is one of the towns of Gujarát. The two words form a witticism or
pun. The play on the word *Parmár* is evident. The other play is on

---

[1] "Parmár," the name of a Musalmán Rájpüt tribe, and a play upon the words, *par*,
" *wing*," and *mar*, mover, or killer, meaning mover of wings or destroyer of winged
creatures, a very apt allusion to Charji's calling of bird-cather.

the word "Nariád," a nar (or more correctly a nal) being a long hollow bamboo stick with which they catch birds, Narya being also the name of a bird-catching animal (a ferret).[1] Another pun from Amín-ul-Mulk is also celebrated:—

One day Sultán Mehmúd asked the eunuch Khán Jehán to what tribe he belonged. He said he was very young when he was captured, and did not remember. Malik Amín said, he knew the tribe of Khán Jehán. The Sultán asked what it was, Malik Amín said, he belonged to the tribe of "Bádhel." Now Bádhel is a tribe of Rájputs, and the word *bádhel* or *vádhel* in the (Gujaráti) Hindi language means also cut or castrated. The Sultán laughed much, and ordered a reward of some *lákhs* of dáms to be given to him.

To continue: Álam Khán and Wajíh-ul-Mulk and Mujáhid Khán and Mujáhid-ul-Mulk, who were the chief men of the State and the army, resolved among themselves to undertake to keep watch over the Sultán by turns: that one day Álam Khán should keep guard over the Sultán, the next day Shujá-úl-Mulk, the brother of Álam Khán, and Wajíh-ul-Mulk, the third day Majáhid Khán and Mujáhid-ul-Mulk Behlím who were brothers, with Ázam Humáyun who was the son of an adopted sister of Álam Khán. According to this plan they guarded the Sultán, and so continued to look after him after their return to Ahmedábád. The Sultán, who was fond of polo or *chaugán*, sometimes wished to have a game. There was an open place for polo playing, in the Bhadr Palace, and he used to play in it; but to go out of the gates of the Bhadr was impossible for him.

Shujá-úl-Mulk, brother of Álam Khán, used sometimes to chaff and make fun of Mujáhid Khán Behlím, who was a fat man with a large paunch. Nisár-ul-Mulk Ghori, the manager of the estates of Mujáhid Khán and his brother did not relish and was always offended at these jokes against his master. The force contributed by Mujáhid Khán and Mujáhid-ul-Mulk to the Gujarát army was ten or twelve thousand cavalry, and the brothers held a thousand villages of Sorath for the upkeep of this force. One day, the nobles in council assembled, said among themselves that it was not politic to keep on the Sultan in that way, and that they should better draw a red-hot iron across his eyes (that is blind him) and set up some other

---

[1] Naryád, Narya, or Nurya is a ferret or a mungoose, a quadrupedal bird-catcher, as Charji was by profession a bipedal one.

boy as sovereign in his place ; others suggested it would be better still to divide the kingdom among themselves. No sooner said than they began to parcel out the provinces of the kingdom amongst themselves, saying : " This one shall have this province, and that one the other." Nisár-ul-Mulk, who was the chief man of the meeting, asked what districts they were going to apportion to his master. Shujá-ul-Mulk facetiously observed : " Mujáhid Khán's paunch does not require an increase of estates, there should, on the contrary, be some decrease from what he already enjoys." Mujáhid Khán passed this off as a jest, and the nobles dispersed. Although Mujáhid Khán did not care for these words, his manager Nisár-ul-Mulk was hurt, and said that, although Shujá-ul-Mulk had said the words seemingly in jest, yet they disclosed his inner thoughts on the principle that "a vessel exudes nothing but its contents.[1]" So said he, he knew what feelings they entertained towards his master.

"To check the evil ere it harms is best,
Regret is vain when it is passed arrest."

Nisár-ul-Mulk used to frequent the presence of the king more than the other nobles, and the consultation of the nobles to draw a redhot needle, through his eyes, had reached the king's ears. On hearing this, the Sultán wept and became painfully anxious as to his fate, and said he would much rather they killed than blinded him.

One night Nisár-ul-Mulk told the Sultán that he was a devoted slave of the Sultán's, and that he had something to tell him if he was willing to hear. The Sultán was at first afraid that he might say something in the same way in which the son of Mukbil Khan did, some time ago, as has been mentioned above, and which, he feared, might lead to greater severity on the part of his custodians. So he said guardedly : " What have you to say to me, and what can I do ? " Nisár-ul-Mulk said : " The Sultán of the world must have heard of the resolution of the nobles ? Your majesty has either to accept blindness or to think how to save yourself from this evil ? The Sultán said : " Who is going to help me." He said : Mujáhid Khan and Mujáhid-ul-Mulk, who have ten or twelve thousand horse ready for service." "If," said he, " the Sultán commands, I shall bring them all armed and equipped. When an hour of the night remains, the Sultán should mount in state elevating the royal umbrella and go and storm the

---

[1] This is the Arabic proverb—"Every vessel exudes what it contains."

houses of Âlam Khán and Wajih-ul-Mulk, and order them to be plundered. These two will be sleeping the sleep of security, and we shall God willing, either capture them alive before the enemy has time to assemble, or send them forth to wander in the wilderness of exile." The Sultán said : "Then let Mujáhid Khán and Mujáhid-ul-Mulk come and enter into agreement with us. They were haply present, as that night was their turn of duty with Ázam Humáyún, the relative of Âlam Khán. So the two nobles with Nisár-ul-Mulk came and took their oaths of fidelity on the Kurán. The Sultán said : "Ázam Humáyún is also present, how will you keep this secret from him?" Nisár-ul-Mulk, saying he would send him off to his house, rose and went to Ázam Humáyún and entered into friendly discourse with him. It so happened that in those days, Ázam Humáyún was fascinated by the charms of a female singer, and used always to talk to his friends of his love and passion for her. Nisár-ul-Mulk drawing him into conversation said to him : "One who has a friend like me (to watch over his interests in his absence) need not suffer (the pangs of separation from his lady-love), " why don't you go and enjoy the company of your mistress ? Your men are present on guard." Ázam Humáyún said : "Âlám Khán sends men two or three times in the night to inquire after me." He said : "Place a pillow length-wise on your bed and spread a sheet over it and order a servant to sit at the foot of your bed and pretend to shampoo you, so that the man from Âlám Khán will think you are asleep and go away." Ázam Humáyún did so, and Nisár-ul-Mulk going back to the Sultán told him he had sent him home and had placed five hundred of his own men in the hall of audience and had posted as many thousand well-armed horsemen iu the Nikúr Bazár, and that the Sultán should, as agreed upon, mount, at the time fixed, and go to the houses of the traitors. He said he would despatch the men of Ázam Humáyun that were on guard before that, and that, God willing, they should gain their object.

The Sultán did just as was agreed upon. When an hour of the night remained, he mounted, and elevating the royal umbrella over his head, he placed the elephants bearing the big kettle drums in front and issued forth. When the people of the city saw the king, they came forth in crowds from every nook-and-corner and assembled in great numbers. The Sultán gave the order for the houses of the traitors Âlám Khán and Wajih-ul-Mulk to be plundered, and that they might be driven out of the city. Nisár-ul-Mulk at the head of his men preceded the Sultán, who followed him slowly. The houses of Álám Khán and Wajíh-ul-Mulk were without the city walls outside the Jamálpúr gate. They had spent the night at a dancing party, where, having drunk wine, they were now securely immersed in sleep. They never suspected what calamity the womb of this fateful night would bring forth for them, as the Sultán was their prisoner and they had three or four thousand veteran horsemen of tried valour devoted to their cause, mounting guard over him every night, and the whole army of the kingdom under their orders. Forgetful of the fact, that—

"When evil fortune grasps the neck,
The veins of the neck become chains."

They did not think any one in the world could harm them.

They say that the men of Álám Khán and Wajíh-ul-Mulk's households were sound asleep. When the uproar arose Álám Khán got up, and, coming to the vestibule, saw that the city vagabonds had entered his house and were crying out : "The orders of the Sultán are that these rascals should not issue forth and must be captured alive."

Álám Khán was in a state of ceremonial uncleanness[1], so emptying over his head a vessel of cold water, he mounted the horse of one of the orderlies on guard and issued forth. He saw several horsemen advancing towards him. He attacked and slew one of them and the others giving way he rode off. The horsemen joined by some others again pressed in his pursuit. When they came up to Álam Khán they would have fallen upon him and despatched him, but two of his faithful retainers, who had accompanied him, Sáleh Muhammad Aláh-diya the slayer of Charji, and the brother of Sheikh Arzáni Multáni, both turning back, engaged the horsemen in a hand-to-hand combat and were slain. This check gave Álam Khán time to escape; but the members of his family, great and small, were taken prisoners.

---

[1] The law of Islám ordains two purifications. The *ghusl* or major purification and the *wudhu* or minor one. The first, required to be performed in extraordinary cases (such as cohabitation or emission of the semen for men and after child-birth or courses for women) consists in the repetition of certain formula with the total immersion of the body in water. The second to be performed before prayers consists in the washing of the mouth, the face, the hands and feet and other parts of the body in a certain formally prescribed manner and order.

It is related by respectable authorities of Gujarát, that there was a man named Kabír Muhammad, who had passed the greater portion of his life, and had grown grey in Âlam Khán's service. He had witnessed the lights and shades of Fortune, and observed the legerdemains of the times and the trickery and the fox-like cunning of the world. When Âlam Khán got the Sultán within his power, and confined him within the limits of the Bhadr-walls, and set Âzam Humáyún to watch over him, with five or six thousand devoted and veteran troops, who remained always on guard out of the twenty-eight thousand horsemen set apart by Âlam Khán for that purpose, and when Kabír Muhammad saw that Âlam Khán himself took up quarters outside the city walls, in the Asoria quarter of Ahmedabad, and entrusting the watch to his nephew Âzam Humáyún occupied himself in luxury and pleasure and wine and wassail, then, they say, this Kabír Muhammad warned Âlam Khán. "Sir!" said the old man "you have caged a lion and yourself lounge at ease at home, entrusting him to other hands! Either proceed yourself to watch over him, or take better care of him, and remember what happened before, and fear the day when he breaks his chains, and sets the whole world by the ears On that day no one will (consider it worth his while to) oppose him." Âlam Khán gave him no reply, and, as all the army and all the great nobles were on his side made light of his wise words, and thought them craven counsel. Yet Kabír Muhammad was a brave man. He had seen the reflection of the aspect of the events of this day in the mirror of his experience. From the beginning of this plot against the Sultán this wise man used to sit up every night from sunset to sunrise, armed and accoutred, at Âlam Khán's house, expecting this evil moment every night for the last five years, till the black hour really came. Just before the army came to Âlam Khán's house, some unknown person ascended a half-ruined minaret near the Jamálpur gate and called out in a loud voice that the Sultán had given up Âlam Khán's house to plunder. Âlam Khán, who had passed the whole night in revelry and debauch, had dropped into a heavy sleep towards the latter part of the night, when this voice fell on the ear of Kabír Muhammad, who at once going up to the Khán's zanánah called out to the inmates to immediately wake up the Khán, as in a moment the Sultán would be there. The personal attendant present waked up the Khán, who asked what the uproar was. Kabír Muhammad said, "It is the same turmoil that I had anticipated from the beginning. The caged lion has

snapped his chains, come out soon." Álam Khán coming out mounted
Kabír Muhammad's horse and set out. Four horsemen blocked the
Khán's way. The valiant old man attacked them, and disabled three
out of the four. The one that remained put an end to Kabír
Muhmmad's life. This, however, gave Álam Khán time to distance
his pursuers. God's mercy on the loyal Kabír Muhammad, and his
valuable experience !

The house of Wajíh-ul-Mulk was also plundered, but his family
concealed themselves and could not be found. They say that
when the Sultán reached the Nikúr Bazar, he sent Aiyúb Khán, the
brother of Násir-ul-mulk, to call Afzal Khán, the old retired minister,
who lived in a house in that quarter. When the Sultán reached the
door of his house, he came forth and kissed the royal stirrup, and
followed the retinue. Till then he had not set foot out of his house,
as has been mentioned above. They say, that the Sultán had hardly
reached the Jamálpur Gate, when the city people met him carrying
loads of the timber, wood-work of Álam Khán and Wajíh-ul-Mulk's
houses, and saying that the traitors had escaped and their houses
were plundered.

COUPLET.

"A rabble mob is like a fire
Destroying where it goes."

The Sultán then returned to his palace. This event happened in
the year H. 952 (A. D. 1545).

After overcoming Álam Khán and Wajíh-ul-Mulk, the conduct
of public affairs again returned to the Sultán's hands. Álam
Khán fled to Pethápur, which is a village belonging to a
Hindu chief. He wrote from Pethápur to Daryá Khán, who
had taken up residence in the Dakhan, expressing regret and
repentance for his past conduct, and stating that he was conscious
that his sufferings were the inevitable and direct result of his
actions. He now asked Daryá Khán to come soon that they might
both combine and do something. Daryá Khán was in a miserable
condition in the Dakhan. He used to dispose of his valuable diamonds
at cheap rates, and pass his days on the proceeds. When he came to
know that he was wanted by Álam Khán, he at once set out by forced
marches, and they met at a village of the name of Naipura. Daryá
Khán said, it was with mature consideration, he used to keep the Sultán

in confinement. Âlam Khán said: "Recall not the past, [1] we must do something to avenge ourselves." Daryá Khán said: "We are moneyless, Alp Khán is your friend, and lives in the town of Uklesar (five or six miles from Broach, on the river Narbada). Go you to him and see him, and if you can, meet with Imád-ul-Mulk also. This is very advisable, as you will be able to get some money, also from them, which is very necessary."

Âlam Khán with 500 horse marched quickly and reached Uklesar, and going straight to Alp Khán's house, alighted there. Alp Khán was then at Broach with Imád-ul-Mulk. Âlam Khán sent word to Alp Khan's family, saying: " Give them my blessings and ask them to send me some food, for I am hungry." Now, though Âlam Khán and Alp Khán were close friends, yet at this time as Alp Khán was in the service of the Sultán, and Âlam Khán an outlawed rebel, to send him food and show him hospitality was fraught with danger. What, on the other hand, could Alp Khán's people do? Alp Khán's family, and household, his treasure, and his elephants were in this town, and here was Âlam Khán (an old friend) who had turned up quite suddenly. How could they refuse him such a thing as a meal? So the people of Alp Khán made preparations for Âlam Khán's food, and sent a man to Alp Khán explaining matters.

Alp Khán said: "Does this man want to ruin me too with himself?" He mentioned the circumstance to Imád-ul-Mulk. Now, Imád-ul-Mulk owed his return to power and property to the good offices of Âlam Khán as has been mentioned above. He could not be ungenerous to Âlam Khán, and sent word to him to say that it was not meet that he should have come in that fashion. As, however, he had come, he might re-cross the Narbada and meet him. Âlam Khán did so, and Alp Khán and Imád-ul-Mulk went and met him. Âlam Khán said: "Alp Khán, is it right in the sight of God that I should be in such misery, and you in such ease?" Alp Khán replied: "Now, by your coming you have made me your equal (i. e., dragged me down to a par with you" Âlam Khán said, still the advantage was on his side, and there was no equality, as he had escaped alive from the Sultán's claws, while Alp Khán was yet within his power, and that if he still did not go out against him (the Sultán)

---

[1] The text has the Arabic proverb: Al-mází-lá-yuzkáro—the past is not to be remembered.

he would not leave him alive. If, said he, Alp Khán wanted to live, he should act in concert with him. He added : "It was at Imád-ul-Mulk's desire that I killed Charji, except Charji's death no crime can be laid at my door." Imád-ul-Mulk said: "It was out and out crudeness of understanding on your part. If you killed Charji, you had no reason to be neglectful in keeping watch over the Sultán. Now the chain has slipped from the lion's neck, and he won't take the noose again." Âlam Khán said : "Let by-gones be by-gones, I shall try now not to fail in whatever I undertake." After great discussion, Imád-ul-Mulk and Alp Khán gave some money to Âlam Khán and dismissed him. Âlam Khán returned to Daryá Khán, and recounted all that had happened. Daryá Khán said : "It was not only to bring funds that I had sent you to these nobles. There was also this motive, that from the day you should meet them the names of these dear friends also should be written down side by side with ours (in the list of rebels), and that they should not have the face to join the Sultán, and would have *nolens volens* to make up with us." And it happened that this news did ultimately reach the Sultán, and threw him into considerable anxiety.

About this time a petition from Imád-ul-Mulk reached the Sultán, that Daryá Khán and Âlam Khán were old servants of the State, and it was not becoming that they should have to go to Sher Sháh at Dehli (as refugees). That it was advisable that the Sultán should give them some service on the frontiers. The Sultán agreed to this request of the Malik, when another trick of Âlam Khán broke down this arrangement. When the order for the plundering of Âlam Khán's house went forth, he himself, as has been related above, escaped leaving his family and valuables in the hands of the Sultán. The Sultán entrusted them to the vigilant care of the royal eunuchs and guardians. After a while Âlam Khán sought the support and intercession of Sayad Mubárak Bukhári to get the Sultán's sanction to the exchange of his family for his brother Safdar Khán. Sayad Mubárak moved in his behalf, and obtained the release of his family for Safdar Khán. The Sultán made over Safdar Khán to the Sayad's care, and the Sayad used to keep him with great kindness and courtesy in the upper storey of his own mansion. After some time Âlam Khán sent Sádhu Náyak, one of his followers, to secrotly spirit Safdar Khán away to him. Sádhu came and throwng a rope to Safdar Khán one night, got him down, and carried him off to his brother Álam Khán. At this proceeding Sayad Mubárak was much humiliated and the Sultán thrown into considerable anxiety lest Álam Khán and Daryá Khán and Imád-ul-Mulk and Alp Khán should again combine and raise a disturbance. He sent an order to Imád-ul-Mulk saying that he considered him one of his liege servants 'and that it was not becoming that he should suffer Daryá Khán and Alp Khán to remain with impunity in one of the frontiers of his guarded dominions, and create a fear of sedition. He should, therefore, start immediately ' for the royal presence to consider what steps should be taken against these men. Imád-ul-Mulk wrote an excuse, stating that he would come after making arrangements for the expedition. The Sultán wrote another order summoning him to the capital. This time he wrote back plainly to say that he had committed a great fault in having allowed Álam Khán to visit him, but that his object being to give him good advice was loyal ; as, however, he had done so without the cognizance of the Sultán he considered himself guilty. If the Sultán sent Sayad Áríshah, the son of Sayad Záhíd, the son of Kutbul Aktáb Sayad Burhán-ud-din Bukhári, with his royal parole for his safety he would come under the Sayad's lead. The Sultán went to Sayad Áríshah and asked him to go and fetch Imád-ul-Mulk. The Sayad said : "Your Majesty is a King, and have always to shape your course of action according to the policy of the time. I am a poor devotee whose business it is to pray, and your Majesty need not put me to this sort of trouble." The Sultán placed his hand on the Kuráan and said : "Between you and me is this sacred Word of God, if from any act of mine any harm comes to the life, the living, or the honour of Imád-ul-Mulk." The Sayad told the minister, Afzal Khán : "The Sultán is young and you are experienced and wise, why do you put me to this trouble ?" Afzal Khán said : "Míránji (my dear lord !) I also swear by the Kuráan and vouch for the sincerity of the Sultán's affirmation. You should not allow any concern to approach your heart and take Imád-ul-Mulk by the hand and bring him here."

The holy Sayad set out for Broach, and the Sultán marched against Daryá Khán and Álam Khán who were in the neighburhood of Chámpáner. When the Sayad reached Imád-ul-Mulk, he asked him: "Why did you write that Áríshah should come and take you by the hand. This was not right. Now the Sultán and Afzal Khán have sworn on the Kuráan that no harm should come to your life or

property or reputation. Farther, you know best. I am not much
conversant with the ways and tricks of the world. If you think it is
good for you to go, by all means go with me, if not you are welcome
to say no. Never permit yourself to think 'how can I say nay when
Árishah has come to call me. I must, by all means, go.' It is easy
enough if you do not come with me now. But if you come, and
God forbid something untoward happens, that shame will be the
hardest for me to bear. I am no wind selling *Bhát* to be able to
rip open my belly with a poniard[1] (in case the Sultán does not keep
his word with you), nor have I an army to oppose the Sultán with an
fight for you. I am only a poor *devotee*, and can do little. Whatever
you do, do it after mature consideration and great reflection."
Imád-ul-Mulk said : " Miyánji ! I am now old and infirm, whose door
shall I go to ? The Sultán has sworn on the Kuráan. If he still
breaks his oath and does wrong, it is his concern." So saying he
sounded the drums for the march, and started for the royal presence.
His well-wishers all advised him not to go, saying the Sultán would
never act fairly by him, and that the best thing for him to do was to
go and occupy some frontier town at the head of ten or fifteen thousand horse and there await the turn of events; that Daryá Khán
and Álam Khán and the Sultán were engaged in fighting and that it
was very possible the Sultán may sorely need his help and then
Imád-ul-Mulk could make peace with him on his own terms. But
the Malik would not listen to their words. He said : " How in this
advanced age of mine could I be a traitor to him and prove false to
my salt ? I am an old dependent of this house, how can I harbour
evil against it. The Sultán, I am sure, will not act basely towards me."

When the Malik met the Sultán at Champaner with ten or twelve
thousand horse well armed and equipped, the Sultán was much

---

[1] The Bháts and Chárans are classes of mendicant Hindus, whose profession in
the present peaceful times is to compose poetry in praise of greatmen. In old unsettled
times, when might was right, the Bhat or Charan used to stand security for the performance by the powerful of their promises or contracts with the poor. In cases of
non-performance the Bhat either killed himself or killed or mutilated an innocent
member of his family, ripping himself open in the sight of the promise-breaker and
sprinkling him and his house with the blood. This practice is in Gujaráti called the
Trága. The blood was believed to bring inevitable ruin on the defaulter. The
Mughals very happily termed the Bháts and Chárans *Bádfurásh* or Wind-sellers
from their wordy profession. Abul Fazl in the *Aíni Akbari* calls Birbal a *Bádfurásh*
by caste.

pleased and showed him great kindness and attention. This treatment continued for some days. -One night suddenly the cry arose:—"The Sultán has given orders for the plunder of the camp of Imád-ul-Mulk."[1] Before his men could come round Imád-ul-Mulk's camp was plundered. Imád-ul-Mulk, who, for his intrepid valour, was styled the second Rustam,[2] had not the strength to mount his horse and fly and escape to the fort of Broach or join Álam Khán; so taking the hand of one of his *kahárs* or bearers he told him to take him to the tents of Sayad Mubárak. The servant taking his hand started in the dark night. While being thus led along in the obscurity of the night, the Malik fell into a small well the camp people had dug. In the morning one of the men of the camp going to the well to draw water found a man in the well. He drew him out and did not recognize Imád-ul-Mulk in him. The half-dead noble said : "Lead me to Sayad Mubárak's tents." The man did so, and announced him to the Sayad, who with great warmth and honour took him to his quarters.

The Malik told him, "My Lord Sayad pray go to the Sultán and tell him to emancipate his old slave, and send him to Allah's temple of the Kaába." The Sayad went to the Sultán. He saw the Sultán in great astonishment and indignation making extravagant endeavours and strict enquiries as to the source and origin of this disaster. "For," said he, "I never ordered it, and am determined to find out the perpetrators." Of the plunderers that were arrested, he ordered. the hands of some and the noses of others to be cut off, and ordered that it might be ascertained where the Malik had gone, saying, "If he has joined Álam Khán and Daryá Khán, there will be—God forbid—a great disturbance." At this moment Sayad Mubárak appeared with his information, and the Sultan was much relieved and agreed to send the Malik to the Kaába and sent for him. When he came he gave him in charge of Sídí Barjí and Sídí Amín, the house-born slaves of Jhujhár Khán Habshi, to be taken to Súrat and made over to Khudáwand Khán Rúmi, the fief-holder

---

[1] Sir Clive Bayley on the authority of one of his MSS. states that the cry to plunder Imád-ul-Mulk's camp was, without the Sultán's knowledge, raised by some seditious rascal, and distinctly asserts that the Sultán was totally ignorant of the transaction. See Bayley's History of Gujarát, p. 434.

[2] Rustam, who flourished about the middle of the 6th century before Christ, became the hero of Persian chivalry during the long wars between that country and Túrán and holds the foremost place as such in Persian Poetry.

of these parts, to be conveyed to the Kaâba at the opening of the pilgrimage season. They say these events happened during the fasting month. While on their way to Súrat one day at the time of breaking the fast Sídí Barjí handed his water cup to the Malik. The Malik looked into his face us much as to imply tacitly that it was impolite for him, a prisoner, to drink off his custodian's vessel. Sídí Barji, however, said: " Malik, we are no better than the smallest of your slaves." By this hint he meant to convey the meaning : " What can we do ? We have to submit to the King's orders." Alas ! The world is just such a place ! Now it raises one so high as to make his charger tread the height of the heavens, anon it drives him on foot on sharp stones. He is truly a man who, in whatever condition he be, does not overstep the bounds of propriety and does not allow himself to be fascinated by the wiles of this guileful world.

To continue. They conveyed the Malik to Khudáwand Khán Rúmi on the 27th of the holy month of Ramazán, the year 952 (A. D. 1545). Khudáwand Khán killed the Malik after subjecting him to severe torture. The public now perceived that Ikhtiyár Khán was innocent, and that Imád-ul-Mulk had killed him unjustly as has been detailed above.[1]

After the decline of the fortunes of Imád-ul-Mulk, the Sultán appointed Sayad Mubárak against the rebels Daryá Khán and Álam Khán. The rebels gave battle and were put to flight, and Sayad Mubárak returned triumphant and victorious. The Sultán then honoured Násir-ul-Mulk by appointing him to move against Álam Khán and Daryá Khán, to drive them from the limits of Gujarat. Násir-ul-Mulk pursued them, till he drove them to uninhabited fastnesses and wilds and stopped there some time. At last they went to Sher Sháh Súr, the Afghán-king of Dehli, and the Sultán's power was now firmly re-established.

The above events are thus laconically recorded by Árám, the Kashmirean, in the history called the *Tuhfat-us Súdát*, which he wrote for Sayad Mubárak :—

" *When the age of the Sultán exceeded fifteen years and approached near upon twenty he began to discern good from evil and discriminate his friends from his foes. He then overthrew those of the nobles that were hostile to him and expelled others from the country.*"

_____

[1] See ante. Beginning of Mehmud III.'s reign.

How can such a short notice give a faithful account of the history of the country ?. This humble person has, for this reason, related the events that happened at this period by recording the occurrences as they happened and following the old accounts as far as possible. Although the birth of the writer took place in the reign of the Sultán of blessed end who had made Mehmúdábád his capital and though he was an infant in arms at the time of the Sultán's martyrdom, yet the writer's father and brother Sheikh Yúsuf were acquainted with some of the events which they communicated to him and he completed his record of the others from respectable persons who personally took part in them.

To continue. After consolidating his power, Sultán Mehmúd recalled and gave the place of Grand Vazír to Ásaf Khán, the Vazír of the Sultán Bahádur, whom, on the invasion of Gujarát by the Emperor Humáyún, Sultán Bahádur had sent away with his harem and treasures to Makkah. He made Khudáwand Khán the younger brother of Asaf Khán minister of the general departments and confirmed Afzal Khán Banyúni who was also a minister of the late Sultán Bahádur in his place, and exalted his rank and honours. Although Afzal Khán had no hand in the management of petty affairs, yet the great affairs of the kingdom were never carried out without his advice and consultation. The Sultán also raised the rank of each noble according to his circumstances, services and loyalty. Among these was the noble Sayad Mubárak, the fountain of blessings, who enjoyed the coronet of nobility as well as the mitre of sanctity, and whose mention I shall, God willing, make after that of Sultán Ahmed. The Sultán also promoted Abúji Gujartái to very high rank and ennobled him with the title of Násir-ul-Mulk. He gave Abdul Karím Khán the title of I'timád Khán. This man was the object of the Sultán's confidence, and enjoyed his trust to an extent equalled by none. The Sultán used to take him by the hand and lead him to his harem, and order him to perform services with respect to the dress and ornaments of his ladies though the jealousy of the Sultán was such a ruling trait in his character that if he saw two of his concubines smiling at each other he used to kill them both. With all this he used to entrust I'timád Khán with such services, and the poor man used ever to be quaking and trembling with fear and used to say, "I am but human, God forbid that this practice may lead to an event which may cost me my head." To guard against such accidents when going to the harem of the palace he used to wear below his usual nether garments a pair of steel ring mail-trousers with the trouser string secured by a small padlock, the key of which he used to leave at home. On his return home from the palace he used take the key and open the padlock. When after a long time the Sultán became acquainted with these circumstances, he said : "I'timád Khán why do you put yourself to all this trouble ? I have more confidence in you than that. Why should you have done this ? I conjure you by my head do not act so after this." When he was enjoined by such strong oaths I'timád Khán took several cups of *kaththá*,[1] which is a destroyer of virile powers, and became totally impotent. It is said, while in great favor with the Sultán, that one day when the court was assembled, I'timád Khán came and whispered something to the Sultán. The courtiers and ministers looked significantly at each other. The meeting then broke up and the statesmen dispersed each to his house. The next day and for six or seven consecutive days no one attended the Sultán's ante-chamber. The Sultán wondered whether all his ministers had fallen ill together. At length it appeared that illness was not the cause of their non-appearance. On enquiry they explained : "We carried on the duties of ministers as long as we could; now when we see we have no confidence, we withdraw." The Sultán asked them to give their reasons. "It is," said they, " degrading to us that the Sultán should be whispered to by others in our presence and ministers like us enjoying so little of trust can do but little. The Sultán might give the post whomsoever he can trust better. If not, the Sultán may talk as he wishes in private but should not do so in public." From that day the Sultán apologized and agreed never again to break the rule nor suffer any one to do so. The Sultán ennobled Aká Arslán, originally a Turk from Balkh, by the title of Imád-ul-Mulk, and conferred on him honors and rank. This Arslán was a purchased slave of the Sultán's. The Sultán ennobled the son of Khudáwand Khán Rúmi, who was killed in the port of Diu, with the title of Rúmi Khán. He also ennobled one of his own house-born slaves with the

---

[1] Forbes describes *kaththá* as "the vegetable astringent extract which natives eat with the betel leaves to neutralize the sharp qualities of the chunam or quick-lime which they plaster the leaf with." It is the produce of a species of mimosa (Chadira) Catechu, Terra Japonica." It is used in the form of a potion, as is also used the sap of the plantain-tree to destroy the virile powers.

title of Ikhtiyár-ul-Mulk, and made him captain of the Mughal soldiers. He divided his forces according to tribal divisions and conferred the command of each division on a leader of that tribe. He gave the command of the Dakhanís to Hasan Khán Dakhaní. He promoted Fateh Khán Balúch and granted him great possessions. He thus brought the soldiers and nobles so completely into subjection that no one could disobey or rebel against him.

After this the desire of conquering the country of Málwa entered the Sultán's mind. He took counsel with Ásaf Khán Vazír. Ásaf Khán said : " I shall show you how to come by a country not less, possibly, more important than Málwa. The fourth part of your proper dominions is enjoyed under the name of " *wántá* " by Rájpút *girásiás* (or landholders). These estates comprise lands which can support a standing army of 25,000 horse. These lands, if resumed from the Rájpúts, would increase the army and bring the conquest of Málwa within the range of easy feasibility." The Sultán listened to this counsel and began to attend to the *Girás Jágirs.* The *Girásiás* of Ídar and Sirohi, Dúngarpúr, Bánswára, Lúnáwára, Ráj- pípla, and the banks of the Mahi and Dohad, betaking them- selves to the villages of the frontier, commenced to disturb the country. The Sultán began to strengthen the frontier posts by establishing one at Sirohi, another at Ídar, and at the places named. In a short time neither name nor sign of Koli or Rájpút remained in the country, except those that actually worked at the plough, and these, too, were known by being branded on the right arm, and if any Rájpút or Koli was found without the brand-mark he was killed.

The laws and precepts of Islám were so strongly enforced in the time of this Sultán that no Hindu could ride on horseback in the city. The dress of a Hindu was not complete without his binding a piece of red cloth round his sleeve. Hindu usages and customs, like the obscene rites of the *Holi*, the evil ceremonies of the *Diváli*, and the worship of idols could not be practiced openly. After the martyr- dom of the Sultán the *Grásiás* got hewed out of stone the image of the vile Burhán, the Sultán's murderer, and setting it up as a guardian deity, began to pay it divine worship, saying : " This is our saviour who has saved us from destruction and starvation. For, had the conditions under which we were living lasted one year more, hunger and privation would have given our lives to the winds of destruction."

THE NAMES OF THE GREAT MASHÁIKHS (HOLY PERSONS) WHO LIVED
DURING THE REIGN OF SULTÁN MEHMÚD.

The Sayads of Batwa derive their extraction from Ḳutbi Âlam
Sayad Burhánuddín, the son of Sayad Mehmúd, the son of Makhdúm
Jehánián. Sayad Aríshah was in a direct line descended from
him. Sayad Sálih Muhammad, known as Sayad Cháoji, and Sayad
Âzmatulláh, the second Ḳutub, were at the fourth remove connected
with the above saint, and Sayad Husein was fifth in descent from
Hazrat Ḳutb, with his cousins, Sayad Táhir Muhammad and Sayad
Pir Muhammad, and Sayad Háfiz Muhammad, who were all saints
of their time. And of great Sayads was Amir Sayad Sháh Kamál,
and his father Mir Sayad Sháh Mirza. And there was Sayad Akram
Aàzam, the son of Âdam Âlam, who, though advanced in years,
was indefatigable in search after the knowledge of religion and
the positive sciences. He was a descendant of Sayad Usmán, who
was one of the deputies of Ḳutbul Aḳtáb, Sayad Burhánuddin, who
had honored him with the title of "Sham-í-Burháni" (i. e., the
Light of Burhán). The village of Usmánpúr to the north-west of
Ahmedábád was founded by him, and his tomb in that suburb is
well known. Sultán Mehmúd had great faith in Sayad Âlam as
a spiritual guide and teacher. Sayad Âlam departed this life in the
month of the first Jumád in the year H. 963 (A. D. 1555), Peace be
on him !

Another holy man was Sheikh-Aláh-dád, the Resigned in Providence. Then there was Sheikh Is-hák, who was very scrupulous in
his obedience to the law of Islám. There was also Sheikh Maudúd,
son of Ḳázi Îlmuddin. Then there was Sayad Rájú and Sheikh Ali the
Pious, and Sheikh Muhammad Ghaus, a holy man of the Shuttáriah
order, who traced his succession in the mystic order to which he
belonged to the great saint Sheikh Báyazíd Bustámi, one of the
first mystics of the faith. Then there was the very learned
Wajíhuddín-al-Âlawi, then Khwájah Âbdul Wáhid, and Sheikh Hasan,
the son of Âziz, from the Máwará-un-nahr (the country beyond the
Oxus) from a village of the name of Miánkál. Then there was Sheikh
Máh from Jaunpúr. Then Sheikh Jamál, one of the Sayads of
the town of Banthari in the Dakhan. Then Miyánji, the deputy, in
an unbroken line from Sayad Husein and Bíbí Ârám, who are
enshrined outside the city of Pattan.

There were, besides, many Sayads at Broach, chief of whom was Sayad Ghiàsuddin, and in the port of Súrat was Sheikh Kamáluddin, who was a follower of Sayad Alí Hamadáni.

The Sultán had great faith in the sanctity of pious persons and saints, and not only did he maintain intact the endowments they enjoyed from the times of the former Sultáns, but bestowed new ones on those of them who came from foreign lands and settled in his kingdom, whom he considered deserving of favour.

ACCOUNT OF THE GENEROSITY, LAUDABLE VIRTUES AND QUALITIES OF THE SULTAN, ON WHOM BE PEACE AND FORGIVENESS !

It is related by respectable people, contemporaneous with the Sultán, that he was a great friend of the poor, and took great interest in their condition, having built houses and asylums for them, and deputed servants thereon to take care and watch over their joys and sorrows, and provide for their needs and necessities. If at any time the Sultán approved of any dish, he asked his servants to provide such food for the poor ' fakirs.' If the servants said it was out of question to provide such rich food for the fakirs he used to order a large quantity of such food to be prepared at once and given to the poor. In the cold weather he used to get thousands of good coats prepared and to send them to people of probity and rectitude living in mosques and colleges, and used also to give quilted sheets and counterpanes for night covering. When he heard that some of the ill-conditioned ne'er-do-weals sold them, he ordered very large-sized quilts to be made so that they may cover a number of persons, and that this community of interest should prevent their being sold. He ordered large piles of fuel to be placed in every street and lane, so that the poor may kindle fires, and the destitute should sit by those fires and warm themselves in the streets. He had also ruled that the fruit of every season—like sugarcane, plantains, mangoes, and melons— should be sent to the poor before being brought to the royal court. When he had such kindness for the common poor, it may be imagined what great interest he must be taking in the Sayads and men of merit and spiritual excellence. Many Sayads of the blood of that Sun of sanctity Sayad Abú Bakr-al-Eidrús (on whom be God's mercy !) and others attracted by kindness of the Sultán, severed their connection with their native land of Arabia and came and settled at Ahmedábád (A. D. 1544-45). God Almighty forgive his

31

sins and pass over his faults for the sake of Muhammad, and his children, and his companions—Amen! Lord of the Universe!

It is related that a Musalmán peasant once came to the Sultán, and told him that he was a father of a family of girls, and had not the means to marry them; that he had seen the Prophet (on whom be peace!) in a dream, and that the Prophet had told him, that he had ordered Sultán Mehmúd to give him a hundred and twenty-five thousand *tánkahs*, and by this sign that the Sultán said a hundred thousand prayers of blessings and peace, for the soul of the Prophet every day. The Sultán said: " The gold that thou wantest, I shall give thee, but the sign that thou givest is not truthful." The poor man replied: " I only say what I heard from the lips of the ' Friend of God'." It so happened that the Sultán also subsequently saw the Prophet in a dream, and was told by him that what the man had stated to him was a fact, and that the blessings the Sultán sent him once every day had a thousand rewards, being worded as follows : " God Almighty, bless Muhammad, according to the number of the lives of thy creation, &c." Next morning the Sultán called the man and showed him much honour, and besides giving him what he had demanded, settled a pension on him, God's mercy on him ! Some people relate this as having occurred in respect of Sultán Mehmúd Begda.

ACCOUNT OF THE BUILDINGS OF THE DEER PARK—AND OF THE PLEASURES THAT THE SULTÁN ENJOYED THERE.

They say that when the heart of the Sultán was free from the oppression of the nobles, and there remained no thorn in the cushion of his desires, he moved from Ahmedábád to Mehmúdábád in the year H. 953 (A. D. 1546), and made it his capital. He began to construct there lofty buildings to which he gave the name of *Ahú-Khánah* (Deer-house or park). These buildings extended over an area of six miles in length by three in breadth being of the dimensions of a hippodrome or horse-course.[1] It was a grateful stretch of green at each corner of which he built a palace, the like of which did not exist on the face of the earth. The greater portion of the walls and ceilings of these palaces were gilded, and in front of the gate of

---

[1] Taking the *farsang* at an English league. Richardson Sub-voce, Ibni Khaldún (Prolegomena 22). Al Mas-ú"di (Prairies d'or Arabic text, I. 378) makes a S dhi fansakh one of eight miles.

each house was a road with shops on both sides, and at the door of each shop sat a pretty girl vending articles of luxury and pleasure, delightful viands or delicate flavoured fruit. On both sides gardens were laid out, the trunks and branches of the trees of which were cased with soft coloured velvets and glittering brocades. In these delightful gardens, the Sultán used to pass his time in the company of gazelle-eyed damsels passing like the sun or the moon from constellation to constellation or from palace to palace, and used to engage himself in the pastime of hunting or shooting. On the days of the *I'd* the royal elephants and horses were ornamented with rich trappings and jewelry with an elegance which could hardly have been attempted or thought of by any king at any time.

ACCOUNT OF THE ASSASSINATION OF THE SULTAN BY BURHÁN, THE VILE.

It is related that during the days of the Nativity of the Prophet (on whom be peace!) from the first day of Rabi-'ul-Awwal to the twelfth, the learned and pious men of the city used to present themselves before the Sultán every day from the morning till one quarter of the day, and used to read the Holy volumes of the Traditions of the Prophet recorded by Bukhári.[1] After this, food prepared as an offering for the good of the pure soul of the chief of the Prophets (on whom be peace!) used to be served with all honour before the holy men present, and they used, after partaking of it, to return to their respective homes. On the twelfth, the Sultán himself used personally to wait on them, pouring out water from the ewer held by himself on their hands, the basin being circulated by his great ministers. The nobles, in attendance, served the food on the tablecloth. Believing this to be a banquet to the soul of the Prophet (on whom be peace!) the Sultán used to wait at it on foot, calling all the while for blessings in a gentle voice on the Prophet's soul. After the distribution of perfumes, he used to bestow on his pious guests gold and clothes enough to last them one year if they lived to appear at the next banquet of the Nativity. The dishes were laid on pieces of rich Dakhan (*Himrús*) or striped

---

[1] The Bukhári, or as it is respectfully styled, the Bukhári Sharif is the most authentic and the largest collection of the traditions of the Prophet (on whom be peace!) Next to it in authenticity is held the Muslim. Both the works are named from their collators.

silks and other fine fabrics intended for the Sultán's own ward-robe. After serving as table-cloths at these banquets, the pieces were washed, and the Sultán's annual stock of clothes cut out therefrom for the year's wear. This pious custom had become an established institution from the time of Sultán Muzaffar, the son of Sultán Mehmúd Begda, but Sultán Mehmúd used to improve upon, and exceed in it in everything. The twelfth day of the first Rabi', being the birthday of the Prophet (on whom be prayers and peace!) is by the Arabs called the *Maulúd*. Other nations on another and more mystic principle call it the *Aárás* or nuptials, it being the day on which the loving soul of the Prophet passed away to unite itself with its Beloved—Alláh. The Prophet hath said: " He who celebrates with joy the passing away of the month of Safar (the month previous to the first Rabi'), verily I congratulate him with having won a right to Paradise." Every lover of Alláh the bird of whose soul leaves the cage of life on this day, obtains union with the Beloved (Alláh). On this day, after the learned men had finished the reading of the Holy Bukhári, and the viands of many kinds prepared for them were brought and placed before them and after they had partaken of these and the delicious fruits provided for them they raised their hands in thanksgiving to the Almighty and prayers for the Sultán, and it seemed as if the glory of martyrdom and Divine forgiveness shortly afterwards obtained by the Sultán were the direct results of these prayers. The Sultán, according to his wont, gave them gold and cloth, and retired to his own chamber, and from the fatigue and weariness that had come over him, after the day's work, he lay down and slept. After a short time feeling thirsty he called for a drink of water. Burhán, the ill-fated wretch of evil stock, who was probably biding his time, was present. He brought a poisoned draught and the Sultán unsuspicious of treachery, drained the poisoned cup and again dropped into sleep. After a while, feeling very hot, he awoke and became very sick. He now began to see that he was seriously ill, and said : " Thou wretch! what was this draught thou hast given me." Burhán said : " Fear not, Refuge of the world, it is only the fatigue of the day's work that has overcome you; go to sleep again, so that it may be dispelled." One watch of the night had passed, when the Sultán again went to sleep, when that twice-accursed wretch drove the dagger into his neck and made the Sultán a martyr.

Account of Burhán, and how that ill-fated one entered the Sultán's service, and the fore-sightedness of Afzal Khán in the matter.

I have heard from the respectable people of Gujarát (may Heaven guard the country from all calamity!), who were themselves eye-witnesses of these events or had received accounts of them directly from their ancestors, that the commencement of the fortunes of the wretch Burhán was as follows:—Burhán's father, Pyárá, a man of mean origin, was in the menial service of the Sultán. The most exalted rank Pyárá ultimatley attained to was the superintendentship of the *Bárgír* [1] stables. His son Burhán was a youth not wholly devoid of comeliness, and the Sultán saw him one day and liked him and for two reasons: First, because the Sultán was in those days in the power of his ministers and could do nothing without their knowledge. All his desires lay pent up within him. Even after he gained power and began openly to indulge in pleasure, charms even the most mediocre in men or women, used to fascinate him. Secondly, because from the beginning to the end of his reign it was a trait of this Sultán's character to incline to men of mean origin and low descent. He always acted thus, and promoted men of low birth, as has been mentioned. He promoted the ill-starred Burhán in the same way, and appointed him his shoebearer. One day Afzal Khán, the minister, saw him cleaning the Sultán's shoes, and asked whose son he was. Some of those present said he was the son of Pyárá, the superintendent of stables. The Minister remonstrated with the Sultán against his sudden and unmerited exaltation of the boy to such high rank, but the Sultán said the boy was his houseborn slave, and that he was sure he would never be deceitful or treacherous towards him. The Minister said he discerned evil in his eye, and that he saw that his phyisioguomy, God forbid, omened harm to the Sultán: but the Sultán insisted no worng would come out of him. There always remained a difference of opinion between the Sultán and his Minister regarding the ill-fated boy. When the vile wretch reached the prime of youth he gave himself up to sodomy and wine. As these two crimes are strongly interdicted by the Law of Islam, and their perpetrator liable to punishment, the Sultán had ordered that whosoever from among his ministers or nobles should be

---

[1] The Bár-gírs were horsemen serving on personal stipends, their horses being found them by the State.

found guilty of them, his house should be given up to plunder. As
the unhappy Burhán was fated to commit both these crimes and had
made them his daily practice, the Sultán was one day informed of
them and ordered that the wretch should be built up alive in a
wall. His parents went wailing and weeping to Afzal Khán, the
Minister, praying that Burhán was their only child and entreating
him to intercede for his life for the sake of God. The Khán was
moved, and going up to the Sultán begged for the life of Burhán, and
his prayer was granted, though not a moment too soon, for had he
delayed a moment in obtaining the pardon, Burhán would have been
killed, as they had already built him up to his shoulders in the wall.
As, however, the Divine mandate had gone forth that the Sultán
should suffer by the hands of this ill-fated one, he was saved. It is also
remarkable that with all his foresight and wisdom and deep-rooted
dislike for the boy, that Afzal Khán should have been the means
of saving the life of this cause of evil. Afzal Khán was, however,
always full of trouble and anxiety on his account, and did not approve
of this ill-starred one being in attendance on the Sultán both in his
private and public moments. He also did not like the presence of
the young man at the State councils of the ministers. So he
pretended a little deafness, and said he did not know whether it was
from debility consequent on old age or from some adventitious causes,
but he was afraid there was something wrong with his powers of
hearing. That he was unable to catch anything said in a low
tone of voice and as a person suffering from deafness is also given to
speak loudly, he said it was advisable that Burhán should not be
present at the royal councils, as it was probable that the weighty
secrets discussed there should go out and their revelation cause
disturbance. They used from that time to exclude him on certain
occasions, but that treacherous person did not let a single consultation
pass without somehow or other obtaining knowledge of it. One day
the Sultán said :—" Our ancestors (may God have mercy on them),
after they brought the country of Gujarát within their power,
conquered the forts of the Hindus, such as Chámpáner and Júnágadh.
Now, thanks be to God, much more than that has passed into the
hands of the servants of this state. Let us think of the conquest
of Chámpáner. How much army properly equipped is required
for the expedition, and what treasure." At this time the ill-fated
Burhán was present, and this order of the Sultán's gave him

the cue wherewith he worked out his nefarious end and he did what he did.

It is related that Burhán was very fond of the son of a singer, and on account of his great love for him always kept him by his side. One day, the Sultán was engaged with his harem in hunting in the Deer-park of Mehmúdabád when this ill-fated one was seen under very objectionable circumstances with the singer's son under the shade of a tree with a bottle of wine by his side, obli vious of the possibility of the Sultán's passing that way. It so happened that the Sultán had let loose a hawk after a bird, and that bird took the direction where this ill-fated one was, and the Sultán came in pursuit, and having ocular demonstration of what was going on under that tree, said :— "Son of adultery ! I did not believe what people said about thee, now I have seen with my own eyes ; if God wills, I shall give thee condign punishment." Saying these words, he followed the bird. The wretch having once experienced the weight of the Sultán's displeasure, thought he would not escape alive this time. He began to think of a remedy. Then the thought that he should kill the Sultán before he could kill him, came to him. As the influence and position of the vile wretch had reached such a pitch that all the articles of the Sultán's food and drink and intoxicating drugs were in his keeping sealed with his seal, the idea of poisoning the Sultán dawned upon his mind as the most , feasible plan of escaping from the consequences of the Sultán's wrath. The morning following the night on which the Sultán saw him in that evil state, was the 12th of the month of Rabi-úl-awwal, the birthday of the Prophet and his re-union with his loved Creator. The Sultán, according to his wont, used to be engaged every day from the 1st of the first Rabi to the 12th of that month in the sevice of the Sheikhs. So he forgot all about the evil conduct of Burhán, witnessed by him during the chase on the 11th of the aforesaid month. On the 12th of that month the Sultán was the whole day on his feet in the entertainment of the Sheikhs. After the conclusion of the entertainment, when the Sultán bade adieu to the Sheikhs, he retired to his chamber, and, seeing Burhán present, asked for some intoxicating drink or drug. Burhán went and brought a confection and jar of water, both mixed with poison. The Sultán ate of that poisoned drug and drank of the poisoned water and went to sleep. After a while the Sultán felt indisposed and became sick, and said: "Oh wretch ! What sort of drug is this, and

what sort of water? What hast thou given me?" The ill-fated
wretch came forward and said, "Oh Refuge of the world, you have
for the last two days been fatiguing yourself, and that has touched
your Majesty's brain. There is nothing to be afraid of, eat a little
more of the confection and seek repose." The Sultán did so and
went to sleep, not to rise till the down of the Day of Doom. In
addition to all this when the Sultán went to sleep, the wretch ran his
knife across his throat, and made him a martyr, and earned for himself
eternal damnation.

Since the treacherous thought of seating himself on the throne
of Gujarát had entered and hatched in his brain, he killed several
ministers and nobles, the pillars of the State, in that night, and in the
morning proposed fearlessly to disclose his fell intent, and making the
discussion of the plan for the conquest of Chámpáner his pretext,
he began to think to what class of people to attach himself. There
was a troop of men called "*Bág-márs*" or tiger-slayers. It consisted
of one thousand two hundred strong, being formed in the reign of the
late Sultán of blessed memory. They were directly under the orders
of the Sultán, without the intermediacy of any minister or noble. He
sent for some of the leaders of this band and concealed them in a
chamber, enjoining them in the name of the Sultán to cut down every
one, noble or simple, who should enter that room. He said he would,
in reward for this service, make them independent for life. Having
given these instructions he came out and sent a man to fetch Ásaf
Khán, the prime minister, who for firmness of purpose and soundness
of judgment was so distinguished, that had Ásaf,[1] the son of Baráchia
been alive he would have been unworthy to hold a candle to him.
Burhán instructed the man to tell Ásaf Khán that he was directed
by the King to say that it was a long time he had ordered him to
arrange a meeting for the discussion of the conquest of Chámpáner,
but that nothing had been done. That the King had assembled
all the ministers for a consultation regarding that business, and
they were waiting for him. Ásaf Khán got up immediately on
hearing these words and followed the man. When he came to the
Palace the base plotter ran down to him, and saluted him, and said,
"My dear Diván (minister) his Majesty has convened all the ministers
to at once arrange and reduce to a workable form the proposal for
the conquest of Chámpáner." Saying so, he led him to that room.

---

[1] The Ginni minister of King Solomon.

When Asaf Khán saw a number of people sitting in that room, he believed the story of that false, faithless, traitor, and unsuspectingly entered the room to be immediately cut down by three of the bravoes inside. In this way twelve of the great ministers and famous nobles of Gujarát (of whom, had even one survived, the Kingdom of Gujarát would not have passed out of the hands of the Gujarátis) were killed at one place and in one night.

To continue: When Burhán sent a man to fetch Afzal Khán, Afzal said to his messenger: "Thou speakest not the words of the Sultán, and the Sultán does not call people at this time of the night; thou talkest nonsense." The man returned and communicated the words of the Khán to the traitor. He again sent the man with a pretended message purporting to be from Ásaf Khán, and stating: "This conduct of yours is not good. The more I incline towards you, the more you hold yourself back. At any rate you must come now as the ministers and nobles have all assembled and are waiting for your arrival to decide on the conquest of Chámpánir." When the Khán again tried to excuse himself, his wife objected, saying, "When the king wishes your presence, why do you hold back?" He said, "Oh simpleton! the man's words smell of blood, and I am sure the message the man delivers is not from the tongue of the Díván. If you do not want me to live press me to go, for the words of the man are not devoid of artifice and guile. But the Khán's wife insisted, yet the Khán did not go. Meanwhile, the traitor sent a third message to him saying, that the Sultán said, that if the Khán did not come, that he (the Sultán) would go to him, as all the assembly was waiting for him to come. Still the Khán wanted to send an excuse, but his wife, and Shirwán Khán Bhatti, whom he had adopted as a son, and exalted in rank, came and pressed him to go, saying that if he did not go the Sultán would be offended. The Khán however told them that he smelt treachery, yet agreed to go as they pressed him so hard. He then sent for all his children and followers and took his last farewell of them, and having asked for their forgiveness he went and sat in his palanquin. When he reached the palace, the traitor came to meet him and as shortly ere this there had been a little estrangement between Afzal Khán and the Sultán, though no important business was settled without Afzal Khán's consent, he thought perhaps the Khán would be pleased to hear of the assassination of the Sultán. So

32

advancing, he said in a coaxing way: [1] "Dear Khán, God Almighty has removed the enemies; if, therefore, you only give me a helping hand, the whole of the country of Gnjarát will come under your rule without a partner." When Afzal Khán heard these words, he said: 'Oh wretch! oh son of adultery! what is it you are thinking of? I smell blood from your words, thou accursed one be quick and show me my master!" He said, "Oh Khánji! you always suspect me of evil. What have I done to your master, come along, your master is seated in this room with a number of the nobles in council." The Khán, a man of a pure soul and excellent qualities, went into the room and the accursed ones made him a martyr. And now, this wretch was entirely at ease. He donned the royal garments, and having sent for the party of his bravoes he broke the padlock of the Sultán's jewel-room which was full of precious stones, and gave them skirtsfull of jewels, and the special riding horses of the Sultán, and promised to advance them all to the rank of nobles in the morning. When two or three hours of the night remained, he dismissed them all by the wicket, and said, "Whoever does not join us I shall give over his house to plunder, I shall then send for the learned men and get the *Khutbah* (sermon) to be read and the coin to be struck in my name."

Shirwán Khán Bhatti, who had sent Afzal Khán (to his death) by his persistence, remained with his family waiting for his return. At dawn, he issued out of his house to obtain news as to what had happened. When he arrived at the head of the lane leading to the Bazár, he heard the tumult of the Sultán's approach in State and thinking it was veritably the Sultán he began to dismount to salute him. But it was Burhán, who called out to him in a loud voice, "Shirwán Khán! do not alight from your horse, but let the office of Afzal Khán, and his titles be auspicious to you!" Shirwán Khán at once gathered what was meant by these words. He tried to advance towards him, but the band that surrounded him would not suffer him to do so. Burhán, however, said, "Shirwán Khán is one of us, let him come that he may kiss my feet." On hearing this speech of the traitor, the fire of wrath blazed up in the heart of Shirwán Khán. He rode up to him and making his horse curvet slightly dealt him such a sword cut on the waist as cleft him in twain

---

[1] A portion of the text next following, being only a repetition of the above account, is omitted.

and he fell from his horse. The company of Tiger-slayers that formed his retinue dispersed. Some of them fled, taking their wives and families with them, and some of them were made to follow that accursed one to hell. There fell a panic and confusion in the city, nobody knew what the night big with events would bring forth, until the break of dawn when all the nobles with Shirwán Khán assembled in the house of Itimád Khán and all unanimously went to the palace and first took charge of the treasure and handed it over to a responsible person. They then went to the king's private chamber and saw the Sultán lying dead and all present could not restrain their tears. Going to the other chamber they saw the mangled bodies of the nobles and ministers. They committed to the dust the mortal remains of the Sultán, on whom be God's mercy! in the mausoleum of Sultán Mehmúd Begda, which is at the foot of the domed tomb of the chief of Saints, Sheikh Ahmed Khattú, and the bodies of the nobles and ministers were conveyed to their own resting places and buried.

These events occurred at Mehmudábád, on Friday night, the 13th of the month of the first Rabi in the year H. 961 (A. D. 1554). The Sultán was ten years old when he mounted the throne of the kingdom, and reigned eighteen years, and was killed in the twenty-eighth year of his age. The letters of the words *Hakikun-bish-Shahádat*, the worthy of matyrdom, form a good chronograph of the event. Sheikh Yahya the *Mufti* has also composed the two following poetical date scripts :—

> When from this world king Mehmúd turned his face,
> And passing straight to paradise his banners there unfurled,
> Amidst his faithful ministers and with his martyr throng
> He reigns supreme in heaven with his regal umbrella spread over him.
> I asked of myself the year and date of his departure.
> The answer was : ohr Yàhyá hear ! [1]
> The King has gained a martyr's crown. (*Sultán Shahádat Yáftah*).

The following is the date-script of the three kings who died in this same year :—

> Three monarchs did the self same year expire,
> Kings who by their justice had made the land of Ind a heaven.
> The first was Mehmúd, lord of Gujarát fair,
> Who like his Fortune was in prime of youth.
> The second was Islám Sháh, the Dehli King,
> Who did in Ind possess imperial power.

The third was Nizám-ul-Mulk Bahri,
Who like a Chosroes o'er Dakhan land held sway.
If you do ask the year of their deaths,
It is : the death of rulers Great and Kings (Faut-i-Khusrawán). [1]

They say that Burhán had sent for I'timád Khán also, but that I'timád Khán thinking that it was too late and untoward an hour of the night for him to be summoned by the Sultán, suspected some evil and was too sagacious to go.

Others of the people of Gujarát have related that when Burhán was satisfied of his success in killing the exalted King, he became secure and happy and fancied himself the centre of popular hopes and expectations. He extended his hands towards the property of the Sultán and donned the royal garb on his vile body and unclasping the jewelled necklace from the handsome neck of the deceased Sultán he bound it round his own, and like a dog seated himself on one after another of all the jewelled chairs of the Sultán. He pulled before himself the gold basin of the Sultán and began to perform his toilet. Then he set to ape at government, bestowing the royal steeds with their gold and silver housings and bridles on his accomplices and gave orders to release the prisoners. The small number of the hungry and needy men who had joined him owing to the pressure of poverty, when they saw that this would not last till the morning, with one mind, took the horses and gold bestowed on them and took to flight. The ill-fated Burhán was left to enjoy his state with a small number of his friends. In the meantime the terrible news began to spread among the people and reached the ears of the state counsellors such as Imád-ul-Mulk who commanded the Turks and Jhujhár Khán and Alif Khán Habashi, the captains of the Abyssinian guards. They writhed with pain, like a hair on fire, and taking at once to horse proceeded to the royal palace. It is related that a panic like that of of the Day of Resurrection fell on the city. On reaching the place these nobles secured the treasury, placed it in charge of a body of trusty Arabs, and turned to punish the accursed Burhán. It so happened that the accursed one also, with some men, who had joined him, went forth. Shirwán Khán Bhatti, who was one of the great nobles of the late Sultán, was seen by him approaching from an opposite direction. The doomed Burhán called out to Shirwán Khán, saying, " Come,

---

[1] A portion of the text next following, being only a repetition of the above account, is omitted.

Shirwán Khán, you are in the nick of time, I shall enrich you for life." Shirwán Khán said: " I come ! " and spurring his horse forward dealt Burhán such a blow on the shoulder with his sabre as to kill him at once and send him to jahannam, whither his companions also were made shortly to follow him by being mercilessly sabred. This happened in A. H. 961 (A. D. 1554). They say that this rascal used outwardly to conduct himself with such piety, that the Sultán used sometimes to make him his leader in prayers. One day the Sultán sent Burhún at the head of a party of body servants to arrange for a hunting trip to the strip of land lying between Cambay and Dholka. On the return of the party Burhán went to Dholka and passed the night swilling toddy in the company of low singing women. When the Sultán came to Dholka one of the servants told him what had happened. The Sultán indignantly said : " Base cur ! I considered thee a man of piety and prayed in thy leading, and thou hast proved thyself such a hypocrite. Thou deservest again to be built up in a wall." Burhán had more than once ere this tasted the horrors of being built up in a wall and was, when at his last gasp, begged off by some of the king's associates. The wretch knew that if he again received this punishment it would be his last. Hence his determination to kill the Sultán.

They say that a *qalandar* had foretold Burhán his future, saying, that one day the royal umbrella of Gujarát would be unfurled over his head. This baneful augury remained ever since working in Burhán's foolish head till it brought him to this ignominious end. But God knows best.

ACCOUNT OF THE NOBLES WHO, AFTER THE DEATH OF THE SULTAN OF BLESSED MEMORY, ADMINISTERED THE GOVERNMENT OF THE COUNTRY.

It is related that when the Sultán became a martyr and his chief ministers and nobles also obtained the crowns of martyrdom, the only one of the great nobles who lived to be the cause of the peace and prosperity to the country and the people was the holy and exalted personality of Sayad Mubárak, may God exalt his glory ! He used to keep up a wonderfully strong army and great state. His army consisted chiefly of Bukhári Sayads of the same extraction and fraternity as himself besides Fauládi Patháns, whose chiefs, Músa Khán and Sher Khán, were famed for valour. The Sayad used to pay them

great respect and attention, and they also on their side used to
behave as his sincere and loyal spiritual followers. There was also a
troop of Afgháns of the Lodi and Shirwáni tribes, like Shah-báz
Khán and others, who were brave and strong in battle . Of the sons
of Sheikhs the most beloved of His Holiness the Sayad was Sheikh
Muhammad *alias* Sheikh Manjhú, the father of this humble person the
writer who, in secular matters, was his agent, and in matters spiritual
one of his chief followers. If I were to relate all the miracles and
deeds of the Sayad it would fill a volume. Hereafter, if occasion offers,
I may write a little regarding it if God wills. In short, there
were all classes of men in my lord's service. There were in his service
nearly ten thousand horsemen so effective and brave, that if they had
to do battle with an enemy consisting of a rock of fire they would
assail him with the mettled power of their scimitars, or if the enemy
opposed to them consisted of a boisterous sea they would swallow
him down like a bowl of water.

The next leading noble—the support and refuge of the other
nobles—was I'timád Khán, who, at the time of the assassination of
the Sultán, was carrying on the duties of prime minister and regent.
The next was Imád-ul-Mulk Rúmi, who had under him a strong
and well equipped body of Turks.

Another noble of exalted rank was Alif Khán Habashi. Then
there was Malik-ush-Shark Gujaráti and Ikhtiyár-ul-Mulk, the chief
slave-noble of the Sultán. All these the Sayad brought round and
reconciled with one another according to the (Kuránic) command
"take counsel in all your affairs." They consulted and took counsel
together in state affairs. They asked of I'timád Khán, who was a repository of the Sultán's secrets, to tell them if the late Sultán had any
male issue. If so, they proposed that he should be raised to the
throne and administer the kingdom of his ancestors. If there were
no male issue, but if any of the ladies of the Sultán's harem were
pregnant, that they would wait till her accouchement. Perchance
Heaven may vouchsafe a son, so that the exalted rule of the Sultánate
may not pass out of the glorious line of Sultán Mehmúd of blessed
end. I'timád Khán said that the Sultán had no male issue nor was
he aware of any of his ladies being with child. Then the nobles
proceeded to select a suitable heir from among the Sultán's kinsmen
who should be fit for the dignity and honour of the throne. They
proposed Ahmed Khán, saying he was the only one of the Sultán's

relatives worthy the honour of royalty, and they resolved to send for
him despatching Razi-ul-Mulk to fetch him. Razí-ul-Mulk drove
away in a horse-chariot with such lightning speed that he reached
Ahmedábád in less than two hours. When he arrived before Ahmed
Khán's house he saw that prince standing before a Banyá's shop his
skirt full of some millet which he had just purchased to feed his
pigeons. Razí-ul-Mulk alighting from his chariot invited Ahmed
Khán into the vehicle, and seating him therein turned round and
drove away. The nurse of the Khán set up a great wailing and
crying : "Who is this man and where and why does he take my
prince. They told her that he was being taken to a place where
to-morrow crowds should kick their heels before his ante-chamber
dying to gain but unable to obtain admission. In short, they took
him thus to Mehmúdábád.

ACCESSION OF SULTAN AHMED SHAH II., SON OF LATIF KHAN, AND GRANDSON OF SULTAN AHMED I., THE FOUNDER OF AHMEDABAD.

It is related by historians and writers of annals that the Sultán
was seated on the throne of the Kingdom of Gujarát at Mehmudábád
between the two prayers[1] on the 15th of the month of the first
Rabi' in the year A. H. 961 (A. D. 1553) with the unanimous consent
of the nobles with the title of Ahmed Shah II. and by the auspicious
hand of Sayad Mubarak.

COUPLET.

It was when sixty-one years had passed over nine hundred
That Fate said to the King Ahmed—" The kingdom is thine ! "

On the same day the King was initiated as a spiritual disciple
of Sayad Mubárak.

After the throne of Gujarát was adorned by the accession of this
king, it was agreed among the nobles that as he was of tender years
they should divide the country and the treasure among themselves
and remain each one in his own fief to prevent the possibility of any
friction or disturbance. It was suggested that this course was the more
desirable, as at this time Islám Sháh, king of Dehli, was dead, and his
wife's brother Mamríz Khán having killed his (Islám Shah's) son Firúz

---

[1] Between the two prayers—is between the Afternoon and the Vespers or the
4 o'clock and the sunset prayers, the 'Asar and Maghrib.

Firúz Khán had usurped the throne under the title of Muhammad Sháh A'dil. He was a young and ambitious king who had recently risen to sovereignty and power, and it was possible the conquest of Gujarát might suggest itself to his young mind. It would be best for each one of the nobles to keep his contingent of men ready and remain alert in his estate, while I'timád Khán should carry on the duties of minister and regent and remain near the king.

When the nobles had divided the country and the treasure and the royal elephants and horses, twenty-two millions of Gujarát tánkas, which are equal to twenty-two hundred thousand Akbari tánkás, and gold and gold articles and jewels, fell to the share of his holiness Sayad Mubárak. The agent of the treasurer put all these valuables into teak boxes and brought them locked and sealed to the house of the Sayad, and said that his principal would come to-morrow and count and deliver them over formally. The Sayad rising, looked at all the boxes, and said, that they were all properly locked and sealed. He then asked for a hatchet. One was immediately produced, and he ordered the lock of the boxes to be immediately smashed. At this moment, Muhammad Zainuddín, the treasurer, said, that the contents were up to that time not counted and that the next day his principal would come and count them over and that the matter had best be postponed till then. The Sayad, however, said : Wonderful must the fool be who defers such a matter for the morrow. "A whole night," said he, " intervenes, and if Mubárak dies during the night, who will divide these monies?" He made a sign to the men to immediately smash the locks. They did so, and made separate heaps of the gold and jewels, while the Sayad occupied himself in saying his noon prayers. After the prayers, he sat on his cushion, with a bow and a small blunt arrow in hand, with which he made signs directing the division. By the time of the afternoon prayers, the Sayad had divided and given away all the gold and jewels among his men. If any one were to collect all the instances of the Sayad's generosity, their narration would require a separate volume. This is but an incident out of many.

To resume :—When Mubárak Sháh, king of Asír and Burhánpúr, heard how the Gujarát nobles had elected Ahmed Sháh as king, and how having consigned him to confinement had divided the country and treasure among themselves and were enjoying themselves, Mubárak Sháh collected an army and set out from his capital for Gujarát.

On learning this the Gujarát nobles taking Ahmedsháh with them sounded the trumpets for a march and issued forth to repel the invasion of Mubárak Sháh. It was agreed that I'timád Khán with Alif Khán Habashi, should attend the victorious stirrups of the Sultán, that some of the nobles should form the right and some the left wing of the army and that the force of Sayad Mubárak should form the van. They went by forced marches and halted at Ránpúr-Kotáh, a village of the district of Broach, about fifteen miles from the city on the bank of the river Narbadú. Mubárak Sháh arrived and encamped on the opposite bank. Nothing but the river intervened between the hostile armies. Násir-ul-Mulk seeing the state of affairs, observed to the nobles of his party, that the issue of the battle depended on Sayad Mubárak. He desired them to do no more than watch the conflict. It was certain he argued, that the kingdom of one of the two belligerents would fall into his hands. One of the two results, calculated this wily reasoner, was bound to happen. Either the Sayad would win or Mubárak Sháh. The party defeated, he concluded, should be considered as destroyed, the victorious side would at any rate become much weakened. Násir-ul-Mulk reasoned he would have the victor at his mercy, and removing him from his way, he hoped by God's help to become master of both, if not one of those two kingdoms. If, thought Násir-ul-Mulk, Mubárak Sháh beats the Sayad, and the Sayad is defeated or haply killed, or if even he lives, he will remain with wings broken and feathers ruffled. Then, hoped Násir-ul-Mulk, he would beat back Mubárak Sháh and the kingdom of Gujarát, without any partner, would fall into his hands a ready prize. Having settled this design with his own men, Násir-ul-Mulk sent a message to Mubárak Sháh stating that all the nobles of Gujarát were agreeable to his wishes to elect him king of Gujarát, except Sayad Mubárak. That if Mubárak Sháh defeated the Sayad alone he would gain his wishes and that all the nobles would go over to him and be his servants. When the Sayad came to know of the machinations of Násir-ul-Mulk, he became desirous of peace and sent a message to Mubárak Sháh, stating, that he was a descendant of the Prophet and that Mubárak Sháh was the offspring of the Commander of the Faithful Al Fárúk [1] and that war between them was not meet. That

---

[1] The Khándes kings were the descendants of the second Khalifáh and successor of the Prophet, Umar Ibnal Khattáb (A. D. 634-643 H. 13-23) whose surname was Al-Fárúk or the Separator of injustice from justice, i.e., the Just.

on his own part he, the Sayad, was unwilling to fight, and that if Mubárak Sháh was of the same mind too, they should make peace and help each other. Whatever proposals of peace however the Sayad made failed of effect owing to the previous instigations of Násir-ul-Mulk.

The Sayad then sent for Maulána [1] Rúh-ud-dín, the preceptor of Mubárak Sháh, in whom he had great confidence, and spoke to him about the peace. The Maulána said he too had this wish at heart but that he was not sure his intercession would be successful unless the Sayad sent with him one of his men to join with him in delivering the message, of the result of which he would inform him. My Lord the Sayad ordered my father saying, "Miyán Manjhú! Go you, please, and convey to Mubárak Sháh my message." My father said it was not likely Mubárak Sháh would listen to his words when he did not heed the counsel of Mulla Rúh-ud-dín, who was his religious preceptor and the chief of his nobles and advisers. The Sayad saying: "He will certainly agree to what you will say," repeated the Fátihah (the opening chapter of the Kurʼan) and dismissed him. My father with Mulla Rúh-ud-dín went to the court of Mubárak Sháh. The Mulla left my father behind and went to announce, my father to Mubárak Sháh. He was asked what sort of a man my father was. The Mulla returned reply stating my father was "a man of noble appearance and dignified and respectful mien who held the post of agent to the Sayad and was well-known and esteemed among the people of Gujarát." Mubárak Sháh then said, all his nobles and ministers kept standing in his presence and asked what my father proposed to do. The Mulla coming, explained this to my father, who said, that Mubárak Sháh's nobles and ministers were all his dependants and servants, but that my father had come as an emissary from the Sayad and that if he was sent for to the presence he would surely deliver the meassge he was charged with by the Sayad sitting. If not, my father said, "Mubárak Sháh, should send one of his confidential men to him who might hear his message and deliver it to his master." The Mulla went and told his master that my father was not the sort of man to permit himself to be subjected to such harsh etiquette and my father was called in and having performed

---

[1] The word literally means Monseigneur and is applied to people of spiritual excellence or note.

all that the rules of courtesy required, was desired to be seated. He
then conveyed the blessings and compliments of the Sayad and
Mubárak Sháh asked him to deliver the message of the Sayad. My
father said that the object of the Sayad was that there should be
peace and that there should be no bloodshed between Musalmáns.
Mubárak Sháh, then said, he had some questions to ask of my father, of
which he should first give replies and then deliver himself of his
mission. The first question was : " Is the greatness of the Sayads due
to their connection with the Prophet, their maternal grand sire or
owing to their relationship with Ali, the son-in-law of the Prophet,
their paternal ancestor ?" My father replied, "Because of their
connection with the Prophet." " In that case," said Mubárak Sháh,
" I am also the daughter's son of the Sultán of Gujarát, if nobody
remained from his line, then the kingdom of Gujarát by inheritance
descends to me. Why then have you passed over a successor of mature
age and understanding for a boy? What fault did you find in
me ?" My father said : " This case exactly resembles the case of
Sultán Násir-ud-dín of Dehli." The king asked, "In what manner ?
My father replied :—"When the life of Sultán Ghiás-ud-din of Dehli
reached its close, his son Násir-ud-dín was Governor of Bengal and was
there and Násir-ud-dín's son, Muîzz-ud-dín, was at the capital with his
grand-father. Sultán Ghiás-ud-din, made his testamentary disposition
to the ministers and nobles. He told them that the country of India
was large and wide and that lest there should be a disturbance ere
Sultán Násir-ud-dín should arrive he made over the sovereignty of the
country to his grandson in supercession of the claims of his son on
whom he confirmed the sovereignty of Bengal. He requested them
to obey his grand-son, and be loyal to him in the management of the
difficult affairs of the kingdom. They all agreed, some with good will,
others with ill-will. After the death of Sultán Ghiás-ud-din, Sultán
Muîzz-ud-dín Keikubád was seated on the throne. This news reached
Sultán Násir-ud-dín and it did not please him, as Bengal is a
subordinate province of Dehli in the same way as Burhánpur is to
Gujarát. Sultán Násir-ud-dín collected an army and marched
towards Dehli and when Sultán Muîzz-ud-dín learned of his father's
expedition he also issued from Dehli with an army to oppose him.
The father encamped on one of the banks of the river Sarwar and the
son did so on the other. Sultán Násír-ud-dín sent a message

to his son. Khwájah (Amír) Khusrao [1] who was in the retinue of Sultán Muîzz-ud-dín in this expedition, has described what passed between father and son in verse and has given the poem the name of Kirán-us-Saädain (the Conjunction of the two auspicious Stars). Some of the lines containing a substance of the parental message run as follows:—

VERSES.

" My son! give up thy hostile thoughts,
Thy scymitar lower for I'm the Sun :
Look not with anger at my prior rights,
For anger holds no place in our code,
How can my Sire's crown go down to thee ?
From him I claim't as thou wilt claim from me ;
If this design from thine own mind hath sprung,
Turn thee to God in lowly penitence,
But if thy acts from ill-advice proceed,
Then hearken not base interest's venomed words.
Thou'rt young in years and crude in wisdom's ways,
Thou needest guidance yet for many days,
A child, though clever and wise to high degree,
Is still, a child, though, he [2] a prophet be "

The reply sent by Sultán Muîzz-ud-din Keikubád to his father ran :—

Quickly to this rebuke the angered king,
Returned like answer by his noble's hand,
A sharp reply he penned,
Sword edged and bitter as the cup of death,
" Oh ! thou !" the letter said—" who art
Greater than greatness' self, founder of fame.
The throne I hold is not mine own to give
Empire is barren though the fates be big [3]
With changes. Kingship is no heritage,
Else wert thou my king now. 'Tis gained by valour,

---

[1] The poetic account written by Amír Khusrao of this meeting is called the Kirán-us-Saädain or the Conjunction of the two auspicious Stars. Ibni Batûtah (A. D. 1333) gives (Elliot's History of India, III. 596-97) a more intelligent account of this meeting. He says that the father and son met at Karra on the banks of the Ganges, and that Násir-ud-dín encamped on the Karra side of the river. See also Amir Khusrao's account. Elliot III, 524-25.

[2] This couplet is a literal rendering of the Arabic saying الصَّبِيُّ صَبِيٌّ وَلَوْكَانَ نَبِيّاً
" A child, will be a child, though he may be a prophet."

[3] The words, " Dominon is barren " from an old Arabic proverb meaning rather differently from the "Divine right of kings" that there is no heredity in kingdom. The pregnancy of the Heavens is another oriental mode of speech or metaphor. The Easterns ascribe the birth of all events favourable or untoward to the revolution of the skies.

No more a child in one step I have reached,
Kingdom and manhood both. I am become,
Great by the call of Allah, have gained the throne
Of age, though young in years and younger still in fortune."

Let it, began my father, not remain secret from your enlightened mind that empire and kingdom do not go by hereditary succession. They depend on fortune. Heaven has, in this case, decreed dominion for Ahmed Sháh. It, therefore, does not behove you to take objection. Mubárak Sháh said : " If the kingdom was Ahmed Sháh's, why then did you divide among you his horses and elephants and his treasures?" My father said that kingdoms and states depended on the army and when the army was flourishing and prosperous wealth was in its right place. He added : " We feared that Islám Sháh, the king of Dehli, being dead and Muhammad Sháh who had killed his son and successor and usurped the throne being a young ruler and an ambitious and knowing that of all princes he is the only one possessing an army superior to our own, might turn his thoughts to the conquest of Gujarát we made ourselves ready to receive him never dreaming that you would march against us. When the conversation reached this stage, Mubárakshah said to his minister Kámil-ul-Mulk : " He means by these words that they have made preparations to fight the king of Dehli, what power have I to fight them and they do not know that with the exception of Sayad Mubárakshah all the Gujarat nobles are in secret league with me." My father said : " The army opposes the king when it is ill-equipped and down-hearted. Your Majesty may ascertain, that from the time of Sultán Muzaffar I. till the time of Sultán Mahmúd, the Martyr, no king has had so well equipped and large an army. It is, therefore, difficult for so good an army to entertain thoughts of treachery towards its master." The king said : " What, if I show you the petitions of all of them ? " My father said : " They must not be written by them, but some evil-disposed persons, who have the habit of writing such letters, when two armies meet, that on both sides dissensions may arise. But such things must not be believed. Had there been any truth in the writings two or three at least of the so-called malcontent nobles must by this time have joined your Majesty. It is surely high time they should have come, for to-morrow the battle is going to take place. When will they come else. These things are the doings of the subordinates and have no weight. The Sayad interferes only for the good and peace of the Mussalmáns. If not, none of the Gujarat nobles have any wish for peace." At this the king became silent. After a time, he told his minister Kámil-ul-Mulk gently to tell the envoy that he had used many hard words in his conversation, but that as he had conveyed them in the style of the wise and the eloquent they had pleased his Majesty and that he agreed to peace. That the envoy was to come and receive the dress of honor and take his leave and that he was to return to-morrow (to Mubárak Shah's camp), when the king would march away. Kámil-ul-Mulk came and took my father to the corner of the tent and there repeated to him the words of the king and gave him the dress of honour with forty thousand Muzaffaris in cash. My father said he would willingly wear the dress, but that he should be excused the money. Kámil-ul-Mulk went and communicated this to Mubárak Sháh, who asked him to tell my father that the people of Gujarát acknowledged with equal honor the rewards conferred by Sultán Bahádur and his (Mubárakshah's) brother Muhammadsháh. Why did my father object to their acceptance? My father said that he was acting according to the inclinations of his master, who, in treating his guests always gave away the plate vessels and table-cloths and other things in and on which the banquets were served. That the Sayad never sent back for these articles lest the guest should put himself to the trouble of giving vail money to the servants who went for the articles. "When," said my father, "my master observes this rule for menial servants, I, who am one of his higher servants should certainly have a regard for his wishes." Mubárakshah highly approved of my father's conduct and dismissed him and he returned to my lord the Sayad and related to him the whole of what had happened. The Sayad was much pleased at the success of my father's mission, and bestowed on my father a horse, an Arab of the name of Táús or the Pea-cock, the pink of the royal stables and a favourite of the late martyred Sultán, after whose death the Sayad had specially begged for and obtained it. He also bestowed on my father a jágir of twenty-five lákhs of Tánkahs, [1] which he asked my father to spend in the rejoicings of the marriage of his sons, and on no other account. In short, the Sayad having informed I'timád Khán and other nobles of peace being concluded, in the morning sent Sayad Háshim and Sayad Mubárak and Sayad Abul Khair Bukhári and my father to Mubárakshah, to request him to retire as promised which he did. The army of Gujarát also

---

[1] The Tánkah was $\frac{1}{100}$ of a rupee. See Gazetteer History of Gujarát, Musalmán Period. Vol. I. Part. I., p. 224. Note 2.

marched back to Ahmedabad. They, however, divided into two parties, one party acknowledged the chiefship of I'timád Khán and
allied themselves to him, the other attached themselves to Násir-
ul-Mulk and followed him. The Sayad joined the chief of the
Gujarát nobles I'timád Khán. Hasan Khán Dakhani, a powerful
noble joined neither party. When the army reached its camp
from which next day they were to march to Baroda I'timád Khán
sent his agents to Hasan Khán and having persuaded him took
him to the Sayad's tent. Násir-ul-Mulk also had sent his
agent Atak Khán to Hasan Khán to try and win him over to his side,
but before Atak Khán reached him Hasan Khán had come to the
Sayad. Atak Khán also followed him there and told the Sayad:
"It does not become you outsiders to set the nobles one against
the other and cause ill-will and disturbance among the people of
Gujarát. While Násir-ul-Mulk breathes no one can claim to be the
Vazir of Gujarát. Why do you throw yourself into destruction?"
asked he, and with these words grasping with one hand the waist of the
Sayad he sought his dagger with the other. On this the kinsmen and
followers of the Sayad fell on him and would have despatched him
had not the Sayad forbade them, saying: "If God wills I will kill this
doomed one in the field of battle." The assembly now dispersed, and
each one went to his own quarters. On hearing this Násir-ul-Mulk
was much moved and said that while the Sayad supported I'timád Khán
he would not gain power. "I must" thought he, "play such a game
as to destroy the strength of I'timád Khán." This however was not
possible without in the first instance crushing the power of the Sayad.
After encompassing the Sayad's ruin he calculated, I'timád Khán
would fall an easy prey. On the day the army reached the vicinity of
the town of Baroda he issued secret orders to the men of his army
to remain ready armed. The Sayad being ignorant of this design,
his men imperfectly armed, marched on incautiously in one direction.
I'timád Khán was at the head of his forces following the Sayad
at the distance of a mile. On the other side Násir-ul-Mulk was
marching with his men. When they reached the encamping ground
Násir-ul-Mulk having joined the other nobles who were intimate with
him, stood in the way of my lord the Sayad as he advanced from
the other side. Atak Khán, the unfortunate, who was mentioned
above, came in the van of the army of Násir-ul-Mulk and began
the action by falling on the Sayad's army, but his brave Sayad's

drawing their swords defended themselves and killed the wretch
and routed his army. At this time Násir-ul-Mulk came up with
30,000 well equipped sabres and a great battle ensued and a
number of fine men chiefly the Sayad's kinsmen fell, notable
amongst them being Sayad Muzzammil, his younger brother Sayad
Háshim and Sayad Muhammad the brother's sons of the Sayad,
and Sayad Muhammad, the son of Sayad Fidá and others. At that
time the cavalry of the Sayad did not amount to more than two
thousand, his other army being scattered never dreamed of the
possibility of such a conflict. I'timád Khán fell short of offering the
Sayad any help. How could two thousand half-armed horsemen hold
against thirty thousand, well armed and equipped. At last the well
wishers of the Sayad, seizing his bridle, led him out of the field and
turned his face towards the Khánpúr Wánkáner ford and there crossing
the river Mahi went to Kapadwanj which was one of the dependencies
of his fief. I'timád Khán avoiding to give battle followed in the
Sayad's wake and arrived at Kapadwanj. Many nobles of I'tmád's
party joined Násir-ul-Mulk. Sultán Ahmed being himself in his power
Násir-ul-Mulk returned thence to Ahmedábád in great pomp and
circumstance by forced marches and there established himself. His
pride and arrogance now reached such a pitch that he did not think
much of any of the nobles. He arrested Zeinuddin, the brother
of Afzal Khán the minister and fined him and seized and imprisoned
and demanded gold of Sadr Khan, brother of Mián Abdus Samad,
the counsellor of Sultán Mehmúd, who in those days was appointed
(by the nobles) minister of Sultán Ahmed. After two months
Násir-ul-Mulk advanced with Sultán Ahmed and with the whole
army of Gujarát towards Kapadwanj, with the intention of expelling
the Sayad and I'timád Khán from Gujarát and encamped at the
village of Kamand, a village of the Ahmedábád division, about
fifteen miles from the city. On hearing this news the Sayad
and I'timád Khán convoked their well-wishers in counsel. I'timád
said he had with him no more than four thousand horse and
the enemy was coming at the head of fifty or sixty thousand. To do
battle against such odds would, he feared, bring no good. They
should, he advised, go to Muhammad Ádil Sháh, King of Dehli. It
was agreed that they should go to Dùngarpúr, the frontier of which
is contiguous with Gujarát and thence to Dehli. The council
unanimously resolved on this. The Sayad got up without saying yea

or nay and going inside consulted Bíbí Álam Khátún, the wife of Sayad Mírán, son of my lord the Sayad and told her what I'timád and the others had advised.

The lady said, " Who am I to advise on such a matter, but as you command me I shall say what my heart prompts me to say. You will be pleased to inform me what is your present age?" The Sayad said he was fifty-eight years old. The lady said, "The age to which the children of the Prophet generally reach is three score or three score years and ten. After that term it is well known they do not live long. For what span of life then" asked she "do you leave your country, your honour and reputation, and repair to the ruler of Dehli ? And will he not say that you have gone to him fleeing from a cowardly grain-selling trader ?[1] It is best to resolve on surrendering your life. Risk a battle. If the time of your death has arrived, die. You will win martyrdom. If not, well then, you have the power to choose." On hearing these words the manliness of the Sayad was moved. He returned at once to I'timád Khán and reassembling the council said, he had resolved not to turn his back from Násir-ul-Mulk and had vowed so before God. I'timád Khán said, " What harm can our fighting do to Násir-ul-Mulk ? " The Sayad said: "My dear Khán ! you stand at our backs and see and do what you think best after I am killed." I'timád remained silent, and the Sayad called his kinsmen and ordered them to arm themselves for battle. As many of the Sayad's brotherhood were killed in the battle of Baroda and many were lying wounded, he selected five hundred veterans, and resolved to surprise the enemy during the night of the next day. At this juncture my father brought a letter from Sayad Husein Bukhári, who at that time was the occupant of the seat of the Saint at the Shrine of the Saint Sayad Burhánuddin Bukhári, from Batwa. It advised the Sayad to give battle to Nasír-ul-Mulk without fear and stated that according to (the Kuraánic verse) " How many a small party has by the grace of God overcome a large one ! " That victory was to be the Sayads. That this favourable result was prophesied by the saint, Sayad Burhánuddín and that the details of it would be communicated by Sheikh Manjhú (my father). These were as follows :— When Násirul-ul-Mulk was about to issue against the Sayad and

---

[1] Násir-ul-Mulk was probably a convert to Islám belonging originally to the Bania class.

34

Ítimad Khán, Sayad Husein went to him and dissuaded him from so doing. But he said :—" Of all things do not put me to the shame of refusing you this. I have made an unalterable resolve to dislodge Sayad Mubárak from Kapadvanj. At this, my Lord the Sayad, being hurt, said : " Then all of us Sayads will take Sayad Mubárak's part. The whole army of Gujarát are our religious followers. Let me see what guideless [1] person has the auda. city to oppose his religious teachers ! " Saying so Sayad Husein got up and came to his own residence. All the great Sayads of Batwa as well as of Ásáwal, in all six or seven hundred strong, made ready to go and prepared to march next morning. That night the Sayad met the saint Kutbi Âlam, in the spiritual world. [2] The Kutb said : 'Sayad Husein, you need not go to the help of Sayad Mubárak. We have sent for him and to-morrow he will come! " My father, coming from Dholka, had been to pay his respects to Sayad Husein on the way and he communicated the above to him and gave him an armour to be given to the Sayad and gave him one for himself. When my father reached the Sayad he said all that he was directed to say. The Sayad regarded Sayad Husein's words as Divine Revelation and made himself ready. That very day the effects of the prophecy became apparent. Imád-ul-Mulk Rúmi and Alif Khán Habashi, the men who had charge of the person of the Sultán, said to one another, " This Násir-ul-Mulk wants to remove the Sayad from his way to power. After he has done that it will be our turn next ! The best thing therefore for us, is to make up with the Sayad and remove this thorn, Násir-ul-Mulk, from our path." That same moment they sent a confidential man of theirs to the Sayad with a message to the effect that " Násir-ul-Mulk, lulled by the pride of the strength of his army fancies himself so secure that he drinks wine every evening before going to bed. The nobles to whom he entrusts the patrol duty are also as incautious and negligent. If you are brave enough to march out at night and fall on our camp about day-break, we shall take the king with us and go over to you and shall

---

[1] To be without a spiritual guide is considered a sign of moral turpitude, so great, that Bē Pír, one having no spiritual guide, is a term of opprobrium.

[2] This has a double meaning. It is possible from the words : " That night " that the Sayad saw his saintly ancestor in a dream. But the probability from, the mention of the words in the text of " World of Spirits," Álami Raúháni, is that the Sayad put himself into a contemplative trance (Murákibah) and thus met his ancestor.

attack Násir-ul-Mulk and matters, God willing, shall end as we desire ! ''

The Sayad communicated this to I'timád Khán. But I'timád Khán said, that it was not advisable to rely on such overtures without the intermediacy of responsible men and without an agreement strengthened by oath. The Sayad said that as he had already resolved to pursue this course without this offer from I'mád-ul-Mulk and Alif Khán Habashi, he would certainly turn out that night relying on God. I'timád Khán said, '' I cannot in that case accompany you, you may take Tátár Khán Ghori. '' This Tátár Khán Ghori was a man of I'timád Khán's confidence and not devoid of courage. My Lord the Sayad said, '' Let Tátár Khan Ghori also be with you. 'Verily God is with us.' '' [1] Repeating with these words the Fátihah, or opening chapter of the Kuráan, he mounted and with five hundred valorous horsemen issued out. The distance to be traversed was nearly twenty miles. In the morning they came in sight of the camp of Násir-ul-Mulk. They saw the pickets, and the flank commanded by Shamsher-ul·Mulk Doláji, who was armed and on guard. My Lord the Sayad, opened the action by attacking him. A hot hand to hand skirmish ensued, in which Shamsher-ul-Mulk fought well, but when his men heard that the Sayad personally commanded the surprise party they took to flight and Shamsher-ul-Mulk was carried away wounded from the field. An uproar arose in the camp of Násir-ul-Mulk and the report of Sayad Mubárak's arrival spread on all sides. At this juncture I'mád-ul-Mulk and Alif Khán Habashi, taking the Sultán with them, joined Sayad Mubárak. The Sayad requested them to follow while he went ahead to attack the tent of Násir-ul-Mulk. Information was given to Násir-ul-Mulk, that the Sayad was on his camp. Násir-ul-Mulk got on a kettle-drum horse and took to flight. Thus the gate of Victory was thrown open to the courage of my Lord the Sayad. Ay verily !

'Tis not the turning skies above that rule the fate of man,
But human virtues strong to do whatever courage can ! [2]

Except Násir-ul-Mulk, the whole army submitted to the Sayad. Mounted messengers were sent to inform Ítimád Khán and he also came and met the Sayad. Next day the Sayad and Ítimád Khán turned towards Ahmedábád. When they came to the city and

---

[1] A verse of the Kuráan Innal-láha-maáná.
[2] That is, by the revolution of the Heavens.

arrived at the Tir-polia Gates [1] which form a famous quarter in the city of Ahmedábád, a merchant coming up grasped the Sayad's knee, and said : "The generous, when they make a promise fulfil it." [2] The Sayad smiled. I'timád Khán was present and asked what he meant. The Sayad said, Ítimád Khán, please pass an order on a certain banker of the city to pay this man 12 lakhs of tánkás (Rs. 12,000) and I shall explain to you this circumstance which is a wonderful one. Ítimád Khán ordered a banker to pay the man this sum. The explanation of the matter was this ; Before the victory, some Afgháns had brought several Arab horses for sale to Kapadwanj. The Sayad asked to buy the horses on credit, but the owners would not give them. The Sayad offered to increase the value by one-third, but still the merchants would not hear of parting with them, so gloomy was the aspect of the Sayad's affairs at that time. One day the dealers attended an entertainment given them by the Sayad. One of the Afgháns was a seer who could read futurity by divination by means of the shoulder-blades of sheep. He took up a shoulder-blade and told his companions that he saw in it that the Sayad would be victorious and advised his companions to sell the horses at two-fifths more than their value. The Sayad said : " You were unwilling when I offered you one-third more and how is it that you now offer me at two-fifths of their nominal value ? Next day his companions also brought their horses and all the Afgháns agreed to part with them on the condition, that when he entered Ahmedábád victorious, the Sayad should pay them the price before entering his mansion. The Sayad agreed and bought the horses at 12 lákhs of tánkás and he kept his promise.

To continue :—After his defeat Násir-ul-Mulk went to the district of Chámpáner. My lord the Sayad having bestowed upon my father the honour of a turband and the insignia of a standard and leaving him at Dholka to look after his estates there went with Ítimád Khán in pursuit. Násir-ul-Mulk went to the hilly tracts of the Pál and there falling sick departed this life. At this time Ikhtyár-ul-Mulk who was left in charge of the city on behalf of I'timad Khán, combining with Hasan Khán Dakhani and Fateh Khán Balúch raised a disturbance by setting up as Sultan the king's uncle by name Sháhúji. When this news reached my lord the Sayad he turned from Broach towards Ahmedábád. When he arrived at Mehmudábád, eighteen miles

---

[1] The modern " Tín Darwázah. "
[2] This is an Arabic proverb—Al Karímo-isá wa-áda w fá.

from Ahmedábád, the rebellious nobles taking Sháhúji with them issued from the city and encamped at the village of Rubrah, six miles from Ahmedábád. My lord the Sayad called my father from Dholka. At that time there was a darvish of the name of Sayad Ahmed Makhdúm, at Dholka. My father before starting went to take leave of him and asked him to pray for him. The darvish said: " Go you. Victory is for the Sayad. But before the battle Í'timád Khán, wishing to join the enemy will separate himself from you and a great panic will seize your army, but all will end well." My father was struck with amazement at these words, as he knew that Ítimád was the head of our army and my lord the Sayad was fighting as much for him as for himself. Why then should he fly and fall away and if he should desert the army how could it remain together. With these anxieties weighing heavily on his mind my father went to meet the Sayad. While yet on his way he learned that Ítimád had quitted the army. This news was in a manner the harbinger of victory, so he presented himself with joy before the Sayad and related what he had heard from the Sheikh. The Sayad told my father that when the sound of my fathers kettle-drums reached his ears he drew the omen of victory from my father's arrival and that my father strengthened the hope by bringing with him the holy man's prophecy.

To continue :—When the victorious army arrived and encamped at Mehmúdábád, an epistle reached Ítimád Khán from Hasan Khán Dakhani and Ikhtiyár-ul-Mulk, stating that Sultán Ahmed was a disciple of the Sayad and that his being king was good for the Sayad but a matter of perfect indifference for Ítimád Khán and for them. So they invited him to join them, stating that they had elevated Ahmedsháh's uncle to the throne, an elevation by which he could as well profit. At this instigation Ítimád Khán, without consulting any noble or commoner, at once left and went to Ahmedábád. As soon as this news reached my lord the Sayad, he at once sent his own son Sayad Mírán, and Sheikh Máh to persuade Í'timád Khán to return. They travelled fifteen miles from the camp and overtook Í'timád Khán and asked him the reason of his opposition. Í'timád Khán said : " Each one of the nobles is inclined to sedition : whom and how many shall we oppose ? I propose to withdraw into retirement, you and your army may do what you like." At this time the Sayad also arrived and said to Í'timád Khán :—" We are risking our lives for your honour, and you treat us in this way." With these persuasions they

brought I'timád Khán back to the camp. I'timád Khán wrote to
Fateh Khán Balúch and Hasan Khán Dakhani that it was not well
for him to remain in the company of Ikhtiyár-ul-Mulk, and invited
Fateh Khán to his side. Fateh Khán Baluch went over to I'timád Khán.
Hasan Khán Dakhani, however, said that the king (they were fighting
for) was of his elevation and the shame of the defeat, in case it happened,
would be his. So the next day the drum for the battle were sounded
and the two armies faced one another. Ikhtiyár-ul-Mulk with Sháhji
fled the field and Hasan Khán Dakhani, who had never turned back
to enemy fell on the field. My lord the Sayad victorious and triumphant, with Sultán Ahmed and the other nobles went to Ahmedábád.
After these events the nobles divided the kingdom of Guzarát
among themselves. They appointed the city of Ahmedábád with the
territory around it for the expenses of the Sultán. The districts
of Kadi, Petlád, Nadiád, Babyal, Rádhanpúr, Sami and Múnjpúr,
Anhilwára and Godhra, and the province of Sorath were conferred on I'timád Khán and his Guzarát followers. I'timád Khán
rewarded Tátár Khán Ghori by the bestowal on him of the province
of Sorath and gave the districts of Rádhanpúr and Sami and
Múnjpúr and Anhilwárá to Fateh Khán Balúch. He conferred the
district of Nadiád on Malik-ush—Sharq and assigned some of the
dependencies of Jhálawúr in lieu of salary to Alif Khán Habashi.
The country of Pattan and the port of Cambay, with its eighty-
four villages, the districts of Dholka, Goghá and Dhandúka and
Chámpánér and Sarnál (or Thásra), Bálásinore and Baroda and
Kapadwanj fell to the share of my lord the Sayad. My lord the
Sayad having taken Músa Khán and Sher Khán the Fauládis under
his patronage gave them the districts of Pattan. Broach and Surat
as far as the frontiers of Sultáupúr, and Nazarbár fell to the lot of
Imád-ul-Mulk Rúmi and Imád-ul-Mulk Rúmi gave Baroda to Alif
Khán the Abyssinian and gave the port of Surat to Khudáwand
Khán Rúmi, who was his wife's brother. Morassa and similar petty
districts were given to the Gujarát nobles who were the followers of
I'timád Khán. The Sultán and I'timád Khán remained in the city
with I'timád Khán as his minister and every one, glad of his share,
went to his estate. My lord the Sayad went and took up residence at
a place of the name of Sayadpúr he had populated in the vicinity of
Mehmúdábád.

    After some time had passed thus, Álam Khán Lodi, who had gone to Dehli in the time of Sher Sháh Pádsháh with Daryá Khán and on whom Sher Sháh had bestowed estates in Málwa, as has previously been described, returned to Gujarát. Daryá Khán died in Málwa and Álam Khán in consequence of some act he had committed found Málwa too hot for him. He made his arrival known to my lord the Sayad, saying that he had returned to this country in the hope of his kindness and support and was only waiting for his permission to join him. The Sayad wrote in reply to say that he was welcome but asked him to wait a few days where he was to enable him to consult the other great nobles to invite him. Álám Khán, who was in a very impoverished state, without waiting, went and joined the Sayad and made his son, Qutub Khán a disciple of the Sayad. The Sayad, without taking Álam Khán with him, went to Ahmedábád and said to I'timád Khán that since Álam Khán had come in hopes of their support, that he and I'timád Khán should provide for him. I'timád, who did not at all like this sudden arrival of Álam Khán, remained silent. He and Imád-ul-Mulk were both sorely vexed with the Sayad. I'timád Khán said to the Sayad that Álam Khán was an intriguing man who would not, he was afraid, be satisfied with anything they would do for him. It was not politic that after the establishment of peace they should allow such a man to re-enter Gujarát and again sow the seed of discord. My lord the Sayad said that Álam Khán had suffered much on account of his former failings and had doubtless repented and given it up before coming to Gujarát. He added that it seemed to him contrary to generosity and manliness to now repel him. Since I'timád Khán could not help agreeing to what the Sayad said, he said that he would do what the Sayad desired, but he added that he was sure they would have to rue the course they were following. The Sayad requested them to remember that Álam Khán was once a great man, the powerful minister of Sultán Mehmúd, and that he now agreed to serve them. He said that it was a good thing to have such a man with them. I'timád Khán said he would send for Imád-ul-Mulk Rúmi from Broach to consider about an estate for Álam Khán. A man was sent to fetch Imád-ul-Mulk and when he came the question of an estate was mooted. Imád-ul-Mulk said his own estates were not sufficient for his men and that he must be excused from giving a share out of them to another. After much discussion this agreement was made that the Sayad should give the districts of Baroda and Chámpáner from his own fief to Álam Khán and Aâzam Humáyún who was reputed as Álam Khán's half brother. I'timád Khán gave the district of Godhra to Alif Khán Khatri, who was a follower and companion of Álam Khán. Álam Khán dismissing his pride served I'timád Khán so zealously that they became close friends. I'timád Khán gave Álam Khán the house of his son which was contiguous to his own so that they may always be together. After this I'mád-ul-Mulk returned to his estates and my lord the Sayad returned to Sayadpúr and gave a piece of his territories of Jhálawar to Alif Khán Habashí who went to Jhálawár. Some days passed in this wise when Alif Khán laid the foundation of discord. He collected all the jágirdars of those parts and usurped authority over all the country of Jhálawár not giving ear to the frequent written messages of I'timád Khán not to be obnoxious and self-willed. At last I'timád Khán and Álam Khán collected an army, and taking the Sultán with them, marched against Alif Khán. They, however, did not inform Sayad Mubárak of this and did not pay him any attention and on his part the Sayad took no notice of this. Alif Khán at the head of three thousand horse made a manly stand, giving battle in the vicinity of the town of Viramgám, but being defeated escaped safely. I'timád Khán with a large force had encamped about eleven miles off but Alif Khán on the pretence of going out to meet him to negotiate peace went away to Dholka where he became the guest of Sayad Mírán. Taking leave thence he went by way of Cambay and having crossed the Gulf of Cambay took refuge with Imád-ul-Mulk at Broach and thence went and took refuge with my lord the Sayad. I'timád Khán returned to Ahmedábád. On hearing this Imád-ul-Mulk also started from Broach for Ahmedábád in company with my lord the Sayad. His Holiness pleaded for Alif Khán with Imád-ul-Mulk, and taking the district of Bahyal from I'timád Khán, gave it to Alif Khán. For some time after this peace and contentment reigned.

After some time it struck Álam Khán to remove I'timád Khán from his position and placing him in confinement, to himself take his place. Álam Khán took counsel of his followers regarding this. One of these who was a well wisher of I'timád Khán apprized him of it. Acting on this news I'timád Khán made Álam Khán quit his son Sher Khán's house and Álam Khán went to his own mansions outside the city walls near the village of Asáwal and fortified the place substantially and began to make overtures of friendship to Imád-ul-Mulk. One day Álam Khán said to Imád-ul-Mulk that it was desirable to get rid of I'timad Khán. I'mád-ul-Mulk pretended to agree with this proposal, but in his heart he began to hate Álam Khán. When Alam Khán saw that there was no chance of Imád-ul-Mulk agreeing to his proposal about I'timád Khán, he dropped his designs against I'timád Khán and commenced to plot the ruin of Sayad Mubárak. He said to Imád-ul Mulk, " Until you can remove Sayad Mubárak your power will not be firmly established." Imád-ul-Mulk also persuaded I'timád Khán to collect an army and attack Sayad Mubárak. I'timád Khán and Imád-ul-Mulk and Álam Khán and all the nobles of Gujarát issued forth from the city of Ahmedábád with the resolution of crushing the power of the Sayad and encamped at the Kánkaria Tank, close to the city. This news reached the Sayad. He said to my father, " Go you and first meet Álam Khán and then I'timád Khán and to each of them say after salutation, " Whenever you go on an expedition you inform me, but you have not apprized me of the object of this exepedition. Please to inform me of your present designs and against whom this army is about to march. See what answer they give. From that I shall shape my course." My father first went to Àlam Khán's house and gave him the Sayad's message. Álam Khán hung down his head and said, " Why do you ask me? You are acquainted with their designs." My father asked, " From whom then shall I learn ? The Sayad expects he has no greater friend or well-wisher than you. If you don't inform me, who will? He then replied " Miyán, Manjhú all the nobles of Gujarát are agreed that until the Sayad is ruined evil will not be banished from Gujarát." My father said : " Alláh make it easy ! But what side will you take in this business ?" He said : " The general side, the side of the majority." My father returned : " My dear Khán, if this is the return for kinduesses done to you by your benefactor then the truth is on your side !" He got up and took his way to I'timád Khán's tent. On the way he encountered Imád-ul-Mulk going away from I'timád Khán's tent in great state. No sooner his eyes fell on my father Imád-ul-Mulk exclaimed: " Miyan Manjhú, I always used until now to wear one sword, but now that I am going to fight Sayad Mubárak I have had, look you, to wear two ! " and placing his hand on the hilts he showed them. My father said : " The swords you have worn are instruments sacred to the children of the Prophet, on whom be peace ! Let us see what results they bring forward." [1] Then he said :

---

[1] The profession of the sword has Ali, the son-in-law of the Prophet, as its tutelary head. He is the guardian saint of the son of Mars and in the latter-day wars of Islám his name, *Yá Ali*! was the martial warcry.

"If you have come to see Alam Khán and I'timád Khán, you may see them, but after seeing them don't go away without seeing us." My father went to the tent of I'timád Khán and delivered the Sayad's message. I'timád Khán opened his budget of complaints of Álam Khán, saying, "Whatever was done was done by him. However much we told him and warned him that Álam Khán was a man from whom one must always look out for intrigue, the Sayad never gave ear to our words of warning. What is now to be done. The Sayad never did let well alone. I always was and still am the Sayad's friend. Convey my blessings to he Sayad and tell him whatever is done is done by Álam Khán. We none of us are agreeable to it. You may go and see Imád-ul-Mulk also and after that come to me to take your leave." My father went to Imád-ul-Mulk, who outwardly said some very harsh words. He then got up and went into privacy. He called my father there who said to him that he whom the Sayad considered his best friend and well-wisher had turned out to be his greatest foe, who wanted to either kill or expel him. "What," said Imád-ul-Mulk, "could we do?" The Sayad never listened to our warnings. You may go and give him our blessing. To-morrow we march from here and encamp on the banks of the Khári and thence we shall send some confidential men of ours to the Sayad. The nature of the Sayad's reply shall decide the matter. My father took leave and coming back to I'timád Khán he repeated to him the conversation he had just had with Imád-ul-Mulk. I'timád Khán confirmed the truth of Imád-ul-Mulk's assurances and bade my father adieu. My father, returning to the Sayad, repeated the words he had had with each of them to him. My Lord the Sayad asked my father what he thought of the words of Imád-ul-Mulk. My father said he seemed to him to insinuate that he wished to play Álam Khán false. The Sayad, however, said he had no confidence in Imád-ul-Mulk's words and knew him to be of a shifty and deceitful character. So the Sayad prepared for battle. He had four or five thousand cavalry about him who all placing their trust in the Lord of Host determined to dies. The next day they heard that the army of Gujarát had come and encamped on the banks of the Khári. When two or three hours of the night had passed, five Abyssinian horsemen came enquiring after my father's residence. Somebody having pointed them out the house, they came to the door and enquired after my father. The porter said, he was gone to my Lord the Sayad. The Abyssinian said : "Hasten thou and tell him softly that Ankus Khán Habashi has come and wants him." The porter did as desired. My father told my Lord the Sayad. He said : "Miyán Manjhú ! I cannot believe that Imád-ul-Mulk is my well-wisher. God grant there be no fraud in all these messages and missions which may turn out to our hurt." My father said that Ankus Khán was the agent of Imád-ul-Mulk and that his sending him at such a time with such secrecy was not without some wise object. "We ought at least to send for him and hear what he has to say." The Sayad desired my father to go and bring him if he was so inclined. My father went to Ankus Khán, who said : "Miyán Manjhú only a small portion of the night remains now and we have to return to Imád-ul-Mulk in such a way that no one should come to know of our having gone out. So you take me to the presence of the Sayad that we may tell him at once what we have to say." My father complying, brought him before the Sayad. Ankus Khán, on arriving in the presence of the Sayad produced a copy of the Holy Kuráan from below his arm, and said : "Imád-ul-Mulk has sent you his blessings and said that the object of this expedition against you was to teach you to discriminate friends from foes. This you will have come to know. Now please ride out with us towards our army : we shall with I'timád Khán bring Sultán Ahmed to you in the way and shall thence turn back and fall on Álam Khán and shall either capture him alive or kill him. Here is the Holy Kuráan between us and there is no untruth or doubt in this." On this understanding the Sayad gave Ankus Khán leave and in the morning, having donned his armour, he went forth. Imád-ul-Mulk and I'timád Khán, with Sultán Ahmed, met the Sayad near the village of Kanij, about five miles from Sayadpúr and having divested their bosoms of all ill-feeling, they marched against Álam Khán. The Sayad sent Sheikh Ahmed Diváni to Álam Khán to say that evil is never productive of good. He who does good finds good in return and he who does evil finds nothing but evil. What you intended for others has gone against yourself. Now you should return to your estates. After consulting with the nobles we shall send for you." Álam Khán said : "You are now coming out against me. How can I go without giving battle." However much the Sayad advised him to desist, he commenced to fight. Aázam Humáyún, who was his half-brother, and his eldest son

Qutub Khán and many Afgháns were slain and Álam Khán being routed fled to Chámpánēr. The nobles pursued him, but he eluded their pursuit by entering the mountains of Pál; so the nobles returning from Chámpánēr came to Ahmedábád.

When Mubárak Sháh heard of the above state of things he allied himself with Nihál Khán, of Berár, and brought an army against Gujarát. On hearing this news the nobles taking Ahmed Sháh with them marched to repel Mubárak Sháh's invasion. Since the army of Gujarát had. always the reputation of being victorious over the army of Burhánpúr and the Dakhan, when the Gujarát army reached the village of Ráná-kot on the bank of the Narbada, Mubárak Sháh not caring to measure strength with it, retired to Pilúgám, a village about five miles from the Narbada. Some nobles, such as Changíz Khán son of Imád-ul-Mulk and Sarandáz Khán of Mándu crossing the river pursued the fugitive army and having plundered some of its baggage returned. The army of Gujarát, also recrossing the Narbada and going to Jívgám, halted there in the open country for some days. In the meantime Álam Khán in obedience to an invitation from Sher Khán Fauládi, issuing from the mountains, went along the hilly tracts to Pattan. Músa Khán, the elder brother of Sher Khán, was in the service of my Lord the Sayad. Sher Khán uniting with Álam Khán seized on the district of Kadi, which was a holding of I'timád Khán. This news reached I'timád Khán on his way back from the Narbada banks. I'timád Khán wrote to Ikhtiyár-ul-Mulk and Daráykhán Habashi who were in and about Ahmednagar (Amnagar) to expel Álam Khan from his Kadi estate. Ikhtiyár-ul-Mulk assembled an army, and marched against Álam Khán. Alam Khán came out, gave battle, and was killed, and Sher-Khán fled and returned to Pattan.

After a while the army that had marched against Mubárak Sháh returned to Ahmedábád. In this going and coming Sultán Ahmed entertained several men in his service and bestowed titles on others. He gave Yúsuf Khán Habashi the title of Aázam Humáyún and offered a title to Sheikh-ul-Islám, who was a Bukhári, which he did not accept. He gave his own younger brother, Abdur Rehmán, the title of Sádát Khán, and appointed him his deputy. All the executive power and administrative authority were still in the hands of I'timád Khán. Imád-ul-Mulk though he aspired to equality with

I'timád Khán and took care that no orders passed independently by the Sultán should become effective. Three or four thousand of the trusty followers of l'timád Khán and Imád-ul-Mulk night and day kept watch and ward over the Sultán by turns : sometimes Imád-ul-Mulk kept the Sultán in his own surveillance, at others I'timád Khán gave him over to the charge of his followers. As the Almighty had decreed the ruin and extinction of the race of these two nobles he first planted discord and jealousy in their breasts and they began to wish each other evil in spite of their sworn compacts and covenants of mutual good-will. For the least prospect of gain they used to forget their mutual obligations and compacts. On such grounds they always squabbled with each other and fancied their advantage lay in these mean bickerings. The Sayad, as far as in his power lay, tried to maintain peace between them, espousing usually the weaker side, but as it was otherwise ordained by an All-wise Providence they did not desist from their mean and petty diff rences. They placed the saw of discord at the root of the tree of their prosperity and worked it on. In a short time neither name nor trace remained of them, and the truth of the blessed Kuráanic verse : "To whom belongeth the dominion of the Day ? To the One All-powerful Allah!," became manifest. Some days passed in this manner. At last the flames of envy and discord broke out high between I'timád Khán and Imád-ul-Mulk. Sultán Ahmed thought that he had no escape from the power of I'timád Khán and made friends with I'mád-ul-Mulk. This displeased I'timád Khán. About this time some Abyssinians killed Tughluk Khán, one of the intimate and powerful followers of l'timád Khán, in obedience, doubtless, to a hint from Imád-ul-Mulk. l'timád Khán, much hurt, went out of the city, and though Imád-ul-Mulk himself followed him and humbly persuaded him to return, he went to Mehmúdábád with the intention of going away to Mubárak Sháh. However much the Sayad also dissuaded him from his intention, he would not be appeased. He went to Mubárak Sháh and taking Mubáraksháh with him advanced at the head of an army against Gujarát. Imád-ul-Mulk, with Sultán Ahmed and the nobles of his faction, came to Mehmúdábád and told the Sayad that the country of Gujarát was a gift of the Sayad's ancestors to the dynasty, that Sultán Ahmed especially was elevated by him to the throne, and that it was but proper that the Sayad should now take the leading part to protect his honour. The Sayad joined them, and they arrived by forced marches at Ránpúr Kotáh. From this place they wrote to I'timád Khán to say that he might be sure that in case the country went to the hands of Mubárak Sháh that monarch would not maintain him in the power and position he enjoyed under Sultán Ahmed. "Why then," asked they, "should you change the duty born of the rights and privileges enjoyed for so many years for ingratitude?" It so happened that Imád-ul-Mulk had already begun to rue the step he had taken as he had come to find that Mubárak Sháh was very miserly of soul, and that what I'timád spent in a day equalled the monthly expenses of Mubárak Sháh. His well-wishers advised him that to give up the administration of Gujarát for the service of such a close-fisted ruler was folly. So he wrote back in reply that as Mubárak Sháh had collected an armament for his help something must be done which could as well save his respect as compensate Mubárak Sháh. He proposed that the districts of Sultánpúr and Nazarbár should be given to Mubárak Sháh. After much dispute this was resolved upon, and Sultánpúr and Nazarbár were given to Mubárak Sháh, who on his part gave I'timád Khán the towns of Dharangáon and Erandol and Nanádar which is celebrated for its fine muslins and waistbands and other textile fabrics. I'timád took his leave of Mubárak Sháh and came back to Sultán Ahmed and resumed his former position. The army returned to Ahmedábád, and for some time affairs went on smoothly.

After some time the Sultán found that his object of taking part in the administration of the country was no more gained by his joining Imád-ul-Mulk than it was by his union with I'timád. So he again placed himself in the hands of I'timád Khán. He took counsel of Sheikh Yúsuf Habashi who had the title of Aâzam Humáyún and Sheikh Salím Bukhári, who were his trusted advisers. They said he ought to get out and go to his Holiness Sayad Mubárak and that it would then become incumbent on the Sayad to advocate his cause. Sulàtn Ahmed left Ahmedábád and went to the Sayad. The Sayad told Sheikh Salim that it was not proper to have brought the Sultán in that manner to him. "If this," said the Sayad, "was your intention you ought to have given me notice of it some time ago. I could then have made my arrangements." They replied that the Sultán was afraid of his life and had come to him to take refuge with him : that he had no time to do as the Sayad suggested he ought to have done.

The Sayad said it was a senseless and childish act and feared it would bring him into trouble. " Who," added the Sayad, "knows what results are fated to follow this act and whom Heaven will befriend. What, however, is to happen shall happen; now that our king has come to us he is right welcome."

About this time Háji Khán Afghán, one of the famous nobles of Islám Sháh, king of Dehli, flying before the conquests of Humáyún, with five thousand horse and 150 picked elephants and with equipments and provisions to match, came to Gujarát. The Rána Rája of Chittaur came and blocked his way with forty thousand horse and asked him to give up forty maunds of gold, his big famous war elephant Bhata the best of his elephants, and his concubine Rang Rái, the prettiest dancing girl in his harem. As he carried all his property and possessions with him, Háji Khán agreed to give up the elephant and the gold, but he flamed up at the demand of the concubine and determined to die rather than surrender her. He fought heroically and God made him victorious over the strong odds of the Rána and he reached Gujarát in success and triumph. When he reached Pattan I'timád Khán and Imád-ul-Mulk thought that it was in anticipation of Háji Khán's arrival that the Sayad had sent for and secured the person of Sultán Ahmed. They therefore agreed to unite and destroy the Sayad before he could effect a junction with the army of Háji Khán. Marching out in the night they encamped at a little distance from Sayadpúr. Now when the districts of Gujarát were divided amongst the nobles and when Chámpáner and Pattan fell to the lot of the Sayad, my father had advised him to elect one of these two strong positions for his residence, as he foresaw that the rulers of Ahmedábád would often be unfavourable and hostile to the Sayad and if they wished to injure him he could well oppose them from a fortified place. Sayadpúr, on the other hand, was but eighteen miles from Ahmedábád, and in case of hostilities the rulers of Ahmedábád could in one night march out and attack the Sayad, while yet some of the Sayad's army leaders were at Pattan and some at Chámpáner and would take time to unite. The Sayad said to my father : "We harbour not evil against others; how can others think of wronging us." My father said that in this world of evil the unforeseen was always sure to happen. The fact was that the climate of the place (Sayadpúr) so pleased the Sayad that he did not move from the place and as has been mentioned above, gave Pattan to Sher Khán and Músa Khán Fouládi and Chámpáner to Álam Khán Lodi. In short, when

I'timád Khán and Imád-ul-Mulk, at the head of some thirty thousand horse, with a strong park of artillery, came and encamped near Mehmúdábád the Sayad sent them a message, stating that it was not at his invitation that the Sultán was with him and that they might themselves come and ascertain and dispel the cause of the anxiety that weighed on the Sultán's mind and take him away with them. That he, the Sayad, had nothing to do with the Sultan's move. They replied, however, that if it was not at the Sayad's wish the Sultán had joined him, that then the Sayad might send him back. That the matter was one between them and the king and that the Sayad was quite an outsider who had nothing whatever to do with the matter. The Sayad said that he neither aimed at the post of minister nor aspired to the regency and did not wish to quarrel with them, but that the King to whom he as well as they owed equal allegience, had come to him a suppliant fugitive fleeing for life and that he could not well send him back to them *nolens volens*. He again requested them to come over to the King and allay his fears and take him with them. But they were afraid lest Háji Khán and Sher Khán Fauládi, who were coming together should on reaching the Sayad take his part. With these considerations they began to fire the guns they had already pointed towards the Sayad's village and the Sayad had to take the field. It so happened that the path up the opposite bank of the river across which the Gujarát army had encamped was very steep. The Sayad allowed his horse to ascend it, which he did with difficulty. Sayad Hámid, the grandson of the Sayad, followed on horse back. He was a young man, only twelve years of age, was heavily armed, and his horse was also covered with a heavy coat of mail. It was with difficulty he climbed the steep bank, but when near the top the foot of his horse slipped and fell and the young Sayad, detached from his seat, fell some distance from his horse. His men alighted to render him aid, but this accident created a crowd which blocked up the narrow path-way up the steep and no one could follow the Sayad who thought his men were following close behind him. The Sayad advanced some distance, reaching the place where the advanced guard of I'timád Khán was standing. Coming face to face with them, they recognized him, surrounded him and slew him. Sayad Hámid in the meanwhile having remounted and ascended the steep, did not see his grandfather, though he and his men searched awhile after him. He became alarmed, his army

being placed in the predicament of a body without a head or a
sleeve without an arm. His men dispersed. Sayad Mírán, who
commanded the van, having charged and routed the forces opposed
to him, passed through the city and again returned to the field to find
that his army was defeated. He therefore left the field for his house
and accidentally arrived at the spot where the body of his father
lay in the dust and saw Sídi Saíd, an Abyssinián slave of Sayad
Mubárak's, seated near the body holding the head on his lap. They
took up the body, wrapped it in a scarlet sheet and buried it on the
spot. [1] Sayad Mubárak's grave stands there to the present day.
Sayad Mírán took his followers with him and went in the direction
of Kapadwanj.

Sultán Ahmed, leaving Sayadpúr, went to Ahmedabad, but Aâzam
Humáyún, who commanded the advanced guard of the Sultán, engaged
with the enemy and fighting gallantly fell on the field of battle.
Sayadpur was given up to pillage, but acting on the custom of the
people of Gujarát the soldiery did not annoy the families of chiefs and
nobles and refrained from plundering their houses. The victorious as
well as the defeated armies, both entered Ahmedábád and after a few
days people interceded and peace was declared. But after a little
while the same strife arose and war and conflict began to rage.

After the death of my Lord the Sayad three of his miracles became generally known. One was this:—Whenever the Sayad used
to suffer from bodily pain or ailment such as fever or diarrhœa and
his friends showed their grief by crying or wailing for fear of losing
him he would forbid them, saying that he had always been assured by
vision from his ancestors that he would die a martyr. Now as the
Muhammadan nobles of Gujarát almost always fought for wordly
ends and aggrandizement and selfish objects, these words of the Sayad
used to be received rather incredulously by those present and seemed
rather impossible. But the sequel proved the truth of his prophesy.
God Almighty, to combine in him the rank of martyr with that of
a Sayad, brought Sultán Ahmed, who was the Ruler of the period to
the Sayad seeking redress from the hands of his oppressors and his
oppressors followed him. Up to the time of battle the Sayad
kept on sending messages of peace, but from their arrogance

[1] According to the Musalmán law, the body of a martyr must be buried either as
described above or in the bloody garments in which he has expired.

86

and their consciousness of superior strength and armament the oppressors refused to listen to his righteous appeals and hastened to battle and made the Sayad a martyr. Another marvellous miracle of the Sayad was his foreknowledge of his end. When he mounted his horse for the battle, he took off his turban and wound it round the head of his grandson, Sayad Hámid, saying: " To-day is the day of my martyrdom; henceforth be this turban yours." The third wonder was that in this battle, he, by accident, fell and was buried at a spot where during life he had often expressed a desire to be buried. More miracles and marvels are ascribed to him, than this brief history has the space to contain. Be it not concealed that Sayad Mubárak obtained the wreath of saintliness and its bounties from the pilgrim of the two sacred temples (Makkah and Madínah) Sayad Abdul Wahháb. When Sayad Mubárak was living with the Háji it once so happened that a large party came to see him and there was not sufficient food to satisfy them all. The Sayad sent for many kinds of food from the market and his own house and gave it over to the men of the Háji's kitchen. The Háji, according to his wont, ordered up all that was in the house to the table and the quantity of food that was served was sufficient for all. The Háji, after the departure of the guests asked his officer of the kitchen how he had been able to cater for such a large number of guests so quickly. He said: " As many guests had come, Sayad Mubárak sent for much of the food and entrusted it to me and I added it to the usual quantity." The Háji was very pleased at this and said to Sayad Mubárak : "The gates of Heavenly mercy are at present open to my prayers, ask what thou wilt." The Sayad said: "I am unable to retire from the world to attain to salvation from the seclusion of the cloister. It is my desire to be able to get union with the Lord from the back of my charger, that is, in the midst of active life." The Háji said: "Sayad thou hast asked for both, *i. e.*, greatness in this world and salvation in the next, and thou hast gained them!"

> " The monkish cowl why needst thou wear.
> To show thy saintliness?
> In thy heart monkish virtues bear
> And don the soldiers' dress." [1]

---

[1] These are the famous lines by Saádi *Hájat ba kuláh i baraki dáshtanat nist, Darwísh sifat básh o kuláh i tatarí dár.* � The literal rendering of the lines is :—

" Thou hast no need to wear the monk's worsted cowl,
Have the virtues of a darwísh and put on a Tartar's (*i. e.*, a military) cap."
Their meaning is most happily expressed by the Latin saying :—
Cucullus non facit monachum.

By the blessing of the word of that pure hearted preceptor God advanced the Sayad's prosperity in both worlds. The Sayad became a devout worshipper and so scrupulously regular a prayer-sayer that he used to perform his ablutions and prayers though, being subject to diarrhœa, he used of cold nights sometimes to be moved twenty times before retiring to bed. Though a great noble and a powerful chief and the Lord of many servants, horses, elephants and great wealth, the Sayad was so free of his substance that at the beginning of every new year when he expected his revenues, he had never a pice in his treasury. This was because he paid up those who had claims upon him at once without caring for the balance in his treasury. I have heard my father say that one night the Sayad was much disturbed. He turned in his bed from side to side courting slumber yet contrary to his usual habit, he could not sleep. He asked those in the room what they thought was the reason of his wakefulness. Each assigned a cause, but the Sayad was not satisfied. He sent for his treasurer, Mahmúd, and asked him if he had any ready money in the treasury. He replied that so many thousand *tánkahs* had that night arrived from such and such a village, of which he (the treasurer) did not apprize him as it was too late. The Sayad said that was the reason of his sleeplessness. He desired the treasurer to bring the money and divide it that instant among those to whom it was due, that is, his pensioners and poor retainers and forthwith fell asleep. After his martyrdom the Sayad one night appeared in a vision to my father and said, "Miyán Manjhú! Do you know? God Almighty has for four reasons accorded me a lofty station among the saints: first, on account of my being a Sayad ; second, on account of my martyrdom ; third, on account of my constantly keeping my body in a state of ceremonial purity, and last, because of my being ever ready to sacrifice everything in the way of God. Now in this after-life, whenever the martyrs are deputed to help in the conquests of Islám, I am also sent. But for the wars in the country of Gujarát I only am appointed and I remain and help on the side for which Allah has ordained victory."

After the martyrdom of my Lord the Sayad, I'timád Khán and Imád-ul-Mulk and the whole of the Ahmedábád army went to that city and Músa Khán Fauládi went to Pattan. After a few days Imád-ul-Mulk sent for Sayad Mírán and brought on the tapis the matter of the bestowal of a fief on him. While he kept procrastinating for

two months, his ministerial officers took possession of Pattan and its
districts which the late Sayad had allotted to Músá Khán and Sher
Khán Fauládi, and the other provinces of the Sayad's fief were taken
charge of by the men of Imád-ul-Mulk and I'timád Khán. The agents
of my Lord Sayad Mírán all the while kept waiting on Imád-ul-Mulk.
One day my Lord Sayad Mírán said to my father that his agents were
constantly waiting on Imád-ul-Mulk who kept them fascinated with
promises. He asked my father to go to Imád-ul-Mulk and find out his
real intentions as regards his affairs. My father went and met with
such exaggerated courtesy and politeness at Imád-ul-Mulk's hands that
he smelt from it the sense of the old Arabic proverb : " Too much
politeness denotes ill will." ³   At the time of his taking leave, Imád-
ul-Mulk said to my father : " Be assured about your estates. I am
going to consult I'timád Khán about the matter to-day to bring about
its settlement."   At the time of taking leave, my father went and sat
near Behrám Khán, the Abysinian, an agent of Imád-ul-Mulk, who
had great friendship for my Lord the Sayad and who, sitting behind
Imád-ul-mulk, beckoned to my father to go to him. My father went in
such a manner as to avoid the notice of Imád-ul-mulk who, having
dismissed my father, had turned, and occupied himself with others
present in the assembly. Thinking my father out of hearing, Imád-ul-
mulk said *sotto voce* in an ironical tone :— "The Mírán wants me to give
him estates.   He does not know that I have not sent for him here to
make a master of him but to reduce him to beggary !" My father heard
every word of this speech which fell from Imád-ul-mulk's lips, and
returning to Sayad Mírán related every thing to him from beginning
to end. Despair took possession of the Mírán's heart, and his army also
became weak. He asked my father what he thought should be done.
My father was a great friend of I'timád Khán. He said that they had
hitherto paid so much attention to Imád-ul-mulk that they had wholly
neglected I'timád. My father suggested that he should be permitted to
interview I'timád Khán and see what he said in the matter. My father
went to I'timád Khán and informed him of the facts. I'timád Khán was
a sincere friend of the Sayad's also, but when Sultán Ahmed fled to the
Sayad he feared lest through his aid, the Sultán should become power-

---

³ The words of the proverb are كَثْرَةُ التَّوَاضُعِ مِنَ النِّفَاقِ *Kathrat-ut-tawásu-*
minán nifák.

ful and ruin him, Imád-ul-mulk being also oppressed by the same fear joined I'timád Khán and marched against the Sayad and the Sayad was killed. This turn of events now became a source of anxiety to I'timád. Whenever during the Sayad's life I'timád had a difference or quarrel with Násir-ul-mulk or Imád-ul-mulk, he used, with the Sayad's help, to make up with them, and no one could injure him. Now with an eye to the same benefits from my Lord the Mirán, he said that the intentions of Imád-ul-mulk were not unknown to himself but that if Abdul Karím Khán (I'timád Khán's name was Abdul Karím) lived a week more he would arrange the Mirán's affairs within that time. I'timád Khán, whenever speaking of himself, used to style himself by his original name of Abdul Karím. My father returned to the Mirán and communicated to him the reply and he began to make preparations. According to his promise I'timád Khán appointed five districts as the portion of my Lord the Mirán. They were (1) Dholka, (2) Kapadwanj, (3) Bahyal, (4) Sarnál or Thasra, (5) Bálásinor. This displeased Imád-ul-mulk and he said to Ikhtiyár-ul-mulk, "We give you Kapadwanj, Sarnál (Thasra) and Bálásinor," and gave Bahyal to Jhújhár Khán the Abyssinian. These two nobles hastening to the places before the men of Sayad Mirán, took possession and the district of Dholka only remained for the Mirán. In the meantime the seed of discord took root between Imád-ul-Mulk and I'timád Khán in another way. Sultán Ahmed entered into some secret conspiracy with Imád-ul-Mulk who sent for his son Changíz Khán from Broach with an army. I'timád Khán sent for Tátár Khán from Júnágadh. Changíz Khán coming from Broach encamped at Mehmúdábád, and Tátár Khán came as far as Sánand, ten miles from Ahmedábád. Imád-ul-Mulk asked I'timád Khán, as his nephew (meaning Imád-ul-Mulk's son Changíz) had come as far as Mehmúdábád, if he would honour him by going with him to meet him? I'timád said, Imád-ul-mulk might go and he would follow. So Imád-ul-mulk went. I'timád sent Malik-ush-Sharq to bring Tátár Khán to the city before the return of Imád-ul-mulk with Changíz Khán. Malik-ush-Sharq drove fast in a horse carriage, reached Sánand and brought Tátár Khán to the city before Changíz Khán. Shortly after this Imád-ul-mulk brought Changíz Khán also to the City and the seed of discord that had taken root now developed branches and leaves. By degrees matters went so far that Imád-ul-mulk mounting cannon up the royal palace of the Bhadra, pointed them at the mansion of I'timád Khán. Thus threatened

I'timád Khán leaving his house and the City went to Sarkhej and
thence went and encamped at the village of Suljápur in the Kadi
division, about fifteen miles from Ahmedábád. He there invited Músa
Khán and Sher Khán. and Háji Khán from Pattan and Fateh Khán
Balúch from Rádhanpúr, and having assembled his forces from the
districts, he came and encamped near Bári Narsanjpúr. He now sent a
message to Imád-ul-mulk, directing him to proceed at once to his
estates, and warning him that in case actual hostilities broke out he would
not even get that. Imád-ul-Mulk, seeing that opposition was useless,
went to Broach. Sultán Ahmed remained in the city and I'timád Khán
entering the city, placed his own guards over the Sultán and, fearless of
others, took his seat on the royal cushion. All the nobles except Imád-
ul-mulk submitted to him. He gave half of the district of Kadi to Háji
Khán, and attached him to his side. He gave Músa Khán leave to go
to Pattan and sent Fateh Khán Balúch to Rádhanpúr. Imád-ul-mulk
lived for some months at Broach, where he heard that Khudáwand Khán
the brother of his wife being struck with an aberration of the brain
had become excessively oppressive at Surat, where he was Governor.
The people of Surat complained to Imád-ul mulk against his tyranny
and asked him to redress their wrongs. Imád-ul-mulk led an army
against him and besieged him and fighting continued for some months.
At last when Khudáwand Khán saw that none of the Ahmedábád nobles
gave him any assistance, he opened proposals of friendship and negotia-
tions of peace with Imád-ul-mulk, agreeing to give up the fort of Surat
to him and invited Imád-ul-Mulk as a guest. Imád-ul-mulk, on
the strength of his relationship with Khudáwand went into the
castle and became his guest. Getting him thus within his power,
Khudáwand slew Imád-ul-mulk by treachery on the 27th of the holy
month of Ramazán A. H. 966 (A. D. 1559) and his army retired to
Broach. After three or four months Changíz Khán, the son of Imád-
ul-mulk, collecting an army went to Surat and beseiged Khudáwand
Khán. As he could not produce any effect by the investment, Changíz
Khán had to call in the Portuguese by ceding to them the Gujarát
dependencies of Dún (Damaun) and Sanján (St. John) as a price for
their help. The Portuguese brought a large navy and blockaded the
way of the sea by which provisions reached the fort. Khudáwand sore
pressed came out and met Changíz Khán, who slew him in
retaliation of his father's death at his hands and took possession of
the fort of Surat.

About this time Alif Khán, the Abyssinian, died. The Abyssinians, whose chief was Jhujhár Khán, gave Alif Khán's son the name and titles of his father and settled him in that position. This displeased Changíz Khán as he was not consulted in the matter. Changíz Khán marched against Jhújhár Khán and Alif Khán at the head of an army. The Abyssinians fought and were defeated and a famous elephant of the Habashi of the name of Udai-Mangal fell into Changíz Khán's hands with his standards and kettle drums and the town and territories of Baroda. In the elation of victory Changíz named two of his dogs Jhujhár Khán and Alif Khán and tied the silken cords and tassels of their standards round the dogs' necks.[1] The Habashis repaired to I'timád Khán and he provided them with estates out of his own. After some time I'timád Khán led an army against Changíz Khán who retired into and submitted to a seige in Broach. At last Tátár Khán Ghori became a mediator and begged that Baroda should be restored by Changíz Khán to I'timád Kbán, and that after peace was concluded Changíz should return. Although Tátár Khán pressed him much I'timád Khán would not consent to these terms. Tátár Khán mortified at this, wrote to Sher Khán and Músa Khán (Fauládi) secretly stating that if I'timád Khán was successful in wresting Broach from Changíz Khán, he would not suffer them to remain in Gujarát and suggesting that they should try and beat Fateh Khán Balúch, on whom I'timád trusted for the safety of Ahmedábád and on the strength of whose arms he was brow-beating Changíz. After crushing Changíz, Tátár Khán said, I'timád would address himself to bring about their destruction.

COUPLET.

To check the evil ere it harms is best,
Regret is vain when it is passed arrest.

When Músa Khán and Sher Khán received this advice from Tátár Khán and other nobles, they marched against Fateh Khán Balúch. A battle was fought near Rádhanpúr, in which Fateh Khán being defeated, took refuge in a place named Dhúlkote[2] near

---

[1] The standard is an object of great veneration approaching almost to worship to the Indian Soldier. He swears by his *Nishan* (standard) and on holy days and Thursdays burns frankincense below it.

[2] Nothing beyond a mound now (1897) exists of this fort. It is now known by the name of *Fateh-kot*, probably after Fateh Khán Balúch. Traditions still linger in Rádhanpúr that the fort or mound is a relic of the ancient site of Rádhanpúr, which is said to derive its name from the temple of a Hindu deity called Radan-Deva, once the resort of an annual pilgrimage.

Rádhanpúr.   On hearing this news, I'timád Khán leaving Broach
to take care of itself came to Ahmedábád, and began to think
seriously as to how to dispose of Sultán Ahmed, who had begun
to incline towards foreigners, many of whom had assembled in
Gujarát. He apprehended great trouble if the Sultán went forth and
joined them. The truth was, that Sultán Ahmed, who was a man
of mean capacity, could now no longer conceal his designs. He
used, when in drink, to draw his sword and strike at the stocks of
plantain trees saying : " With this blow I sever the head of I'timád
Khán; thus I would slay Imád-ul-mulk." In the same absurd way
he used to say he would slay Wajíh-ul-mulk or Razí-ul-mulk, who
were councillors of I'timád Khán and thus the Sultán used to keep up the
impotent farce repeating the names of all his nobles. Wajíh-ul-mulk
and Razí-ul-mulk on coming to know of this, determined to dispose
of Sultán Ahmed before he could slay them. They say that at this
time Sultán Ahmed had got to be so independent that he used to go
out to hunt whenever he pleased, three or four miles out of the city
and used to present himself at any hour at I'timád Khán's house.
Trembling and quaking I'timád used to go out to receive him and used
to treat him with great mildness and though Wajíh-ul-mulk and Razí-
ul-mulk used often to press I'timád Khán to kill the Sultán, he used to
put them off. One day they secretly sent a message to Sultán Ahmed
to say that if he would promise them the ministry they would adopt
measures to slay I'timád Khán. The Sultán foolishly gave ear to and
entertained their proposals and promised them the post. This they
communicated to I'timád Khán, who however still said that unless he
heard it with his own ears he would not believe it. They asked him
to their house, where they said they would invite the Sultán so that
he might hear with his own ears what passed between him and themselves. I'timád Khán agreed to this and they sent a message to the
Sultán saying that if they went to him there would be about him many
spies of I'timád Khán, who would be sure to communicate all to him.
So if the king came alone to the house of Wajíh-ul-mulk which adjoined
his palace, they would make agreements and ratify them by oaths
and begin to act in the matter. They sent for I'timád Khán first, and
put him into an adjoining chamber and closed the door on him and placed
by the door a throne for the Sultán to sit on. They then called the
Sultán, who came alone and sat on the throne. The conspirators now
introduced the subject of the plot. The Sultán in the simplicity

of his heart began artlessly to discuss the point so that I'timád Khán heard it with his own ears. He immediately opened the door and discovering himself said :—What evil have I done you that you seek my life ? On seeing I'timád Khán the Sultán's soul flew from his body with fear.

I'timád Khán made a signal to his slaves to knock him down and despatch him and they did so. He then ordered the body to be taken and thrown on the sands between the palace and the river Sábarmatí and to be left there. This happened on Monday night on the 5th of the month of Shaábán A. H. 968 (A. D. 1560) and from the numerical value of the words مَقْتُول شُد بیگناه *Maktúl-Shud-bígunáh,* "he was killed innocent," can be drawn the date of the above event.

In the morning they gave out that the Sultán had fled. After a search, they said that the Sultán was killed by dacoits who had thrown his body on the Sábarmatí sands. After a while, they took up the body and buried it in the shrine of Sultán Ahmed, the builder of the city of Ahmedábad.

> " The crown's a bauble so pleasant to wear,
> But at the cost of life 'tis dear." [1]

ACCOUNT OF I'TIMÁD KHÁN RAISING SULTÁN MUZAF-FAR TO THE THRONE AFTER THE ASSASSINATION OF SULTÁN AHMED II., AND I'TIMÁD KHÁN'S EXPEDITION AGAINST MÚSA KHÁN AND SHER KHÁN FAULÁDI AND THE DISSENSIONS BETWEEN THE GUJARÁT AND THE FOREIGN NOBLES.

It is related that in the month of Shaábán A. H. 968 (A. D. 1560) after the assassination of Sultán Ahmed II. I'timád Khán seated Sultán Muzffar on the throne, and after some months in order to avenge the wrongs of Fateh Khán Balúch, he set out with an army against. Músá Khán and Sher Khán. But after his foul atrocity all the nobles had become disgusted with I'timád Khán and said among themselves that one who had killed Sultán Ahmed in this way would not scruple at murdering another. They apprehended he would next think of killing them after destroying Músa Khán and Sher Khán. They, therefore, resolved to see that no harm came to Músa Khán and Sher Khán and believed that therein lay the popular welfare. All the nobles

---

[1] Lines quoted from a Ghazal of Háfiz.

except Alif Khán and Jhujhár Khán Habashi, who were partisans of I'timád Khan, joined them in this plot. On arriving near Pattan, Músa Khán and Sher Khán intrenched themselves within the city for a seige. I'timád Khán laid siege and ordered that the city wall and the fort should be battered down by cannon. His holiness Sayad Mírán, Háji Khán, and Ikhtiyár-ul-mulk proposed peace and though they tried hard to persuade him to this end I'timád Khán would not listen. So they informed the Fauládis that their best and only course was now to fight it out with I'timád Khán and that they might be sure they (the nobles) would not take I'timád's part in the battle, but would, on the contrary in the midst of the engagement, turn their bridles and retire from the field. The forces of Músa Khán and Sher Khán did not number more than one thousand five hundred horse while those of I'timád Khán exceeded them by over twenty thousand. All of I'timad's men were, however, discontented and down-hearted and that was why I'timád Khán's business fell through. When Músa Khán and Sher Khán went forth to battle they were opposed by the van of I'timád Khán's army which consisted of the Abyssinians who fought gallantly but were defeated. Seeing the Habashi route the whole army was so panic-struck that in whatever part of the field they were located, I'timád's men turned and fled. They say Háji Khán with great fool-hardiness stood his ground, saying he had never in his life turned back to foeman and would not do so now. Muzaffar Khán Shirwáni who was his chief officer, came up to him and catching hold of his bridle turned him back saying : " Do you wish to give the ruffians of Gujarát an opportunity to handle the corner-ends of the scarves of your Afghán ladies?" (Meaning, did Háji Khán not see that if he was killed he would place his poor Afghán ladies at the mercy of the lust and rapacity of the Gujarát soldiery?) Then it was that Háji Khán helplessly turned and departed. They say that the Rána Rájá of Chittaur used always to pray that Háji Khán should be defeated by no one, since the Rána (as has been mentioned above)[1] was defeated by the Khán. When the Rána heard of the defeat of the Khán, he would not touch food for two days until he was assured that the Khán's turning away was an act of discretion and that he had retired without fighting. Then only did the Rána return to his usual habits.

To resume :—When I'timád Khán saw that this retirement, from the battle-field of every nobleman, was not devoid of pre-arranged

[1] See page 279 ante.

treachery, he also turned back and came to Ahmedábád and the baggage of an army twenty thousand strong, fell into the hands of fifteen hundred horse who thus gained as much strength as I'timád Khán became proportionately weak. This occurred in the month of Zalikaád A. H. 968 (A. D. 1561.) I'timád Khán now resumed the estates of Háji Khán, who being offended went over to Sher Khán and Músa Khán. The Fauládis observed : " We were two brothers hitherto, now we are three." They divided the country from two to three shares and gave a share to Háji Khán and from the advent of Háji Khán they gained great strength. I'timád Khán again sent for Tátár Khán from Júnágadh. He promoted a clerk of the name of Habíb and styled him I'tibár-ul-Mulk and gave him one thousand horse. This Habíb was a strong-minded man. He entertained two thousand horse, employing good and gallant men and became the chief of I'timád Khán's army. I'timád again collected men with a view to be revenged on Músa Khán and Sher Khán Fauládi, but none of the nobles would join him, even Tatár Khán, whom he had raised from the dust was unwilling to act against the combined nobles and tried to dissuade him from his purpose. This was the cause of ill-will springing up between I'timád and Tátár Khán, who on the pretence of bringing his army from Sorath, asked leave to go. This further displeased I'timád Khan. I'tibár-ul-Mulk entreating I'timád Khán to give Tatár Khán leave to go to Sorath was also considered by I'timád as one of his evil-wishers and summoning him up to his balcony one day I'timád Khán killed him. He attacked the house of Tátár Khán and gave it up together with the house of Áráish Khán, the grand-son of I'tibar-ul-Mulk, to plunder. Tátár Khán getting news of these proceedings had just time to mount a horse, bare-backed and escape to Sarkhej. Áráish Khán flying from his house escaped to Dholka with the Habashis in hot pursuit. When Tatár Khán reached Sánand he also saw that the Habashis were at his heels. Sayad Kabir, who was Tatár Khán's agent following him with thirty-four horsemen arrived at Sánand. He gave out that Tátár Khán had entered the fort and giving Tátár Khán four horsemen told him to fly anywhere to a place of safety as the Habashís would seek him out in the fort. It happened just as Sayad Kabir had foreseen. When the Habashis came they enquired after Tártár Khán's whereabouts, and on being told he was in the fort, they surrounded it and sent word to I'timád Khán that they had secured Tátár Khán and would presently capture and bring him. Surrounding the fort they commenced fighting. Sayad Kabír fought with them till the time of the vespers prayers. When, however, he saw that a great army had arrived and that by that time Tátár Khán must have been able to seek a safe refuge somewhere, he sent a message to the besieging Habashís, saying that if their quarrel was with Tátár Khán, he was not there. That he against whom they were fighting was Sayad Kabír, and that if they wished he would come out and see them. They said, "Come." The Sayad then issued out and the Habashís, taking him with them, went to I'timád Khán and explained what had happened. I'timád Khán approved of Sayad Kabír's conduct. "It is thus a servant should serve his master" said he and giving him a dress of honour dismissed him.

To resume. While these events were taking place, my lord Sayad Mírán left Ahmedábád and went to Dholka, and from Dholka he proceeded to Dhandúka. Tátár Khán had taken up residence at Ránpúr near Dhondúka where the Sayad went and joined him and they went to Músa Khán. I'timád Khán now again led an army against Músa Khán. Músa Khán, coming out of Pattan, gave battle to I'timád Khán in the vicinity of the village of Jhotána, about twenty-seven miles from Pattan. I'timád Khán was again defeated and returned to Ahmedábád. This took place on the 21st of Zil Hajjah in the year of the Hijrah 969 (A.D. 1562). Músa Khán came and encamped at Jhotána, a village of the division of Kadi, which belonged to the Khán. Sayad Mírán intervened and took half of the division of Kadi which belonged to Háji Khán from I'timád Khán and restored it to Háji Khán and made Músa Khán to retire from Jhotána. Tátár Khán went to Sorath, and I'timád Khán having given assurances of friendship to Sayad Mírán, sent for him, and the Sayad went to Dholka.

After a short time I'timád Khán sent for Changíz Khán and having gained him over again marched with him against Músa Khán and Sher Khán. In this expedition a quarrel occurred between Changíz Khán and Alif Khán Habashi, which almost reached the limits of bloodshed. Changíz observed that if the officers of I'timád's army gave him this treatment while yet Músa Khán and Sher Khán were in power, what was he to expect from them after the destruction of Músa Khán and Sher Kháu? He made secret overtures to Músa Khán and Sher Khán. At this time, however, Músa Khán fell ill and died on the day I'timád Khán reached Dhanoja, a village fifteen miles from Pattan.

Changíz Khán said it was not generous to attack an enemy labouring under such a grievous bereavement and calamity. As it was on the strength of Changíz's arm that I'timád Khán had set out on this expedition, and as he saw through the existence of some secret compact between Changíz Khán and Sher Khán, I'timád Khán now saw no other course but that of returning to Ahmedábád. Changíz Khán returned to his own country and my lord Sayad Mírán to his estates.

Some time after this Mirza Ibráhím Húsein and Mírza Muhammad Husein and Sháh Mírza, the grandsons of Sultán Husein Bàbakara of Khurásán, who were vassals of the great Pádsháh Jaláluddin Muhammad Akbar and who had revolted, came to Changíz Khán. Mírza Ashrafuddín Husein, one of the grandsons of Khwájah Ahrár, who had some time since severed his connection with Akbar had also come to Músa Khán and Sher Khán. As the army of the Fauládis consisted for the most part of Afghán levies and as the Mírzás did not like their rough Afghán ways he left the Fauládi court and after passing some time in the companionship of my lord the Sayad Mírán he also went to Changíz Khán in consequence of an invitation from him. With men of this stamp assembled round him, Changíz Khán entered into a compact with Sher Khán to dispose of I'timád Khán and divide the country between themselves, the territories north of the Sábhar being allotted to Sher Khán and those south of the river to Changíz Khán. Sher Khán advanced towards Ahmedábád from Pattan and Changíz Khán from Broach. My lord Sayad Mírán himself went to Sher Khán sending his son Sayad Hámid to Changíz Khán to dissuade both from taking this step. Sher Khán, acting on the counsel of the Sayad, stopped at Kadi thirty miles from Ahmedábád, but Changíz Khán, regardless of all advice advanced. I'timád Khán coming from the other side with the Sayads Mírán and Hámid as far as the river Khári, about eight miles from Ahmedábád, a battle took place. As the ground on the banks of this river is covered with a thick growth of prickly-pear and cactus-bushes the victory or defeat of the portions of the army engaged could not be seen from the position taken up by the main forces. The forces of Changíz Khán that opposed those of I'timád Khán defeated them, but on being attacked by those of Sayad Hámid were defeated and fled together with their leader Changíz Khán to Mehmúdábád, ten miles from the field of battle. On the other side I'timád Khán being defeated by Changíz Khán fled with his army to Ahmedábád. No one remained on the field of battle except Sayad Mírán and Sayad Hámid and Juneid

Gurzani (Kázráni?), the nephew of the Afghán Suleimán Khán, the
ruler of Bengal and behind them in one corner of the field remained
Iktitiyár-ul-Mulk with two thousand horse, without having engaged
with any one at all. While Sayad Hámid having fought and won the
battle with such a small number was surveying the field from an emi-
nence with a few men and his men scattered over the field were
engaged in plundering, a party of five hundred Habashi horse and
an elephant suddenly appeared on the scene, cautiously and slowly approaching the Sayad. The Sayad asked who these men were. Some one
said they were a party of men from Alif Khán Habashi's army, who
were returning after the pursuit of Changíz's fugitive army. As night
had advanced the dispersed forces were from all sides collecting
round this force so that in a short time nearly two thousand horse came
round it. Sayad Hámid thinking that the army that was collecting was
Alif Khán's, said to my father: "Miyán Manjhú! go to Alif Khán,
and after my congratulations to him for the victory ask him to remain
in the field so that the scattered forces may rally." My father ran to
the party and asked whose army that was. When they told him it
was Alif Khán's, he asked the elephant driver to give him way to go
to the Khán and to convey to him the Sayad's congratulations for victory.
The elephant driver made a sign to his animal who threw his trunk at
my father (intending, no doubt, to catch him). My father was thinking
of fighting him when the son of Hamzah the Turk who was the slave
of the late Sayad Mubárak, and who after his martyrdom had entered
the service of Changíz Khán, recognized my father and placing his
hand on the knee of my father,[1] said: "Why are you in this army?
It is the army of Bijli Khán, the Abyssinian, who is an officer of
Changíz Khán and who has ordered his men to give out that this army
belongs to Alif Khán, so that those dispersed should rally round it and
his army gather size. Pray, take yourself away." My father turning
rein left the army and reaching my Lord Sayad Hámid related the
facts to him. Sayad Hámid sent word to Ikhtiyár-ul-Mulk
stating that the forces that were forming opposite were those
of Bijli Khán and that if he joined and advanced they should
if God willed, gain an easy victory. This hypocrite was only
in appearance a friend of I'timád Khán's, being in reality a

_____

[1] The way in which a man belonging to a humbler walk of life embraces his superior
in position. He bends himself down and touches the knee where an equal would
embrace and touch the shoulder.

partisan of Changíz Khán's. He entertained a deadly hatred for the Sayad. He simply replied that the forces were not Bijli Khán's but that Changíz Khán himself was present with them, that his main forces were defeated and that he was not strong enough to again cope with him. Though Sayad Hámid pressed him much he would not agree. When the Sayad's friends saw that there was now no remedy they took his bridle and turned him from the field and went away. The fate of the engagement was now reversed. I'timád Khán taking Sultán Muzaffar fled to Morása which is forty-five miles from Ahmedábád and next morning Changíz Khán entered the city. At this time Sher Khán also coming from Kadi encamped on the other side of the Sábarmati and Changiz Khán went and met him. Finally, as agreed upon between the two the country to the north of the Sábhar was assigned to Sher Khán and the territories to the south to Changíz Khán. Sher Khán, now returned to Kadi but Changíz Khán remained at Ahmedábád.

About this time Báz-Bahádur, the Afghán, who was for sometime king of Málwa and who had been defeated and expelled thence by the forces of the Emperor Akbar came and entered the service of Changíz Khán. Junnáid Gurzáni also entered Changíz Khán's service. Changíz Khán ascended the throne of Sultán Mehmúd and began to enjoy himself and to shower gifts on all around him. Although, son of a slave of Sultán Mehmúd's, this Changíz Khán had a right royal presence and a heart so generous that he used to remind the people of Gujarát of the times of Sultán Bahádur. The day Abdulláh Khán Aurang came to him from Málwa, flying before the armies of Akbar, two of Changíz Khán's ships arrived from Jaddah : he gave them both to Abdullah Khán as a gift of his hospitality. His minister, a Banya of the name of Súja, said to him : " Khánji ! had you glanced over the cargo of these ships before giving them away you could have formed some estimation of my services." He replied : " Granted that both these ships come laden with gold mohars of one coinage, they can not be more richly laden. The moment they come in port your services are acknowledged." He was a comely young man of pleasant conversation and a presence full of dignity. He had made justice and fairness his principles of conduct so that in his time the hand of oppression was inert. One day a Mughal, one of the intimates of Mirza Sharfuddin Husein, carried off the daughter of a poor man, who came and complained to Changíz Khán. The Khán forthwith

sent his Cháushes [1] to capture and bring the offender to him. When
the man was brought Changiz ordered him to be taken and crucified.
Mirza Sharfuddín Husein begged hard for his life but the Khán
said : " Mírza! there are many men like you here and each has
a Mughal following.   To-day it is a soldier of yours has done this and
you expect me to pass over his fault, to-morrow another soldier will do
the like and I shall be expected to pass over his crime also.   Then it
will become hard indeed for God's creatures to live ! Whatever other
desire you have be it on my eyes and head (*i.e.*, I shall happily) place
it within your reach but pardon me if I cannot comply with this
request of yours." He ordered the Mughal to be immediatly taken
and impaled. After this none of the soldiers ever presumed to commit
an act like this. This humble person (the writer) has seen with his
own eyes the army of Changiz Khán encamped near the Kánkaria-tank
in the midst of cultivated fields with a crop of *jawári* (sorghum
vulgare) standing on them.   Many of his horsemen had picketed
their horses just on the borders of these fields with *jawár* trees
standing on them. The army remained encamped there for eleven
days yet nobody had the presumption to break a single *jawár*
stock or leaf and throw it before his horse.   In a short time Changíz
grew so much in power that Sher Khán repented having ruined
I'timád Khán.

When Ahmedábád became assigned to Changíz Khán he went
personally to Dholka and brought my Lords Sayad Mírán and Hámid
with all respect and reverence to Ahmedábád.   All the favoured servants of Sayad Mubárak who at that time happened to be with Sayad
Mírán obtained an audience with the Khán. My father on account of
his friendship or I'timád Khán would not wait upon Changíz Khán
(I'timád's rival).   My father's friendship for I'timád Khán was known
to all the nobles of Gujarát and that was why my father did not go
from Dholka with Sayad Mírán to Ahmedábád. After four days
had thus passed one day Sheikh Yúsuf, the elder brother of this humble
person (the author), who was skilled in poetry went to pay his respects
to Sayad Hámid and was taken by Sayad Hámid with him to
Changíz Khán. The Khán was pleased and made enquiries after my
father. "Where," said he, " is Miyán Manjhu ?" I do not see him."
My brother said he was not very well. The Khán said in a joking

---

[1] A cháush is a petty Arab officer, a centurian.

manner : " Perhaps the water of the Pál has disagreed with him."
He implied by this that my father being a friend of I'timád Khán must
have accompanied him to the Pál mountains. In fact the remark of the
Khán's had a double *meaning*. In the first place I'timád Khán was
known to have gone to the Pál and in the second place the waters of
the Pál were so proverbial in Gujarát for their injuriousness that on
seeing an emaciated yellow visaged person it was common to ask
him if he had been drinking the water of the Pál. My brother
replied that it was exactly on account of the climate that my father
did not go with I'timád Khán and he (my brother) had to go instead.
When he heard Changíz Khán talking in this (kind) way (about my
father) Sayad Mírán said to my father : " Miyán Manjhú the present
circumstances demand that you should go and see Changíz Khán.
So one day my father went with Sayad Mírán. My father was
shown great respect and treated with much consideration, being
given a place by Changíz Khán at his side and questioned with
great warmth. After a while dinner was announced. The dinner
cloth was served with pickles of all kinds. Razí-ul-Mulk who has
been mentioned above was seated near Changíz Khán on the other
side. He whispered gently to the Khán that my father was very
fond of pickles, though in fact my father so hated every thing
sour that he abstained from food cooked in a vessel in which
anything sour was cooked, even after it was well washed and nothing
sour cooked in it with the present meal. Owing, however, to this
hint from Razí-ul-Mulk the Khán used to select tit-bits from his own
plate of pickles and place them before my father saying : " This is
delicious, " and so on : My father out of politeness took the pieces
from the Khán's hand and could not but eat them. When this
happened several times Razí-ul-Mulk said to the Khán : " Khanji !
It is perhaps after three years that Miyán Manjhu has broken
through his rule of abstinence from sour food." The Khán apologized
to my father and turning to Razí-ul-Mulk said : " Malik, if that
was the case, why did you tell me the contrary" ? My father said :
"My dear Khán ! to do so is the Malik's business and calling. But it
matters little ; in this case the acids will do me good on the principle
of the couplet :—

COUPLET.

The deadly stake if fired by friendly hands,
Turns hellish flames to airs from heavenly lands."

38

The Khán was at heart a gentleman. He was very pleased at the recital by my father of this couplet and asked him to repeat it and remained seated with him long and became very friendly with him.

To resume. At this time Mírán Muhammad Sháh Asiri at the instigation of I'timad Khán collected a large army and marched against Ahmedábád. Changíz Khán seeing that he had a powertul enemy to cope with sent Sayad Hámid son of Sayad Mírán to I'timád Khán asking forgiveness and inviting him to come and resume his former place and dignities ; adding that a foreign enemy had come against them whom it was advisable for them to unite and expel. Mírán Muhammad Sháh at the same time sent his vazír Zeinuddín to I'timád Khán stating that it was simply to help him that he had come and requesting him to join him and stating that he had no wish beyond reinstating him and expelling Chang:z Khán. I'timád Khán was much exercised as to which side to join. He marched with haste from Morása, and coming to Maâmúrábád met Zeinuddín. He told Zeinuddín he was going in consequence of his invitation and assured Sayad Hámid that he was coming in obedience to his call. Up to Maûmúr-ábád the road of the emissaries of the adversaries lay together. There he halted. Mírán Muhammed sháh, marching from Baroda crossed the Mahi and advancing by forced marches came and encamped at Jetalpúr, which is nine miles from Ahmedábád. At this time the greater part of Sher Khán's forces under the command of his son Muhammad Khán were in the districts of Kadi and Víramgám. Sher Khán sent a fleet camel-rider to quickly fetch his son and deceitfully sent a message of welcome to Mírán Muhammad Sháh, stating that he and his brother nobles were all longing for his arrival and requesting him to halt for two days at the place ; he then was to permit of his taking a favourable opportunity of joining him. Mírán Muhammad Sháh deceived by these sweet words of Sher Khán halted for two days. The day after Sher Khán's despatching this message Muhammad Khán came with a large army of Afgháns and joined his father. Changíz Khán, issuing from Ahmedábád marched against Mírán Muhammad Sháh and halting about three miles from the hostile camp, sent a party of Mughals under Mírza Ashrafuddín Husein to try the enemy with a discharge of arrows. The Mírza went and engaged them smartly with his sharp shooters. From the morning up to the time of the evening-prayers no one in the army of Muhammad Sháh was able to alight from horse-back. On seeing this, Mírán Muhammad Sháh without informing any one in his army, fled at night with some of his chief companions. In the morning when this news became public a party of the Mughals went in pursuit and the soldiers of Changíz Khán who were stationed in Broach and Baroda took up the pursuit as they heard the news. The elephants, camels, horses and treasure of Muhammad Sháh's camp fell into the hands of the soldiers of Chang´z Khán and of his the Rájputs and Koli allies. Of the chief men of Muhammad Sháh, some were killed and others taken prisoners. This news reaching Ítimád Khán at Maâmurábád, he turned back with Sultán Muzaffar and returned to Morása and being unable to remain even there he crossed the Gujarát Frontier, and went over to Dungar-púr. Changíz Khán, victorious and triumphant, remained at Ahmedábád and Sher Khán at Kadi. Ikhtiyár-ul-Mulk, who was at Maâmúrábád being confirmed in his estates was called by Changíz Khán to his presence. The fiefs of Jhujhár Khán and Alif Khán Habashis who were the followers of Ítimád Khán were restored to them. When the Habashis came to Changíz Khán he went forth to receive them with great honour and re-assured them. Except I'timád Khán all the great nobles of Gujarát came and rendered obedience to Chang´z Khán and proffered their allegiance to him. The position of Changíz Khán became so great that men like Mírza Ibráhim Husein and Mírza Muhammad Husein and Sharfuddín Husein, Báz Bahádur Súr and Junneid Gurzáni, (Kúzráni ?), each one of whom entertained aspirations to royalty, entered his service. The nobles of I'timád Khán's party also came and submitted to him and all the country from the banks of the Sábhar to the confines of the province of Sultánpúr and Nazárbár came within his rule.

Thoughts of ruining Sher Khán now entered Changíz Khán's mind : for how happy are the words of the poet :—

VERSE.

The beast of the field when it knoweth its might,
And gaineth its end is contented and quiet ;
All creatures when free from pressing alarm,
Save man lust no further for evil or harm ;
But man! he desponds when his substance doth wane,
When it waxes he wastes it and grabs at more gain.

When Sher Khán learnt of these thoughts of Changíz Khán he was pained and became anxious. About this time too, Bijli Khán began to show signs of faithlessness.

This Bijli Khán, was an Abyssinian eunuch, who was a slave of Changíz Khán's mother. Changíz Khán's father had educated and brought him up and had raised him to nobility. On the occasion of the victory mentioned above gained by Changíz Khán, he bestowed on Bijli Khán the port of Cambay. But the mother of Changíz Khán coming to him from Broach (to congratulate him) on the same occasion Changíz took the port from Bijli Khán and presented it to his own mother. This sorely offended Bijli Khán. It is well known that every animal when castrated loses its viciousness, except man, who, when deprived of virility, increases in vice and turpitude and especially on being emasculated young the innate evil of his nature increases a hundred-fold. Bijli Khán taunted Jhujhár Khán and Alif Khán Habashis with dastardliness, saying that he was surprized to see them so devoid of spirit as to have submitted to Changíz Khán who had given his very curs their names and turned their banners into dog collars. He also insinuated that Changíz was thinking of killing them. It would be well if they anticipated him in the matter, otherwise they had better prepare for departure from this world. On hearing this, Alif Khán and Jhujhár Khán determined to kill Changíz Khán before he could kill them, though the truth was that Changíz Khán, far from entertaining the remotest idea of killing them held them in an exceedingly warm and sincere regard. He had given back to Alif Khán his elephant Udai Mangal, which he had captured in the battle of Baroda, restored to them all their estates and not a day passed without his bestowing on them some valuable present such as a horse, a sword, or a dagger. He addressed them by the endearing title of brothers while on their part they were only biding their time to take his life.

One day, it so happened, that both these nobles, with strong retinues went to Changíz Khán's house and said: " Dear Khán, this is a fine day for (Chaugán) a game of polo." "What is there to prevent us ?" returned Changíz Khán, and ordering his horse he rode out unceremoniously. Very few of the soldiers of his own body-guard were present at this early hour of the day, the whole of his guard having after their night duty dispersed in the morning to their homes, to attend to their private needs or to say their prayers. Changíz

Khán rode forth with a very slight following. He was riding in the middle with Alif Khán on his right and Jhujhár Khán on the left, forty or fifty *Chaúshes* or Arab foot soldiers formed all his retinue and the army of the Habashis followed in the rear in a compact mass. When they had gone a few paces from the mosque of Farhat-ul-Mulk, which is situated between the Three-Gates and the Bhadra, Alif Khán and Jhújhár Khán interchanged signals and Alif Khán said : " Khánji ! this Arab that I am riding is a late importation and has very easy paces, just see ! '' With these words he gave his horse the spur. While Changíz Khán's attention was thus occupied, Jhujhár Khán drew his sword and dealt Changíz Khán a blow which cleft him obliquely from the shoulder to the waist and he dropped from his horse, dead. This happened in the year A.H. 976 (A.D. 1568). The Habashis going to Changíz Khán's residence took possession of all his property, his horses and elephants. The Commanders of Changíz Khán's forces, the Mírzas and all others, wherever they were, mounted and took their way to Baroda. Pure is God ! Glory to God ! the sun of Changíz Khán's state set in a moment and the steed of his rule turned its head towards oblivion !

To resume : After this event Alif Khán and Jhujhár Khán got possession of Ahmedábád. Sher Khán Fauládi, who was at Kadi, came and encamped on the other bank of the Sábarmati and sent a message to Alif Khán and Jhújhár Khán, asking them to give up the city to him and he said he would deliver over their estates to them. They agreed to immediately surrender the citadel and the royal palaces known as the Bhadra to Sher Khán's men, and to give up the city also the next day. But in the meantime some of Sher Khán's Afgháns entered the city and began to lord it over and oppress the inhabitants. The Habashis said they could not agree with such men and they wrote to I'timád Khán to come at once. I'timád Khán marched hastily and came to Ahmedábád with Sultán Muzaffar and closing the gates, opened a cannonade and musketry-fire against Sher Khán. The men of the city who were in the royal citadel of the Bhadra were turned out by dint of this firing. At last my lord Sayad Mírán interfered and brought about a peace on the terms that existed between Sher Khán and Changíz, namely, that the country to the South of the Sábarmati was to belong to I'timád Khán and the territories on the north to Sher Khán. On these terms peace was restored. Sher Khán returned to Kádi, and my lord Sayad Mírán to Dholka.

I'timád Khán and the Habashis remained in the city. Gradually the Habashis became so headstrong that they took possession of the richest suburbs of the capital and quietly annexed those of I'timád's villages that bordered on their possessions. They thought very little of I'timád Khán, saying. "We have restored you to Ahmedábád ; but for us you could not have dreamed of being here." When I'timád Khán saw power thus slipping from his hands he withdrew in disgust to the upper storey of his house and discontinued seeing the nobles and the soldiers. Alif Khán, Jhújhár Khán and Ikhtiyár-ul-Mulk went several times to his doors and demanded an interview, but he sent word that he had retired from the world and taken to a corner of his house, that he had nothing to do with the administration of the country of Gujarát and that they were free to carry it on as best they could. If they were not inclined to allow him even that little corner of his house in peace, he said he was ready to leave it and go the way he had come. When I'timád Khán resolved to take this course and Sher Khán betook himself to Kadi the Mírzás, Ibráhím Husein, Muhammad Husein and Sháh Mirza made themselves masters of all the territories lately owned by Changíz Khán and laid an obstinate siege to the castle of Broach. Rustam Khán Rúmi, a loyal servant of Changíz Khán, entrenched himself in the castle and fought most manfully defending the fort for one year. Rustam Khán Rúmi asked help of I'timád Khán and Sher Khán, but none of his numerous appeals for succour had any effect. When nobody came to his aid he made peace with the Mirzás, surrendered the fort of Broach and submitted to them and the castle of Surat also fell in to the hands of the Mírzás. Ibráhim Husein Mírza took up residence at Broach. Muhammad Husein Mirza at Baroda, and Sháh Mírza at Chámpáner, thus dividing among themselves the whole of the country from the south of the Mahi to the borders of the territories of Sultánpúr and Nazarbár. They quartered an army of only five hundred Mughal horse on this immense fief. The number of the men posted on these extensive lands was so small that the salary of one man used to range from 60,000 to 70,000 or even a hundred thousand Mehmúdi Changízís."[1]

---

[1] The revenues from Surat, Broach, Baroda and other districts South of the Mahi were returned in *Changízís* a coin varying in value from something over $\frac{2}{3}$rds of a rupee to slightly less than $\frac{1}{2}$, the revenues from Rádhanpúr and Morvi were entered in the Gujarát accounts in *Mahmúdis* a coin nearly identical in value with the *Changízís* The customs dues were returned in a gold currency, the *Ibráhímís* of the value of 9. S. (Rs. 4½). and the tribute in *Húns* of about 8.S. (Rs. 4). Under the Gujarát Sultáns the accounts were kept in *Tánkás* or $\frac{1}{100}$th of Rupees while under the Mughals *Dáms* or $\frac{1}{40}$th of rupees were used. See page 219,222. Notes 2, part I, Vol. I, *Bombay Gazetteer.*

They had many fief-holders enjoying as salary revenues as large as those shown above. Nearly four years passed in this manner when the fire of sedition arose from the ambition of Sher Khán. With the hope of taking Ahmedábád Sher Khán in H. 980 (A. D. 1573) advanced against the city, and encamped near the Narsinghpúr postern of the city. It was in this year also that Sayad Mirún left this perishable world for the eternal abode. As long as he lived he used to take the part of the oppressed against the oppressor and tried to restrain the powerful from aggression. If his peaceful endeavours failed he used to fight for the weak against the strong and root out the evil. When he retired behind the curtain of non-existence there was no one to restrain the power of evil-minded persons. Matters went from bad to worse and the flames of dissension broke out and rose so high in Gujarát as to envelope and consume all.

When Sher Khán, with twenty thousand Afghán horse came and beleaguered the city with the object of expelling I'timád Khán, and taking possession of the city himself, Alif Khán Habashi, falling out with Jhujhár Khán over the division of the property of Changíz Khán left the city and joined Sher Khán. Sayad Hámid took the side of Sher Khán. Sultán Muzaffar, seeing that the balance of power inclined in favour of Sher Khán, went over to his side. Sher Khan seating him on the throne, stood by him baton in hand and sending for all the nobles made them do obeisance to the Sultán. The Sultán thought this would last but the Afghán nobles had become so greedy of rank and power that submission to royalty was remote from their thoughts. The new regimè only lasted a day. The next day Sultán Muzaffar was made to take his seat behind the curtain of seclusion like a secluded anchorite.

I'timád Khán on seeing Sultán Muzaffar also go out of the city, sent Wajíh-ul-Mulk to fetch Mírza Muhammad Husein, who was at that time at Baroda, agreeing to pay the Mírza 500 *Ashrafís* (gold coins) for each day's march of his army after leaving Baroda for Ahmedábád, and to hand over to him the reins of the Government of Ahmedábád after the defeat of the Afghán army. He also wrote to Mírza Ibráhím Husein who was at Broach stating that the Afgháns had grown so powerful as to have laid seige to Ahmedábád and that Sultán Muzaffar had also joined them. He pointed out to the Mírza that he (the Mírza) too was a scion of royalty and requested him to come with

an army, beat back the Afgháns and receive from him the charge of
the Government of Gujarát. Up to that time he promised to pay
the Mírza five hundred *ashrafís* a day. He sent with Wajíh-ul-Mulk
certain jewels to the Mírzá as presents. While writing thus to the Mírzás
I'timád Kháu sent a like message to the great monarch Akbar Sháh,
beseeching him to come with all possible despatch to Gujarát and take
over a country which was his own. He added that he was reduced to
such straits by the Afgháns who had besieged Ahmedábád that to spite
them he would otherwise have to deliver over the city to the Mírzás.
Mírzá Muhammad Husein delayed to come, but Mírza Ibráhím Husein
hastened at I'timád Khán's call with three or four thousand brave and
well-equipped horse and alighted at the Khamdarol Palace without the
city walls. The Mírza made it a rule to send every morning a batch
of a hundred cavalry to the field against the Afghán guard with orders
that fifty out of them should go out and take their stand in view of
the Afgháns while the other fifty should from time to time assail the
Afgháns with a cloud of arrows. On the part of the Afgháns a force
of two or three thousand horse used to go out against them. The
Mughal sharpshooters harried the Afgháns with clouds of arrows and
whenever the latter charged them took to their heels. This mode of
warfare was kept up every day from morning to evening prayers. At
night when the guards of either side returned to their quarters thirty
or forty well mounted Mughal horsemen from their out-posts would
attack Sher Khán's camp and cause great havoc and commotion in the
Afghán camp by a discharge of arrows and return to their quarters.
Not a day passed without ten or twenty men being killed in the Afghán camp, the Mughal losses being insignificant even in the wounded.
In the morning again even before sunrise the Mughals were ready as
sure as ever in the field fighting bravely. On the Afghán side, three or
four thousand horsemen sweating under the weight of their armour used
all day to remain ready on horseback, not having the time even for a
drink of water at ease. When some days passed thus, the Afgháns
became quite weary. Mirza Ibráhím Husein now received information
that Kíka, a Banya minister of Sher Khán and who was given by
him the title of Muwáfir-ul-Mulk, was escorting treasure from
Pattan and that he would that day encamp at Hájípúr, fifteen
miles from Ahmedábád. He also heard that the escort were careless,
thinking that the army of Ahmedábád being besieged could
not issue from the city. The Mírza sáid to himself: "This is the

time to strike a powerful blow. Consulting I'timád Khán and taking with him Zain Khán Kokah, the son of Ikhtiyár-ul-Mulk, he issued at midnight from the Ídar gate with three hundred of his Mughals and marching rapidly reached in the morning a place which the enemy had just marched from. Their tents and equipage were just taking their departure and many of the escort were falling in to march forward. When the noise of the arrival of the Mírza reached them they fled, without making a stand. An Afghán officer of the name of Ibráhím Khán, a man of honour, stood his ground with his men and fell fighting on the field. The Mírza took the treasure, the elephants and the baggage, and leaving by a road about three miles higher up, went to Ahmedábád. In the morning, some time after daybreak, news reached Sher Khán of Mírza Ibráhím having gone during the night against Muwáfir-ul-Mulk. Sher Khán himself hastened to help but by the time he reached Kíka's camp, the Mírza had returned safe to his camp, with the booty. As usual, the intrepid Mírza's hundred Mughal horsemen appeared that morning on the field to fight as if nothing uncommon had happened. On seeing this Sher Khán and his army were confounded and dismayed. Though the Mírza showed himself capable of such brilliant prowess and daring enterprise, he was burning to inflict a reverse of some kind on Sayad Hámíd, he having twice been defeated by the Sayad. At this time the Sayad was one of Sher Khán's auxiliaries and was present with his army and his entire property and family were at Dholka, the main road to which though it was about twenty miles to the south of Sher Khán's camp, there was another road to it which was not more than four miles distant from Sher Khán's camp. Every night the Mírza used to try to go by this shorter road to Dholka to put his project into execution. Certain spies however used to bring the information to the Sayad who used to cross the Sábarmati and start to where the two roads met, about seven miles from the camp and seven from Ahmedábád, and to take his stand there with his army drawn up in order. The Mírza on his part, getting information of this, used to retire, and the Sayad, after waiting till the dawn, used to return to Ahmedábád. This happened several times, after which a feeling of indifference and carelessness came over the Sayad and his men. Some used to wear their armour, others to carry it with them on led-horses, some used to follow the Sayad, others to join him after his reaching the tryst. It so happened that one day news was received that the Mírza had started for Dholka. The

39

Sayad mounting with all possible haste soon reached the place mentioned above. That night the Sayad had got on his greaves, but had not on his coat of mail and some of his men were indifferently armed and some followed him a little distance behind. The Sayad sent a message to Alif Khán Habashi and Sádát Khán Bukhári (who were probably his officers at Dholka) informing them of the Mírzas having started for Dholka and also of himself having done the same, requesting them to be prepared. These two officers on getting the message sent their men on and hastened behind them. Arriving midway they sent on Odu, the son of Abul-Fateh and Ahmed, the son of Odu, to press on with the news of their arrival. These men, Odu and Ahmed, were veterans of tried courage and ripe experience. They were given a following of seventy or eighty men and the leaders went on slowly and at ease. Odu and Ahmed proceeding with haste reached their destination. At this time a camel-rider coming up sharp from behind overtook them. They asked him who he was. He said he was the Rabárí [1] of Alif Khán, who had sent him on to go and ascertain how far the Sayad had come and said he was returning with the information to the Khán. At this time there were about two hundred and fifty horsemen with the Sayad, but they were all his relatives and kinsmen, men of courage and intrepidity in whose eyes war was a sport and battle an entertainment. There was also a middle-sized elephant of the name of *Pák,* an animal that had not reached the season of "*masti.*"[2] They kept this animal to the fore with a man holding a torch mounted on him to direct those of their men who happened to be at a distance. It so happened that this torch was observed also by the enemy for some time when their spy reached them and informed them: "Yonder goes the Sayad with a small party!" The Mírza and Rustam Khán Rúmí, whom they styled the second "Rustam" (both on account of his great physical strength and his bravery and Imád-ul-Mulk, son of Ikhtíyár-ul-Mulk, who was a young and intrepid warrior with seven or eight hundred mounted Mughal archers and Turks (Rúmís) with fire-arms and Gujarát swordsmen came up to the Sayad's small army. The Sayad had just left Páli (Páldi?) and

---

[1] The *Rabáris* being a class of Hindu camel-breeders are preferred in Gujarát as camel-trainers and camel-riders.

[2] The word "*masti*" literally means wildness, lustiness, and in the language of elephant-drivers signifies maturity of age when at the natural breeding or rutting season this monstrous animal becomes so wild and reckless as to be unmanageable.

was passing a narrow path in a cactus jungle between that village and Maroli, some six miles from the camp, when the Mughals coming from behind, shot a cloud of arrows, the Turks, a volley of musketry-fire, and the Gujarátis charged on their horses and a cry went forth that the enemy was up on the Sayad's army. It, however, so chanced that to the right of the Sayad there was a little space between him and the cactus bushes and on the other hand there was some level ground. The Sayad retiring there sent for his coat of mail, but as he put his right hand into it, an arrow struck on the coat and sank into his hand like a thorn into a rose and another struck him on the greaves and passing through them pierced his knee. The Sayad drew out the arrows with his own hands telling nobody of his wounds. He put on his coat of mail and his brave kinsmen grasping their bows gallantly responded with a discharge of arrows. The Sayad took his place on one side of the cactus wall and the enemy on the other side and the birds of destruction began to fly about on either side and to pick up lives like grains of barley. The kinsmen of the Sayad like flying sparks in that narrow place helped one another in the melee. At this time Sayad Sádát Khán Bukhári with seventy or eighty well equipped horsemen came from behind to the help of the Sayad and joined in this gallant fight. The brother of the writer, Sheikh Eúsuf did active service with the Sayad in this battle and received two wounds; one over the other on the elbow. He used to say that the battle raged very hot for about an hour or more, when the elephant destroying the partition of the cactus brake, the brave kinsmen of the Sayad rushed sword in hand over it with cries of Allah! Allah! and attacked the enemy and after much fighting repulsed him from that place. Retreating behind another cactus brake the Mughals made another stand and the action was renewed by a discharge of arrows from both sides. Here also the same order of battle was repeated till the elephant again broke through the cactus hedge and the enemy being again attacked at close quarters was repulsed only to take shelter behind another patch of the cactus and renew battle in the same way. At this time the turmoil and din of the battle reaching the ears of Odu and Ahmed, who were in advance, they came charging in a compact mass and joined the battle. The Sayad said: "Now my lads! it is your turn, fail not my lion-hearted men!" and the men charged without delay and on the principle of the proverb that to disperse the ranks of a beaten enemy a word of challenge is enough, put to flight the troops opposed to

them. Victory fell to the lot of the Sayad. In this fight many fine
men of the Sayad's fell. Of these three men were of high rank and
of the brethren of the Sayad, Sayad Abd-us-Salám Rasúldar who held
the most exalted rank with the Sayad. Of the brave officers of the
Sayad, Eúsuf Shámi and Sayad Reihán, who was the Sayad's wife's
brother, were killed. On the side of the enemy also many fine men
fell on the field of battle. One of them, a young man of the name of
Dalu or Dabu Sultán, a youth of renown, was killed by an arrow shot
by the Sayad. The Sayad's arrow piercing through the breast plate of
his cuirasse passed through his coat of mail and causing a great deal
of hemorrhage projected on the other side from the back. When the
breeze of victory blew on the banners of the Sayad and his anxiety
subsided, the arrow wound on the knee-cap which he had received
early in the fight, now owing to loss of blood began to assert its effect.
The Sayad said : " Take me down from my horse," but do not
remove me till morning from the field of battle." Immediately on
being laid down on the ground he fainted and remained in that
state till morning. At daybreak, Sher Khán and the whole
Afghán army arrived on the scene of last night's action and placing
the Sayad in a litter, they brought him to camp applauding and
praising his high courage. The Sayad's charger, a noble Arab of the
name of *Duldul*,[1] was during last night's action struck by a musket
ball, which piercing through the chest had passed out at the flank.
But the noble animal did not fall till its master was taken down its
back, when it fell and expired.

At this time, news was suddenly received that the victorious
standards of Akbar Sháh had reached Disa, which is thirty miles from
Pattan. This information first reached Mirza Ibráhím Husein who
communicated it to I'timád Khán. He stated that the wars they were
hitherto waging were after all of no dread import. If one of them
was victorious and the other worsted there was no material fear. They
were in the end sure to come round to a state of peace and amity
and every one would return to his place. That now the country
was going to the hands of the emperor Akbar and they would be
extirpated root and branch. He said he had heard the emperor was
coming at the head of but a small force and that if they effected an

---

[1] *Duldul* was the name of the famous and faithful charger of Ali and it was
perhaps in imitation of his ancestor that the Sayad had given his steed this auspicious
name. It was also the name of the mule which, together with the coptic slave-girl Maria,
was presented by the ruler of Egypt to the Prophet.

amalgamation of forces with Sher Khán and placed him (the Mirza) in the van, they would try an issue with the emperor, and see on which side victory inclined and which side the Almighty was pleased to favour. I'timád Khán, however, did not agree to this, and the Mirza departed to his own estates. When Sher Khán and his Afgháns heard of Akbar's advance, they left the camp at once for Pattan the Afgháns without even taking leave of Sher Khán, as their wives and children were in that town. The sons of Sher Khán, Muhammád Khán and Badr Khán, also departed towards Pattan, leaving Sher Khán on the field at the head of an army whose number did not exceed forty strong. Sher Khán now came to Dholka, as far as which place Sultán Muzaffar accompanied him. But, when Sher Khán left Dholka for Sorath Sultán Muzaffar left that town to present himself before Akbar, a proceeding in which the nobles of Gujarát had preceded him. On his arrival at Pattan the Emperor sent Ein-ul-mulk Hakim to I'timád Khán and the nobles that were still with him to persuade them and bring them to him. He sent Sayad Muhammd, the son of Sayad Abdur Rahím Bukhári to assure him of the Imperial favour and to bring Sayad Hámid Bukhári to the Court. I'timád Khán and Ikhtiyárul Mulk and Alif Khán and Jhujhár Khán had the honour of waiting upon the great king in the vicinity of the town of Kadi and the next day Sayad Hámid had the honour of joining him at the village of Hújipúr, near the town of Kadi. Alif Khán and Jhujhár Khán were placed in confinement by the Emperor's men. The soldiers of the Imperial army thinking that the Imperial anger extended to all the nobles of Gujarát fell on their camps and plundered most of their baggage. When this news reached the Emperor he ordered the spoliators to be severely punished and reassured and consoled I'timád Khán. These events occurred on the 23rd Rajab A. H. 980 (A. D. 1573.), and according to the *Abjad* [1] calculation the (Hijrá) date can also be gathered from the words *Nuh-sad-o-hashtád* (that is nine hundred and eighty). After the arrival of his Imperial Majesty at Ahmedábád the mother of Changíz Khán came from Broach and complained [2] that Jhujhár Khán had unjustly slain her son and begged the just monarch

---

[1] The *Abjad* is the name formed from the first four letters of an arithmetical formula, each letter of which represents a certain numerical value from one to a thousand.

[2] According to other histories of Gujarát, the execution of Jhujhár Khán, under the orders of Akbar did not take place till after the capture of Surat by that monarch in A. D. 1573. Bombay Government Gazetteer, Vol I., Part I., 266.

to redress her wrong. As her complaint was just the king ordered Jhnjhár Khán to be cast under the foot of an elephant and killed. After a sojourn of some days, leaving Mírza Azíz Kokaltúsh in Ahmedúbád, Akbar went to visit Cambay and I'timád Khán, taking a week's leave to collect his men and things and follow the Emperor, remained behind. Ikhtiyár-ul-Mulk, who was a disappointed man, told him that he could not reconcile himself to live under the new rule and had made up his mind to take himself out of it somewhere. He asked I'timád to accompany him if he liked. I'timád said he could not do so. Ikhtiyár-ul-Mulk went to the hills of Lúnáwára and I'timád kept his promise and joined the Emperor at Cambay. Some of his nobles represented to Akbar that though I'timád had not fled on this occasion he would surely fly in the end. I'timád Khán was placed in confinement by some of Akbar's nobles.[1] Akbar went from Cambay to capture the fortress of Surat. When after crossing the Mahi the Imperial camp reached Baroda, a *firmán* or order was issued to summon Rustam Khán (the gallant defender of Broach), who was with Ibráhim Mírza at Broach. When the Mírza came to know of this, though there was a compact, ratified by an oath on the sacred Kuráan between them he killed Rustam Khán and took the road to Upper India along the slopes of the Chámpáner hills. When this news reached Akbar in the neighbourhood of Baroda he sent off a detachment in pursuit of the fugitive Mírzá and starting himself also in pursuit overtook the fugitives with only thirteen horsemen at the town of Sarnál, which is at the head of a narrow precipitous and impregnable defile, before the detachment he had appointed could do so. Although the Mírza was at the head of three or four hundred cavalry, he took to flight after making a slight stand. As the Emperor had marched from a considerable distance Mírzá Ibráhim Husein was able to get away. The Imperial party put up at the fort in the town and returning to the camp again resumed the march to Broach. After taking possession of the fortress of Broach, the Emperor departed for Surat. A deputy of

---

[1] According to the Tabakát-i-Akbari (Elliot's History of India, V. 343) I'timád was placed under the charge of that straitlaced noble, Shahbáz Khán Kambo. For the severely austere though rugged and brave character of this noble man which furnishes a striking contrast to the easy and elastic religious opinions of the generality of Akbar's courtiers, see Blochman's Áini-Akbari, p. 401. He never took any pains to conceal his contempt for the new-fangled I'láhi faith founded by Akbar and for its followers though he was often in disgrace for it.

Mírza Ibráhím Husein of the name of Ham-zabán, who held the place, intrenched himself within the castle. Mines and trenches and approaches were constructed and battle and conflict ensued.

At this time Muhammad Khán, son of Sher Khán Fauládi, who with his family had betaken himself to the mountains of I'dar, having got round a force, took this opportunity of falling upon Pattan. Sayad Ahmed Khán Bárha, one of the Imperial nobles who was in charge of that city intrenched himself in the citadel commonly called the Old Fort. Muhammad Khán took possession of the Jehán Panáh fort.

When Ibráhím Husein Mírza went to Hindustán, Muhammad Husein Mírza separated from him, and crossing the Mahi by the Sáran and Dhwáran ford and leaving Cambay to the left, passed through the districts of Dholka and Dhandúka to Ránpúr. Sher Khán returning from Sorath joined Mírza Muhammad Husein. They went and effected a junction with Muhammad Khán at Pattan, forming an army of nearly 10,000 horse. From Ahmedábád, in obedience to Imperial orders, Mírza Azíz Koká started with the following nobles : Nawáb Qutbuddín Khán, Muhammad Khán and Sayad Muhammad Bukhári, and Sayad Jaâfar Bukhári, the elder brother of Nawwáb Azud-ud-Daulah Sheikh Muhammad Bukhári, the grandson of Háji Abdul Wahháb, Sháh Budágh Khán, Naurang Khán and others. These nobles went by consecutive marches, reached the vicinity of Pattan and gave battle to Sher Khán. Sayad Muhammad Bukhári and Sayad Jaâfar, the elder brother of the Nawwáb and Sheikh Faríd fell on the field after performing deeds of great heroism. On the other side many Afgháns were killed. Though the Nawwáb was victorious, the victory was dearly purchased by the loss of two such brave spirits.

After his defeat Sher Khán went to Sorath while his son Muhammad Khán, with a body of Afgháns concealed himself in the I'dar hills. Muhammad Husein Mírza withdrew to the Sultanpúr and Nazarbár frontier, and the Nawwáb returned victorious and triumphant to Ahmedábád.

About this time Ham-zabán left the fort of Surat, and did himself the honour of kissing the Imperial feet. His Imperial Majesty entrusting the Castle of Surat and its dependencies to Quilíj Muhammad Khán, and the viceroyalty of Gujarát to Khán-i-Aâzam (Mírza Azíz Kukaltásh) turned his footsteps towards the capital, that is, Ágra.

Estates were given to the following nobles in Gujarát and according to the following details :—

To the Khán-i-Aázam (Mírza Azíz Kukaltásh):—Ahmedábád with Pitlád and several other districts.

To Nawwáb Mír Muhammad Khán, better known as Khán-i-Kalán or the Great or Senior Khán :—The district of Pattan.

To Nawwáb Qutb-ud-dín Muhammad :—The district of Broach.

To Nawwáb Aurang-Khán:—The distrct of Baroda.

To Nawwáb Aurang Khán :—The district of Baroda.

To Sayad Hámid :—The district of Dholka, the sub-district (tappa) of Khánpúr, and the district of Sami. (a)

For Sayad Mehmúd Bukhári, according to previous custom, a salary in cash was appointed. Other districts were assigned in fief to the rest of the nobles.

The nobles of Gujarát had not long enjoyed their estates in peace when Ikhtiyár-ul-Mulk and Muhammad Khán, the son of Sher Khán Fauládi, with his Afgháns, issued out of their shelter in the I'dar hills. The Nawwáb Khán-i-Aázam went to Ahmednagar, which is fifteen miles from I'dar, to check them. At this time Muhammad Husein Mírza marching rapidly from near Nazarbúr, captured the fort of Broach. Nawwáb Qutbuddín Muhammad was then at Baroda. On getting this news the Viceroy Nawwáb (Mírza Az'z) directed Sayad Hámid Bukhári, Nawwáb Naurang Khán, Báz Bahádur and Sheikh Muhammad Ghaznavi to join Nawwáb Qutbuddín with a select body of their troops and repel the Mírza. This force effecting a júnction with that of Nawwáb Qutbuddín Muhammad at the village of Asámli, which is seven miles from Dholka, marched against the Mírza, who with three hundred horsemen was at Cambay. The writer of these lines took part in this expedition in the following of Sayad Hámid. When they reached the vicinity of Cambay it was so agreed that the Army should enter the city by different gates, that Qutb-ud-dín Muhammad should get in by the Broach gate, and Naurang Khán by the Ahmed-ábád gate, Báz Bahádur and Sheikh Ghaznavi, by the same gate, while

_____

(a) The large number of Bukhári land owners and cultivators in Sami is thus easily accounted for. Being the برادري (fighting brotherhood or clansmen) of the Sayad, lands must have been allotted to them there, and to this is due the nominal rent they pay to H. H. the Nawwáb of Rádhanpúr.

Naúrang Khán and that Sayad Hámid should enter by the sea-port postern of the Custom House. Each one according to agreement repaired to his post. The Mírza having posted some of his forces to attend to the two gates, confined himself to the Custom House gate and when Sayad Hámid advanced against it he issued out and gave battle. The Mírza fought bravely but was repulsed. Three times he sallied out of the gate and as often was he repulsed after a hand to hand fight with the Sayad's army. At the other gates too the battle raged from morning to the early part of the evening. At last the nobles without deciding the fate of the day retired some distance from the city and encamped for the night. During the night the Mírza marched out and effected a junction with the forces of Ikhtiyár-ul-Mulk, and Muhammad Khán, who had come out to meet him from I'dar. The Nawwáb, who was in their wake, now returned to Ahmedábád and was there besieged by the enemy. Qutb-ud-din Muhammad and Sayad Hámid also marching quickly, entered the city. This seige lasted for two months. At last the Emperor Akbar marching from Ágra with a small number of men, came up on the ninth day to Ahmedábád, and the enemy who up to this time shone like a bright star, paled and disappeared before the victorious rays of his solar effulgence. Some of the enemy's men took to flight and others took the road to non-existence. Of those who wended their way to the land of oblivion were Mírza Muhammad Husein, Ikhtiyár-úl-Mulk and Daryá Khán, and some others of their chief men. His Imperial Majesty entered Ahmedábád in triumph and after a stay of three or four days, entrusting the Government as before to the Khán-i-A'zam (Mírza Azíz Koka), departed for the seat of government at Ágra. This event took place on Wednesday, the 4th of Jamádil Awwal, A. H. 981 (A.D. 1574).

This time the Emperor took Sayad Hámid with him together with all his family and property and bestowed the district of Dholka on Wazír Khán and appointed him against Amín Khán Ghori, who then held the province of Sorath to wrest that country from him. Wazír Khán went and fought with Amín Khán, but having lost many good men, returned without success to Ahmedábád, and thence to the presence of the Emperor. The Viceroy (Mírza Azíz Koka) enjoyed the government of Gujarát for two years and some months. After that period, in the same year (A. D. 1574-75) Wazír Khán was entrusted with the Government. Wazír Khán's tenure of the viceroyalty lasted two years, during which there was no order in the administration of the country. After this the government of Gujarát was entrusted to Shaháb-ud-din Ahmed Khán, in the year A. H. 984 (A. D. 1577). This viceroy constructed forts and garrisoned posts in the *Mehwás* country, and brought the country under order and control, lawlessness became rare, and the people began to enjoy the blessings of comfort and peace.

Fateh Khán Shirwáni, a man who had few equals in his day for courage, who was the Chief of Amín Khán's army, being offended with Amín Khán, came to Shaháb-ud-din Ahmed and offered to wrest the country of Sorath and Júnágadh from Amín Khán if an army was placed at his disposal. The viceroy placed his nephew, Mírza Khán with an Army of four thousand horse under Fateh Khán's command. When Fateh Khán reached the territories of Sorath, Amín Khán sent agents to him to say that he was ready to pay tribute and hold a part of his country as an estate and give up the rest to them, on the understanding that he must be allowed to retain the fort of Júnágadh, which was his home, for his children. After consultation the Imperial officers answered that to take Júnágadh was the chief object and end of their expedition. This prevented their coming to an amicable settlement. Marching rapidly Fateh Khán on the first day took the city of Júnágadh, which is also styled Mustufa-ábád. Amín Khán strengthened his position to undergo a seige in the fort. It so chanced, however, that Fateh Khán fell ill and his ailment in a few days carried him away from this evanescent world. The Mírza, raising the seige, went to Mangalore, a town thirty miles from Júnágadh and besieged the fort of that town. Amín Khán asked the aid of the Jám who sent Jasa his minister at the head of four thousand horse to his help. Amín Khán issuing forth, marched towards Mangalore. Mírza Khán retired to Korínúr, whither Amín Khán followed him. Mírza Khán giving battle was defeated with great loss. The whole of his baggage fell into the enemy's hands, and he returned with a few wounded followers, to Ahmedábád.

At this period Sultán Muzaffar, having escaped from the surveillance of the Imperial servants, came to Gujarát and remained for some time in the country of Narwári, the capital of which is Rájpípla. Leaving that place also for fear of Shaháb-ud-din Ahmed Khán, he went to Lúmbha Káthi, at the village of Kheri, or Khíri

---

[1] The country possessed by petty Rajpút or Koli land-holders, more or less free from direct Imperial control is called the "*Mehwás*"

under the Súrdhár division of the province of Surath, and there took up his abode.

After some time the government of Gujarát was taken from Shaháb, ud-din Ahmed and entrusted to I'timád Khán Gujaráti. Shaháb-ud-din started for the capital. At this time a party of about seven or eight thousand Mughal horse, detaching themselves from Shaháb-ud-din Ahmed, remained behind at Ahmedábád. The names of their leaders were Khalíl Beg, Mír Eúsuf, Muhammad Badakhshi, Quádir Beg, Abáligh Uzbak, Mír Ábid, Mír Kae Khán, Mughal Beg, Khájah Abdulláh, Tarsún Beg, Míram Beg, Ghazanfar Khán, Qurbán Áli Bahádur and Mirza Ábdulláh and Teimúr Husein. After agreeing among themselves, these men represented to I'timád Khán that they had separated from Shaháb-ud-dín and remained behind ¡n the hope of obtaining service under him and that if he provided for their remuneration they would remain in his service. I'timád Khán said that his orders were that the salaries of the mounted soldiers should not exceed Rs. 10 per mensem ; that they were all Mughals and this pay would not be sufficient for them. He asked them to look out for themselves. These men now thought to themselves : Shaháb-ud-dín has left us behind and I'timád has left us in the lurch; where are we to go? Let us betake ourselves to Sultán Muzaffar and bring him out and lay our hands on plunder. Let us see whom fortune favours." They left Ahmedábád with this intention, and went to Dholka, and from Dholka to Khíri, to Lúmbha Káthi. They entered into agreement with Lúmbha and Sultán Muzaffar and taking Lúmbhá with three or four thousand Káthi horse they marched against Ahmedábád. This news reached I'timád Khán, on Monday night, the 25th of Shaâbán. I'timád leaving his son Sher Khan in Ahmedábád went with speed in pursuit of Shaháb-ud-din to turn him and bring him back with him. He reached Shaháb-ud-din Ahmed who had encamped at Kadi the same night. Shaháb-ud-din, however, told him he had made over the charge of the country and its cares to him and had nothing now to do with it, that he was returning in consequence of being recalled. When I'timád Khán pressed him hard, he said he would return only on condition of I'timád Khán writing (to the Emperor) that the enemy was about to retake the country and that he (I'timád) could not make any opposition and had to re-entrust the government to Shaháb-ud-dín Ahmed. Unless I'timád Khán was willing to subscribe to these terms Shaháb-ud-dín said he would not interfere and I'timád might cope with the enemy or not, as he liked. It was no concern of his. Monday and Tuesday were passed in these discussions. On the other side, Sultán Muzaffar arrived before Ahmedábád on Wednesday, the 27th Shaâban, before the Ráikhad Gate, where the city wall was a little delapidated, and had not been repaired. They were now repairing it and Mujáhid Khán Gujaráti was supervising the work, and guarding the place. The Mughal in the army of Sultán Muzaffar alighting from their horses rushed towards the breach. After a little fight Mujáhid Khán turned his face and fled and Sultán Muzaffar got into the city. Sher Khán, who was sitting at the Chaukhandï near the Bhadra mounted and attended by a small number of men, fled. When he had gone as far as the house of Sheikh Bhathri, he espied a band of Muzaffar's Mughals advancing towards him and again turned rein and fled. Sultán Muzaffar went and resumed his place and became master of the capital. This took place in the year A. H. 991 (A. D. 1584-85). When one watch of the night had passed some of the followers of Sher Khán coming to I'timád Khan, related the above events to him. I'timád Khán now gave Shaháb-ud-dín in writing all that he wanted him to do. Shaháb-ud-dín Khán thought to himself, that the cause of all this revolution were a handful of soldiers who were in his service, and who had mostly not received at his hands aught but good. He thought, therefore, that they would not oppose him and that immediately on hearing of his return, they would come and meet him and the revolt would be suppressed, and he would be reinstated in his former office. With these hopes he returned that same night to Ahmedábád and at dawn on the 20th of Shaábán, reached the other side of the river at a place called the Bári-chah (or postern). Most of his men being accompanied by their families, occupied themselves in pitching the tents, and in bringing down their families from the carts in a manner so secure and careless that they had not on even their armours or arms. Shaháb-ud-dín Ahmed was every moment expecting the information of Sultán Muzaffar having left the city immediately on hearing of his arrival and of his Mughals coming humbly and peniten-tially to take up their old places in his following. These men on the other hand, having become masters of Ahmedábád, were already, dreaming dreams of nobility, each one of them, thinking : "Than myself no one is greater. [1]" When the sound of Shaháb-ud-dín khán's

---

[1] This is an Arabic proverb *Aná-wa-là gheiré* انا ولا غيري = *literally* " I (am great) and none else."

kettle-drums reached Muzaffar's ears he was afraid lest his late partisans should hand him over to Shaháb-ud-din, so he prepared to take
himself away. But the men coming placed their hands on the Sacred
Kuráan and assured him of their loyalty and besought him to go out
with them and witness their prowess against the enemy. In case of
their being defeated, they said, he might do as he pleased. Sultán
Muzaffar coming out of the Khánpúr Gate stood on the Sábarmati
sands, and the whole population of Ahmedábád turned out to a man
to witness the fight. Shaháb-ud-dín Ahmed and I'timád Khán mis-
took the townsmen for an army of soldiers. The Mughals now
sallying forth began the fight and with very little ado routed Shaháb-
ud-din Ahmed and I'timád, who, with a small following reached
Pattan, leaving all their baggage behind to the enemy as booty. Their
soldiers also went to the city and entered Sultán Muzaffars service
who now remained at Ahmedábád. He conferred great honours on
the Mughals who were the means of his success and bestowed on them
titles and estates, and salaries befitting their rank. He gave Mír Ábid
the title of Khán-i-khánán and Khalíl Beg that of Khán-i-Zamán.
He styled Mír Yúsuf Badakhshi Bahádur Khán and Mughal-Beg Khán-
i-Daurán, Quadr Beg-Khán-i-Aázam, Khájah Abdulláh Khán-i-
Jehán and Tarsún Beg-Adham Khún, Miram Beg-Afzal Khán and
Qurbán Ali Bahádur-Kalích Khán, Mírza Abdulláh-Ásif Khán, Teimúr
Husein-Bhái Khán. Mír Kai Khún and Ghazanfar Khán remained
content with their former titles, but Tígh Bahádur would not be
satisfied with any. Many persons obtained titles, called themselves
nobles and gave themselves no small airs.

POETRY.

A mouse one night in dream did see
Himself into a camel turned ;
At morn he rose full filled with glee,
To show his size to all he burned.
While bustling thus from place to place,
He met a camel with a load,
And straining hard to go its pace,
He stalked along the selfsame road.
By chance from off the camel's back
Of barley-corn did roll
On the vain mouse a hard-filled sack
That crushed it's soul.
So man in power, like boys at play,
Fills a brief part and flits away.

Sayad Daulat who was the servant of Kalyán Ráo of Cambay, collecting an army, possessed himself of Cambay and obtained much money from that port.   He entertained nearly four thousand horse and sent a petition to Sultán Muzaffar who in return sent him the present of a horse and a dress of honour with the title of " Rustam Khán" and ordered him to remain where he was and that he would send for him when wanted.   When some days passed thus Nawwáb Qutb-ud-dín ·Muhammad, who was then at Nazarbár, heard of these events and came by forced marches to Baroda.   Sultán Muzaffar, leaving Mír Ábid behind him at Ahmedábád, on the 17th: of the month of Zil-Quaâdah of the same year, departed for Baroda.   Sayad Daulat joined him near Nariád, with four thousand horse.   On hearing of this Nawwáb Qutb-ud-din Muhammad sent Muhammad Afzal Khán and Muhammad Mírak with three hundred horse, to occupy and hold the ford of Khán-púr-Bánkáner against the advance of the enemy.   They went to the place ordered, but being in secret league and correspondence with Sultán Muzaffar, after a little show of fight took to flight.

When the Sultán reached the neighbourhood of the city of Baroda, Nawwáb Qutb-ud-dín marched out with his officers (who were only outwardly the friends of the Nawwáb but really the partisans of the Sultán), to oppose the Sultán.   When the Nawwáb came to know the true feelings of his army he returned and entered the fort of the city. Sultán Muzaffar, with about twenty thousand horse and foot, and a numerous following of Kolis and Rájputs, beseiged the city. The Khán notwithstanding the inimical feelings of his men, held the fort for two and twenty days and made almost superhuman efforts to maintain his position.   But what could one man do against such odds ? On the twenty-first day of the seige Afzal Muhammad Mírak and Chárkas Khán Rúmi from their batteries sent a message to Sultán Muzaffar stating that as long as they remained on their batteries the people of the city having an eye on them would guard their batteries.   They asked the Sultán to send for them on the pretence of negotiating a peace.   They requested Sultán Muzaffar to send also for Zeinuddín Kambo (who was a relative of Shahbáz Khán Kambo,) and was sent out with I'timád Khán from the court and was sent by Shaháb-ud-din Ahmed and I'timád Khán on their defeat to bring Qutb-ud-din to their help against the enemy.   During the seige this Zeinuddín was making sincere and faithful efforts in the Imperial cause.   They also asked the Sultán to send for Sayad Jalál Bhakhri (who was one of the faithful followers of Qutb-ud-dín Muhammad), and for Khwájah Yahyá, Agent of Naurang Khán. That he was to pretend to imprison Afzal Muhammad Mírak, and Khájah Yahya, and kill Zeinuddin Kambo, and Sayad Jalál Bhakri, and the next day assault the fort, and no one, said he, would raise a finger in its defence and he would gain his object. The Sultán did as advised. Nawwáb Qutb-ud-dín Muhammad sent a deputation of the five persons above enumerated. The Sultán put them in confinement as soon as they came. The next morning he threw Zeinuddín Kambo under an elephant's foot, but Sayad Ahmed Bukhári who was with the Sultán, interceded with the Sultán for the life of Sayad Jalál Bhakhri and took him to his quarters. The Sultán mounting his horse, gave the order for all his nobles to assault the fort. They brought the cannon that they had got from Ahmedábád to bear on the fort. The state of the Khan's army has been described above, still for some days the Khán tried hard alone to do his best, but the cannonade levelled the fort to the ground and the enemy entered the breach. The Nawwáb now retired to the citadel and was beseiged there. The next morning the Sultán took an oath on the sacred Kuráan to spare the life of the Nawwáb and with a promise to that effect, sent for him. The Khán went over to the Sultàn, who, at the instigation of some interested persons, imprisoned the Khán and his sister's son Sayad Jalál-ud-dín and after a few hours killed both of them. After a sojourn of two days at Baroda the Sultán on the third, marched towards Broach and alighted near the city. The mother of Nawwáb Naurang Khán, with some of her slaves, was in the Broach fort. On the third day of the siege these traitorous slaves came to the Sultán and gave up the keys of the fort of Broach to the Sultán and all the Nawwáb's treasure fell into the Sultán's hands. He remained for fifteen days at Broach. Presently news was received that Khán Khánán, the son of Byram Khán, was under orders from the Emperor coming by forced marches from Jhálore. The Sultán turned his footsteps towards Ahmedábád, and arrived there on the 6th Muharram A. H. 992 (A. D. 1585-86), and on Monday the 9th, issuing from the city he encamped at Mehmúd-Nagar, nearly two miles from the city of Ahmedábád. On Tuesday he remained there. On Wednesday, Mírza Khán-Khánán leaving Sarkhez on the left, came and encamped near the Sábarmati. The Sultán leaving Mahmúd Nagar crossed the river and encamped near the Mousoleum of Sháh Bhikan, son of Sháh-Álam. On Thursday both the armies

remained encamped.   On Friday they formed their ranks and a battle
was fought in which Allah opened the door of victory to Nawwáb
Mírza Khán Khánán. Amongst the Imperial servants who fell in
this battle, was Sayad Háshim, son of Sayad Muhammad Bárha
His elder brother Sayad Kásim was wounded.   The Sultán being defeated, went to Cambay where nearly eleven or twelve thousand horse
soon rallied round him.   On the 2nd of Safar Nawwáb Mirza Khán
marched from Ahemedábád towards Cambay.   The Imperial army
from Málwa commanded by Sharíf Khán, Kilich Khán and Naurang
Khán, also arrived to co-operate with him and reached Baroda on the
morning of the day on which the Sultán was`defeated.   The writer of
these lines was present with that army. When they received at Baroda
the news of the victory gained by the Imperial arms they remained
there. Nawwáb Naurang Khán and Mírza Záhid, son of Sharíf Khán
made a rapid march against Broach to seize the fortress.   Háji Samad
Khán and Charkas Khán and Násir Khán who held the fort on behalf
of Muzaffar shutting the gates in the face of the Nawwáb, opened a
cannonade and fire of musketry.   Nawwúb Naurang Khán, having
encamped near Broach every day was diligent in the search of means
to worst the enemy, but when Nawwáb Mírza Khán set out for Cambay
he wrote to him inviting him thither, stating that the enemy was again
assembling there in force and that after dispersing them they
would attend to other business. Naurang Khán, therefore, after
a seige of fifteen days set out to join the camp of Mirza Khán at
Cambay, and came up with him at Báreja,   about eleve miles
from Ahmedábád.   Sultán Muzaffar learning of this amalgamation,
left Cambay for Baroda, and from Baroda went and entered,
the hilly tracts of Jhámpa in Rájpipla.   The (Imperial) forces
also went in pursuit of him to Jhámpa where Sultán¦ Muzaffar
made a stand.   As the Málwa army had not taken part in the first
fight, they now tried their best to engage the enemy and succeeding
in doing so gained a victory after a short and easy battle.   The
Sultán was defeated and his army dispersed, and many of his men
entered the service of Mírza Khán, who notwithstanding the magni-
tude of their crime, pardoı ed them.   Others went away to the Dakhan.
All his baggage was plundered by the men of the victorious army and
every one went his own way.   The Sultán could never collect an army
after this and with a few men went to Lúmbha Káthi at Khíri
(in Káthiáwár).   Náwáb Mirza Khán returned victorious to Ahmed-

ábád. At the town of Sínore Mírza Khán heard that Háji Samak and
Charkas Khán and Nasír Khán were still in the fort of Broach.
Nawwáb Shahábuddín Ahmed Khán, Kilích Khán, Sharíf Khán
and Naurang Khán were appointed by him at the head of the whole
of the Málwa army against Broach, he himself returning to
Ahmedábád. The Emperor conferred on Mírza Khán the title of
" Khán-Khánán. " After these two victories and from that day to this
his power, dignity and state have been on the increase. God
Almighty give him long life and perpetuate his greatness to the
Day of Judgment !

The abovementioned nobles went and besieged Broach. When the
beseiged were reduced to great straits one night Nasír Khán and
Charkas Khán fled, Nasír Khán having killed Haji Samak by treachery
lest he might join the Imperial nobles. The horse of Charkas Khán
becoming bogged in the mud of the Narbada he was captured and
beheaded. Nasír Khán escaped, and the fort was captured. Sháhábuddín
Ahmed Khán now went to Málwa because that country had been
bestowed on him in fief and the other nobles returned to Ahmedábád.

After his defeat and retirement to Khíri Sultán Muzaffar went to
Amín Khán, the son of Tátár Khán Ghori, of whom mention has been
made above. Amín Khán alloted to the Sultán the town of Gondal,
which was (then) waste, as a residence and the Sultán lived in the
fort of that village, hoping that Amín Khán would help him.
Amín Khán, however, said he could not command means sufficient
to equip an army, and that if the Sultán gave him two hundred
thousand *Mehmúdis*, he would organize an army and place himself
entirely at the Sultán's service. The Sultán sent him two hundred
thousand *Mehmúdis*—but Amin Khán took the money and failed to
perform the promise.

When the Khán-i-Khánán learned that Muzaffar was still hanker-
ing after getting an army around him he led an expedition to Sorath
against the Sultán.[1] The emissaries of Amín Khán and the Jám came

---

[1] The text here, as far as it relates to the Káthiáwár campaign of the Khán-i-Khánán, and up to the word *Barah*, is, according to the late Colonel J. W. Watson, rather
vague and inaccurate. According to him, though the text somewhat incorrectly writes
it *Baràh* برا the word is evidently a copyist's error for *Barda* بردا. Were it not
so, and had the کو or hills referred to been the Girnár the Viceroy would have
chastised Amín Khán. The efforts of Khán Khánán were directed against the Jám, in
whose territories lie the Barda hills. From the data before me, it seems that Colonel
Watson's objection is well founded.

41

and stated to the Khán Khánán that their principals had harboured the
Sultán in their territories only to keep him from brigandage. That if the
viceroy went against the Sultán personally or sent an army he was
welcome to do so—it was no business of theirs. The Viceroy only wish-
de them to remain where they were. He would see to all the rest
himself, provided they agreed neither to give the Sultán shelter nor
passage through their territories. Agreeing to these terms the agents
made engagements to that effect and the viceroy set out on his expedition. When he reached the village of Upleta, fifteen miles from
Júnágadh, he heard that Muzaffar had entered the Barda hills. The
Viceroy left his camp behind and marched on with a light following.
When he reached the defiles of the hills, he sent a party of his men to
enter and reconnoitre the different spurs. Sultán Muzaffar however,
had some time ere this left the Jám's country and entered Dánta,
which is the residence of seditious Kolis. Abhai Chandra Rájput,
a Chohán, and some of the Sayads of Bárha, like Sayad Lád Khán
and Sayad Bahádur who were left to guard the city of Ahmedábad
and its dependencies, went and fought with Muzaffar, who being
deefeated, again entered the Narwári country (Rájpípla). As the Jám
had not kept to his agreement of not harbouring the Sultán in or letting
him pass through his territories and as the Sultán had passed through
them to Dánta, the Nawáb leaving the Barda hills drew an army against
the Jám. The Jám quaked at this intended advance of the viceroy
and making up his mind to die, with fifteen thousand horse and
twenty thousand foot came and encamped outside his capital of Nawá
Nagar. In the language of the Musalmáns of the Jám's country
when the Jám himself determines to die and with his children and property goes out to oppose the enemy, the practice is termed *láwah*
(Gujaráti લાઈ). The Nawáb ultimately returned to Ahmedábád after
taking from the Jám the elephants that had fallen into his hands when
Mírza Khán, nephew of Shaháb-ud-din Ahmed was defeated as has been
above described by Amín Khán. Some horses were also given by the
Jám in addition by way of compensation and penalty to the viceroy.

In the year 999 A. H. (A.D. 1592-93) Khán Khánán was recalled
to the court and the government of Gujarát was conferred on the
Nawwáb Khán-i-Ázam.

Sultán Muzaffar again returned to the neighbourhood of the
Jám's territories and after waiting a year the Khán-i-Ázam led an

army against the Jám, with the intention of expelling Sultán
Muzaffar from that country or of capturing him. He put Nawwáb
Naurang Khán and Mírán Sayad Kásim Bárha in advance and followed them in person. The writer of these lines was also in this expedition. Naurang Khán and Sayad Kásim advanced and encamped
before Morvi.

The Nawwáb himself was near Víramgám. Amín Khán being
dead, his son Daulat Khán went and joined the Jám. Sultán Muzaffar
also with an army of Káthís and with Bhárá the Jám came to his
aid and a large army assembled. For some time messages passed
between Naurang Khán and the Jám to the effect that he should
expel Sultán Muzaffar from his territories and never suffer him
to re-enter them and to give some good horses by way of tribute.
But proud of his large army, the Jám did not consent to this. Naurang Khán and the Mírán wrote to this effect to the Khán-i-Ázam,
who in a rage at once marched against the enemy, making light of
their strength. He halted one day at Búthiri, nearly five miles from
the enemy and it so happened that that day the monsoons broke and
for five days and nights there was a large and continuous downpour
of rain. The ground became so muddy that it was difficult to go
from one tent to another and there was such a puddle of mud and
water between the two armies that a mosquito could not put his foot
on the ground without getting bogged much less a horse or an elephant. The skirmishers of the Jám's army during these five nights
came and killed sometimes a horse, sometimes an elephant and sometimes they wounded men and went off. Grain became so scare as to
be sold at prices as extravagantly high as a *ser* (nearly 1¼ lbs.) to a
rupee. The Nawwáb now held a consultation with the Chief Officers
of the Imperial forces. Some advised an immediate engagement with
musketry and cannon and a pitched battle when the wind blew and
dried the ground. Sayad Kásim said there was but little grain in the
Imperial camp, but there was plenty, in the enemy's; that if they
waited for a pitched battle the men would be disabled by hunger. It
was therefore the best policy not to engage the enemy but to march
on to the Jáms capital, Nawá Nagar, which was stocked with all the
necessities. His family and property also being there, he would be
obliged to leave the place and come to intercept them and then where
ever he opposed them they could fight him. All approved of the
Sayad's advice, and next morning they marched for Nawá Nagar. The

Jám in great anxiety marched away and came and encamped in the
limits of the town of Dhokar, about eight miles from the Imperial
camp and intercepted the route to Nawá Nagar. When this information reached the Nawwáb as the road was heavy with mud and rain-
water it was arranged that the Imperial forces should march three
miles and then encamp to enable them to give battle the next day
When they arrived at the camp agreed upon, it being a rising ground,
they could see the tents and army of the enemy. Sayad Kásim commanded the van and Naurang Khán the right and on the left were
Gújar Khán and Khájah Muhammed Rafi, who were amongst the
bravest men of the day, with several of the Imperial nobels and local
landowners. Mírza Ihtirám, son of the Viceroy, commanded the
rear. The Nawwáb himself and Mírza Anwar were in the front
of the army. When the army of the enemy appeared the Nawwáb
asked Sayad Kásim what to do, as their intention was to fight the
next day The Sayad said if they did not offer battle that day the
enemy would become arrogant. The Viceroy therefore said : " Be it
auspicious ! we shall fight to-day." Reciting the Fátihah, they
advanced, until the van became engaged., Khájah Muhammad Rafi'
advancing quickly, encountered the forces opposed to him, which were
commanded by Áchár, the eldest son of the Jám, and his minister Jasa.
A hand-to-hand fight ensued. While this was raging hot Daulat Khán,
the son of Amín Khán, after directing a cannonade against them, fell
upon Sayed Kásim's Imperialists with many Kolis. A mist now arose,
which like night wrapped the world in darkness in which the swords
flashed and gleamed like falling stars. At this time Khájah Muhammad
Rafi' was killed and the left wing of the Imperial army defeated. The
Jám's minister, Jasú, and Áchár, the Jám's son, having routed the army
opposed to them, attacked the forces under Sayad Kásim. The Sayad,
whose bravery and prowess were proverbial, could not be moved from his
place even by the lightning flashes of swords or by clouds of arrows.
At this time Gújar Khán and Mírza Anwar, commanders of the left
and the viceroy himself, who was at the van of his army, threw themselves upon the enemy, who turned their backs and fled. The son of
the Jám and his wretched minister were both slain and left about 1,500
of their men killed on the field. The names of those who were killed
on the side of the Imperialists are as follows : Khájah Muhammad Rafi'

---

¹ The Fátihah is literally the opening or first chapter of the Kuráan. Its reci-
tation at difficult moments is considered auspicious.

Khájah Sheikh ; Sayad Sharfuddín, nephew of Sháh Abú Turáb; Sayad Kabír, son of Sayad Ali Khún, with thirty or forty men. God bestowed victory on the viceroy.

One of the good deeds in the life of the viceroy, in the annals of whose life there is no lack of bright achievements, was that after the death of Sultán Muzaffar he performed on Monday the 2nd of the month of Rajab A.H. 1001 (A.D. 1594) the pilgrimage (to Makkah). Though he was at that time the viceroy of Gujarút, the best of the provinces of India, and was possessed in the highest degree of all the means of happiness and enjoyment and no nobleman of his time probably enjoyed the friendship and intimacy of the Emperor to such a degree, yet placing all this aside he embarked on a ship at the end of the sailing season when the sea was wild and tempestuous enough to frighten one's soul out of his body. It is said that one day somebody said to him that the sea at the time was so wild and stormy that it seemed to express in inanimate language the warning that whoever ventured upon it in such weather would do so at the risk of his life. But the brave nobleman said that the stormy, raging sea was but a sea of water. If an ocean of fire intervened between him and his sacred resolve he would not be deterred by it. He embarked with his family in such weather and, they weighed anchor and he sailed away. God rewarded the purity of his intentions by landing him safely on the shores of the land of his destination and by bestowing on him the merit of the ordained perambulations round the Kaába at Makka and the visit to Madína.

But to continue: The Jám, the Sultún, and Daulat Khún, fleeing from the field entered the fort of Júnágadh. Next morning the Viceroy went from Dholar to Nawúnagar. The family of the Jám, and his servants had all left and only a few of his servants remained in the city. They were taken prisoners and the city given up to plunder. The next day, the Nawwábs Naurang Khán and Gújar Khán and Mírán Sayad Kásim were sent against the fort of Júnágadh, the Viceroy himself remaining at Nawúnagar. On hearing this news, Sultán Muzaffar and the Jám descending from the fort, set off for the Jám's country, Daulat Khán remaning in the fort. By chance that very day the above-mentioned nobles arrived before the fort of Júnágadh and on that day Daulat Khan, the son of Amín Khán, who was the ruler of the fort, died. His agents and chief officers strengthening the fort, commenced a musketry fire and cannonade.

The Imperial nobles remained for several days before the fortress, when the Viceroy himself coming there, made several attempts to take the fortress. The country, however, being waste, grain became at first very scarce and then unobtainable in his camp. So he relinquished the seige of the fortress and returned to Ahmedábád.

After seven or eight months he again set out for the conquest of Júnágadh. The agents of the Jám came and besought him to pass over the fault of their master and to restore his kingdom to him, in return for which the Jám offered his submission and services to the Viceroy. The Viceroy, agreeing, asked the Jám to undertake to regularly supply his army with grain and advanced and besieged Júnágadh. The Jám regularly sent supplies of grain to the Imperial camp. After three months, the garrison surrendered the fort to the Viceroy and submitted to him.

About this time information reached the Viceroy that Sultán Muzaffar had gone to Jagat, a well known place of Hindú worship on the shore of the salt sea. The Viceroy sent Naurang Khán, Mírza Anwar, and Gújar Kháu after Muzaffar. These officers marching with despatch to Jagat, were informed that the Sultán had gone to Bet. Without halting, the Imperial officers at once pursued the fugitive Sultán to Bet. The news of their advance, however, reaching Síva Vádhel, [1] he destroyed his village, and embarked Sultán Muzaffar with his family on board a ship and was preparing himself to follow in another vessel but as it was low water the sailing of the boats was delayed. The fugitives believed that the Imperial army could not overtake them that day from Jagat but perceiving the approach of the vanguard of the Imperial forces the Vádhel made Sultán Muzaffar to alight and mounting him on a fleet horse and giving him an escort of some of his Rájpúts sent him away. While the Vádhel was attempting to reach the boat himself the Imperial army came up. The Vádhel with forty or fifty men that were with him, fought gallantly and was killed and his family and people were taken prisoners. After the tide rose at high water the boat containing the family and harem of the Sultán sailed away. The Imperial officers came to Arámra, a place belonging to Sagrám Wádhel, the Rájah of Jagat. This man came and met the Imperial

---

[1] This Vádhel Rájput seems, no doubt, to have been a landowner of Bet, though the text is rather vague as to his identity.

officers and asked them to give him a party of their picked men to enable him to pursue and capture the vessel on which the Sultán's family had sailed from whatever place they might have gone to, since all the islands of those parts were under his rule. This request of his had a treacherous motive. He really wished to select the finest men of the Imperial force and take them away and after landing them on some island, to sail away and keep them as pledges for the exchange of the family and property of Síva Vádhel. But God made Naurang Khán to suspect his intentions and he said : "(In that case) Sagrám himself shall remain with me and he may send his own men in these vessels." On this, Sagrám fled, and his treachery became apparent. The Viceroy and Mírza Anwar returned to Júnágadh. The Viceroy now led his army against Morbi. The Jám came and paid his respects while the Viceroy was encamped in the vicinity of Morbi.

At this time information was received that the Sultán was with Bhárá, [1] who had given him shelter near Bhuj which was his capital. The Viceroy drew his forces towards that country. When Bhára heard of this he sent emissaries to beseech the Viceroy not to ravage his territories, as he was ready to surrender Sultán Muzaffar and he eventually did as he had promised. The details of this affair are as follows :—There is a hilly tract about thirty miles from Bhuj where Bhárá had given shelter to the Sultán. When his intentions towards him changed, he sent for a detachment of the Viceroy's men and capturing the Sultán, made him over to them. These men taking the Sultán prisoner, marched towards Morbi. When they reached the town of Dhrole, which is about twenty-three miles from Bhuj on the way to Morbi the Sultán expressing a wish to respond to a call of nature retired to a corner, drew out a razor, which he used to keep with him in his drawers during the predatory life he was obliged to lead and cut his throat and delivered himself from the turmoil and buffets of this mean world. This took place in the year 1000 after the Hijrah (A. D. 1503).

---

[1] Ráo Bharmal I. of Katch. (A. D. 1585-1631.)

INDEX.

A

Aâzam and Muâzzam, of Khurásán at the court of Sultán Mehmúd Begda, 89 ; their work, 89.

Aâzam Humáyún, the relative of Álam Khán, 227 ; cozened by Nisár-ul-mulk, 227, Álam Khán Lodi's half brother, is given Baroda and Chámpáner in fief, 271, 272 killed in battle, 275, 276 ; the title of Yúsuf Khán Habshi, 276 ; killed in battle; 281.

Abdul-Kádir, Kázi, 183.

Abdul Karím Khán, entitled I'timád Khán , 237, 285 ; confidence reposed by Sultán Mehmúd III in, 237.

Abdulláh Changál, Sheikh, his shrine near Dhár, 97.

Abdul Latíf Malik Mehmúd Dáwar-ul-mulk, one of the religious nobles of Sultán Mehmúd Begda, 82 ; an attempt on his life, 82 ; his intimacy with Sháh Álam, 82 ; almoner of Sháh Álam, 83 ; appointed Thánedár of Amrún, 83 ; his expedition against Bhuj, 83 ; his probity, 83 ; his death (A. D. 1509), 83 ; his miracles, 84.

Abdul Wahháb Sayad, gives saintliness to Sayad Mubárak, 292.

Abdur Rehmán, younger brother of Sultán Ahmed II, 276 ; is given the title of Sádát Khán and made deputy, 276.

Abdus-Salám Rasúldár, killed in the battle near Maroli, 308.

Abdus Samad, Mián, the counsellor of Sultán Mehmúd III, 264.

Abú—(the fort of) Sultán Kutbuddín sends a force against, 34 ; restored to Krishna Devada (A.D. 1457), 35 ; Rájá of Sirohi plunders merchants at (A. D. 1486-87), 72.

Abú Bakr, the grandson of Fírúz Sháh, mounts the throne of Delhi (A.D. 1389), 5 ; struggles for the throne between him and Sultán Muhammad, 5 ; revolt of his army, is imprisoned, 5 ; and dies in prison, 5.

Abú Bakr-al-Eidrús, Sayad, leaves Arabia and settles at Ahmedábád (A.D. 1544-45) 241.

Abúji Gujaráti, entitled Násir-ul-mulk, 237.

Abúji Náik, afterwards Wajíh-ul-mulk, confidential attendant of Sultán Bahádur, 185.

Abul Fazl, his account of Bahádur's death, 200 (note 4) ; calls Birbal, a Bád-furúsh, 234.

Abu Turáb, Sháh, a man of high intellectual attainments in the court of the Gujará Sultán, 168.

Achár, the eldest son of the Jám of Navánagar, in the battle against Khán-i-Aâzâm, 324, slain in battle, 324.

Adam Sultán Afghán Khán defeated by rebels against Sultán Ahmed (A.D. 1410), 11.

Adhámrá, a village near Jagat, Sultán Mahmúd Begdá at, 61 ; full of snakes, 61.

Ádil Khán, alias Malik Násir, the ruler of Asírgarh and Burhánpúr, invades Gujarát ; repelled by Zafar Khán, 6.

Ádil Kháu Fárúki I, son of Mubárak ; Mahmúd Begdá's campaign against (A. D. 1499), 75 ; dies without male issue, 76.

Ádil Khán, the title assumed by Álam Khán, son of Ahsan Khán, supported by Sultán Mehmúd Begdá, 76 ; established in the Government of Asír and Burhánpúr, 77 ; one of the family of Malik Rájá assumes the title of, 76 ; also entitled Aâzam Humáyún, 93 ; visits Sultán Muzaffar II at Morámli, 93 ; son-in-law of Sultán Muzaffar II, 93 ; sent against the Ráná of Chittaur, 101 ; engaged in the Málwá campaign, 106, returns to Asír, 106.

1

C

D

F

Faríd, Malik, son of Imád-ul-Mulk, story of, and Sultán Ahmed I., 16; distinguishes himself at the battle between Sultán Ahmed and Hoshang of Málwa, 17.

Farishtah, the History of, references to, 7, 11, 21, 24, 34, 52, 59 60, 65, 67, 162, 163, 164, 174, 911.

Farrah, a Kandhár village, Sayad Muhammad Jaunpuri dies at, 91.

Fateh Khán, son of Fírúz Sháh and father of Sultán Ghiás-ud-dín, 4.

Fateh-Khán, surnamed Hoshang, a cousin of Sultán Muzaffar, 13; sent against the Ídar rebels, 12.

Fateh-Khán, son of Sultán Muhammad and Bíbí Mughli, 36, 38; half brother of Sultán Kutb-ud-dín, 36; born (A. D. 1455), 23; protected by Sháh Álam, in his early years, 36; miracles worked on and in behalf of, by Sháh Álam, 37, 38; raised to the throne by the nobles as Sultán Mehmúd (afterwards Begda), 41. (See Mehmúd Begda).

Fateh-Khán, Governor of Pattan, 110.

Fateh-Khán, an Afghán, of the Lodi tribe, admitted to an audience by Sultán Bahádur, 164.

Fateh-Khán Balúch, places Sháhúji on the throne of Gujarát, 268; encamps at Rúbráh, 269; I'timád Khán bestows estates on, 270; defeated by Sher Khán and Músa-Khán Fauládis, 287.

Fateh-Khán Budhú, ruler of Sindh, the Gujarát Sultán's cup-bearer and son-in-law of Sultán Muzaffar, does not join Imád-ul-Mulk, 145; his wife Ráje-Áyishah, 136.

Fateh-Khán, Shirwáni, Chief Officer of Amín Khán's army, 314; comes to Shaháb-ud-dín, 314; expedition against Júnágadh, 314; dies, 314.

Fatehpur, Burhán-ul-Mulk escapes to, 44.

Fattúji, surnamed Muháfiz Khán, his counsel to Daryá Khán, 210, 219; at the battle of Dáhor, 219; goes to Chámpáner with the treasure and women of Daryá Khán, 221; being defeated, takes shelter in the Mauliya-fort, 221; is imprisoned and sent to Surat, 221.

Fauládi Patháns, in the service of Sayad Mubárak, 253.

Firangis, the (Portuguese), create a disturbance in Bassein and Máhim, 75: defeated at the port of Chaul by Malik Ayáz, 75; destroy the fort of Diu built by Malik Ayáz, 84; their power in the Gujarát ports, 85; Is-hák, son of Malik Ayáz Governor of Sorath, reported by his brother Iiás to be about to make over the fort of Diu to, 157; a vessel of theirs captured at Diu by Kiwám-ul-Mulk (A. C. 1527) and the men taken prisoners, 159; they are converted to Islám, 159; they build a fort at Diu, 198; their treacherous assassination of Sultán Bahádur and his attendants. (A. C. 1536), 199.

Firang-Khán, a Portuguese convert to Islám of the name of John de St. Jago, 193— and note.

Fírúz-ábád, Ghiás-ud-dín, grand-son of Sultán Fírúz Tughlak crowned at, 4.

Fírúz, Bahmani, Sultán of the Dakhan, his campaign against Bíjánagar with the help of Sultán Ahmed I., 21; died (A. D. 431).

Fírúz, Jám of Thattah, comes to ask aid of Sultán Bahádur, 161.

Fírúz-Khán, son of Sultán Islám Sháh, killed by Mamríz Khán, 255.

Fírúz-Khán, Dandáni, ruler of Nágor, dies (A. C. 1451), 33.

Fírúz Sháh, Sultán, uncle's son of Muhammad Tughlak, fond of hunting 1; his hunting adventure, 2; ascends the throne of Dehli (A. C. 1345), 4; hands over the reins of Government to his son Muhammad Khán, 4; dies, 4.

G

Gadái, Malik, sent to the relief of Nágor, 34.

Gágráon, Sultán Bahádur orders Munhammad Sháh Asíri to march to and capture, 176; Saint Miyán Mítha enshrined in, 176; Sultán Bahádur at, 177.

Gálnah, fort, Bahádur Khán at, 160.

3

I

army of Bukhári Sayads and Fauládi Patháns, 253; also of Afghán, Lodi and Shirwáni tribes, 254; Sultán Ahmed Sháh II the spiritual follower of, 255; the generosity of, 256; makes peace with Mubárak Sháh, 257, 262; takes advice of Bibi A'lam Khátún, 265; receives a letter from Sayad Husein, 265; attacks the army of Ná ir-ul-Mulk, 267; goes to Ahmedábád, 267; story of him and horse-merchants, 268; returns to Ahmedábád, 270; his share of the kingdom of Gujarát, 270; at Sayadpur, 270; receives, A'lam Khán Lodi, 271; arranges some estates for him, 271, 272; gives refuge to Alif Khán, 272; plot for the ruin of, 273, 274; but saved by I'timád Khán and Imád-ul-Mulk, 274, 275; defeats A'lam Khán, 276; overthrown by Imád-ul-Mulk and I'timád Khán, 279, 280; is slain in battle, 280; the miracles of 281, 282; obtians salvation, 282; the sanctity of, 283.

Mubárak Khán, son Ahmed Sháh, joins the court of Sultán Mahmúd of Málwá, 26;, mediates between Sultán Kutb-ud-dín and Mahmúd Khilji (A. D. 1451), 26.

Mubárak Khán, brother of Muhammad Sháh, in confinement at Biáwal, 205; treacherously murders his nephew and ascends throne himself, 207, 208.

Mubárak, Malik, entitled Iftikhár-ul-Mulk, 91.

Mubárak Sháh, the king of Burhánpúr, 211; harbours Imád-ul-Mulk, 211; asked to capture Imád-ul-Mulk, 211; the reply to Daryá Khán of, 211; gives battle to Daryá Khán at Dangri, 211; defeated at Dangri, 211; withdraws to the fort of Asír, 211; King of Asír and Burhánpúr, 256 ; his expedition against the nobles, 256, 262; the offspring of Al Fárúk, 257; makes peace with Sayad Mubárak, 257, 262; his invasion of Gujarát, 276; retires to Pilúgám, 276; with I'timád Khán invades Gujarát, 277 ; compensated, 278.

Mubáriz-ul-Mulk, the title of Nasírshádi, 91.

Mubáriz-ul-Mulk, the title of Malik Husein (q. v.), 108.

Mubáriz-ul-Mulk, the title of the son of Nizám-ul-Mulk, 153.

Mufarrah Khán, Nizám, viceroy of Gujarát, 5; entitled Rásti Khán (q. v.) 5.,

Muftib-ul-Mulk, son of Malik Tawakkul, noble of Mehmúd Sháh, raised to the post of Imád-ul-Mulk, 155.

Mughal chiefs, the list of, at Ahmedábád, 315; go to Sultán Muzaffar, 315.

Mughals, defeat Jám Fírúz, king of Sindh, 162; Sultán Bahádur harbours refugees from, 164; invade Gujarát under Emperor Humáyún, 186, 197; are driven out of Gujarát, 198; length of their occupation, 198; again invade under Akbar Sháh, 309, 311.

Muháfiz Khán, Jamál-ud-dín, the armour-bearer, entitled as, 59; the grandfather of the author of Tárikh-i-Bahádur Sháhi, 59; his success, 59; made viceroy, vazir, 59; executes Bhim, Rájá of Jagat, 63; Ahmedábád entrusted to the care of, 72.

Muháfiz Khan, see Fattáji.

Muháfiz Khán Bakkál-Imád-ul-Mulk sends to the out post of Dhanej to prevent Bahádur Khán, 153; joins Latíf Khán against Bahádur Khán, 155; defeat and flight of, 157;

Muháfiz Khán, Charji, the birdcatcher (q. v.), so entitled by Sultán Mehmúd III, 218.

Muhammad, the Prophet, disputed tradition concerning, 49, 50; the nativity of, 121.

Muhammadábád, Chámpáner so named, 67; built by Sultán Mahmúd Begdá, 67; its beauty, 68; capital of Gujarát, 150; Bahádur Khán at, 159.

Muhammad Afzal Khán, sent against Sultán Muzaffar, 318; intrigues with him, 318.

Muhammad Bukhári Sayad, Sádát Khán obtain grant of Batwa from Sinkandar, 149.

Muhammad Bukhári, Sayad, sent by Akbar against Sher Khán, 311; killed in battle near Pattan. 311.

Muhammad Hayát, vakil of Malik-ut-Tujjár Dakhni, rejects Bahádur Giláni's offer of marriage, 73; killed by the assassins of Bahadur Giláni, 74.

Muhammad Hisám-ul-Mulk Khájah conspires against Malik Shaában and Sultán Mahmúd Begdá, 42.

Muhammad Husein Mírza, grandson of Sultán Husein Bábakara of Khurásán comes to Changíz Khán, 293; called by I'timád Khán, 308; separates himself from Mírza Ibráhim, 311; goes to Ránpúr, 311; joins Sher Khán, 311; defeated near Pattan by the nobles of Akbar; 311; captures Broach, 312, 313; at Cambay, 313; flees from there and joins Ikhtiyár-ul-Mulk, 313; dies (A. D. 1574), 313.

Muhammad Ikhtiyár, Malik, one of the companions of Sultán Mahmúd Begda's youth, 79; refuses the title of Khán, 79; leaves the work, 79, 80; becomes a Saint, 81, 82.

xxxvi INDEX.

6

xlii INDEX.

ERRATA AND ADDENDA.

For the word *Delhi* read *Dehli*, page 1, lines 16, 18, 21; page 5, lines 12, 13, 18; page 7, lines 2, 6, 15, 32; page 8, lines 7, 14; page 9, lines 5, 28, page 100, para. 3, line 10; page 149, para. 1, line 2; page 54, para. 2, line 4; page 186, para. 1, line 11; page 187, para. 1, line 3; page 190 para. 3, line 2.

Page 2, para. 1, line 4, for *art* read *arts*.

„ 4 „ 1, „ 2 „ *747* ,, *749*

„ 4 „ 1 „ 2 „ *1345* ,, *1348*

To note 1, p. 4, add : Bayley's MS. gives A. H. 749, as the date of Mohammad Tughlak's death but gives the real date to be H. 752 (A. D. 1351) and this is correct. See Bayley's Gujarát 71 and note 4, p. 71.

At page 5, line 1, for *Sherpura* read *Sher-púr*.

At page 13, line 2, read *Saád-ul-mulk* for *Saád-ul-mul*. Line 14 *Saád-ul-mulk*, for *Sáád-ul-mulk*.

At page 13, line 3, para. 3, for *Afgán* read *Afghán*.

At page 13, line 19, read *Dandáni* for *Dandani*.

At page 13, line 30, for *Sátarsál*, read *Satarsál*.

At page 15, line 32, for *Nasir* read *Nasír*.

At page 15, line 19, for *Sháms Khán* read *Shamskhán*.

Page 16, line 15, after *agents* read *to* instead of *in*.

Page 16, line 23, read *drawing* for *pulling*.

At page 25, line 17, the words *prayers and* are superfluous.

At page 26, line 17, for *ruler* read *rule*, line 35 read *Kuráan* for *Kurán*. Also at page 32, line 18.

At page 20, line 18, instead of *be lasting* read *last*.

At page 22, para. 1, last line, for *strived* read *strove*.

At page 22, line 1, para. 2, for *having* read *he had*.

At page 22, line 13, para. 2, for *of* read *with*.

At page 23, line 1, para. 1, of the opening chapter for *of* read *after*.

At page 27, line 2, for *Palri* read *Pálri*, line 9, for *would* read *could*.

At page 28, line 4, the word *he* is superfluous ; line 16, the word *kind* is superfluous ; line 23, delete *com* after *grain* and add the words *of corn*.

At page 29, Note 2, for *meohed* read *Mash-had*.

At 30, para 3, line 6, for *Imád-ud-din* read *Alú-ud dín*.

At page 31, line 30, for *their* read *his*.

At page 32, line 15, for *safar* read *Safar*.

At page 32, Note 2, for Laba read *Láha*.

At page 33, line 5, for *then* read *when*.

At page 34, line 22, the word *and* between the words *Malik* and *very*, is superfluous.

At page 35, line 31, insert after the word *this* the figure 1 for note 1.

At page 36, line 14, for *urned* read *turned*.

At page 37, line 6, after *in* read *the*. In the same page and line for *palaces* read *palace*.

At page 38, para 2, line 8, *now* after Sháh Alam is superfluous.

At page, 39 para 3, line 9, for *its* read *his*.

At page 40, para. 4, line, 3, read *o* for capital *O* and in line 4, read *and* after 1458-59, Note 1 *Farrásh* for *Farrush*.

At page 41, line 11, read the word *a* between given and high ; line 10, for *at* read *of* ; line, 14, delete the word *reducing* ; line 18, instead of *in* read *into* ; line 26, instead of reading the word *him* after *deprivest* read it after *it* and before *thou* ; line 27, for *Shekk* spell *Sheikh* ; para. 2, line 3, read *Shadbán* for *Shubaán*.

At page 42, para 4, line 4, for *Khájá* read *Khájah* ; para 3, line 8, remove *his* from after *with* to *his*.

At page 43, line 14, for *elephants* stables read *elephant stables*.

At page 46, line 9, read *Khájah* for *khaja*.

Page 47, line 6, instead of *Illadáwand Khan* read *Khudáwand Khán*.

Page 48, line 1, for *Koranic* spell *Kuranic*; line 2, for *Mecca* read *Makkah*.

Para. 2, line 12, insert after the word *by*."

Para. 3, line 1, for *tha* read *the*.

Note 1, after chap. insert *I*.

Note 2, between the words *for* and *peace* insert *the*.

Note 3, for *Saádi* read *Saádi*.

Page 49, para. 2, line 7, for *Shija* read *Shafá*.

Page 50, para. 2, line 22, for *horses* read *horse*.

Page 51, para. 1, line 5, delete *the* between *but* and *Sultán*.

Page 52, para. 1, line 1, omit the inverted commas after " Dakhan." Note 1, insert *it* after *describes*.

Page 54, para. 3, line 5, for *Maghrebi* spell *Maghrib*.

       „ 3, „ 9, for *Khanjár* spell *Khanjar* and for *Jamdhár* spell *Jamdhar*.

       „ 3, „ 15, for note of interjection after *Mahábala* substitute note of interrogation.

       „   „ 20, after *hunting* insert *and*.

Page 55, para. 1, line 20, spell *Ghiás-ud-din* for Ghriásud-din.

Page 56, Note 1, instead of *harbs* spell *harbo*.

Page 58, para. 1, line 9, for *Hazrát* spell *Hazrat*.

Page 58, para. 2, line 1, for *Janágad* spell *Júnágadh* ;
line 16, for *onmand* write *command.*
Page 61, line 28, for *Mehamúd Sháhi* read *Mehmúd Sháhi.*
Page 62, para. 2, line 15, for *Musalmán* read *Musalmáns.*
Page 65, para. 2, line 1, for *Junágad* spell *Júnágadh.*
line 6, between the words *of* and *chief* insert *the.*
Page 66, para. 2, line 6, between *and* and *dagger* read *the.*
Page 67, para. 2, line 9, for *paper* read *sheet.*
Page 68, para. 1, line 21, for *chamli* read *chameli.*
Page 68, para. 1, line 23, for *Borsal* read *Borsali.*
Page 68, para. 1, line 32, after *Chámpáner* insert *which.*
Page 75, para. 2, line 2, for *Fárukhi* read *Fárúki.*
Page 75, para. 4, line 1, for *Chauls* read *Chaul.*
Page 79, para. 2, lines 13, 14, 16, twice in line 19, 21, 26, 28, 35, read *Mulla* for *Mullah.*
Page 79, para. 2, line 34, read *way* for *why.*
Page 80, para. 1, line 6, for *valuable* read *valuables.*
Page 83, para. 1, line 2, between *Masuúd* and *his* insert *for.*
Page 83, para. 2, line 3, for *hi* read *his.*
Page 84, para. 2, line 17, for *of* read *over.*
Page 85, para. 2, line 17, *Misprint.*
Page 92, Note 1, for *Yádgar Beg* spell *Yádgár Beg.*
Page 96, para. 1, line 8, for *of* write *for.*
Page 99, para. 1, line 21, insert *a,* after the words *God willing.*
Page 105, para. 3 line 1, for *Muzaffúr* read *Muzaffar.*
5, delete the word *thus* between *master* and *they.*
Page 106, para. 2, line 23, delete *and* between *fatigues* and *after.*
Page 115, para. 2, line 8 for *muslin* read *Muslim.*
11, for *wha* read *what.*
18, for *on* read *one.*
Page 116, para. 3, line 10, for *tanzí* read *tanzíl* 14, for *the* read *that.*
Page 117, para. 1, line 25, for *nd* read *and.*
Page 118, para. 1, line 8, delete *the* after *night.*
para. 1, line 9, after *Sultán* insert *Mehmúd Begda.*
Page 125, para. 1, line 3, for *Mullahs* spell *Mullas.*
line 7 for *Mullahs* spell *Mullás.*
Page 129, Note 1, line 2, reverse the â in âmal.
Page 131 para. 2, line 12, for *Mullah* spell *Mullá.*
Page 137-138.
Page 139, para. 2, for *Katili* read *Katili.*
para. 2, line 10, for *Delhi* read *Dehli.*
para. 4, line 2, for *Delhi* read *Dehli.*

4

ERRATA AND ADDENDA.

Page 140, para. 2, line 2, for Delhi read *Dehli*;

para. 4, line 2, for *Khān* read *Khán*.

Page 141, para. 1, put the words *the Emperor Bábar* in parenthesis.

Page 141, para. 3, line 6, delete the comma after Imád-ul-Mulk.

para. 4, line 1, for *Latif Khán* substitute *Latíf Khán*.

line 3, for *Amirs* read *Ami'rs*.

line 4, for *Shirzah* read *Sharzah*.

line 5, for *horses* read *horse*.

Note 1, lines 2, and 3, for *Rana* read *Rána*.

line 3, for *Bhim* read *Bhím*.

Page 142, para. 1, line 1, for *Latif* read *Latí'f* and for *Shirzah* read *Sharzah* the same on line 3.

line 6, for *Amirs* read *Amírs*.

line 11, for *Katbi* read *Kutb-i*.

line 12, .for *Makhdum* read *Makhdúm*.

Page 142, para. 1.

line 21, for *told me* read *communicated it to him*.

para. 2, line 6, before *the* place inverted commas.

,, line last, delete comma after *market*.

Page 143, line 8, for *were* read *had*.

line 19, for *Kuthi* read *Kutb-i*

line 39, after *in* insert *to*.

Page 144, para. 1, line 1, delete the commas after *Muhammad* and *servant*.

para. 8, for *on* read *at*.

Page 147, para. 1, line 2, for *Id* read *I'd*.

Note 1, for *Id* read *I'd*.

Page 148, para. 2, line 2, for *man or woman* read *men or women*.

Page 151, para. 1, line 3, for *horses* read *horse*.

Page 152, para. 2, line 2, for *I'd* read *I'd*;

para. 2, line 27, for *Shirzah Khan* read *Sharzah Khán*.

Page 154, para. 5, line 11, for Kabírrul-Mulk read *Kabír-ul-Mulk*.

Page 155, para. 1, line 11, for *Khush-Kadám* read *Khush-Kadam*.

Page 156, para. 3, line 8, for *Id* read *I'd*.

Page 170, para. 1, line 3, for *he* read *the Sultán*;

line 12 delete the comma after the words *Vazír Ikhtiyár Khán*;

para. 2, line 10, for *tánkás* read *tánkahs*.

Page 171, para. 1, line 1, for for Rabí-ul-Akhir read *Rabí'-ul-A'khir*;

line 4, insert . after *Jamád-ul-Awwal*.

Page 172, para. 1, line 27, insert *for* between *asked* and *orders*.

Page 173, para. 1, line 22, after the word *alive* insert " ;

26 for *Bahadur* read *Bahádur*.

Page 181, para. 1, line 14, for *produced* read *reproduced*.

Page 184, para. 1, line 7, delete *a* before *conduct.*

Page 184, para. 1, line 6, for *have* read *has.*

Page 187, para. 1, line 3, note 1, line 3, read *Hushang* for *Husbang.*

Page 191, para. 1, line 11, for *animal* read *bird.*

       para. 2, line 9, for *attack* read *assault.*

       para. 2, for *moreovr* read *moreover.*

Page 192, para 2, line 16, for *words* read *word.*

Para 2, line 35, for *hinder* read *harm.*

Page 202, para. 1, read *his* for *h.*

    „   „ 3, read *invited* for *nvited.*

    „   read *say* for *siad.*

Page 204, para. 1, read *Muhammad* for Muhammád.

Page 208, in the heading of the chapter read *Mehmúd III* for *Mehmúd.*

    „ new chapter line 12. The second *from* is redundant.

    „ line 16, *Mehmúd III* for *Mehmúd II.*

Page 212, line 18, read *mistake* for *mistak.*

Page 224, line 5, the word *and* after *came* is superfluous.

Page 225, para. 3, line 6, for *Majahid* read *Mujahid.*

Page 232, para. 2, line last, for *throwng* read *throwing.*

CPSIA information can be obtained
at www.ICGtesting.com
Printed in the USA
BVHW030909300821
615581BV00001B/8